ARCHITECTURE AND JUSTICE

AF755271

Ashgate Studies in Architecture Series

SERIES EDITOR: EAMONN CANNIFFE, MANCHESTER SCHOOL OF ARCHITECTURE, MANCHESTER METROPOLITAN UNIVERSITY, UK

The discipline of Architecture is undergoing subtle transformation as design awareness permeates our visually dominated culture. Technological change, the search for sustainability and debates around the value of place and meaning of the architectural gesture are aspects which will affect the cities we inhabit. This series seeks to address such topics, both theoretically and in practice, through the publication of high quality original research, written and visual.

Other titles in this series

A Life in Education and Architecture
Mary Beaumont Medd
Catherine Burke
ISBN 978 0 7546 7959 2

The Dissolution of Place
Architecture, Identity, and the Body
Shelton Waldrep
ISBN 978 1 4094 1768 2

Nationalism and Architecture
Edited by Raymond Quek and Darren Deane, with Sarah Butler
ISBN 978 1 4094 3385 9

Forthcoming titles in this series

Church in Concrete
Roman Catholic Church Architecture in Britain, 1955–1975
Robert Proctor
ISBN 978 1 4094 4915 7

Architecture as Civil Commitment:
Lucio Costa's Modernist Project for Brazil
Gaia Piccarolo
ISBN 978 1 4094 5462 5

Architecture and Justice

Judicial Meanings in the Public Realm

Edited by

Jonathan Simon
University of California Berkeley, USA

Nicholas Temple
University of Huddersfield, UK

Renée Tobe
University of East London, UK

Routledge
Taylor & Francis Group
LONDON AND NEW YORK

First published 2013 by Ashgate Publishing

2 Park Square, Milton Park, Abingdon, Oxon OX14 4RN
711 Third Avenue, New York, NY 10017, USA

Routledge is an imprint of the Taylor & Francis Group, an informa business

First issued in paperback 2016

Copyright © 2013 The editors and contributors

Jonathan Simon, Nicholas Temple and Renée Tobe have asserted their right under the Copyright, Designs and Patents Act, 1988, to be identified as the editors of this work.

All rights reserved. No part of this book may be reprinted or reproduced or utilised in any form or by any electronic, mechanical, or other means, now known or hereafter invented, including photocopying and recording, or in any information storage or retrieval system, without permission in writing from the publishers.

Notice:
Product or corporate names may be trademarks or registered trademarks, and are used only for identification and explanation without intent to infringe.

British Library Cataloguing in Publication Data
Architecture and justice : judicial meanings in the public
realm. -- (Ashgate studies in architecture)
1. Correctional institutions--Design and construction.
2. Justice. 3. Symbolism in architecture.
I. Series II. Simon, Jonathan. III. Temple, Nicholas.
IV. Tobe, Renée.
725.6-dc23

Library of Congress Cataloging-in-Publication Data
Architecture and justice : judicial meanings in the public realm / [edited] by Jonathan Simon, Nicholas Temple and Renée Tobe.
pages cm. -- (Ashgate studies in architecture)
Includes index.
ISBN 978-1-4094-3173-2 (hardback : alk. paper)
1. Public architecture. 2. Architecture and state. 3. Justice, Administration of. I. Simon, Jonathan, 1959- editor of compilation. II. Temple, Nicholas, editor of compilation. III. Tobe, Renée, editor of compilation.

NA9050.5.A73 2013
725'.15--dc23

2012034190

ISBN 978-1-138-24648-5 (pbk)
ISBN 978-1-4094-3173-2 (hbk)

Contents

Figures and Tables

FIGURES

TABLES

Contributors

John Bass is Associate Professor of Architecture at the University of British Columbia School of Architecture and Landscape Architecture. His work addresses contested landscapes, and uses visual tools and techniques to describe relationships between environmental and industrial practices, physical and historical events, spatial and social practices, and political and economic structures. He does this work in the geographies of California water policy and infrastructure, coastal British Columbia's First Nations territories, and Punjabi agricultural settlement.

Peter Blundell Jones was educated at the Architectural Association in London, and has been involved in practice, criticism and teaching. In 1973–74 he wrote the first book on Hans Scharoun, and in 1978 he joined the Cambridge Department of Architecture, moving in 1988 to London's South Bank University, then in 1994 to a chair at the University of Sheffield. He has published widely in journals, and his books include *Modern Architecture through Case Studies* (two volumes), and monographs on Hugo Häring, Gunnar Asplund, Günter Behnisch, Peter Hübner and the Grazer Schule.

Peter Carl trained at Princeton and, after a Prix de Rome, taught first at the University of Kentucky and then the University of Cambridge. He recently moved to London Metropolitan University where he directs the PhD programme in Architecture. His research interests revolve around architectural and urban order and their philosophical interpretation.

Jonathan Charley lives and works in Glasgow where he is currently Director of Cultural Studies in the Department of Architecture at the University of Strathclyde. He studied Architecture in London and Moscow and publishes mainly on the political and social history of buildings and cities. His most recent work was the co-edited volume *Writing the Modern City* (2011) that explored the relationship between architecture, literature, and modernity, and a collection of his essays, *Memories of Cities*, published by Ashgate in 2012.

Keith Crawford is an Economics and Social Research Council funded doctoral candidate at the University of Nottingham. His research is in the field of the law and economics of corporate insolvency and banking, with a particular interest in how procedure and regulation impact upon stakeholder behaviour.

Raymond Geuss was born in Evansville, Indiana (USA) in December 1946 and studied in New York and Freiburg/Br, West Germany, as it then was, taking a PhD in 1971. He has taught in faculties and departments of Philosophy and Political and Social Sciences at various Universities in Germany, the USA and the UK including Heidelberg, the University of Chicago, Hamburg, Princeton University, Frankfurt/M and Cambridge. In 1982–83 he was a fellow at *Wissenschaftskolleg zu* in Berlin. In 1993 he emigrated to the UK and was naturalised here in 2000. He is the author of *The Idea of a Critical Theory* (1981), *History and Illusion in Politics* (2001), *Public Goods and Private Goods* (2001), *Outside Ethics* (2005), *Philosophy and Real Politics* (2008). In 2009 a collection of his recent papers entitled *Politics and the Imagination* was published by Princeton University Press. Some recent, as yet uncollected papers include 'Blair, Rubbish and the Demons of Noon-Tide', in *Redescriptions* (2008), 'Goals, origins and disciplines', in *Arion* (2009), and *Vix intellegitur* in *Cambridge Literary Review* (2009).

Catherine Hamel is an Associate Professor in Architecture at the University of Calgary, Canada. Her interests lie in the potential role of architecture as an instrument for social reconstruction. Themes investigated include identity and estrangement in post-war contexts; memory in the scarred body; the voicing of political experiences in public space. These topics are explored through teaching, drawing, collaborative making, and writing. What agitates her is not the sides people take, but the lines they draw in order to be able to take them. She loves the sound of laughter …

John Hendrix is a Professor of Architectural History at the University of Lincoln, UK, and a Lecturer at Roger Williams University, US. He is the author of *Architecture as Cosmology: Lincoln Cathedral and English Gothic Architecture*; *Robert Grosseteste: Philosophy of Intellect and Vision*; *Architecture and Psychoanalysis*; *Aesthetics and the Philosophy of Spirit*; *Platonic Architectonics*; *Architectural Forms and Philosophical Structures*; *The Relation Between Architectural Forms and Philosophical Structures in the Work of Francesco Borromini in Seventeenth-Century Rome*; and *History and Culture in Italy*.

Yvonne Jewkes is a Professor of Criminology at the University of Leicester, author/editor of *Prisons and Punishment* (2008, Sage), *Handbook on Prisons* (2007, Willan), and *Captive Audience: Media, Masculinity and Power in Prisons* (2002, Willan). Publications on prison architecture include (with Philip Hancock) 'Penal aesthetics and the pains of imprisonment', *Punishment & Society*, 2011, 13(5);

'Penal Aesthetics and the Art of Prison Architecture', in Leonidas K. Cheliotis, *The Arts of Imprisonment: Control, Resistance and Empowerment* (2012, Ashgate) and (with Helen Johnston) 'The Evolution of Prison Architecture', in Yvonne Jewkes *Handbook on Prisons* (2007, Willan).

Helen Johnston is Senior Lecturer in Criminology and Co-Director of the Centre for Criminology and Criminal Justice at the University of Hull. Her research interests lie in the history of imprisonment particularly in local prisons, prison staff and prison architecture. Her current project is concerned with the personal and financial costs of imprisonment between 1850 and 1940 (with Professor Barry Godfrey and Dr David Cox). She is editor of *Punishment and Control in Historical Perspective* (2008, Palgrave Macmillan) and co-editor (with Professor Yvonne Jewkes) of *Prison Readings* (2006, Routledge).

Lisa Landrum is Assistant Professor in the Department of Architecture at the University of Manitoba, Canada, where she teaches history, theory and design. Lisa earned a PhD and post-professional Masters in the History and Theory of Architecture from McGill University in Montreal, and a Bachelor of Architecture from Carleton University in Ottawa. Her research and publications explore the dramatic origins of architectural theory and the dramatic underpinnings of architectural representation. Landrum is also a Registered Architect in New York State and the Province of Manitoba.

Linda Mulcahy is a Professor at the London School of Economics, University of London. She was previously the Anniversary Professor of Law and Society, School of Law, Birkbeck College, University of London. She has published extensively in the field of dispute resolution. Her most recent work on architectural design and law include 'The Unbearable Lightness of Being? Shifts Towards the Virtual Trial', *Journal of Law and Society*, vol. 35(4) (2008): 464–89; 'Architectural Precedent: Manchester Assize Courts and Monuments to Law in the Mid-Victorian Era', *Kings Law Journal*, 19 (2008): 525–50; 'Architects of Justice: The Politics of Court House Design', *Social and Legal Studies*, vol. 16(3) (2007): 383–403. Her forthcoming book *The Place of Law: The architecture of the law court and its relationship to due process*, Routledge, was published in July 2010.

Zarina Patel has a joint appointment as a Senior Lecturer with Environmental and Geographical Science and the African Centre for Cities at the University of Cape Town. Her research is concerned with various dimensions of the meaning and practice of sustainable development in local level planning in South African cities. Her research focuses on three interrelated areas: interpretations of sustainable development in theory and practice (rhetoric); environmental governance as it applies to the transition to sustainability (practice); and tools for decision-making (implementation).

Richard Patterson was formerly Assistant Head of the School of Architecture and Design and Academic Programme Leader for Architecture at the University of Brighton. He was born in San Francisco in 1945 and graduated with a degree in Fine Art from the University of California at Davis. Patterson completed his BA (Cantab) in Architecture, the AA Dipl qualifying as a registered architect in 1980. His publications are concerned with architectural semiology and the linguistic precursors of architectural principle. Patterson's own practice, was concerned with the restoration and refurbishment of seventeenth- to nineteenth-century buildings.

Emma Rowden is a Research Associate with the Justice Research Group, University of Western Sydney. She has a background in media, performance and architecture. Her current research examines perceptions of inclusion, safety, comfort, fairness and respect within institutional environments. Rowden recently completed her doctoral studies at the University of Melbourne, exploring the impact of video-mediated communications and the distribution of the space of the trial on court design.

Jonathan Simon is the Adrian A. Kragen Professor of Law, UC Berkeley. His books include *Governing through Crime: How the War on Crime Transformed American Democracy and Created a Culture of Fear* (Oxford University Press, 2007) and the forthcoming, *Mass Incarceration on Trial: Human Rights and the Future of Imprisonment* (New Press, 2013).

Baroness Vivien Stern, CBE is currently a member of the Parliamentary Joint Committee on Statutory Instruments. In 2009 Stern was invited by the UK Government to conduct a review of UK rape laws and produced the subsequent report The Stern Review. She lists her political interests as criminal justice, foreign affairs, human rights, international development, penal reform, and prisons, and has written several books, including *Creating Criminals: Prisons and People in a Market Society*; *Bricks of Shame: Britain's Prisons*; *Failures in Penal Policy*; *Imprisoned by Our Prisons: A Programme for Reform* (Fabian Series); *The Prisons We Deserve* and *A Sin Against the Future: Imprisonment in the World.*

Gabriela Świtek is a lecturer in the Institute of Art History, University of Warsaw. She completed her PhD in History and Philosophy of Architecture at Cambridge University (1999). She is an author of *Writing on Fragments: Philosophy, Architecture and the Horizons of Modernity* (2009), editor of *Avant-garde in the Bloc* (2009), *Transfer* (2006) and *Zachęta 1860–2000* (2003). Since 1999 she has been curator and chief of the documentation department in the Zachęta National Gallery of Art in Warsaw. In 2006 she curated the Polish Pavilion for the tenth International Exhibition of Architecture in Venice.

Nicholas Temple is an architect and Professor of Architecture at the University of Huddersfield, with research interests in the historical and cultural contexts of architecture. He has previously taught at University of Lincoln, Liverpool University, Nottingham University and University of Pennsylvania. Temple has been a Rome Scholar in Architecture (1986–88) and a recipient of the Paul Mellon Rome Fellowship (2012). His published works include *Disclosing Horizons: Architecture, Perspective and Redemptive Space* and *renovatio urbis: Architecture, Urbanism and Ceremony in the Rome of Julius II* (Routledge, 2007 and 2011).

Renée Tobe is Head of Architecture at University of East London. She received her AA Diploma and qualified as a chartered Architect in 1990. Tobe completed her PhD in History and Philosophy of Architecture at Cambridge University (2001). Published work investigates graphic novels, literature, film and television and the forthcoming *Architecture, Film and the Spatial Imagination* (Ashgate).

Clinton David van der Merwe is a lecturer and the PGCE Coordinator with the School of Education at The University of the Witwatersrand, Johannesburg. He teaches Geography and Geography Teaching Methodology to teachers in training. He is reading towards a PhD at The University of Johannesburg, in South African Heritage Tourism and remains interested in Heritage, Sustainable Development and Urban Renewal or Regeneration – as well as the linkages between the three in place, time and space.

Foreword

Baroness Vivien Stern

A collection of scholarly pieces on architecture and justice is long overdue and very welcome. Thinking about the architecture of police stations, courtrooms and prison cells leads to reflections on the meaning of these places, what purposes they serve and what they say about the political culture of the country where they are located. In most West European countries prisoners are held in small locked rooms called cells. In Russia however cells are only used for punishment and prisoners there normally live in large dormitories. In some countries prisons will be designed with a corridor of small bedrooms, so the prisoners can meet their partners in private. In others architects will need to design a visiting area where prisoners communicate with their visitors as best they can through a grille in a dividing wall. These differences matter.

In Perth in Western Australia in a quiet residential neighbourhood is a women's prison. Few would recognise it as such. The women live in one storey houses set in flower-filled gardens with fountains. In the centre of the grounds is a circular building open at all times for private reflection or for religious services. There is a welcoming library building with a children's corner, a health centre and a restaurant which is used for eating out when families come to visit and also for training of prisoners in catering skills. The reception area resembles the reception area of a quiet small hospital. On arrival there is no strip-searching. The incoming prisoners wait in a sitting room for various prison staff members to come and talk to them about the prison and how it works.

Even though we may not know how well the women are treated by the staff or by each other we can say with some confidence that the built environment of the prison gives a message to those arriving there. It says, 'You are worth something. You are entitled to treatment that is respectful and humane.' It also gives a message to those working there. It tells them, 'The people you are guarding are fellow human-beings'.

In Texas is a women's prison that gives a different impression. The women there live in warehouse-type dormitories with about 100 beds in each. Each woman has a bed, a small cupboard and about half a metre of personal space next to the bed. When the pressure of such confinement becomes unbearable and the woman fails to conform she will be moved to a grey stone three-storey block with rolls of razor wire between the storeys and little natural light. Her home will be a cell with a slit in the heavy steel door through which she can be viewed, and from which she will be let out once a day to walk round a wire cage in the central well of the building. What women can take from their built environment is clear. 'You are not wanted. Society has no use for you. You are entitled to very little and we do not accept any obligation to treat you with humanity and respect.'

Architecture and design matter.

Prisoners are in a very vulnerable situation, taken from their families and communities to live with strangers, at the mercy of others for all their basic needs, and with little access to the outside world. Therefore they are specifically protected by the international human rights framework. For the past sixty years the international community has accepted that no-one shall be subjected to inhuman or degrading treatment or punishment. International law requires that 'all those deprived of their liberty shall be treated with humanity and respect for the inherent dignity of the human person'. Manifestly many prisoners in all regions of the world are not treated that way. Whose responsibility is it therefore to protect the human rights of prisoners? Is it just the state which takes away their liberty? Is it also the state officials who administer the prisons? Do those who design and build brutal grey three-storey blocks with an internal exercise cage bear any responsibility for the human rights abuses that such a building gives rise to?

Doctors and medical professionals working in prisons have standards and guidelines that govern their conduct. From their own professional organisations and from the United Nations have come rules that preclude medical workers from becoming involved in or contributing to torture or inhuman treatment. In 1981 and again in 2000 the World Medical Association resolved that it was unethical for doctors to participate in capital punishment, in any way, or during any stage of the execution process. Do architects have similar codes of ethics? Do architects face any discouragement from their profession if they are contracted to design a death chamber? Maybe such an initiative may be stimulated by this book.

Prisons are a universal expression of the state's power to use legitimate force over its people. All countries have prisons or if they are very small they put their prisoners in the prisons of a neighbouring country. Prisons are recognisable as places of captivity where cruelty and ill-treatment can take place. But quite ordinary buildings can also be the site of illegitimate force, of egregious human rights abuses by states. In Chapter 19, *Politics and Architecture*, Raymond Geuss describes very well the decision to turn the building that was the head office of the makers of the gas chambers used by Germany in the second world war into premises for the University of Frankfurt and the measures used to decontaminate it. It needed to be 'symbolically detoxified' with a permanent exhibition about its history and the naming of one part of it after a forced labourer who had worked for the gas chamber makers before it was felt to be appropriate for it to house an institution of learning.

A similar example of a building that needed to be 'detoxified' can be in seen in Cambodia. A school in the capital Phnom Penh was used by the Khmer Rouge as a torture chamber and massacre centre. It is now a genocide museum where visitors can come and see the rows and rows of black and white photographs of the people tortured and killed there and view the torture implements in the walls and the floors. Turning this school into a museum and a place where respect can be shown to the numerous dead is another way of decontaminating a building that has been a site of human rights atrocities.

Architecture and justice then meet in many ways. The style and structure of buildings is interwoven with what takes place in them. The design of buildings to be used for criminal justice purposes can reflect human rights values, open justice, and respect. Alternatively they can instil fear and become the site of torture and institutionalised cruelty. Courtrooms can suggest that justice is for everyone and all are equal before the law. Or they put into stone and glass the idea that the law is an instrument for maintaining the power of the powerful and the legitimacy of the status quo. Some buildings can be put to such monstrous uses that the echoes remain long after the abuses have stopped.

This book illuminates these themes and many more. I hope it is widely read.

Acknowledgements

In November 2009 University of Lincoln supported by the University of East London, hosted a conference that explored subjects of Architecture and Justice. This publication extends the original discussions from the fields of criminology, international law, philosophy and architectural history and theory. This publication includes only a small fraction of the discussions that arose in the course of the conference and some fascinating insights into the subjects are left out. We would like to thank all the speakers who contributed to the conference, many of whom travelled from different continents as well as different countries in order to present their thoughts. In particular we extend our gratitude to the keynote speakers whose papers are not presented here but whose thoughts and practical interpretations added to the debate: Stephen Quinlan, of Denton Corker Marshall whose Manchester Civil Justice Centre, completed in 2007, sparked a round of discussion, and Professor David Wilson, former HM Prison Governor and now Professor of Criminology. We also owe a debt of thanks to those who contributed in different ways, in particular to Mani Lal who formatted all the images in this book.

Introduction

The papers presented in this volume expound on the links between architecture and justice, articulating the provocative and sometimes ambiguous juncture between the two, seek to draw out the formal language of justice, and examine the effects that architecture has on both the place of justice and on individual and collective experiences of judicial processes. In bringing together disparate disciplines this book aims to be evocative, informative and educational for both form givers (architects) and law givers (legal, judicial, and criminological practitioners). Baroness Vivien Stern, who gave the opening keynote address at the conference (from which these papers originate), remarked that this was the first time she had been invited to speak to a combined audience of architects, lawyers, and criminologists. Her sometimes uncomfortable remarks, about the contributions of architecture in the creation of both a just and unjust society, set the tone for the debate in which each speaker was held under 'surveillance' by a watchful and critical audience. A silent voice in these discussions was Michel Foucault, whose *Discipline and Punish* has inspired countless students of architecture with its detailed and imagistic descriptions of prisons and punishment, offering a range of different readings for criminologists, lawyers and architects.[1]

The structure of this volume develops from the particular to the universal – from local situations to unbounded dispositions. Hence the chapters are arranged in escalating increments of scale, from the intimate, often personalized (and depersonalized) scale of a single prison cell, to the courtroom where justice is meted out, through cities that are registers of justice in the civic order and the social realm and concludes with deeper discussions of the nature of both justice and injustice. Drawn from a multitude of philosophical, political, juridical, theological, historical, cultural, psychological and architectural interests, the book provides a platform on which to debate the relationships between the ceremonial, legalistic, administrative and penal aspects of justice, and the spaces that constitute their settings. These relationships moreover are not always assumed as stable or unquestioned. Indeed, historical claims of a universality – or standard – of justice are often predicated on the basis of enforcement through violent or intimidating means; that questions of mercy or salvation are intimately bound to various forms of punishment, whether through the infliction of physical pain, public shame/humiliation or forced confinement.

In the modern democratic world justice is fundamental to our notions of societal order; that is to the order that is sustained between us as responsible citizens, without recourse to force or violence. There is a strong assumption that justice is something to which we have an unassailable and absolute right. Yet justice is not a concept that lends itself easily to universal definition, or to codification. It is rather subject to judgments which are deemed morally right before a mutually accepted authority, in conformity to shared reasoning and values.

The problematic relationships between a universal concept of justice, whether instituted through religious doctrine, democratic systems of government or an autocratic regime, and the actual deliberations of justice – actualized through judgments made by a judge or a jury – underlines the central role that architecture plays in conveying the solemnity and legitimacy of the occasion, and ultimately of the judicial outcome. In essence, architecture provides the setting in which to situate – and declare – important moments of decision-making and their consequences. At the same time, we should be aware that architecture both frames – and is framed by – justice. Building practices, which involve bringing disparate parties (architects, surveyors, planners, clients and users etc) together for a shared/common purpose, are explicitly bound by judicial processes; laws that are both written (codes of professional conduct, planning law etc) and unwritten (the ethical responsibility of architects to society at large). What is arguably at stake in this bureaucratization of justice is succinctly summarized by Peter Carl: '... the truth of the legal trial is neither the winner nor the loser of the context, but the re-affirmation through the context of lawfulness.'[2] It is this quest for lawfulness, and ultimately of our search for a just society, that is at the heart of this series of essays.

Part 1 in the volume, 'Prisons and Prison Cells', examines the distinction between incarceration and correction, between penitence and the penitentiary. It traces prison design and suggests that there may be other forms of control that are more efficacious in the expressions of justice. Yvonne Jewkes suggests that prison architects face acute, paradoxical challenges. Not only must they design prisons that fulfill the brief issued by government ministers, who prioritize low cost and high security before anything else, but they must also meet public expectations about what prisons should look like. At the same time their designs must aid rehabilitation as well as deliver punishment. Helen Johnston discusses how the architecture of the prison has developed historically. Prison space has been contested and used to reflect the competing philosophies of punishment of the time. She describes how the prison 'cell' became the main space for this transformative regime whether underpinned by ideas of reform or deterrence. Oscar Wilde's invocation of 'humanity's machine' and the dark and narrow cells in which we dwell, informs the next chapter as well.[3] Here Gabriela Świtek expounds on the Piranesian fantasy as the basis of a rich body of literature inspired by the impossible, labyrinthine and endless spaces of the *Carceri*. Historical and contemporary developments of prisons and visions of Bentham's panopticon reflect descriptions of imagined dwelling places, and shed light on visual culture. Nicholas Temple's description of the transformation of Lincoln Castle into a prison, and the use of the nearby Lincoln Cathedral as a courthouse and prison, reveal often overlooked aspects of judicial and punitive practices in the early modern world and their implications in the relationship between canon and civil law. Focusing in particular on the punitive role of the Lincoln Castle, Temple examines the governorship of the gaol under John Merryweather who used the surveillance tower for both guarding prisoners and as a personal astronomical observatory, a dual function that speaks volumes about the ambiguous relationships between appearance and function in the varying acts of surveillance. The prison chapel, still preserved intact, was designed so that prisoners were isolated from their fellow inmates and could only observe the minister. An example of Wilde's 'humanity's machine' described earlier, the psychological effects of this confinement (highlighted during a short visit to Lincoln Castle by participants from the conference), remind us of the effectiveness of certain design strategies to instill feelings of extreme claustrophobia and isolation – in the face of legitimate punitive and judicial practices.

The following part, 'Courtrooms and Courthouses', brings the discussion into the place where justice is meted out, and the symbols of both justice and authority in courtrooms and courthouses. Justice framed by Architecture forms the basis of this section, and the symbols of both Justice and authority expressed on or framing the architecture are recurrent themes. Justice implies an imposition of an authority, and cultures and societies create architectural forms for this expression. Linda Mulcahy asks what contemporary courthouses should 'look' like and whether we are required to 'recognize' justice in architectural form. Just as the previous part examines the distinction in architectural decision making between external and internal design, Part 2 offers different codes for courthouse presence and courtroom layout. The discussion of whether and how courtrooms may be 'read' draws from distinctive internal planning that dictates circulation routes and separate rooms where those who once rubbed shoulders are now kept apart. Design guides for courtrooms standardize how a courtroom should be experienced to maintain neutrality of design so that the justice is the same wherever it is practiced, the principle being that if the place where justice is decreed looks identical, then the justice will be standardized as well. Keith Crawford discusses the courtroom as place to practice authority through symbol and civic code based on Revolutionary France and the *Palais de Justice*, where the seat of the judge, the authority of law, becomes the magistral of the law faculty lecture theatre. In contrast to this discussion of physical imposition, Emma Rowden questions whether there is still a place for the physical courtroom, or if justice can be rendered 'virtual' as effectively. In the virtual court it is difficult to determine when justice begins, and without symbols of authority there is mistrust of the fairness of the court.

Implicit within this section on Courtrooms and Courthouses, is the notion of authority and how it is expressed in architecture. Spatial form and symbolism informs the conceptions of social justice discussed by Zarina Patel and Clinton van der Merwe, who examine Constitution Hill in Johannesburg, South Africa. Constitution Hill, once military garrison, then Boer fort, became a jail that housed at different times, Mahatma Gandhi and Nelson Mandela as well as other less iconic offenders whose very imprisonment represented the injustice of the society, and is now a tourist attraction. Symbols of justice and the path to freedom and redemption question the individual's place in the society, and form a backdrop for the South African Constitution. This discussion of architecture and ritual expressed through codified building forms is seen through the veil of the typically authoritarian representation of justice in architecture, in the form of the Chinese yamen, where Peter Blundell Jones discerns a transition (expressed in the gatehouse) between the public realm and the lawcourt. The need for continuity and tradition in judicial matters is typically expressed in the ceremonial trappings of the courthouse and in the language of the legal document and demonstrates the inseparability of administration and law-keeping. In the yamen, before imposing judgement, the law keeper determines the truth through seven tactics of detection, evocatively named as: the hook, the raid, the attack, intimidation, browbeating, comparison, and compelling, codified in a legal manual for magistrates.

Part 3, 'Civic and Societal Order', offers reflections on the dialectical character of the contemporary city looking at how it has developed from nineteenth century consumerism, of 'ownership' and material consumption, the crimes associated with these appropriative spaces, through to examinations of how imagery imposes justice and exposes injustices. The space of justice becomes the space of the theatre of the public realm; that we also refer to as the space of the city. Jonathan Charley expounds on how politics, power, and the edifices of justice in three European cities are inextricably linked to the history of the slave trade, colonization and the plantation economies of Africa and the Americas. Just as Foucault's *Discipline and Punish* sits as a constant companion throughout the book, two other texts inform much of the writing. One of these is David Harvey's *Social Justice and the City* describing social processes and spatial forms.[4] Richard Patterson applies Harvey's special and social anthropology to urban semiology and linguistic structures in social expression and a spatialization of knowledge. Another text, John Rawls' *A Theory of Knowledge*, sets the *mise en scène* for Jonathan Simon's chapter that begins by rejecting the pre-conceptions of ideologies and policies that shape prisons and courtrooms, and demonstrates how home ownership and crime are interconnected in surprising ways, contextualized with the economic crisis and politics of the current era.[5] John Bass's chapter exposes the role of photography and images in investigating colonial 'preemption' of Native settlements in Western Canada. These images although possibly staged, offer spatial evaluation of both truth and injustice. Catherine Hamel's poetic and abstract expressions of justice, politics and boundaries evocatively rounds off the debate.

The final part, 'Philosophical Questioning of Propriety', concludes these discussions by casting light on our human condition of being individuals in a globalized society where justice is a central political concept. Peter Carl looks at the concept of fairness and equity through a discussion of temporality, symbolic order, measure and spatial ordering by Hammurabi in ancient Mesopotamia, and then in Plato's *Republic*, with its proposals for the just well-ordered state. He questions whether Justice itself is subsumed in a black hole of laws and law-giving, of control and contracts, or remains firmly in the centre of architectural form and thought. Renée Tobe's commentary examines different translations of Plato's *Protagoras*. No matter the asymmetry of meaning between civic justice and citycraft, political skill, or citizenship our capacity for urban life is always requisite on common sense and justice. In Lisa Landrum's chapter, classical Greek plays featuring architect-protagonists provide exemplary dramatizations of the quest for justice, peace and social order. This relation of symbolic justice is developed in the medieval cathedral and expressed through light and spirit expounded on by John Hendrix through a reading of justice as the good through the experience of Lincoln Cathedral. The final chapter, by Raymond Geuss, questions our desire 'to know' and our quest for truth in a world that is unstable and insecure. Geuss examines freedom and politics in relation to architecture and the city. While we can turn away from an image of injustice or close a book that describes an uncomfortable truth, we can not avoid the architecture and cities we construct for ourselves.

This publication includes only a small fraction of the discussions that arose in the course of the conference. One subject that we were not able to include here described in detail is the experience of the Supermax prison. The sensory deprivation (the little lockable room where a prisoner is placed so that two inmates did not pass in a hallway, for example) and the details of the minutely controlled routine of each day are both fascinating and compelling. It is worth highlighting here briefly the impact of reading about the Supermax prison on one of the editors to this volume:

> *While sitting in the British Library Reading Room, after having finished the relevant chapter, I looked up and 'felt' the materiality of the space, the feel of air movement, the colour, texture, sounds of people turning pages, the clothes and hair of the readers around me, the lighting. It was as if the world, the one we take for granted, described as 'asleep on the back of a tiger' was suddenly brought into existence for me and I had woken up. I never felt so free and so rich and so lucky. I sat for some minutes, just looking.'*

In another part of the world, the ferry from San Francisco to Larkspur, a highly priced and desirable area of real estate in the West coast of the USA, passes right in front of the State prison of San Quentin, somewhere inside of which is an execution room where people are put to death and someone, maybe an architect, has determined the shape and form, decided how it should be painted, whether or not it has carpet on the floor and what kind of lighting it has. It is a chilling thought.

People are incarcerated all over the world. As architects we look at prisons as 'typologies' or try to make them better places to be in. Traditional discussions of Architecture and Justice designate prisons and courtrooms. We hope that this publication will open up future discussions about how the cities and environments we build for ourselves are expressions of notions of 'justice', and that we are responsible for not just the cities we live in, but how and why we live in them.

NOTES

1 Michel Foucault, *Discipline and Punish: The Birth of the Prison*, trans. Alan Sheridan (London, 1991).

2 Peter Carl, 'Architectural Design and Situational History', in Adam Hardy and Necdet Teymur (eds), *Architectural History and the Studio* (London, 1996), pp. 74–89, esp. p. 81.

3 Oscar Wilde, *De Profundis, The Ballad of Reading Gaol and Other Writings* (Ware, 1898/2002).

4 David Harvey, *Social Justice and the City* (Baltimore MD, 1973).

5 John Rawls, *A Theory of Knowledge* (Cambridge MA, 1971).

PART 1
Prisons and Prison Cells

1

The Aesthetics and Anaesthetics of Prison Architecture[1]

Yvonne Jewkes

INTRODUCTION

This chapter synthesizes perspectives from the field of critical organization studies with those from criminological studies of prison design and the lived experience of imprisonment. It brings together these distinct areas of scholarship in order to consider the proposition that prison spaces are layered with meaning and that prison design has a profound psychological and behavioural influence on prisoners, prison staff, and the communities in which prisons are located. Mindful of Elaine Scarry's call for an intrinsic link between 'beauty and being just' the aim is to explore meanings conveyed by carceral spaces and to reflect on both the monotonous, anaesthetizing effects of penal architecture and design, and the potential civilizing, rehabilitative role they can play.[2] The chapter is in two parts. First, it will first consider 'space as symbol', or the multifarious penal philosophies that can be seen reflected in the form and fabric of prison buildings, and 'space as practice', or what 'aesthetics' means within a penal setting. Then the chapter will discuss some of the difficulties facing those who want to rethink prison design, and will examine the competing discourses influencing contemporary prison architects. It will explore the idea that, while most penal institutions are commonly (and accurately) characterized as sites of control, abuse and neglect, prison designers might consider adopting an emerging philosophy – 'humane architecture' – which has recently transformed many public institutions, including hospitals and healthcare centres. Given that its advocates believe that humane architecture has a rehabilitative impact on patients, it begs the question of whether it might have similarly positive effects on prison inmates. However, prison architects face a particularly acute challenge, for not only must they design institutions which fulfil the client's brief (the clients for the most part being government ministers and private security companies, both of whom will prioritise value for money and security imperatives before anything else) but they must also meet public expectations about what a prison should look like. Prison designs which enhance dignity and promote rehabilitation through a normalized aesthetic may not appear sufficiently punitive to a public with an appetite for punishment.[3]

PENAL AESTHETICS: SPACE AS SYMBOL AND SPACE AS PRACTICE

The architecture of incarceration traditionally has been inscribed with symbolic meaning that seeks to secure the acquiescence of society at large as well as that of convicted offenders. Whether gothic cathedral, monastic citadel or castellated fortress, the purposefully scripted exteriors of eighteenth and nineteenth century prisons incorporated symbolism that had a 'see and beware' function, warning the community at large to refrain from committing crimes lest they too should end up within the monstrous institution's imposing walls. Indeed, the internal life of inmates was a secondary consideration to the symbolic meaning transmitted by the external façade to society at large and inside these splendid palaces was a highly restricted economy of space as prison accommodation became increasingly enclosed and claustrophobic. Arguably no other type of building employs the concepts of 'outside' and 'inside' quite as dramatically or self-referentially (in the sense that one interpellates the other) as the prison, and the penal philosophies of the late eighteenth and nineteenth centuries – based on principles of austerity, isolation, silence, remorse and reform – are evident in the juxtaposition of the prison's cathedral-like exterior and the minuteness of private interior space within. Echoing Jeremy Bentham's (1791/1843) famous belief that morals could be reformed, health preserved, industry invigorated and instruction diffused 'all by a simple idea in architecture', Daniel Nihill, Governor and Chaplain of Millbank Penitentiary in the mid-nineteenth century, proclaimed that good behaviour among his prisoners was maintained 'with the passive instrument of the building itself'.[4]

The conceptualization of the prison cell as a restricted subterranean space, a place of death or entombment, is common in academic studies of imprisonment. The disparity between the upward gaze toward the vast, vaulted, chillingly austere exterior[5] architecture and the downward gaze into the darkness of the coffin-like cells is beautifully illustrated by the following quote from a twentieth century prisoner:

> *The whole is an enormous enclosure of space, top-lit from secular clerestories, and, at the far end of the halls, by gargantuan round-headed windows rising atria-like from floor to ceiling... One feels like some rare exotic bird, trapped in an intricate gilded cage; a metaphor not inappropriate as the hammer beamed roofs frequently resound to the flapping of real birds, curious and unfortunate enough to have found their way into these vast basilicas of human discontent. It is once inside the cell that the prisoner really begins to feel the oppressiveness of these city fortresses... more often than not, living space for 23 hours a day, seven days a week, averages 800 cubic feet; that is, 8 x 13 x 9. Roofs are shallow arches, so it easy to imagine oneself on the Orient or Trans-Siberian Express taking some never ending journey to the edge of the world. These cells look like gutted sections of railway carriages without the panoramic windows. The only window in evidence here is sunken into the back wall, too high to look out of, and usually double-barred. Standing underneath this aperture, one glances up at Oscar Wilde's 'little tent of blue the prisoners call sky.*[6]

Of course, the paradox of their external splendour and internal squalor is still keenly felt by the thousands of inmates still held in them but, ironically, the aesthetic qualities of Victorian prison buildings have never been more appreciated by the free community than they are two centuries after their construction. The British government is considering selling off many large Victorian prisons such as Pentonville, Brixton, Wandsworth and Wormwood Scrubs; a venture that is estimated to be worth £350 million. It has not been revealed what these prime sites might be turned into, but one can well imagine that if converted into apartments with the façades kept intact, they are likely to appeal to the kind of affluent young professionals who stay in the boutique hotel housed in the former HMP Oxford. Here, the aesthetics of imprisonment are considered so desirable that rooms have been converted from the old cell blocks with views of the prison's former exercise yard, as well as a 'luxury suite' in the governor's house. The hotel group's publicity material leaves the potential guest in no doubt about the 'charms' of staying in a former jail:

> *Perhaps the most striking of all Malmaison hotels, Oxford is as close to staying in a prison as it gets (without the real thing of course). Your eye will go immediately to the original heavy metal studded doors, while once you enter the main atrium and see the wrought ironwork stairs and three inch thick steel doors, you could almost forget that you're on a break – and not actually doing time.*[7]

Ironically, here, the aesthetics of incarceration are considered highly desirable but for earlier occupants of HMP Oxford and, indeed, for most prison inmates, penal aesthetics might more accurately be described as *an*aesthetics, whereby the senses are blunted or depressed.[8] In the UK, anaesthetic design is perhaps best exemplified by the prisons established in the 1960s and 1970s, such as Albany, Long Lartin and Gartree; all of them functional, featureless and concrete. As Peter Wayne puts it:

> *[P]erennially water-stained walls; crisscrossed with miles of razor-wired fencing; and sheltering under the ultimate anti-escape devices – highly strung threads of orange, red and yellow balloons to stop invasion by helicopter; an archipelago of identical... blocks.*[9]

Many of these prisons were established at the height of penal welfarism and they echo the austere styles of high, progressive modernism.[10] Whether their design simply reflected what was considered to be humanely functional and most likely to meet the therapeutic goals of punishment at this time, or whether it was a knowing strategy to reassure the public that penal welfarism did not equate to leniency, is open to debate. Either way, they share a melancholy and sometimes brutal external appearance while, inside, they are characterized by bland uniformity in colour, texture, lighting and levels. Even more recently, since the early 1990s, the introduction of the Private Finance Initiative (PFI) has paved the way for contracts to be awarded for the entire design, construction, management and finance (DCMF) of a prison, and new penal institutions have been built with the imperatives of efficiency and security in mind, while keeping costs to a minimum. Prisons operated by Serco, G4S and Kalyx all share a countenance that is antithetical to their Victorian predecessors, yet not as stark and sombre as the post-Mountbatten (1966) prisons. Dull, unassuming and uniform in appearance, the typical hallmarks of prison exteriors built in the last twenty years are vast expanses of brick, few (small) windows and no unnecessary ornamentation or decoration. In general they look rather like private hospitals, no-frills chain hotels, or the kind of nondescript corporate HQ you might expect to find in a business park.[11]

Prison historian Sean McConville asks whether it is morally acceptable for ugliness, vulgarity or mere indifference to be part of punishment given that one of the core values of our civilization is a belief in the beneficent effects of beauty.[12] His conclusion is that, like supporters of the separate system a century ago, we are spared the need to make decisions about prison aesthetics but now, in addition to 'the passive instrument of the building', we have a 'routine grinding of politics, administration and public expenditure priorities' overseen by an 'impersonal' and 'dispassionate' system, that counteracts the need for petty vindictiveness.[13] While this is true, the restrictions of cellular confinement remain unchanged even in the most recently-constructed prisons, and many prisoners are 'doubled-up' in rooms which are no bigger than cells with sole occupancy. Indeed, Henri Lefebvre's comment that 'space commands bodies, prescribing or proscribing gestures, routes and distances to be covered' seems particularly apposite in the context of the cramped cells, gated wings and walled exercise yards of a 'typical' closed prison.[14] We may no longer subject prison inmates to the treadwheel or prevent them from communicating with each other but the disciplinary power underpinning nineteenth and early twentieth century institutions, is retained within the architectural logic of prisons and continues to influence penal design, despite being abandoned in penal policy and practice almost a century ago.[15]

The designing of prisons that blend in with their characterless environs may be, in part, an attempt at counteracting the controversy and NIMBY-ism that inevitably arise when proposals to build a new prison are announced.[16] The highly visible prison might be a constant reminder to society of the perils of transgression but it also arguably generates disproportionate fears about inmate escapes, an influx into the area of 'undesirables' visiting prisoners, and ex-inmates settling into the community in which the prison is situated on completion of their sentence (striking at the heart of middle-classes fears about local property values plummeting). For all these reasons, aesthetic considerations have been submerged by the imperative to disguise penal institutions; they simply merge with the environs, whether urban or rural. The camouflage effect is further achieved because, at the same time as the prison has become increasingly indistinguishable from its surroundings, urban design has taken on the features of the carceral with gated communities, visible surveillance systems, and fortress style security paraphernalia.

Mike Davis characterizes contemporary prisons as 'melting into the architexture' of the city and 'becoming architecturally naturalized as aesthetic objects'.[17] The notion of the city and the prison merging finds ideological[18] form in Michel Foucault's rhetorical question; 'is it surprising that prisons resemble factories, schools, barracks, hospitals, which all resemble prisons?',[19] and also in the title of an article on the criminalization and control of young, lower-class black men; a 'deadly symbiosis' formed 'when ghetto and prison meet and mesh'.[20] The spaces and places of urban landscapes are further evoked by Michel de Certeau who characterizes institutions as one of the primary sites in which the powerful construct and exercise their power, but the weak create their own 'spaces' within those places; making them temporarily their own as they occupy and move through them.[21] In some prisons in the UK, the long, narrow corridors that connect different wings and run past association rooms – sometimes out of the sight of staff in the wing offices – are known as 'the streets'. In these spaces, groups of prisoners congregate to replicate some of the activities they might engage in on the streets outside, that is, hanging around doing nothing except marking their patch.[22]

Prison design that incorporates spaces where prisoners can associate with each other while remaining beyond the sight of staff would be unthinkable for the architect of today. In the medium and low security prison estates, mid-twentieth century discourses of therapy and rehabilitation have given way to new ideas concerned with helping prisoners to change and improve as a result of their own efforts, backed up by systems of privileges or penalties to be administered for good and bad behaviour and by the introduction of new technologies which augment staff powers to reward or punish. Spatial organization is instrumental in this strategy of 'responsibilization', and the new generation of prison architecture seeks to incorporate features of situational crime prevention into design; for example, discrete housing units staffed by officers who operate informally and interact with inmates in the living area while having a clear sight of all cell entrances. This model of direct, informal supervision by officers – often referred to as 'dynamic security' – is aimed, not simply at aiding surveillance and control, but also at facilitating communication between staff and inmates, so that the role of officers is no longer to watch and respond to inmate problems, but to predict and prevent them.[23] In the 'deep' end of the prison estate on the other hand – that is, high and maximum security – inmates have little or no contact or communication with each other or with prison staff, and officers enforce secure custody conditions with the aid of architecture designed to deprive the senses (including long-term isolation of individuals considered a 'risk' to themselves or others) and militarized weaponry.

RETHINKING PRISON DESIGN: TOWARDS A 'HUMANE ARCHITECTURE'

> *It is only the agencies responsible for the construction of prisons and jails, one of the costliest building types to construct, that frequently indicate no desire to incorporate architecture into their facilities and in some cases actively discourage it. It has been our experience, in several recent designs, to have clients mandate that certain degrees of bleakness (one could argue ugliness) be incorporated.*[24]

This admission from an American architect that he is frequently discouraged from incorporating 'architecture' into correctional facilities and is sometimes even encouraged to design in elements of bleakness or ugliness reminds us of something so obvious that we that we take it for granted: environments are *thought* before they are built.[25] As the quote underlines, one of the most difficult issues for an architect commissioned to design prisons to overcome is an apparent total lack of concern on the part of the client as to a fundamental goal of the profession: the artistic and aesthetic endeavour to create spaces which can improve, enhance and nurture the lives of those who come into contact with them.[26]

Conversely, an enduring problem for academics and other 'experts' when voicing opinions about the benefits of building aesthetic considerations into the architecture of incarceration (or any number of other 'civilizing' influences or humanitarian measures) is that the accusation can be levied that one is simply tinkering at the edges and doing nothing of substance to challenge the institution of the prison itself. This is a dilemma familiar to prison reformists. Given the upward trend in prison population numbers in the United States and in most European countries over the last two decades, even groups that were set up with a strong abolitionist agenda have been forced to switch their focus to reducing further expansion of the penal system, and making prisons more humane, which can cause some reformists discomfort. It is a predicament that has also penetrated discussions about prison design among architects and planners. In the US an organization called Architects/Designers/Planners for Social Responsibility (ADPSR) has called for a boycott of all prison design, construction and renovation on the grounds that the current prison system is 'a devastating moral blight' on society, and an 'overwhelming economic burden' to taxpayers which 'has no place in a society that aspires to liberty, justice, and equality for all'. San Francisco-based architect Raphael Sperry, President of ADPSR, is unequivocal about his aims, arguing that architects should be engaging in:

> *... making our country and our world a more sustainable, prosperous and beautiful place ... Saying 'no' to prisons is a very important part of that. Saying we're going to make prettier prisons, it's not part of that. It's neither here nor there.*[27]

The call by ADPSR for a boycott has generated heated debate within some of the main firms contracted to design and build correctional facilities, as well as more widely among members of the American Institute of Architects (AIA).[28] Unsurprisingly, most architect and construction firms are unwilling to go as far as turning down lucrative contracts, even if privately they have reservations about aspects of prisons and imprisonment. In many cases, the professional architects commissioned to design and construct correctional institutions are themselves 'anaesthetized' as they must desensitize themselves from not being able to deliver a full aesthetic experience.[29] However, Michael Fuller, a senior associate at global architects HOK, refutes the suggestion that he is compromised or constrained by the particular demands of designing prisons, and is unapologetic about the firm's commitment to building facilities that are responsive to the 'the kinds of crimes and populations we are finding'.[30] In his opinion, improving correctional facilities is a more realistic goal than simply refusing to build more prisons, and he claims that HOK are at the cutting edge of prison design because they are finding innovative solutions for dealing with specific prison populations, for example, sex offenders. Frank J. Greene of Ricci Greene Associates and the AIA Academy of Architecture for Justice agrees: 'America might not need more prisons, but it desperately needs better ones'.[31]

Most architects and penal reformers who share the views of Fuller and Greene underline the importance of design that is sensuous (that is, appeals to the senses). They emphasize that facilities should be in tune with the seasons; warm or cool as appropriate and maximizing natural daylight. Direct access to outside space is also widely considered vital to a sense of well-being. Over the years, many penal experiments have been instigated which attempt to reflect progressive regimes and aspirational aims in innovative, sensuously rich environments. For example, at the prison in Brest, France, efforts have been made to improve the psychological quality of inmates' life, resulting in:

> *... a spatially stimulating environment that is filled with light and colour wherein the confined inmates can move about with more freedom. Bright colours are applied to surfaces throughout the building...the cell interiors are of a lighter, softer tone that is accentuated by colour features.*[32]

On a similar theme, Brians Penitentiary in Barcelona, Spain, has adopted a model of 'functional flexibility...[in] a setting that is conducive to personal development and positive change'.[33] Its architects have achieved this by incorporating elements of unevenness and differing horizons in the belief that 'distances and shadows help to create an environment with less spatial repetition to ward off monotony'.[34] In prisons in the Netherlands (for example, De Geerhorst and Breda), imaginative use has been made of glass in roofs and floors which maximizes light and space (while, it must be said, increasing opportunities for surveillance and security), and at Rotterdam's De Schie Penitentiary, the bright interior paintwork is reminiscent of Southern climates.[35] In the UK, the privately run HMP Peterborough, which opened in 2006, has rejected the usual green-grey paintwork of institutional conformity, and instead has a bright colour-coding system to identify the purpose of its different areas. With its low-rise design, natural lighting, healthy living and alternative therapy centre, and artificial trees placed in the workshops and education block, Peterborough prison more closely resembles a shopping centre than an archetypal jailhouse. Cells have been designed with as few ligature points as possible to reduce suicide, each cell is fitted with an intercom linked to the wing office, rather than the more usual simple call button, and prisoners can control the lighting in their cells.[36]

While many European countries have examples of prisons that strive to incorporate aesthetics, rather than anaesthetics, some of the most striking examples of progressive penal experimentation are to be found in Scandinavia, whose countries have an exceptionally low prison population and a reputation for striving to make prison conditions approximate those on the outside as far as possible, rather than degrading and dehumanizing the individuals within.[37] For example, the buildings which make up high-security Halden prison in Norway have been designed to maximize the natural resources available, including the forest in which it is situated. As an architects' news website puts it, the prison has a 'sensitive landscape, light buildings, with much local timber on display, and shockingly large windows [which] allow prisoners a dialogue with their surroundings'[38] Large bar-less windows (including in one of the two segregation blocks) might be 'shocking' to many, but every facet of Halden prison is purposefully designed to normalize the environment for those who live and work within its walls (which, incidentally, are rounded at the top so as not to appear too hostile, according to the prison's governor, Are Hoidal.[39] Since it was opened by the King of Norway in April 2010, Halden has been the focus of much controversy, much of which has emanated from the fact that many regard Halden's comfortable living quarters with fully-fitted kitchens, sofas and flat-screen TVs as inappropriately conceived indulgences to an anti-social population[40] (see, for example the see *Daily Mail*'s report on the 'world's poshest prison'.[41] Ironically, and somewhat paradoxically, opprobrium from the Norwegian media and public focused not on home comforts and aesthetic considerations but on the number of foreign prisoners initially held there. Not only was it not their own criminals who would be enjoying the well appointed prison but, as Norwegian Broadcasting (NRK) reported, most of those held at Halden and taking part in its enlightened rehabilitation programmes would not contribute to Norwegian society on their release because they will be deported.[42] As a result of public dissatisfaction with this situation, Halden has changed its policy and is now taking offenders from its own boundaries.

Another penal experiment was the Dóchas Centre (aka Mountjoy Women's Prison) in Dublin. Opened in 1999 to house about 80 women in medium security conditions, Dóchas (meaning 'hope') promised to usher in a new penological era within the Irish prison system. With an aim of encouraging the women held there to take responsibility for their lives and successfully reintegrate into the community on release from prison, the Dóchas Centre also set out to be different from traditional penal institutions: it had no high external wall, no barred windows or barbed wire and no visible external indication that it was actually a prison. The 'exercise yard' was a garden around which the inmates' accommodation – situated in five houses – was situated in intimate proximity and with an emphasis on domesticity. Phoenix, the fifth house, provided private bed-sitter accommodation and was intended for long-term prisoners who in the months leading up to their release usually went out to work. With an emphasis on nature, and natural light and sound (including a water feature designed to block out noise from Dublin's north circular road on which the centre was situated), the prison was, as far as the architect who led the project was concerned, a triumph.[43] However, Dóchas has proved to be a short-lived success. In 2006 the Irish Prison Service announced its decision to replace all four prisons on the Mountjoy complex (which included a dilapidated and much-criticized men's prison) with a 'new modern operationally-efficient prison' on a green field site in north County Dublin.[44]

Like Halden, Dóchas might be considered an example of 'humane architecture'; a philosophy that has penetrated the building and design of other kinds of institutions, e.g. hospitals and healthcare centres in recent years. While the nineteenth century prison and hospital shared a disciplinary logic the twenty-first century hospital is based on a very different model of medical power to that of their Victorian predecessors.[45] For example, private health company Circle recently commissioned Foster and Partners to design a hospital in Bath which feels more like a boutique hotel, while AHMM's Health Centre in Kentish Town was shortlisted for the RIBA Stirling Prize in 2009 and architect firm Gareth Hoskins has designed several health centres which embrace the experiential and sensual dimension of architecture.[46] One of the most extensive and well-known projects, however, is the Maggie's Centre initiative, established by architectural theorist and designer Charles Jencks, following the death from cancer of his wife, Maggie Keswick, in 1993. This growing network of cancer care centres – many designed by high-profile 'starchitects' – are not claiming a deterministic relationship between architecture and health. However, Jencks believes that if there *is* an architecture of hope – an architecture that helps one to live longer – it is not to be found in the traditional hospital. Indeed, he has described the space in which his wife received her weekly chemotherapy – a windowless, neon-lit space dictated by the demands of hygiene and efficiency with hard, sterile surfaces, bright, white spaces, long corridors and artificial ventilation systems – as a form of 'architectural aversion therapy'. By contrast, Maggie's Centres are linked by design that is defined by inarguably positive qualities: natural light, space, openness, intimacy, views, connectedness to nature, and domestic in space and feeling.

The parallels between these innovative health centres and progressive prisons are as obvious as are the similarities between traditional hospitals and penal institutions (and any number of other 'total' institutions as Erving Goffman and Michel Foucault remind us). Both are inscribed with narratives about the individuals confined within them, their supposed characteristics and how they are expected to behave. Historically, in both types of institution the needs of their occupants (prisoners and patients) for an architecture that offers the required resources for persons displaced from their routine lives by legal or medical necessity – resources enabling them to nurture their sense of self and maintain the narrative of their lives – has been absent. Instead, the architecture, internal landscaping, fixtures and fittings of traditional hospitals convey messages about illness, alienation, vulnerability and acquiescence to expertise; they encourage conformity and obedience while giving the patient little opportunity to present his or her identity, far less to assert autonomy or resistance to the dominant discourse. Prisons impart similar messages about weakness, subservience and loss of identity, though they may also communicate something crueller and more brutal. Cage-like interiors, dormitories stacked with bunk beds which resemble human filing cabinets, and heavy, vandal-resistant furnishings communicate to inmates that 'you are animals', 'you are sub-human' and 'you are potential vandals' respectively.[47] Even basic healthcare for inmates has sometimes only been provided as an afterthought. For example, in California, prisons in the 1980s and 1990s were designed with little if any consideration to the need for medical space to examine and treat patients; an oversight that subsequently necessitated a massive and expensive building programme to retro-fit a healthcare infrastructure into the penal estate. The most extreme penal environment, the 'supermax' (synonymous with the USA, but also found in other parts of the world, including Australia), incorporates numerous design elements that result in psychic and physical pain on a par with techniques of torture. But the coercive use of architecture to instil total psychic and bodily control over prisoners is not dedicated solely to those individuals designated 'threatening', 'non-compliant' or 'high-risk'. Overcrowded accommodation, physical separation of prisoners and guards, hi-tech monitoring and surveillance, and areas of both sensory deprivation and sensory overload can be found in many prisons around the world that hold inmates who are not deemed a high security risk. Conventional penal aesthetics may thus simply reinforce criminal and criminalized identities to a prison population who will (mostly) return to society.

In contrast, one of the most striking similarities between the Maggie's Centres and Halden and Dóchas prisons is their emphasis on 'normal', domestic spaces. In all of them, kitchens are especially important and all the things that commonly go on in kitchens – cooking food for oneself and others, drinking tea, having informal talks around a kitchen table – are viewed as an important form of rehabilitation and therapy. An emphasis on domestic space has also been found in many 'progressive' prison regimes in the UK; among them, Parkhurst C Wing, Glen Parva, Gartree and Grendon Underwood therapeutic communities, Blantyre House resettlement prison and Barlinnie Special Unit. In these institutions, regimes were based on individual responsibility and accountability and collective support and solidarity. Prisoners could follow their own daily routine, wear their own clothes, decorate their cells, cook their own food, take delivery of uncensored mail and receive visitors.[48] Yet all of these places have been shut down, fundamentally changed or left on the margins of the penal system because their regimes challenged the retributive, punitive philosophy underpinning penal policy in this country.[49] For example, Barlinnie – established as an alternative to the notorious 'cages' at Inverness prison – became a political embarrassment despite (or perhaps because of) the positive evidence from its prisoners and prison officers that it was possible to rehabilitate those long-term prisoners who were viewed by the political establishment as incapable of redemption'.[50]

For former inmate Jimmy Boyle, 'what made the Unit unlike any other place was the way staff and prisoners were allowed and encouraged to sit down and talk together'[51] a nod to normalization which caused fellow prisoner Johnny Steele to reflect that eventually 'All the bitterness and hatred seemed to have abandoned me; the instinct for revenge, which so often flared up in me, had extinguished. This was all I needed to get out of life, this friendly, loving feeling, this human feeling that had been gone from my life for so long'.[52] Here again we might draw parallels with humane health centres. For founder of Maggie's Centres, Charles Jencks, we need medical environments to cure us, but 'we also need to feel like people again, rather than patients'.[53] The question arises, then: shouldn't we be purposefully designing penal institutions which make convicted offenders – the vast majority of whom will come back into society – feel like people again rather than prisoners? One of the key problems for the prison architect is that he or she has formal clients in the form of government ministries and private security companies awarded design contracts, but must also serve further 'clients' in the guise of prison staff, inmates and the wider community in which the prison is located. Of these, only the last may be considered worth consulting and designers do not generally liaise with the actual 'end users' of their designs.[54] In an ongoing climate of populist punitiveness, enlightened penal experiments, including those which employ aesthetic considerations aimed at making prisoners feel like people again frequently prove too controversial to survive in societies where the prevailing public view is that offenders deserve to be held in anaesthetizing, pain-inducing environments.

NOTES

1 Thanks to Jonathan Simon for his insightful comments on an early draft of this chapter.

2 Elaine Scarry, *On Beauty and Being Just* (Princeton NJ, 1999), p. 58.

3 Public expectation is itself complex and contested terrain. Media-fuelled anxiety projecting ideas about 'risk' and 'dangerousness' on to offenders suggests that the general public want to see 'traditional' looking prisons with all the motifs of punishment, retribution and deterrence implied – until they are proposed in their own neighbourhoods.

4 Daniel Nihill cited in Robin Evans, *The Fabrication of Virtue: English Prison Architecture, 1750–1840* (Cambridge, 1982), p. 323.

5 M. Fiddler, 'Projecting the prison: The depiction of the uncanny in *The Shawshank Redemption*', in *Crime, Media, Culture: An International Journal* 3/2 (2007): 192–206.

6 Peter Wayne, 'Prison design in the twentieth century', in Iona Spens (ed.), *Architecture of Incarceration* (London, 1994), p. 21.

7 See <http://www.malmaison-oxford.com>.

8 Karen Dale and Gibson Burrell, 'An-aesthetics and architecture', in Adrian Carr and Philip Hancock (eds), *Art and Aesthetics at Work* (Basingstoke, 2003).

9 Wayne, 'Prison design in the twentieth century', p. 22.

10 Philip Hancock and Yvonne Jewkes, 'Architectures of incarceration: the spatial pains of imprisonment', in *Punishment & Society* (December 2011).

11 Yvonne Jewkes, 'Penal aesthetics and the art of prison architecture', in Leonidas K. Cheliotis (ed.), *The Arts of Imprisonment: Essays on Control, Resistance and Empowerment* (Aldershot, 2011); and Yvonne Jewkes and Helen Johnston, 'The evolution of prison architecture', in Yvonne Jewkes (ed.), *Handbook on Prisons* (Cullompton, 2007).

12 Sean McConville, 'The architectural realization of penal ideas', in Leslie Fairweather and Sean McConville, *Prison Architecture: Policy, Design and Experience* (Oxford, 2000).

13 McConville, 'The architectural realization', p. 10.

14 Henri Lefebvre, *The Production of Space* (Oxford, 1991), p. 143.

15 Michel Foucault, *Discipline and Punish: The Birth of the Prison*, trans. Alan Sheridan (London, 1991); and E. Goffman, 'On the characteristics of total institutions: the inmate world', in Donald Cressey (ed.), *The Prison: Studies in Institutional Organisation and Change* (New York, 1961).

16 Jewkes, 'Penal aesthetics'.

17 Cited in Fiddler, 'Projecting the prison', p. 194.

18 Ideological, not literal as, strictly speaking neither are concerned with form and fabric. For Foucault the common thread that binds these institutions is a disciplinary technology of power while Loïc Wacquant's comparison of urban ghetto and prison is functional, not architectural.

19 Foucault, *Discipline and Punish*, p. 228.

20 Loïc Wacquant, 'Deadly symbiosis: when ghetto and prison meet and mesh', in *Punishment & Society* 3/1 (2001).

21 Michel de Certeau, *The Practice of Everyday Life* (Berkeley and Los Angeles CA, 1984).

22 Yvonne Jewkes, *Captive Audience: Media, Masculinity and Power in Prisons* (Cullompton, 2002).

23 Ian Dunbar, *A Sense of Direction* (London, 1985).

24 Architect Michael Walden of Dworsky Associates, Los Angeles, cited in Spens, *Architecture of Incarceration*, p. 11.

25 Amos Rapoport, 'Vernacular architecture and the cultural determinates of form', in Anthony D. King (ed.), *Buildings and Society: Essays on the Social Development of the Built Environment* (London, 1980).

26 Spens, *Architecture of Incarceration*, p. 11.

27 T. Fuss, 'Rethinking prison design: is it time to throw away the key to prison architecture?', in *LA Architect*, May/June (Glendale CA, 2006): 64.

28 Fuss, 'Rethinking prison design'.

29 Dale and Burrell, 'An-aesthetics and architecture'.

30 Ibid.

31 Ibid.

32 Spens, *Architecture of Incarceration*, p. 123.

33 Ibid., p. 115.

34 Ibid.

35 Ibid.

36 Jewkes and Johnson, 'evolution of prison architecture'.

37 John Pratt, 'Scandinavian exceptionalism in an era of penal excess', in *British Journal of Criminology* 48/2 (2007): 119–37.

38 See <http://www.worldarchitecturenews.com>.

39 *Time*, 10 May 2010.

40 It should be noted, however, that despite the lack of spatial and architectural repression at prisons such as Halden, 'modern' does not necessarily and unequivocally equate to 'better'. In fact, Hancock and Jewkes (2011) argue that such experiments in flexible, aesthetically sensitive penal design may engender their own distinctive 'pains of imprisonment' and represent an extension of state power over the individual; one all the more inhuman due to its apparent absence.

41 See <http://www.dailymail.co.uk/news/worldnews/article-1277158/Halden-Prison-Inside-Norways-posh-new-jail.html>.

42 See <http://www.newsinenglish.no/2010/05/25/shocking-lack-of-prison-security/>.

43 Barbara Mason, 'A gendered Irish experiment: grounds for optimism?', in Frances Heidensohn (ed.), *Gender and Justice* (Cullompton, 2006).

44 *Irish Prison Service* (2006), p. 35.

45 Foucault, *Discipline and Punish*.

46 See <http://www.garethhoskinsarchitects.co.uk/projects/health>.

47 Christine Tartaro, 'Watered down: partial implementation of the new generation jail philosophy', *The Prison Journal* 86/3 (2006).

48 Joe Sim, 'Barlinnie', in Yvonne Jewkes and Jamie Bennett (eds), *Dictionary of Prisons and Punishment* (Cullompton, 2008).

49 Ibid.

50 Ibid.

51 Sim, 'Barlinnie', p. 22.

52 Ibid.

53 Cited in the *Guardian*, 6 May 2010.

54 Hancock and Jewkes, 'Architecture of Incarceration'.

2

Architecture and Contested Space in the Development of the Modern Prison

Helen Johnston

Each narrow cell in which we dwell
Is a foul and dark latrine,
And the fetid breath of living Death
Chokes up each grated screen,
And all, but lust is turned to dust
In Humanity's machine.

(From *The Ballad of Reading Gaol* by Oscar Wilde)[1]

INTRODUCTION

This chapter will examine the changing place of architecture and the contested nature of prison space across 100 years of the development of the modern prison.[2] Prisons in the eighteenth century were often places of disorder and disease; inmates paid for their entrance, food, lodgings, release; gaolers profited from the fees and those prisoners with little or no family or support lived a meagre existence.[3] Prisoners were held until their court appearance, or until they were transported overseas to the colonies or publicly executed for their crimes. Those imprisoned for a short prison sentence or until debts were paid were simply detained; the function of the prison was detention and prisons, at this time, did not claim to do any more than secure custody. The architecture of such prisons was largely unimportant; prisons had to be secure but had little meaning beyond this function.

During the eighteenth century, it was probably the architecture of the gallows used across the country, or the permanent Triple Tree at Tyburn that had a more symbolic place in the minds of the populous with regard to the operation of punishment. But by the end of the century, this began to alter as the prison and more importantly, for this chapter, the architecture and spatial planning of the prison was transformed and the prison was placed at the centre of a new philosophy of punishment.

There were various reasons for the shift towards the use of imprisonment, some philosophical, others more practical responses; there was a decline in the use of execution by the beginning of the nineteenth century and public executions were ended in 1868, by which time it was often only those convicted for murder that were actually hung. Sending prisoners overseas and banishing them to one of the colonies for their crimes had also fluctuated in use, transportation to America had ended with the War of Independence in the 1770s and although the discovery of Australia had relatively quickly become the replacement, it too as a convict destination was under scrutiny in the early decades of the nineteenth century and had all but ended by the 1850s.

The 'birth' of the prison was a significant shift in the way in which the modern world saw the treatment of those who committed crimes, a movement away from the barbarous infliction of physical pain in public, whether that be execution, flogging, stocks, or pillory, towards a system of punishment that reflected the supposed civilisation of the nation and Utilitarian ideas about proportionality in the law, sentencing and punishment. As outlined, it was also a practical response to the problem, it was not deemed appropriate to execute offenders in the numbers in which they had in previous generations; indeed the system of capital punishment was seen as unjust and barbaric, often resulting in a lottery as to who actually stood at the gallows.[4] Various mechanisms operating throughout the criminal justice system meant that a person may not be executed, despite the large number of capital offences (about 250 offences: 'the Bloody Code'). Legislation was minutely defined so many of these statutes did not result in offenders being put to death. Some offenders could claim immunity through an old concept of 'benefit of clergy' but only for the first offence. At trial, juries were reluctant to convict if they thought the offence did not deserve such a punishment, or if there was an error in prosecution, or they judged stolen goods to be of lower value; thus removing the possibility of a capital sentence. In addition, at sentence the judge may reduce sentence to transportation or it could be reduced through a plea of mercy to the King.[5]

Although transportation had been fairly widely used, as a sentence and for those reprieved from death, it was also becoming apparent that prisoners could not be sent abroad as the former colonies no longer wanted the 'dregs' of English society. Therefore, by the early to mid-nineteenth century, England was faced with a new, and what was for some, uncomfortable reality; prisoners would have to serve their sentences in prisons in this country and many of them would at some time be released in this country. This briefly summarises just some of the conflicts and complex questions which confronted penal commentators and social observers in this period.

What was important for the prison at this moment in history was that it developed from a holding and detention function to a place in which the offenders could potentially be transformed by the regimes and routines within the prison walls. The architecture and design of prisons became central to the way in which the transformation of offenders would occur and to the changing penal philosophies and practices in the following years. As this chapter will discuss, different penal philosophies came to prominence at different times, the new prison architecture which began in the late eighteenth century had to embrace these shifting penal ideologies and practices. Architectural meaning in internal construction and external façades became multi-layered; communicating ideas of reform, punishment, deterrence, state power often at the same time but with one or another philosophy at the fore. Predominantly focussing on the nineteenth century, this chapter will focus on internal prison architecture and space in three distinct but linked moments in the development of the modern prison. It will consider first, the period of prison 'reform' at the end of the eighteenth and beginning of the nineteenth century; second, the height of the use of the separate system in the 1830s and 1840s; and finally, a period of severely deterrent prison regimes, from the mid-nineteenth century, through the centralisation of local prisons in 1877, to 1895 when the Gladstone Committee on prisons began to challenge the deterrent regime and promote the idea that prisons could be both deterrent and rehabilitative.[6] In each of these periods, all key in the development of the modern prison, architecture and design of space in prisons was fundamentally important to the regime and became deeply embedded into the way in which prisons operated.

Unlike the United States, where a large scale prison building programme of 'Big House' prisons such as Sing Sing occurred in the early twentieth century, there were few prisons built in England. In the twentieth century, new prisons were located in disused army barracks, airfields, military hospitals or country houses, where buildings were adapted for the purpose rather than newly constructed. As John Pratt has argued the prison 'disappeared', becoming increasingly invisible, remote and cut off from society.[7] New progressive thinking in the early twentieth century saw the development of open prisons and ex-military facilities suited the requirements and so the first complete new build was HMP Everthorpe in 1958, which originally opened as a borstal.[8] Some 'new-generation' prisons appeared from the 1960s onwards, HMP Holloway was rebuilt in the 1970s but the architectural design was its fundamental flaw, since then, most have conformed to the traditional spurred design.[9] In the twenty-first century, there has been more discourse on penal aesthetics and humane treatment in prison building but this exists alongside a discourse for more security and in a terrain where new prison builds are likely to be undertaken by private companies.[10]

However, it is important to remember that the prisons of the nineteenth century still play a central role in current prison system, local prisons built in the Victorian period, such as HMP Liverpool, HMP Wandsworth; two of the largest prisons in Western Europe, and HMP Hull, HMP Leicester, HMP Birmingham, HMP Leeds, HMP Wormwood Scrubs, 'have not been consigned to the history books; thousands of prison inmates still live, sleep and work in these monoliths of the Victorian penal imagination'.[11]

ARCHITECTURE AND PRISON SPACE IN THE PERIOD OF REFORM

The architectural development and prison designs of the early reform period in the late eighteenth century were not just about providing a moral environment in which prisoners' behaviour could be potentially altered, in the preceding decades there had also been a widespread concern about disease and health in the post-reform gaols and houses of correction. Much of the squalor, disease and the poor conditions in which prisoners were housed as well as the deficiencies of administration were exposed by reformers such as John Howard and Elizabeth Fry in the late eighteenth and early nineteenth century. Howard was concerned with the spread of disease and poor health in prisons but he was also interested in improving the moral environment, ending the debauchery, association and drunkenness he had observed.

Broadly speaking, the changes in prison design and space came in two phases; in the early phase came designs influenced by the concerns about the physical health of prisoners, particularly concern about gaol fever and an influential design by Jeremy Bentham, his plan for the 'Panopticon' prison. In the second phase, prison design and architecture was more deeply embedded in the regime and was thought to encourage the transformation of the prisoner through inward religious and moral reflection influenced by Evangelical thought, as demonstrated in the use of the separate and silent systems of the early nineteenth century (discussed in the following section).

From the mid-eighteenth century, the architecture of prisons was being altered due to the concerns about health. As Robin Evans has pointed out in the years up to 1795 there was widespread prison building in England, at least 45 new gaols and bridewells were constructed and these projects were undertaken by magistrates at the local level and not by the government.[12] This was partly due to the end of transportation to America (the number of prisoners in gaols and houses of correction had increased and the hulks (prison ships) were overcrowded and had a high mortality rate), but was also due to the concern about the spread of 'gaol fever'. Although it remained clear that prisons should be 'places of terror' and the external architecture of the prison should convey this, there was concern that 'gaol fever' could escape the prison walls and infect the populous. Therefore prison architecture and design focused on the prevention of the spread of disease by the use of ventilation, 'salubrity and airiness' determined prison construction, as it was believed that the putrid air in prisons was the cause of contagion.[13]

The work of pioneering prison architects such as Stephen Hales, who installed ventilation devices and bellows at various prisons across the country, can also be seen to influence the recommendations of reformer Howard, made in the latter decades of the eighteenth century. Howard recommended that prisons should be built in open country, perhaps on a hill or close to running water, and that the building itself should be divided into pavilions for different classes of prisoners, each pavilion raised above ground on arcades to allow the flow of air around the building.[14] One example of a prison which embraced all the principles of design and location recommended by Howard was Shrewsbury prison, built in 1793. Shrewsbury prison was built (and still stands) on Castle Hill, near to the River Severn, and internally the prison was designed around four main courts and other smaller ones. Each court was surrounded by an arcade with arches, above which were the sleeping cells connected by railed galleries and at the centre of the prison stood the chapel.[15] The prison was designed by William Blackburn, and a local architect John H. Haycock and the construction fell to the then County Surveyor of Shropshire, Thomas Telford. Blackburn was a leading prison architect who designed many of the prisons constructed across the country in the period of reform; he translated Howard's reforms into practical construction.[16]

Howard's influence can also be seen in the 1779 Penitentiary Act; it was resolved that penitentiaries should be built by the government to hold prisoners before transportation (or until a new destination was found) and it was to this tender that Jeremy Bentham submitted his plans for the Panopticon. The Panopticon has probably become the most famous prison design and its influence on prison construction and the construction of other buildings is clearly evident, but it has never been built in the way in which Bentham envisaged, at least not in the UK. The Panopticon design is based on the ideas of surveillance, observation and inspection, the design is of six floors in a circular structure, each floor has cells around the outside and all the cells face an observation tower in the centre of the structure. Prisoners in their cells were therefore observable from the guard tower at all times, conformity induced by the fact that prisoners could not tell at any one moment whether they were being observed or not.

Despite Bentham's long correspondence with the government, the Panopticon was never built and neither were the penitentiaries; in the end the discovery of Australia led to a new penal colony and from 1787 convicts were sent to this new faraway land. The problem of housing large numbers of prisoners in England was largely abandoned until 1816 when the first government penitentiary, Millbank opened for convicts to serve sentences of solitary confinement before transportation overseas. The demise of Millbank was relatively swift as public attention grew to the numbers of prisoners with mental health problems caused by the severe regime.[17] By the time the Millbank experiment had ended and it was converted to a convict depot, penal philosophies had moved on and across the Atlantic the development of new ideas about how prisoners should be treated and could be transformed began to influence architecture and design of prison regimes in this country.

THE SEPARATE CELL: ARCHITECTURAL ISOLATION AND SPACE

The spread of new penal philosophies from the United States to England in the 1820s and 1830s had a fundamental impact on the prison, its architecture and its regimes. Penal administrators, magistrates and social commentators debated the relative merits of two systems of punishment; the separate system and the silent system. Both systems were in use in the US; the separate system at Walnut Street Prison and the Eastern Penitentiary in Philadelphia, and the silent system at Auburn and Sing Sing Prisons in the State of New York. Under the separate system, prisoners were held in separate cells, where they would sleep, eat and work, they would only leave to go to chapel or for exercise. Even then their faces could be covered to prevent recognition, or exercise may be undertaken in a separate yard to prevent contact with other prisoners. Under the silent system, prisoners were held in association during the day and put to labour, but communication was prohibited at all times. Both of these systems operated in the belief that moral contamination should be prevented through the isolation of, or the prevention of communication between, prisoners; young offenders and those in prison for the first time would not be contaminated by the hardened or more experienced offenders confined with them.[18]

One of the first Inspectors of Prisons, William Crawford, had visited penitentiaries in the US operating both systems of imprisonment and presented a detailed report demonstrating his support for the separate system. Crawford and another Inspector, Reverend Whitworth Russell used their position to advance the benefits of the separate system and the establishment of Inspectors of Prison in 1835 allowed the government to inspect and make recommendations to local magistrates who administered prisons across the country.

The architecture of imprisonment was to play a central role, as the attention to detail in the construction of the cells and buildings was crucial to enforce the required degree of separation, isolation (physical and acoustic) and yet maintain space for sleeping and labour within the cell; the use of separate system enforced by architectural isolation in a cell was seen as an important part of not only punishment but also of reformation. As Crawford noted in his report to the government:

> *In the silence of the cell contamination cannot be received or imparted. A sense of degradation cannot be excited by exposure nor reformation checked by false shame. Day after day, with no companions but his thoughts, the convict is compelled to reflect and listen to the reproofs of conscience. He is led to dwell upon past errors, and to cherish whatever better feelings he may at any time have imbibed. These circumstances are in the highest degree calculated to ameliorate the affections and reclaim the heart. The mind becomes open to the best impressions and prepared for the reception of those truths and consolations which Christianity can alone impart.*[19]

The government's second penitentiary Pentonville, opened in 1842 had embraced the use of the separate system and this had been designed into the architecture of the building, by Joshua Jebb (Surveyor-General of Convict Prisons). Even before the first prisoners arrived at Pentonville the new government experiment came under considerably scrutiny in the press. *The Times* was a staunch critic of the new regime, calling the system 'unnecessarily cruel, impolitic and injudicious'[20] and the new cells of isolation held up to offer a space of moral and religious conversion were quickly seen by critics as a source of mental breakdown in prisoners and unnecessary severity. Charles Dickens, who had also observed the separate system in operation in Philadelphia, argued that:

> *Very few men were capable of estimating the immense amount of torture and agony which this dreadful punishment, prolonged for years, inflicts upon the sufferers; and, in guessing at it myself, and in reasoning from what I have seen*

> *... I am only the more convinced that there is a depth of terrible endurance to it which none but its sufferers can fathom, and which no man has the right to inflict upon his fellow creature.*[21]

In the following months, the periods of isolation under the separate system were reduced from eighteen to twelve and then to nine months as prisoners' mental and physical health began to breakdown.[22]

Whilst the use of the separate system may not have been as widespread in practice as some authors have suggested, the Prison Act 1839 did order that all prisons across the country operate the system (it also required each separate cell to be certified by the Inspectors of Prisons) and it is at this point that the use of 'the cell' becomes the central focus of penal philosophy and practice. Across the country, the use of the separate system varied, some prisons like Shrewsbury had, even before the Act, built separate cells and began a slow conversion of the whole of the prison in the following decades,[23] yet other prisons still operated the silent system, or the local magistrates did not, or were not willing to, commit the financial resources required for such a project, it remained the case that the systems and practices in use were diverse.

In practice, the use of the separate system in local rather than government controlled prisons, was not universal, and conversion to the system could be long and protracted but the dominance of the separate system within the penal system was ensured by Prison Inspectors appointed under the Prison Act 1835. These five inspectors and notably, two in particular, Crawford and Russell, began to exert considerable influence and pressure on the local authorities running prisons across the country. They began regular inspections, certified prison rules, advised magistrates and the Home Secretary, they interviewed applicants for posts in government prisons, approved all architectural changes and developments and Crawford and Russell prepared the Prison Act 1839 which pushed through their preferred separate system.[24]

In the US, the silent system won out in the mid-century, but it appears that the use of the systems across the Atlantic were different; in the US the silent congregate system was used in cellular confinement, but in England the silent system was often operated through cellular confinement at night, but during the day, labour was undertaken in large workrooms where the prisoners were in association but silent. Advocates of the silent system like the Governor of Coldbath Fields House of Correction, George Laval Chesterton, were not as convinced by the religious transformation of the separate system and thought that prisoners needed to be taught new attitudes. A system of rewards and punishments came along with the silent system; a more pessimistic view of reform, in which defiance was met with immediate punishment, which was both automatic and increased in severity if the defiance lasted. Chesterton believed that prisoners were 'forced into reflection ... they become penitent and submissive. The lesson is not lost upon them and in the process of time their dispositions are so obviously improved as to attest the valuable benefit of the treatment they have received.'[25]

So, by the late 1830s the separate system and the separate cell had been established by its advocates as a place of potential transformation, the cell was a space in which, under the correct conditions, the prisoner could reflect on their own behaviour, past criminal life and mistakes, repent and look to God for salvation. In 'the solitude of the cell ... alone with God and a wounded conscience, the unhappy man is forced to exercise his powers of reflection, and thus acquires a command over his sensual impulses which will probably exert a permanent influence'.[26]

But by the mid-1840s to early 1850s the separate system was beginning to lose its appeal, the penal philosophy underpinning the system came under attack as long periods of isolation were deemed too severe for the majority of prisoners to endure. On the other hand, it was claimed prisoners manipulated chaplains with false claims of religious enlightenment. Others thought the regime too soft; questions were raised about the amount of food given to prisoners particularly in relation to the daily food given in workhouses and the everyday diet of the labouring poor. But others stuck firmly to their claims that through the separate system: 'a very strong impression on the nervous system is made, and it requires careful watching to regulate it, but we believe that with such watchfulness it not only is controllable, but essential to that change of mind which reforms character.'[27]

However, the decision to choose cellular confinement made in this period was a fundamental moment in the history of the prison. It was at this moment that the way in which architecture and space in prisons were devised and internally organised (at least in the Western world), became the focal point for many of the regimes that followed and continues to remain central to the way in which many prisons are organised today.

DETERRENCE AND ARCHITECTURE

From the mid-nineteenth century until the Gladstone Committee in 1895 prison regimes were dominated by a deterrent philosophy of punishment. Whilst a deterrent element of the prison regime and architecture already existed, the reformative potential of the separate system had been undone and combined with public fears about the 'criminal classes' and the end of transportation gave prominence to a more deterrent penal philosophy.[28] By the early 1850s transportation to Australia had virtually ended and the government had designed a new system of convict prisons where those prisoners who would otherwise have been transported would undergo sentences of penal servitude. Thus from the mid-century existed two systems of imprisonment, the government-run convict prisons and the local prisons for shorter sentences of imprisonment (under two years) which were administered by the magistrates of the county or borough.

Both local prisons and convict prisons from the mid-century were to operate a regime in which deterrence was the primary aim. The reformative potential of the separate system enforced through architectural isolation was lost and although separate cells remained a key feature of the prison regime, they were no longer seen as offering the potentially transformative function of religious and inward reflection that the earlier commentators had hailed. Instead the architecture of isolation in cellular confinement was to form the central part of a regime to deter the offender. The new regime saw the use of the cell embedded into a severe prison regime based on deterrence and uniformity. This regime came from the recommendations of the Carnarvon Committee in 1863 and is often referred to as 'hard labour, hard board, hard fare'; prisoners were put to hard labour for long hours of the day, given low diets and sparse living conditions. The use of cellular space remained; to isolate the prisoner at night or to separate them from others during the day, whilst they were put to hard labour on the crank or making clogs or picking oakum (prisoners were given old rope which they had to untwist and separate by hand this would then be sold on, hence the expression 'money for old rope'). The types of hard labour given varied according to the establishment; convict prisoners may be put to work on the dockyards yet those prisoners in local prisons often completed hard labour in their cells and therefore may have only left the cell for short periods to attend chapel or for exercise. The cell was pivotal within the control of the regime and the cramped, poorly-lit environment loomed large in the memoirs of prisoners in this period. Fraudster, Austin Bidwell, sentenced to twenty years imprisonment in 1873 wrote:

> *[a] little box with a mixture of curiosity and consternation for the thought smote me with blinding force that for long years that little box – eight feet six inches in length, seven in height and five feet in width, with its floor and roof of stone – would be my only home – would be! must be! And no power could avert my fate.*[29]

The cell conditions were sparse; the main furniture was the bed or hammock, although the 1863 Committee replaced them with plank beds and coarse mattresses for short term prisoners and those in the early stages of a long sentence. The pillow of the plank bed was also a piece of wood, nailed to the plank and stuffed with coconut fibre. The early reformers had been concerned about ventilation and circulating air in the prisons but as the separate system had spread, the arcades and galleries of prison had been filled in, separate cells with built-in lavatories were insanitary and poorly maintained or the use of cell buckets resulted in stench and stagnant air trapped in the architecture of the wings.[30]

In 1877, the Prison Act transferred the control of the local prisons from the magistrates to the government. The slow and gradual process of uniformity that had been a concern for most of the century had been overcome, all prisoners in local prisons could be subject to the same conditions regardless as to their geographical location and a system of marks (used in the convict prisons) was introduced. Under the marks system, each prisoner was set a daily number of marks to achieve through labour and good behaviour, through 28 day stage system marks were accumulated, and if the required number were obtained during the period, then the prisoner would pass to the next stage which had some amelioration in the regime. Periods of imprisonment in both convict and local prisons remained focused on deterrence and conditions were harsh. Convict prisoners were still to serve nine months in separate confinement before they were set to penal servitude. In local prisons, most sentences were short, commonly less than one month but frequently less than two weeks, this often meant that prisoners were unable to progress through the marks system and were to experience the whole of their sentence at the first and therefore most meagre stage of the system.[31] One-who-has-tried-them argued in 1881 that:

> *Unless one has experienced it, one can have no conception of the effect of close confinement upon the nervous system. People who have not tried it are apt to say 'Well, it's only for twenty-eight days;' but if they were to try what it was like having nothing but white-washed walls to stare at day after day, and neither book nor employment to take one's thoughts, as it were, out of one's self, I don't think they would say anything about it's being 'only twenty-eight days'.*[32]

The deterrent regime persisted until the Gladstone Committee in 1895 which reviewed prisons in the late nineteenth century; this Committee advocated some alterations in the regime and was based on ideas which bought together rehabilitation and deterrence. Some alterations in the day to day lives of prisoners emerged yet separation and silence was still dominated the regime. Brocklehurst wrote, in 1898, of his twenty-eight day sentence of solitary confinement:

> *Imagine a blind man denied human intercourse, with power of motion only in a space 14 feet by 7, whose only contact with a limited outside world comes through the ceiling, walls and iron door, and you can form a faint idea of what life in prison must be. A prisoner sees nothing beyond the limits of his cell; feels only its discomforts; tastes the prescribed prison fare; hears limited sounds of his strange environment; and smells little beyond the scent of creosote as it exhales from the oakum.*[33]

CONCLUSION

Examining prison architecture and space in the historical development of the modern prison, particularly focusing on the key period between the end of the eighteenth and the end of the nineteenth century, demonstrates not only how prisons operated in the past, but also provides an important insight into the shape of prisons today. As this chapter has shown, the influence and indeed, the continued use of Victorian prisons today, means that these architectural influences remain at the core of our prison system. The lack of prison building and the decline of the prison population in England in the early twentieth century meant that when new developments and a rise in the prison population occurred in the post Second World War era, these Victorian prisons were needed. But it is not simply about the functional requirements of the system, the popular cultural image of a 'prison' is a Victorian prison, long three tier buildings with small windows and an austere exterior, is the 'prison-look' and this is deeply culturally embedded.[34]

The use of cellular confinement as opposed to other collective methods of holding prisoners has also been pivotal in shaping the organisation and management of prison space and regime throughout the following centuries. In the twenty-first century, we can observe the use of such deeply embedded attitudes about cellular architectural and prison space in the construction and use of Supermax prisons across the globe. These spaces confine the 'worst of the worst' prisoners in solitary lockdown for 23 hours per day with little visual stimuli, possession or activities and by design, contact with human beings at a minimum or the use of Supermax isolation for death row inmates to 'prime' the condemned for death in the US.[35] Whilst supermax prisons have not been built in the UK, instead dispersal prisons and high security units are used, elements of supermaxes such as segregation, isolation, surveillance, constant artificial lighting are features which predominate. Such use of the cell and the architectural enforcement of this space in the twenty-first century and the debates they provoke are strongly reminiscent of some of the historical developments in prison architecture discussed above. The cell is perhaps irremovable in our view of how prisons should be organised. It has been through various incarnations as a space of reform, separation, deterrence and isolation and although often now occupied by more than one prisoner, has remained architecturally the most significant space in the prison.

NOTES

1 Oscar Wilde, *De Profundis, The Ballad of Reading Gaol and Other Writings* (Ware, 1898/2002), p. 136.

2 An earlier version of this article appeared in the *Prison Service Journal* 187 (2010): 9–14.

3 Randall McGowen, 'The Well-Ordered Prison, England, 1780–1865', in Norval Morris and David J. Rothman (eds), *The Oxford History of the Prison – The Practice of Punishment in Western Society* (New York, 1998), pp. 71–99.

4 Victor Gatrell, *The Hanging Tree – Execution and the English People 1770–1868* (Oxford, 1994).

5 Clive Emsley, *Crime and Society in England, 1750–1900* (Harlow, 2010).

6 *Report from the Departmental Committee on Prisons [Gladstone Committee]* (C.7702), vol. LVI, Parliamentary Papers (London, 1895).

7 John Pratt, *Punishment and Civilisation: Penal Tolerance and Intolerance in Modern Society* (London, 2002).

8 Ian Dunbar and Leslie Fairweather, 'English prison design', in Leslie Fairweather and Sean McConville (eds), *Prison Architecture: Policy, Design and Experience* (Oxford, 2000); Mark Leech, *The Prisons Handbook* (Manchester, 2005).

9 Leslie Fairweather, 'Prison design in the twentieth century', in Iona Spens (ed.) *Architecture of Incarceration* (London, 1994); Paul Rock, *Reconstructing a Women's Prison: The Holloway Redevelopment Project, 1968–1988* (Oxford, 1996); Yvonne Jewkes and Helen Johnston, 'The evolution of prison architecture', in Yvonne Jewkes (ed), *Handbook on Prisons* (Cullompton, 2007), pp. 174–96.

10 Fairweather, 'Prison design'; Jewkes and Johnston, 'The evolution of prison architecture', pp. 174–96.

11 Jewkes and Johnston, 'The evolution of prison architecture', p. 191.

12 Robin Evans, *The Fabrication of Virtue: English Prison Architecture, 1750–1840* (Cambridge, 1982).

13 Evans, *Fabrication*, p. 102; also see Jewkes and Johnston, 'The evolution of prison architecture', pp. 174–96.

14 Evans, *Fabrication*.

15 Owen, *Some Account of the Ancient and Present State of Shrewsbury* (Shrewsbury, 1808, republished Manchester, 1972); Jewkes and Johnston, 'The evolution of prison architecture', pp. 174–96.

16 Evans, *Fabrication*.

17 Sean McConville, *A History of English Prison Administration Vol. 1 1750–1877* (London, 1981).

18 William J. Forsythe, *The Reform of Prisoners 1830–1900* (London, 1987).

19 William Crawford, *Report of William Crawford Esq., on the Penitentiaries of the United States, addressed to His Majesty's Principal Secretary of State for the Home Department* (593), vol. XLVI.349, Parliamentary Papers (London, 1834), p. 12.

20 *The Times*, 20 May 1841.

21 Charles Dickens, *American Notes* (London, 1842), pp. 153–4, cited in Helen Johnston, '"Buried Alive": Representations of the separate system in Victorian England', in Paul Mason (ed.), *Captured by the Media: Prison discourse in popular culture* (Cullompton, 2006), p. 108.

22 Johnston, '"Buried Alive"'.

23 Helen Johnston, 'Transformations of imprisonment in a local context: A case study of Shrewsbury in the nineteenth century', unpublished PhD thesis (Keele University, 2004).

24 Forsythe, *Reform*.

25 George Laval Chesterton, *Revelations of Prison Life* (London, 1856), cited in Forsythe, *Reform*, p. 32.

26 Dr Daniel Ritchie, *The Voice of our Exiles; or Stray Leaves from a Convict Ship* (Edinburgh, 1854), p. 4, cited in Phillip Priestley, *Victorian Prison Lives: English Prison Biography 1830–1914* (London, 1999), p. 37.

27 Robert Ferguson, 'Pentonville Prisoners', *Quarterly Review*, 82 (1847): 184–5.

28 Johnston, 'Buried Alive'.

29 Austin Bidwell, *From Wall Street to Newgate* (London, 1895), p. 397, cited in Sarah Anderson and John Pratt, 'Prisoner memoirs and their role in prison history', in Helen Johnston (ed.), *Punishment and Control in Historical Perspective* (Basingstoke, 2008), p. 181.

30 Anderson and Pratt, 'Prisoner Memoirs'.

31 Sean McConville, 'The Victorian Prison, 1865–1965', in Norval Morris and David J. Rothman (eds), *The Oxford History of the Prison – The Practice of Punishment in Western Society* (New York, 1998), pp. 117–50.

32 One-who-has-tried-them, *Her Majesty's Prisons and their Effects and Defects by ...* (London, 1881), p. 264, cited in Priestley, *Victorian Prison Lives*, p. 41.

33 F. Brocklehurst, *I was in Prison* (London, 1898), p. 29, cited in Anderson and Pratt, 'Prisoner Memoirs', pp. 181–2.

34 Jewkes and Johnston, 'The evolution of prison architecture'.

35 Roy D. King, 'The rise and rise of the supermax: An American solution in search of a problem?', *Punishment & Society*, 1/2 (1999): 163–86; Sharon Shalev, *Supermax: Controlling risk through solitary confinement* (Cullompton, 2009); Mona Lynch, 'Supermax meets death row: legal struggles around the new punitiveness in the US', in John Pratt, David Brown, Mark Brown, Simon Hallsworth and Wayne Morrison (eds), *The New Punitiveness: Trends, theories, perspectives* (Cullompton, 2005), pp. 66–84.

3

A Simple Idea in Architecture: On the Principles of Projecting Prisons

Gabriela Świtek

'The world itself is but a large prison, out of which some are daily led to execution', said Sir Walter Raleigh, favourite of Elizabeth I and member of her court, for whom the political meanderings of justice were far from indifferent.[1] He was imprisoned in the Tower, then released, then imprisoned again, sentenced to life imprisonment, until finally they cut off his head. It is no coincidence that his contemporary William Shakespeare compared the state and the world to a prison, lovers to prisoners and love to being shackled in handcuffs.

The prophets of the Old Testament foretold the liberation of those held captive and freedom for prisoners. In Book VII of *The Republic*, Plato housed people in a cave, or in a habitation which he compared to living in a prison: 'in this they lie from their childhood, their legs and necks in chains.'[2] Descartes, in his turn, in developing his moral outlook concurs with stoic resignation in asserting that one should 'first and foremost change one's desire rather than the order of the world'. Or, in other words, in practice if we are sitting in prison, as the philosopher gives us an example, should we in order to achieve peace of mind rid ourselves of the desire for freedom, which is merely the desire to possess 'wings to flutter like a bird'.[3]

Oscar Wilde, when writing his celebrated *Ballad of Reading Gaol* on the basis not just of an aesthetic vision but of his own experiences, described a prison as a place in which each day is as long as a year, which itself is composed of very long days. In *De Profundis* he confessed:

> *I have lain in prison for nearly two years. Out of my nature has come wild despair; an abandonment to grief that was piteous even to look at; terrible and impotent rage; bitterness and scorn; anguish that wept aloud; misery that could find no voice; sorrow that was dumb. I have passed through every possible mood of suffering.*[4]

George Bernard Shaw maintained that a home is like a prison for a girl and like a workhouse for a woman, although this time the claim did not come from personal experience. Evelyn Waugh, the literary inheritor of those cited above and connoisseur of the Oxford climate, maintained in *Decline and Fall* that 'anyone who has been to an English public school will always feel comparatively at home in prison'.[5]

In escaping from Oxford to the picturesque English Lake District, Thomas De Quincey did not succeed in freeing himself from the prisons that oppressed the hallucinations brought on by opium and laudanum:

> *I seemed every night to descend – not metaphorically, but literally to descend – into chasms and sunless abysses, depths below depths, from which it seemed hopeless that I should ever re-ascended. … The sense of space, and in the end the sense of time, were both powerfully affected.*[6]

As Anthony Vidler notes, De Quincey found his alter ego in the person of Giovanni Battista Piranesi. He imagined him hazily under the influence of an account by Coleridge who described to him 'a set of plates from that artist [Piranesi], called his *Dreams* and which record the scenery of his own visions during the delirium of a fever'.[7] Piranesi was climbing up the stairs of a prison, which he had engraved himself; the stairs abruptly came to a halt in a sheer abyss, but higher lay the next stairs where the figure of Piranesi was once again visible climbing strenuously. And so on without end until both the stairs and Piranesi disappeared in the upper gloom of the hall. De Quincy was fascinated by the endless division and self-reproduction of the space of the *Carceri*. Although he never actually saw the drawings, it was they who provided the architectonic backdrop for his narcotic visions.

De Quincey's celebrated account of his conversation with Samuel Taylor Coleridge set off a chain reaction. There are shackles that bind the interpretation of Piranesi's famous *Carceri* in English gothic tales with French romanticism. Mario Praz found the spirit of the *Prisons* in Horace Walpole's *The Castle of Otranto*, in the letters of William Beckford and in the literature of the period of the French Revolution.[8] The influence of Piranesian fantasies has also been identified in the work of Alfred de Musset, Charles Nodier, Honoré de Balzac, Victor Hugo, Charles Baudelaire and Stéphane Mallarmé. Thèophile Gautier imagined Hamlet played on a backdrop of set drawn from the *Prisons* – because after all 'Denmark is a prison'.

Aldous Huxley, the master of dystopia, whose *The Doors of Perception* emerged under the influence of the hallucinogenic mescaline, wrote the introduction to one of the editions of the engravings. In the *Prisons* he saw the reflection of the torpor of the soul.[9] Analysing 'the dark brain of Piranesi', Marguerite Yourcenar stresses that the *Prisons* are not reminiscent of the claustrophobic space of funeral darkness traditionally associated with prison nightmares. They are also dissimilar to the 'cold functionalism of [the] model prison, the sinister banality of concentration-camp barracks … , the image of human crowds penned in the abattoirs of the first half of the twentieth century'.[10]

It is prisons that are never built that become myths of architecture, astutely observed by Manfredo Tafuri in his book *The Sphere and the Labyrinth: Avant-Gardes and Architecture from Piranesi to the 1970s* (1987). The *Prisons*, however, did not become a motivation for the writing of a history of prison buildings, but to the following of their influence, as labyrinths along which artists fumble, on the presentation of space in architecture, and also in other domains. One of the heirs to this myth, for example, is Sergei Eisenstein who found in Piranesi's drawings the potential for film sequences.[11] Drawing on the hazy vision of the *Carceri* presented by De Quincey, Vidler finds them the first appearance of 'spatial uncanny', which is displayed in 'the abyssal repetitions of the imaginary void'.[12]

The prison, thus, was first and foremost an allegory of the human condition, in particular for the state of mind of the romantic artist and all mental, emotional and institutional violations, rather than a theme worthy of great architecture. Indeed, the history of architecture has little to say about this type of building. Vitruvius, the author of the one ancient treatise on architecture says virtually nothing about prisons. In Book V which deals with the principles for the projection of public buildings, there is simply a reminder that 'the treasury, prison and senate house ought to adjoin the forum, but in such a way that their dimensions may be proportionate to those of the forum'.[13] In reality, the history of the architecture of prisons begins with the descriptions of dungeons in citadels and castles, of the cells of town prisons or hulks, but the prison as a noble task for architects appears only in the eighteenth century, when in the name of the public good, a series of other types of public buildings, such as museums, hospitals or factories, also started to emerge.

CESARE BECCARIA AND JOHN HOWARD

In his *Essay on Crimes and Punishments* (*Dei delitti e delle pene*, 1764), translated into English as early as 1767, Cesare Beccaria, a Milanese aristocrat contemporary of Piranesi, inspired by the accounts of Alessandro and Pietro Verri about the torture and horrifying conditions which were the norm in prisons, proposed a reform of the justice system. According to Beccaria the aim of punishment is not revenge, but social adjustment, and he therefore called on governors and lawmakers to establish clear laws and to do away with the death penalty.[14] The law and the penitentiary system were indeed to become a safeguard for the basic principles of the social contract, thus establishing that the members of a society are endowed with free will and reason, and that human actions are predictable and subject to control.

Beccaria's view that long term punishment acts as a more effective deterrent to the committing of a crime than a rapid execution not only had a profound influence on the shape of modern law codes, but also acted indirectly as a challenge to architecture. Given such ideological foundations, it would be necessary to come to terms with a new type of public building. In France, Beccaria's treatise was greeted with enormous enthusiasm, although he himself, apparently excruciatingly timid, did not make a big impression during his stay in Paris at the invitation of Enlightenment intellectuals.

As W.C. De Pauley notes in his essay, 'the best commentary on the principles advocated by Beccaria is the life of John Howard, who translated into action the spirit of his "benevolent" inspirer'.[15] Howard, who began an inspection of European prisons in 1773, died of typhus when visiting Russian military hospitals, but none the less bequeathed to history the work *The State of the Prisons in England and Wales, with Preliminary Observations and an Account of some Foreign Prisons and Hospitals* (1777), which was reprinted on three occasions prior to the end of the eighteenth century. Here he also presented a plan for a prison of rectangular design divided into separate blocks for men, women and young offenders.[16] In the centre of the establishment, Howard situated the house of the gaoler, who was supposed to be an honest and sober minded person, and also a garden and a chapel. The blocks were also divided according to category of crime committed: debtors were divided from felons. Each block was to have its own courtyard, and each prisoner his own cell for sleeping and a guaranteed change of clothing twice a week.

The individual endowed with the task of undertaking the reform, begun by Howard, was the architect William Blackburn. He built seventeen prisons and acted as consultant on another five projects, but did not stay faithful to any one form of construction.[17] He designed prisons in the form of a single block, with interior courtyards, pavilions, polygons and wings departing in a radial form. The great campaign about prisons ended with the death of Howard and Blackburn in 1790. By the end of the century the French Revolution had made its own contribution to the architecture of prisons, not so much through the storming of the inglorious Bastille, as through the return to the spectacle of swift and absolute punishment – the guillotine.

ARCHITECTURE TERRIBLE VERSUS THE PANOPTICON

'If I placed this august Palace above the shadowy lair of Crime, I should not only show to advantage the nobility of the architecture on account of the resulting contrast, but I should also have an impressive metaphorical image of Vice overwhelmed by the weight of Justice.'[18] Etienne-Louis Boullée obtained this contrast, necessary for the expression of the poetry of architecture, by placing the entrance to a prison under the monumental mass of the Palace of Justice. The picture of this never realised Palace is painted with great assiduousness by Boullée in his *Architecture, Essay on Art* from somewhere around 1793. The palace is majestic, as befits its function. Surrounded in 'brilliant light' and placed on a high podium, it 'appears to be part of the Heavens'. It was designed according to an ideal square design, with interior courtyards which, assuring a plentiful supply of air and light, would reinforce the healthy and salutary atmosphere of the whole construction.

Boullée does not, on the other hand, present detailed plans of the level of the underground prisons, since, in his opinion, their arrangement is 'of no great interest'. We are merely informed that the entrance to the prisons is to be at ground level, as if they were 'the precarious tomb of criminals'.[19] His contemporary, Claude-

Nicolas Ledoux, miraculously avoided prison, or even perhaps the guillotine, during the time of the Terror. He went on to design a prison in Aix, but not in his ideal industrial town Chaux; this town was a more developed version of the Royal salt mines in Arc-et-Senans built according to his design in the years 1774–78. In the centre of the circular complex, Ledoux placed the building of the director: an all-seeing manager.

As Barry Bergdoll argues, *architecture terrible*, architecture of a horrifying physiognomy is presented as being the characteristic feature of a prison as a public building of a unique type in the *Cours d'architecture* (1771–77), or the series of lectures by Jacques-François Blondel, Boullée's teacher, given at the Parisian Academy of Architecture.[20] Taking from Germain Boffrand the theory of architectural character, Blondel builds an aesthetic hierarchy of the effects of architecture, based on classical rhetoric and physiognomic treatises. A prison should be repugnant: through its monumentality and the heavy proportions of its elevations it should both deter the committing of a crime, and express the heavy and ensnared fates of the prisoners.

An answer to this physiognomic approach was given by George Dance the Younger in the infamous London prison of Newgate (1768–75) demolished in 1902. Dance, it should be noted, studied in Rome between 1759–64 and met Piranesi during his Italian sojourn.[21] The massive rustication of gloomy elevations without windows and the chains above the entrance gate were meant not only to arouse fear, but also to fulfil the role of an urban spectacle replacing the public acting out of punishment. This place was already a cursed one for, from the 1630s on, successive prisons had been built on this site.[22]

In the *Panopticon* (*Letter VI. Advantages of the Plan*) Jeremy Bentham maintained, showing more concern for the gaoler than for the prisoners, that if Newgate had been designed according to the principles of the Panopticon its inspection would have taken just a quarter of an hour.[23] Newgate was conceived more as a huge, terrible symbol of justice and punishment – thus in line with the sensualist aesthetic, the theory of character, of effect and of *architecture parlante* – than as a practical, architectural resolution of the dilemmas of the penal theory of the day. This spectacular prison was designed before John Howard published *The State of the Prisons* (1777) and Bentham his *Panopticon* (1791). However, aesthetic techniques for the manipulating of emotions and impressions can easily be transformed into a programme for reforming society. Edmund Burke's aesthetic categories of sublime and beauty, and the descriptions of the arousing of feelings of anxiety, fear, power, enormity or the threat of darkness are based on the simple psychological mechanisms presented by Claude Adrien Helvétius: the avoidance of pain and trouble and the desire for pleasure. Knowledge of these mechanisms is vital and is therefore a desirable attribute for a governor, a lawmaker or an educator. Not accidentally, the mechanisms of pain and pleasure considered as sanctions are extensively discussed in Jeremy Bentham's *Introduction to the Principles of Morals and Legislation* (1789) and in his *Theory of Legislation*: '*Evil* is pain, or the cause of pain. *Good* is pleasure, or the cause of pleasure.'[24]

Some see in Bentham's Panopticon an outstanding Enlightenment game with light and shadow. Cells were lit only by a window in the external wall, thus presenting the prisoner in silhouette so that he would be more visible from the central tower. In the centre, 'the guards remained in darkness'.[25] Bentham suggested that sometimes they did not even need to be there, since the prisoners would not know when they were being observed. The Panopticon was thus the most economical in its upkeep since it permitted the reduction of the number of personnel.

MICHEL FOUCAULT AND JEREMY BENTHAM

It is through Michel Foucault's *Discipline and Punish*, and his 'panopticism' and 'incarceration' that the name of Bentham is today one that arouses negative connotations. And taking a glance in University College will not help change this opinion, for there sits Bentham's auto-icon, the embalmed body of a jovial looking old man with a wax head that has become the butt of student humour. We are imprisoned in the modern version of the cave, in a disciplinary society where, as Foucault argues, prisons are similar to factories, schools, barracks and hospitals, which all in their turn are redolent of prisons.[26] But Bentham's utilitarianism was a doctrine of Greatest Happiness, measurable through the Greatest Number of the members of any state,[27] and his theory of punishment was based on the concept of prevention, one that must be less damaging than the practice of bloody revenge.

It is through Michel Foucault that Jeremy Bentham, a philosopher of law, language and ethics,[28] became the architect of all manner of surveillance institutions, even though he never actually built anything himself, and that the Panopticon became worthy of being condemned as an architectural allegory of all-seeing power, of the mechanism of discipline. The first Panopticon was planned, but never completed, in 1786 in Crecheff (Krichev) in Belarus by Jeremy Bentham's younger brother Samuel, a naval architect and engineer, as a workshop ('Inspection House, or the Elaboratory'), not as a prison. The second Panopticon built by Samuel in 1806 in St Petersburg housed a fine arts' school and the design was then copied all over Russia, as was in line with the tsarist theatre of absolutism, but it could hardly be said to have had much of an impact on Russian prison reform.[29] It is noteworthy that Jeremy Bentham's *Traités de Legislation Civile et Penale* (the first edition in French prepared by Etienne Dumont and published in 1802) was translated into the Russian language as early as in 1805. Interestingly, in 1814 Bentham sent a letter to Alexander I, the Emperor of Russia, in which he offered his aid in the field of legislation, but very quickly were his expectations disappointed.[30]

Jeremy Bentham adapted his brother's architectural plans to his prison project, the famous rotunda with a central guard's tower, but his efforts to build a Panopticon in London ended in fiasco. He received twenty three thousand pounds as a compensation for the purchase of the plot lying under the construction. It was there that Millbank prison was built according to a design by William Williams and Thomas Hardwick between 1812–1821. The prison design was reminiscent of a flower with six petals: in the centre was a six-sided courtyard with a chapel, out from which in radial form spread pentagonal courtyards. The prison, which Bentham could not stand, was destroyed in the end of the nineteenth century and on this site now stands the Tate Britain.

Bentham's publication did not have a direct or immediate impact on prison architecture. The French edition prepared by Etienne Dumont enjoyed greater success than the English original.[31] In 1825, Dumont designed a prison in Geneva, destroyed in 1862, which was close to Bentham's concept. As the authors of *English Prisons* argue, the prison closest to the conception of the Panopticon is, however, the small prison for women, the so-called K-wing near to the castle in Lancaster, built between 1818–1821 by Joseph Michael Gandy. It is a semi-rotunda with a centrally situated establishment for the supervisor, and is five storeys high with nine cells in each of them.[32] Pentonville prison in London (1840–1842) built by Joshua Jebb, often cited as built on the Panopticon model, is not a rotunda, but has a central hall from which wings depart in a radial configuration. It was the model for fifty four Victorian prisons. The Koepel (dome) Prison in Arnhem, Netherlands (1882) became well-known due to the renovation project presented by Rem Koolhaas and O.M.A. (1979–1981). As Koolhaas claims, the Arnhem Koepel represents the Panopticon principle in its purest form: 'a single, all-seeing "eye" is placed dead center in a circle of the observed.'[33] Taking things from an architectural perspective, according to Foucault virtually any design of building can become a Panopticon; on the basis of the influential projects for penitentiary institutions developed by Nicolas Philippe Harou-Romain (*Plan for a Penitentiary*, 1840) the philosopher lists in his *Discipline and Punish* a series of possibilities: Bentham's Panopticon understood in the narrow sense, or semi-circular, cross-shaped or star-shaped.[34]

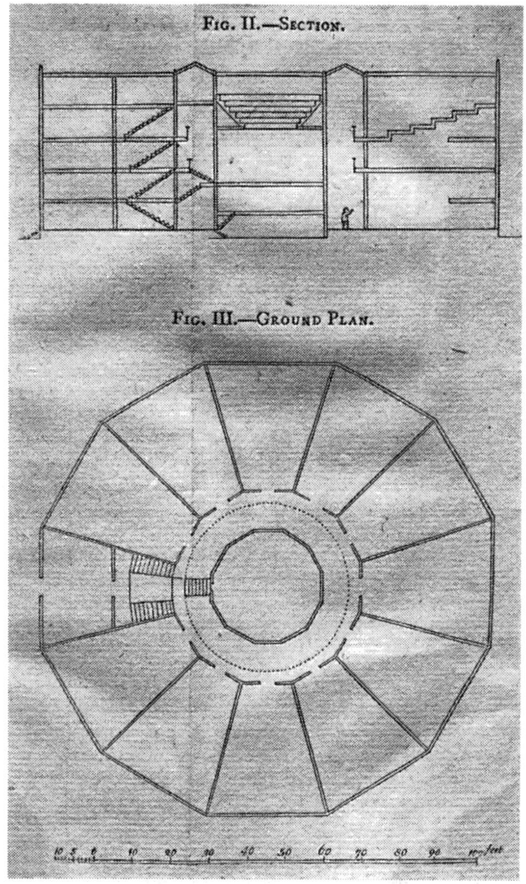

3.1 Panopticon's section and ground plan. Jeremy Bentham, 'Building and Furniture for an Industry-House Establishment, for 2000 Persons, of all Ages, on the Panopticon or Central-Inspection Principle', in *Pauper management improved: particularly by means of an application of the Panopticon principle of construction*, 1812

It was equally due to the publication of *Discipline and Punish* that Bentham went on to become one of the heroes of contemporary visual studies, although Foucault was far from the first in the latter half of the twentieth century to rediscover the Panopticon.[35] Bentham's invisible guard in the tower came to replace the Eye of Providence, was transformed into Big Brother, and the whole world into a prison supervised by the CCTV cameras and satellites.[36] As Nicholas Mirzoeff argues, total visual surveillance does not prevent crime either against individuals or against humanity.[37] What has happened, however, is that prisons

BUILDING AND FURNITURE

FOR AN

INDUSTRY-HOUSE

ESTABLISHMENT,

For 2000 Perſons, of all Ages,

ON THE

PANOPTICON OR CENTRAL-INSPECTION PRINCIPLE.

☞ For the Explanation of the ſeveral Figures of this PLATE, ſee "Outline of a Work, intitled PAUPER MANAGEMENT "IMPROVED;" by *Jeremy Bentham*, Eſq. as printed in ANNALS OF AGRICULTURE, Vol. XXX.

The Ranges of Bed-Stages and Cribs are reſpectively ſuppoſed to run from End to End of the *radial* Walls, as exhibited in the GROUND PLAN: they are here repreſented as cut through by a Line parallel to the Side of the Polygon: in the Bed-Stages, what is repreſented as *one* in the Draught, is propoſed to be in *two* in the Deſcription.

FIG. I.—ELEVATION.

SAMUEL BENTHAM, Knight of the Order of St. George of Ruſſia, Brigadier-Ge
SAMUEL BUNCE, Eſq. Architect of his Majeſty's Naval Works, *delineavit.*

3.2 Jeremy Bentham, 'Building and Furniture for an Industry-House Establishment, for 2000 Persons, of all Ages, on the Panopticon or Central-Inspection Principle', in *Pauper management improved: particularly by means of an application of the Panopticon principle of construction*, 1812 have become destinations for tourist trips, to be visited like museums. In some analyses of contemporary visual culture the Panopticon starts to disappear, leaving behind it little more than ghosts in refugee camps, almost invisible and barely observed, deprived of any sort of social status: 'The internment camps for migrants is becoming the model institution for a range of social practices, just as the Panopticon was the model for nineteenth-century factories and schools.'[38]

Michel Foucault did not attack architects. He did not put them in a single bracket with 'doctors, prison wardens, priests, judges and psychiatrists'. He even opposed Le Corbusier being called a 'crypto-Stalinist'. He saw him rather as a person full of good intentions.[39] Was this not also true of Bentham? In the late eighteenth century Bentham's utilitarianism was not perceived as the root of all totalitarianisms. When Robert Owen bought a factory from his father-in-law in New Lanark on the River Clyde in Scotland, he limited the hours of work, improved the worker's living conditions and created a worker's cooperative. When however he wanted to reduce the returns on the investment of capital, the shareholders protested. They convinced him to buy the shares and create a new enterprise together with Bentham and the Quaker William Allen.[40] As Joseph Rykwert argues, this experience turned Owen into a theoretician of the campaign against the abuses of the industrial revolution. Is it not, however, possible to conclude that Bentham's utilitarianism turns out to be more desirable to those concerned than trade unionism?

The Panopticon, or 'a simple idea in architecture', is universal. Bentham does not write only about prisons, but about all types of institutions that in his opinion require special supervision, such as factories, hospitals, psychiatric hospitals and schools. In a simple way, he demonstrated the usefulness of this structure for other functions, such as increasing the number of floors from four to six. In *Letter XVI* of the *Panopticon*, he also indicates that, dependent on the function, 'the gloomy paradox of crowded solitude might be exchanged, perhaps, for the cheerfulness of a common refectory'.[41] It was not Bentham, however, who began the date on modern forms of public institutions. The debate on the theme of the hospital, for example, began in 1772 when the Parisian Hôtel-Dieu caught fire.[42] It was then that were formed two types of approach to hospitals: one similar to the later Panopticon project, and another, pavilion type, which was more popular and easier to rebuild. In the case of the Panopticon as a hospital, Bentham fully justifies the need for ubiquitous vision. The doctors placed in the position of the observers will have the possibility of full control over the path of treatment, for instance over whether medicines are really given in the right proportions.

The Panopticon is also an idea about long-term construction. Bentham proposed that a building destined to become a factory should be built in iron and glass, be of fire-proof construction, and allow the maximum amount of daylight in order to improve working conditions. For these reasons, it was an important element in the debate over the reform of factory buildings, begun after the huge fire in the Albion Grain Mills in 1791.

The maximisation of production was not based purely on the optimisation of surveillance, but also on a specific division of work. In *Letter X* of the *Panopticon*, Bentham asks a simple question: 'What trades may I put my men to when I have got them?' And he provides an answer by dividing prisoners/workers into four classes dependent on the type of work and the manual workers' capabilities: 'good hands', 'capable hands', 'promising hands' and 'drones'.[43] This fragment sounds rather alarming as our physicality as potential manual workers is reduced purely to our hands, or as if our productivity could be exclusively described 'from the point of view of the hand'.[44] But Bentham is also quick to point out that if it is not a question of punishment, labour should not be forced. In schools, above and beyond the fact that there would be no possibility for cribbing, the youth of either sex would study and sleep under the kind of supervision that any loving parent would dream of. In a boarding-school for young ladies, built according to this ideal plan, gentlemen would assemble in order to choose themselves wives. Bentham, however, has doubts as to whether the liberal spirit and energy of a free citizen should definitely be replaced by the mechanical discipline of the soldier or the austerity of a monk. But in the final account he affirms, as if anticipating Foucault's interpretation: 'Call them machines: so they were but happy ones, I should not care.'[45].

THE PANOPTICON AND THE CELL FOR LIVING

From the mid-eighteenth century, the two paradigms, or rather two mythical types of buildings, have dominated architecture, argues Anthony Vidler in the celebrated essay *The Third Typology* (1977). The first is the primitive hut described by Vitruvius, but evoked by Marc-Antoine Laugier in 1753 in the Roussean version of a return to nature. This was a model legitimising architecture as assuring safe shelter. The second is Jeremy Bentham's Panopticon, an effect of the industrial revolution, which identified architecture with the world of machine production, and with economic and technical criteria. This is a model legitimising architecture as an effective machine for habitation, for work and also for acting out a punishment. As Vidler notes: 'Laugier's primitive hut and Bentham's Panopticon stand at the beginning of the modern era.'[46] Thus, the Panopticon should not be understood in terms of a realised building but in terms of 'the principle of construction' as Bentham himself suggested, or as a 'system of Industry-houses upon a large scale', where the poor were to be maintained and employed.[47]

In 1971, an Italian group of architects, Superstudio, presented a conception of twelve ideal cities, or *Twelve Cautionary Tales for Christmas*, in which the models for safe shelter and effective machines for living were blended in an absurd city-machine in total control over the lives of its inhabitants.[48] The tales about cities are also a variation on the theme of the modern and rational *Existenzminimum*. In the majority of the cities we find cells allotted to a single person, in which sometimes there are no windows, but where a stable temperature and humidity are maintained. In some are to be found forms of apparatus that emit images, sounds and smells. In one version the cells are replaced by ten million crystal coffins, and in an another by allotments a few metres in area where everybody could build the house of their dreams.

The fourth city is reminiscent both of a cosmic Panopticon and a cosmic Odyssey, although the architects do not reveal the source of their inspiration. This is a ring of a diameter of fifty metres. In the central nucleus is a computer that controls the life of the city and steers its journey. The ring is divided into eighty sectors each containing two cabins, with a man sleeping in the upper cabin and a woman in the lower. The inhabitants sleep connected to a machine, which maintains their physical functions, as well as to a dream generator. One complete rotation of a cabin takes eighty years. When the cabin enters the eightieth sector the inhabitants are ejected into cosmic space. At the same time, in the fortieth sector the dream generator stimulates the emission of ovules and sperm. As a result of this mechanically controlled fertilisation are born a woman and a man who occupy the vacated cabins. And thus travels the city-ship on its way to the New Land.

At the end of the twelve tales the architects propose a test. You have to answer the question as to how many of the twelve cities you would like to come true. If the answer is more than nine you are a head of state and the mechanisms of power are perfected within you. From six to nine, you are a cog in the system, functioning perfectly within its mechanism. From three to six, you are a slave, a succubus. From one to three, you are a worm, because you are so scared that you are even afraid to run away. And if none of the cities appealed to you then you have no reason to feel satisfied. All of these cities already exist.

In Superstudio's *Twelve Cautionary Tales for Christmas* one may observe a paradoxical blending of the two architectural paradigms, that of the safe shelter as a modernist *Existenzminimum* and that of the prison cell. This subversive project points to the heart of the architecture of justice. The architecture of justice concerns the principles of projecting prisons as well as designing a homely house and safe environment. Jeremy Bentham's Panopticon principle of construction should be seen, on the one hand, in the historical context of the birth of modern legislation and the claim for the effectiveness of industrial production. On the other hand, due to Michel Foucault's idea of panopticism and its impact on the visual culture studies, the Panopticon appears today as a symbol of total control and visibility. The most demanding task for contemporary architectural discourse is to reflect upon the far-reaching consequences of the Panopticon principles of construction. Bentham referred to his manual workers as 'machines' and put them in the

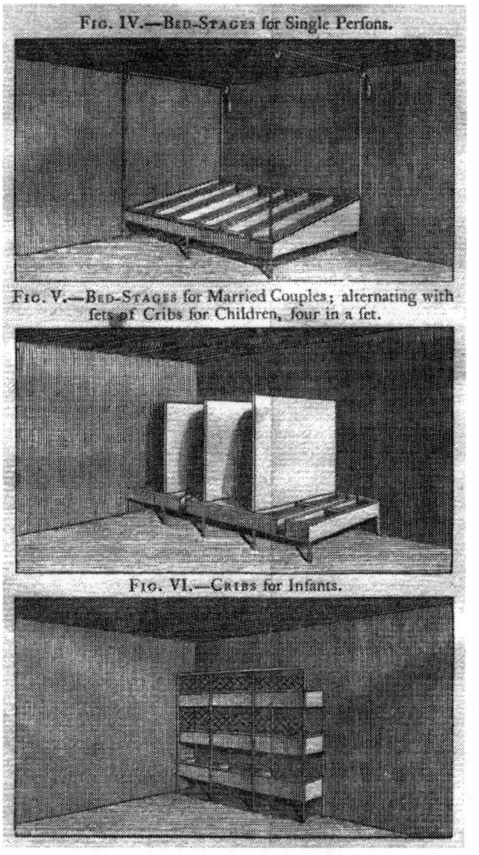

3.3 Bed-stages for single persons, married couples and cribs for infants. Jeremy Bentham, 'Building and Furniture for an Industry-House Establishment, for 2000 Persons, of all Ages, on the Panopticon or Central-Inspection Principle', in *Pauper management improved: particularly by means of an application of the Panopticon principle of construction*, 1812 cells for living, which assured 'preservation of health from infection', 'preservation of morals from corruption', or even 'prevention of unsatisfiable desires'.[49]

This idea should not sound surprising, especially when one recalls the modernist architectural claim for 'machines for living in'.[50] If the Panopticon were borne of 'good intentions', the same could be said of the modernist concept of *Existenzminimum*. What we need today, facing the crisis of late capitalism, is a balanced criticism both of the oldest cultural paradigm (Vitruvius', Laugier's and even Heidegger's primitive hut as a symbol of dwelling) and of the modern type of institution (Bentham's and Foucault's Panopticon as a symbol of productiveness and social control).

NOTES

1 J.M. (John Michael), M.J. Cohen, *The New Penguin Dictionary of Quotations* (London, 1998), p. 325. A version of this essay first appeared under the title 'Annexe to Book V: On the Principles of Projecting Prisons', trans. B. Cope, in Hanna Wróblewska (ed.), *Panopticon: The Architecture and Theatre of Prison* (Warszawa, 2005), pp. 60–73. Reprinted in Polish in Gabriela Świtek, *Aporie architektury* (Warszawa, 2012), pp. 39–51.

2 Plato, *The Republic*, trans. A.D. Lindsay (London, n.d.), p. 207.

3 René Descartes, *Discourse de la mèthode*, in *Oeuvres choisies*, ed. T. (Bar-le-Duc) Contant-Laguerre (Paris, 1879), p. 56.

4 Oscar Wilde, *De Profundis: Being the First Complete and Accurate Version of 'Epistola'* in *'Carcere et Vinculis' the Last Prose Work in English of Oscar Wilde* (London, 1949), p. 78.

5 Evelyn Waugh, *Decline and Fall* (London, 1937), p. 225.

6 Thomas De Quincey, *Confessions of an English Opium Eater* (Ware, Hertfordshire, 1994), pp. 235–6.

7 Ibid., p. 239.

8 Anthony Vidler, *The Architectural Uncanny: Essays in the Modern Unhomely* (Cambridge MA; London, 1992), pp. 38–41, 232.

9 Aldous Huxley, *Prisons. With the 'Carceri' Etchings of G.B. Piranesi* (London, 1949).

10 Marguerite Yourcenar, *The Dark Brain of Piranesi and Other Essays*, trans. Richard Howard (New York, 1984), pp. 108–9.

11 Manfredo Tafuri, *The Sphere and the Labyrinth: Avant-Gardes and Architecture from Piranesi to the 1970s*, trans. P. d'Acierno, R. Connolly (Cambridge MA and London, 1987), pp. 55–90.

12 Vidler, *The Architectural Uncanny*, p. 37.

13 Vitruvius, *The Ten Books on Architecture*, trans. M.H. Morgan (Whitefish, 2005), p. 137.

14 Cesare Beccaria, *Dei delitti e delle pene*, in *Edizione nazionale delle opere di Cesare Beccaria*, ed. L. Firpo, (15 vols, Milano, 1984), vol. 1, pp. 86–95. See also Marcello Maestro, 'A Pioneer for the Abolition of Capital Punishment', *Journal of the History of Ideas*, 34/3 (1973): 463–8.

15 W.C. De Pauley, 'Beccaria and Punishment', *International Journal of Ethics*, 35/4 (1925): 411.

16 Allan Brodie, Jane Croom, James O. Davies, *English Prisons: An Architectural History* (Swindon, 2002), p. 33.

17 Ibid., pp. 41–53.

18 Etienne-Louis Boullée, *Architecture, Essay on Art*, in Helen Rosenau (ed.), *Boullée and Visionary Architecture* (London and New York, 1976), p. 98.

19 Ibid., p. 99.

20 Barry Bergdoll, *European Architecture 1750–1890* (Oxford, 2000), pp. 91–4; Jacques-François Blondel, *Cours d'architecture* (9 vols, Paris, 1771–77), vol. 1, pp. 426–7.

21 Harold D. Kalman, 'Newgate Prison', *Architectural History*, 12 (1969): 55.

22 Brodie, Croom, Davies, pp. 26–8.

23 Jeremy Bentham, *Panopticon*, in *The Panopticon Writings*, ed. M. Bozovic (London, 1995), pp. 29–95.

24 Jeremy Bentham, *Theory of Legislation*, trans. E. Dumont (London, 1904), pp. 2, 20–30. Bentham's *Theory of Legislation* was first published in three volumes under the title of *Traités de Legislation Civile et Penale* (Paris, 1802).

25 Bergdoll, p. 94.

26 Michel Foucault, *Discipline and Punish: The Birth of the Prison*, trans. A. Sheridan (New York, 1995), p. 228.

27 See, for example, Graham Wallas, 'Jeremy Bentham', *Political Science Quarterly*, 38/1 (1923): 48.

28 See Jeremy Bentham, *Legislator of the World: Writings on Codification, Law and Education*, ed. P. Schofield, J. Harris (Oxford, 1998); Janet Semple, *Bentham's Prison: A Study of the Panopticon Penitentiary* (Oxford, 1993).

29 The workshop was planned on the estate of Grigori Aleksandrovich Potemkin, a statesman and the lover of Catherine the Great. See Matthew S. Anderson, 'Samuel Bentham in Russia, 1779–1791', *American Slavic and East European Review*, 15/2 (1956): 165–7; Robert Alan Cooper, 'Jeremy Bentham, Elizabeth Fry, and English Prison Reform', *Journal of the History of Ideas*, 42/4 (1981): 676; Simon Werret, 'Potemkin and the Panopticon: Samuel Bentham and the Architecture of Absolutism in Eighteenth-Century Russia', http://www.ucl.ac.uk/Bentham-Project/journal/nlwerret.htm [accessed 18 July 2011].

30 In the letter of July 1814 Bentham writes to Alexander I: 'The object of this address is to submit to Your Imperial majesty an offer relative to the department of Legislation. My years are sixty-six. Without commission from any Government, not much fewer than fifty of them have been occupied in that field. My ambition is to employ the remainder of them, as far as can be done in this Country, in labouring towards the improvement of the state of that branch of Government in Your Majesty's vast Empire.' After the Congress of Vienna (1815), Bentham became disillusioned. As we read in his comment to the correspondence with the Emperor: 'The Constitution of *Poland* had taken its seat on the same cloud with *Utopia* and *Armata*: that what remained of that unhappy country under its own name, had been finally swallowed up in the gulph of Russian despotism.' See 'Jeremy Bentham, to the Emperor of all the Russias, London, July 1814', in Jeremy Bentham, *Papers relative to codification and public instruction: including correspondence with the Russian Emperor and Divers constituted authorities in the American United States* (London, 1817), pp. 83 and 94.

31 Wallas, 'Jeremy Bentham', p. 54.

32 Brodie, Croom, Davies, pp. 58–9.

33 Rem Koolhaas, Bruce Mau, *S, M, L, XL*, ed. J. Sigler (New York, 1995), p. 237.

34 Foucault, p. 250.

35 Martin Jay, *Downcast Eyes: The Denigration of Vision in Twentieth-Century French Thought* (Berkeley and Los Angeles CA, and London, 1994), pp. 381–3.

36 See, for example, Thomas Y. Levin, Ursula Frohne, Peter Weibel (eds), *CTRL [Space]: Rhetorics of Surveillance from Bentham to Big Brother* (Karlsruhe and Cambridge MA, and London, 2002).

37 See Nicolas Mirzoeff's argument: 'The abduction of the toddler Jamie Bulger from a Liverpool shopping mall [1993] was impersonally captured by a video surveillance camera, providing chilling evidence of the ease with which the crime was both committed and detected. At the same time, despite the theory that constant surveillance provides increased security, it in fact did nothing to help prevent the child's abduction and eventual murder.' Nicholas Mirzoeff, *An Introduction to Visual Culture* (London and New York, 1999), p. 1.

38 Nicholas Mirzoeff, 'Imperium obozów' ['The Empire of Camps'], trans. M. Walkowiak, *Czas Kultury*, 1 (2004): 134.

39 Michel Foucault, 'Space, Knowledge, Power', interview with Paul Rabinow, *Skyline* (March 1982), trans. C. Hubert, in K. Michael Hays (ed.), *Architecture Theory Since 1968* (Cambridge MA and London, 2002), pp. 433–4.

40 Joseph Rykwert, *The Seduction of Place: The History and Future of the City* (Oxford, 2000), p. 58.

41 Bentham, *Panopticon*, p. 75.

42 Bergdoll, p. 119; Foucault, *Discipline and Punish*, p. 212.

43 Bentham, *Panopticon*, p. 52.

44 I refer here to Jacques Derrida's expression. See Jacques Derrida, *On Touching – Jean-Luc Nancy*, trans. C. Irizarry (Stanford CA, 2005), p. 122.

45 Bentham, *Panopticon*, p. 89.

46 Anthony Vidler, *The Third Typology*, in Hays (ed.), *Architecture Theory Since 1968*, p. 288.

47 Jeremy Bentham, *Pauper Management Improved: Particularly by Means of an Application of the Panopticon Principle of Construction* (London, 1812), p. 3.

48 Peter Lang, William Menking, *Superstudio: Life Without Objects* (Milano, 2003), pp. 150–61.

49 Bentham, *Pauper Management Improved*, p. 17.

50 'The house is a machine for living in.' See Le Corbusier, *Towards a New Architecture*, trans. F. Etchells (New York, 1986), p. 4.

4

The Watchman in the Vineyard*
Historical Traces of Judicial and Punitive Practices in Lincoln

Nicholas Temple

INTRODUCTION

Towering above the flat rural landscape of Lincolnshire is the majestic Gothic cathedral of Lincoln that stands as testimony to both human piety and divine worship. Located on the summit of a limestone ridge, and within the precinct of the former Roman settlement, the iconic profile of the cathedral has served for centuries as a potent symbol of the city and its rich history. The dominance, however, of this venerated place of worship overshadows a less apparent topographical relationship that was gradually to define the dual identity of Lincoln as both a pilgrimage destination and a stronghold for defence and incarceration. Partly revealed from the south aspect of the city (from Brayford Pool), the lofty

4.1 View of the upper town of Lincoln today, from Brayford Pool, showing the relation between the cathedral and observatory tower of the castle (left) (photo by author)

bell towers of the minster are counterpoised by the fortified walls of the ancient castle that culminate in the prominent 'observatory tower' on the south side of the east gate. Both cathedral and castle confront each other as two key monuments in Lincoln's history, that speak of the various accords, disputes, collusions and conflicts that have defined the relationships between church and state, canon and civil law, salvation and punishment.

The present investigation examines the history of judicial and punitive practices at both the castle and cathedral, from the Middle Ages to the nineteenth century, in the context of their territorial and topographical relationships. My aim in the enquiry is to trace changes in the various deliberations of justice and punishment in the 'upper-town' of Lincoln, through the agency of architecture, urban space and topography. In particular, the study will demonstrate how acts of justice and injustice were circumscribed by a complex – and sometimes conflicting – interplay between adherence to changing religious/political practices and the emerging instrumental methods of punishment and imprisonment.

CONTESTED TERRITORIES: THE OUTER BAILEY AND THE CLOSE

Relations between the authorities of the castle, cathedral and the larger city of Lincoln were often confrontational, and disputes arose concerning both rights of jurisdiction and the levying of taxes for the sale of goods.[1] The catalyst for these disputes can be identified in the emerging territorial demarcations in the 'upper town', between the outer bailey and the cathedral precinct, which was to persist until 1832 when the precinct was subsumed into the parliamentary constituency of the city, and subsequently into the municipal borough.[2]

To understand the reasons for these earlier territorial and judicial divisions we need first to examine the building of the cathedral in the thirteenth century, when the dean and canons of the cathedral issued a petition (in 1255) to King Henry III for a licence to extend the building eastwards, so that it would breach the old Roman wall of the outer bailey. This initiative formed part of the scheme, instigated by Bishop St Hugh (1181–1200), to reconstruct and enlarge the earlier Norman cathedral in the Gothic style, following its destruction in an earthquake in 1185. However, the dismantling of the city wall, along its eastern and northern frontiers, meant that the minster and its clergy were no longer under the protection of the outer bailey, being exposed to potential attack from outside invaders.

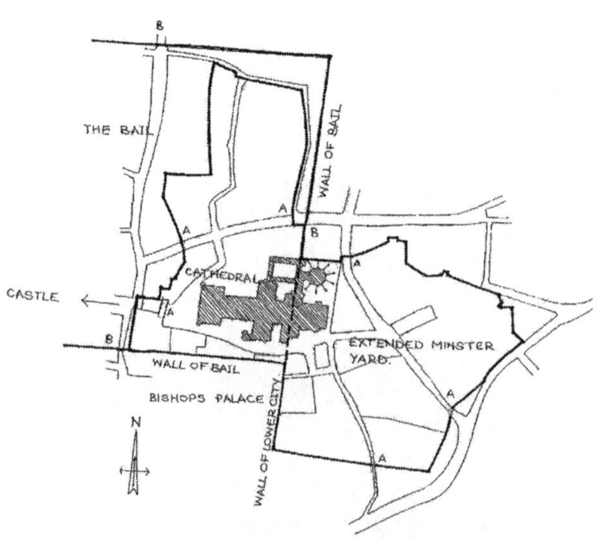

4.2 Plan of the 'Upper Town' of Lincoln (*c.* 1400) indicating relation between the Outer Bailey of the Castle and the Cathedral Close. 'A' indicates locations of gates in the wall of the Cathedral Close and 'B', the gateways into the old Roman settlement (Drawn by author after Francis Hill)

To remedy this threat a further royal licence was granted for permission to build a high wall to enclose the precinct of the cathedral. Initially, this only surrounded the projecting east end of the edifice, but eventually it enclosed the whole cathedral, creating in the process a minster 'close' that was separated from the bailey. Later raised and crenelated in the early forteenth century, with the addition of turrets, the wall was punctuated by a network of six secured gates, some of which still exist today – most notably the monumental West or Exchequer Gate. As part of the royal licence to create a cathedral close the dean and chapter also acquired legal rights of jurisdiction over the precinct which they were to vigorously enforce almost without interruption until the Civil War when disputes arose about the reinstatement of the 'ancient privileges of the close'.[3] As Carl Estabrook states: 'In the tumultuous decades leading up to the civil war, cathedral officials waged a symbolic battle to demarcate and delimit their sacred space more visibly, invoking royal adjudication to fend off the appropriation of sacred symbols by civic authorities.'[4]

4.3 View of the Galilee Porch, with original courtroom on the 1st floor, located off the south transept of Lincoln Cathedral (courtesy of Chris Rees)

These rights included the establishment of a law court, located above the Galilee Porch on the west side of the cathedral's south transept, which had authority over all those inhabiting the close and working within its confines, including clergy and their secretaries:

> *… in a letter sent to the city authorities by Henry II, we learn that the dean and chapter were allowed to hold a weekly court … for every kind of dispute affecting the inhabitants of the Close. They were entirely free from interference, wither by the city or the castle, and were an independent community of their own.*[5]

We should be reminded here that the disputes at the end of the Civil War, over the 'ancient privileges' of the cathedral close (by then considered anachronistic practices), roughly coincided with the abandonment of the nearby castle as a defensive structure and its subsequent transformation into a county gaol and court, a topic for later discussion. In each case we witness significant changes in the judicial roles of castle and cathedral that in one sense could be said to constitute a defining moment in the history of the 'upper-town'.

The trials held in the 'Galilee Court' imposed a range of punishments, including incarceration for serious offenders. It may seem surprising that the cathedral accommodated a prison.[6] Nicknamed 'le Wynde' (meaning narrow lane or passage), and located in the north-west tower, the entrance to the prison was highlighted in a curious drawing executed in 1789 by Samuel Grimm, which shows a group of men (including the renowned botanist Sir Joseph Banks) crossing a ladder to a door in the tower.[7]

Trials within the cathedral precinct were not just limited to the Galilee Court. We know that the Chapter House was also periodically used as a courtroom during the Middle Ages, only here for cases that extended beyond the jurisdiction of the close; in the early forteenth century one of many trials to convict the knights of the heretical order, the Templars, was held here as well as for royal parliaments summoned by both Edward I (1301) and Edward II (1316).[8] Much later the Chapter House was used as a temporary county court, probably during periods when the courthouse in the castle was being reconstructed.

4.4 Samuel Grimm (1786). Sketch of the interior shaft of the northwest tower of Lincoln Cathedral showing a group of men, including Sir Joseph Banks, crossing a ladder to the entrance to the old cathedral prison (courtesy of the Cathedral Library)

Whilst the cathedral, and its walled precinct, enjoyed over many years independence from the authorities of the castle bailey and the city, we know that accommodation within the close was used at various times by officials of the bailey to officiate their own judicial duties. Indeed, during the seventeenth and eighteenth centuries, the lodgings for the judge of the county court were located in various places around the cathedral, including College House which stood on the green near the Chapter House and leased from the dean and chapter.[9] The lodgings were later moved to a house in the 'Minster Yard facing the east end of the Minster'.[10]

What emerges from this brief examination of the relation between the outer bailey and the close is that there existed a fluid – and sometimes contested – relationship between territorial jurisdiction and judicial authority. In spite of the close inter-dependence between cathedral and castle, from the period of William the Conqueror and his loyal Bishop Remigius, the establishment of a bounded enclosure for the minster served as a catalyst for greater autonomy and self-determination for the cathedral authorities. This privileged position was no doubt aided by the declaration in the Magna Carta that: 'the English Church shall be free, and shall have its rights undiminished, and its liberties unimpaired.'[11]

As Claire Breay reminds us, this clause '…confirmed the right of the church to elect its own bishops and other officials, without royal interference. It reflected the powerful influence of Archbishop Langton who was clearly eager to confirm the rights and freedoms of the Church, which John had challenged so persistently earlier in his reign.'[12] Moreover, the mere presence of the Lincoln copy of the Magna Carta (the 'Lincolnia') in the cathedral, where it was deposited in the treasury in 1215 and remained there for over 600 years, is likely to have been viewed by the clergy as further grounds for reinforcing their claim of independence, both from a judicial and political standpoint.[13]

At the same time, however, we should consider the authority of the English Church in the light of the particular and unique circumstances of Lincoln Cathedral's foundation. Unlike Canterbury, Winchester, Norwich and Durham, which emerged as cathedrals from Benedictine monastic foundations, Lincoln was established in response to different needs: 'The vast size of the diocese [that stretched from the Humber to the Thames] required a body of administrators and lawyers to ensure its smooth running.'[14] Hence, Remigius saw the need for this large diocese to have 'a chapter of secular canons, each endowed with a prebend or source of income …'[15] We can only imagine the effectiveness of this significant body of legal experts in the cathedral when challenging any disputes arising with the castle sheriff or city authorities, thereby ensuring the longevity of the ancient privileges of the clergy referred to earlier.

The judicial and punitive actions of the close were largely inconspicuous to the attending worshipper or pilgrim, concealed behind the religious iconography of the cathedral; the prison was largely camouflaged by the monumental Norman west front of the minster, whose eschatological meanings were intimately associated with the symbolism of the triumphal gateway to Heavenly Jerusalem.[16] The courtroom, on the other hand, would have drawn its own Biblical associations from the Galilee Porch to which it forms part; the title 'Galilee' suggests a threshold of a journey of faith that emulates Jesus' journey from Galilee to Jerusalem, or alternatively as a point of departure from where the disciples were 'commissioned' by the 'Risen Christ'.[17] In both cases we see notions of justice and punishment being recapitulated as acts of mercy and salvation. As I suggest elsewhere, '... the criminal represents the sinner par excellence, and is made into a good Christian through his forced penance/sacrifice consequent to trial'.[18]

CIVIL UNREST AND STRATEGIES OF PUNISHMENT

Whilst the Civil War signalled the demise of the ancient privileges of the clergy, that once sustained the judicial and religious codes of conduct in the cathedral close, the eighteenth century witnessed the abrupt closure to what was left of this tradition. This forms part of a more general transformation of the upper-town during the eighteenth and early nineteenth centuries, where cathedral and castle became fragments of a larger socio-political order.

An indication of the direction of these changes can be seen in an incident that took place in 1724. Following the destruction of the central spire of the cathedral by high winds in 1548, there was increasing concern about the stability of the remaining two spires on the west towers. A report by the appointed architect James Gibbs recommended that the west towers should be secured, but that their spires are removed. The implementation of these recommendations provoked a riot in the city. The secured gates of the Close were breached by a mob of five hundred protesters. According to the then Secretary of State, Lord Townshend, the reasons for the riot may not have been just about the proposed demolition of the spires but also a demonstration of the protesters' 'disaffection with the state', its prevailing injustices.[19] If we accept Townshend's assessment then the incident could be said to constitute not just an act of violence but also one of opportunism; trespassing the minster close (ostensibly to protest against the destruction of the spires) provided an opportunity to express more general issues of discontentment. In the ensuing confrontation the sacred precinct became the scene of mob riots against both the dean and chapter of the cathedral, as well as the city authorities.

We should be reminded here of the historical significance of the gateways into the close. Mary Lucas describes the Exchequer Gate in these terms: 'It marks the symbolic entrance to the peace and sanctity of the cathedral where the pilgrim leaves behind the hurly-burly of everyday life beyond the gate.'[20] The tranquillity of the close was abruptly disturbed, and the sanctity of the cathedral violated, by the riot. Consequently, the close was subsumed into the lawlessness of the larger city, which Daniel Defoe describes in rather scathing terms in 1720 as '... an ancient, ragged, decay'd and still decaying city; it is full of the ruins of monasteries and religious houses', even stating that it was scarcely tolerable to call Lincoln a city at all.[21] No longer reserved exclusively for visiting pilgrims as a sacred enclosure, the minster precinct finally concedes to new – more prosaic – priorities; the construction of a turnpike in the eighteenth century, which passes through the close, resulted in 'the dean and chapter giving up their right to lock the gates'.[22] This development provides an important backdrop to examining the later developments of the other enclosure in the upper town – the castle yard – during the early nineteenth century. Whilst the circuit wall of the minster yard was dismantled, and the close absorbed into the larger city, parts of the castle wall were reinforced and the surrounding derelict buildings along its dyke demolished through a programme of slum clearance.

CASTLE AND GAOL

Throughout the Middle Ages, the fabric of Lincoln Castle underwent a number of major additions and alterations, including the construction of more substantial fortified walls, towers and a larger keep, later called the Lucy Tower on the south side of the enclosure. After the Civil War, Lincoln Castle became redundant as a fortification, resulting in the disbandment of its garrison of soldiers. It subsequently accommodated a courthouse and county gaol, the latter used to incarcerate debtors and those who required provisional detention either before a trial or deportation.

A more substantial purpose-built county court was completed in 1776, in the centre of the castle yard, whilst the gaol was located in the north east corner of the yard. As the name implies, the courthouse dealt with cases from the county of Lincolnshire, whilst the trials of those citizens within the city took place in the Guildhall, located in the Stonebow, which contained its own prison.[23] Hence,

4.5 Bronze model of Lincoln Castle, as it appears today, showing Lucy Tower (bottom left), East Gate and Observatory Tower (bottom right), Cobb Hall (top right), Prison building (centre) and Crown Court and West Gate (top left) (photo by author)

whilst the castle and its constable originally had control over the enclave of the outer bailey, defined by the extant boundary stones, the later introduction of a courthouse within the castle's inner bailey gave its magistrates judicial authority over the whole county.[24]

By the late eighteenth century, however, Lincoln Castle was in a ruinous state and was declared by the magistrates as unsuitable for a gaol, partly as a result of the security risks arising from buildings being erected immediately outside its crumbling perimeter wall. Hence a petition was submitted to parliament in 1775 by the city magistrates to enable the trustees to purchase 'the perpetuity of the castle yard for the use of the county for ever'.[25]

It was not until 1831 that an Act was finally passed which permitted the city authorities to buy the castle from the duchy of Lancaster, followed later by a Local Government Act of 1896 that formally concluded – after much dispute – that the castle and its adjacent judges' lodgings lie 'within the city'.[26]

The castle was the setting for a number of public executions. Originally these probably took place on the ramparts at the west gate, as was traditional practice away from the sacred precinct of the cathedral to the east. In 1400 however the west gate was blocked and the site for the executions relocated. By 1817 public hangings were held at Cobb Hall, a horseshoe shaped tower constructed in the thirteenth century and located on the north east corner of

4.6 View of Cobb Hall, from outside the castle walls, and Water Tower in the background (photo by author)

the inner bailey. Significantly, the tower probably served as the castle's prison during the Middle Ages, long before the construction of a purpose built prison in the castle grounds. During public hangings in the nineteenth century, crowds reserved places at the nearby taverns to watch the spectacle, giving Cobb Hall an infamous reputation as a dramatic 'theatre of the scaffold'.[27]

This brief overview of the transformation of Lincoln Castle into a gaol, with its regime of public hangings and assize courts, provides a useful background in which to trace the judicial and punitive practices in the outer bailey. The period of John Merryweather's governorship of Lincoln Castle Gaol, from 1799 to 1830, is especially interesting in this regard. During this period we witness significant changes, some of which were initiated by Merryweather's own personal agenda. A native of Lincoln, Merryweather seems to have possessed a somewhat dubious character, having been both admired and reviled in almost equal measure by his contemporaries. His job as governor of the gaol led to protests from various quarters about his ability to manipulate the system for his own financial gain. As Brian Taylor explains, '[Merryweather's] appointment as keeper of the gaol … meant that he was responsible for debtors, prisoners awaiting trial, and those convicted prisoners who awaited their call to the gallows or the ships to transport them to distant colonies.'[28]

His management of the gaol was highlighted by a series of scandals, most notably allegations of having illicit sexual relations with female inmates and fathering daughters out of wedlock, one of whom lived with him in the governor's residence. At the same time Merryweather was noted for his eccentricities and interests. A keen astronomer, he also cultivated a garden within the castle yard, with the help of inmates, and was a collector of animals and birds, including a peacock. These various character traits and hobbies paint a picture of a man seeking to make his own life within the austere confines of the castle as pleasant and as enjoyable as possible, often at the expense of the inmates over whom he had responsibility.

Under his governorship the gaol underwent a number of alterations and additions which include the following:

1. Judges' Lodgings built in 1812
2. So-called Observatory Tower in 1825
3. Assize Courts/County Hall in 1826

The establishment of permanent lodgings for the judges of the assize court, directly opposite the east gateway and across the castle ditch in Castle Hill, formed part of a gradual process of institutionalisation of court facilities and proceedings in Lincoln. Constructed in white brick, this monumental and rather austere building, situated at the threshold to the gaol and in visible range of the County Court, served as a reminder of the authority of the judge in court deliberations.

On the south-east corner of the castle wall is a substantial mound and tower believed to date originally from the twelvth century. Most probably used as a

4.7 View of the Observatory Tower from the Castle walls (photo by author)

second keep to the castle, it was originally built in timber on a stone substructure. In 1825, with the aid of public funds, Merryweather substantially altered the medieval structure and surmounted the tower with a castellated round turret. Within the turret a cast-iron spiral staircase was installed to provide access to the observation platform at its summit.

The project was funded, it seems, on the understanding that a more effective guard tower was needed at this corner of the castle, to provide a high enough vantage point from which to survey the whole circuit wall. What we know however is that the turret was also used by the governor as his own personal astronomical observatory. As Samuel Bamford states: '[Merryweather] was not an educated man, but had a reputation of being an adept in astronomy. He had a handsome mounted telescope and frequently spent whole nights in star-gazing …'[29]

From the perspective of the security of the gaol, the outward appearance of the so-called observatory tower could be construed as a 'camouflage', designed to deflect attention from its secondary function. Merryweather's attempt to benefit directly from such developments at Lincoln Castle also involved more substantial projects, in particular the construction of the new county hall, following the subsidence of the earlier courthouse – referred to earlier – soon after its construction in 1776.[30]

Robert Smirke, one of the leading architects in Britain at the time, was appointed to undertake the design in the 'Regency Gothic Style'[31] The terms of the contract for the project quickly aroused suspicion, with E.J. Willson claiming that 'There is some hidden intention in these terms [of the contract].'[32] The numerous deceptions that underlie these building projects at Lincoln Castle, during the governorship of Merryweather, partly reflect his management of the gaol. Again Bamford serves as a helpful source here. Imprisoned for his involvement in the notorious Peterloo riots in Manchester, Bamford served twelve months at Lincoln gaol:

4.8 View of the Crown Court from above the east gate (photo by author)

> *All around the prison building I have thus sketched arose high stone walls, some parts of them appearing to be of great age. They comprised ... an area of about eight acres, one part of which was a large green in front of the gaol, on which the prisoners for debt took exercise; in the centre of this green was a shrubbery, and the green was bordered on three sides by a long slip of garden ground, embracing the foot of the wall, appropriated to the use of the governor, and cultivated by the more orderly of the felons. On the wall opposite the governor's apartments was a round tower [Cobb Hall], on which executions took place; and an ancient keep, called Lucy's tower, in the rear of the jail – part of the original fortification – was now kept locked, and was tenanted only by owls, and an immense number of snail shells, which completely formed the floor. In a hollow at the foot of this tower were seen the green heaps above the graves of felons who had died within the prison, and of criminals who had been executed; and on a more level plot behind the Town Hall [County Court], which building fronted the gates at the extremity of the yard, was the place of interment for the debtors, some with stones and inscriptions, and others with only the green mantle of their mother earth lapping over them .... High above the gates and prison walls, at a short distance outside, rose the towers of the venerable and magnificent cathedral. The Lady tower contained a pearl of bells which were only rung twice a year; on Lady and Michaelmas days. They were the sweetest-toned bells I have ever heard ... the tower of the great bell Old Tom ... boomed forth the hours to us, as they too slowly joined the eternity of the past.*[33]

4.9 View of the west towers of Lincoln Cathedral from the grounds of Lincoln Castle (photo by author)

In addition to the activity of cultivating gardens the castle also contained, according to Bamford, some rather gruesome features including a 'curiosity shop' for displaying 'instruments of murder' used in executions.[34] What we can ascertain from these accounts, and our knowledge of Lincoln Castle during this period, is a strange mixture of the macabre and the tranquil. The castle would have served as a constant reminder to the prisoner of his own impending and brutal end, whether enacted in the public and humiliating spectacle at Cobb Hall (clearly visible from the castle yard) or his forced deportation to the colonies. At the same time, the setting underscored the deprivations to his liberty through the monotony of confinement, relieved only by the tantalizing views of the cathedral and the sound of its bells.

Bamford's portrayal of life in the castle yard sits somewhat uneasily alongside a representation of the new County Hall, published in 1837, which depicts the building in a verdant landscape with a roaming peacock. Here, the setting of judicial deliberations is presented as an Arcadian landscape – even a walled Garden of Eden (an ironic metaphor for a prison yard). It seems likely that the author of the illustration was consciously drawing upon a double – if strangely contradictory – connection; firstly the personal legacy of Merryweather (who we know owned a peacock referred to earlier), and secondly the prevalence of this species of bird in Early Christian symbolism to evoke rebirth and the redeemed soul.[35]

4.10 Anonymous, View of County Hall (*c.* 1837) showing peacock in the foreground. (From the Local Studies Collection, Lincoln Central Library, courtesy of Lincolnshire County Council)

The function of the castle, from the early eighteenth century, as a holding point for felons awaiting deportation to the colonies and 'plantations', may well have been partly due to its location within striking distance of Brayford Pool to the south, a busy inland port since Roman times.[36] The good navigation system of the River Witham and Fossdyke Canal (the oldest canal in Britain) that connects Brayford Pool to Boston to the east and Hull to the north (via the River Trent), gave Lincoln a strategically important location in the East Midlands. Before the introduction of the railways, rivers and canals were the principal means of transporting goods to and from Lincoln, which also included prisoners. This activity was also personal to Merryweather who was a shareholder in the Witham Navigation Company, and personally took charge of accompanying criminals by river and canal to seaports bound for Australia and elsewhere.[37] His involvement in this company may have been prompted by an invention he submitted for a patent in 1816, which was a 'means of propelling boats and vessels through the water'.[38]

This broader geographical context of Lincoln Castle further underlines the emerging institutionalisation of incarceration during this time; the gaol benefited from the improved trading and communication routes to the colonies, at the same time as the growing efficiency of sentencing felons and committing them to permanent exile. These developments also closely paralleled more effective methods for hanging criminals; the most well-known, which was first introduced at Lincoln Castle Gaol in the nineteenth century, was the so-called 'long (or measured) drop'.[39]

4.11 View of the Chapel at Lincoln Castle Gaol, designed using the 'Separate System' (photo by author)

During the time of Bamford, Lincoln Castle did not contain a chapel, an issue that was the subject of on-going complaints by the magistrates. However, Bamford's description of the view of the cathedral towers, with the periodic sound of chiming bells, would no doubt have served as a reminder to the prisoners of the rituals of worship during their exercise in the castle yard. With the introduction, however, of the 'separate system', participation in the life of the prison entailed a very different restrictive and repressive regime. This is most provocatively conveyed in the construction of a chapel within the prison building, where each inmate was required to sit in isolation from his fellow prisoners, with only the view of the chaplain conducting the sermon. This arrangement resulted in a design where prisoners were confined to their own compartment – more redolent of a series of stacked wooden coffins than a layout of choir stalls or church pews. The separate system was soon, however, abandoned at Lincoln, as elsewhere in England, as a result of its inhumane treatment of prisoners, resulting in cases of insanity and even suicide. It also, coincidentally, signalled the end of Lincoln Castle as a make-shift gaol; felons were transported to a new purpose-built prison to the east of the city in Greetwell Road.

CONCLUSION

My examination of the history of judicial and punitive practices at Lincoln Castle and Cathedral, through their architectural/spatial adaptations, topographical relationships and shifting territorial jurisdictions, provides an intriguing story of the changing meanings of justice and their various forms of deliberation. It is a story that is both remarkable – in its complexity and spatial richness – and at the same time disturbing in the contradictions and violations it reveals. Underlying the investigation is the principle that comparative history can provide a lens to reveal the way certain buildings, over a period of time, variously serve as spatial registers of justice/injustice, even when these are not made legible or explicit through ritual or corporate action. Beyond, however, the performance of individual spaces as settings for specific judicial proceedings (such as the modern courtroom), the transitional or adaptive spaces of cities, that accommodate both formal and informal renderings of just/unjust acts (sometimes arising from the influence of undeclared or conflicting political, religious and ideological agendas), provide the most productive settings for such an enquiry. What we have learnt from this investigation is the manner in which architecture and urban space are 'implicated' in the pursuit of justice, or conversely how they can just as effectively operate in covert ways to facilitate acts of injustice in the guise of legitimate authority.

The ambiguity of this relationship is made all the more apparent today with the location of the Lincoln copy of Magna Carta in the prison building, where it was transferred in the twentieth century. Displayed in close proximity to the chapel, referred to earlier, we are reminded in this relationship of both the historical distance travelled, between the formalization of law for human rights and the development of institutional methods of punishment and confinement, and the binding topographical and symbolic connections between castle and cathedral, civil law and canon law, testified in the history and associations of the 'Lincolnia'.

NOTES

* With special thanks to Brian Taylor for useful sources and for permission to refer to parts of his unpublished dissertation 'This Disgraceful Thraldom: John Merryweather Keeper of Lincoln Castle 1799–1830'.

1 In 1390, for example, the sheriff of the castle took action against the city mayor for interfering with the affairs of the Bailey, a situation that was not to be fully resolved until the 19th century. E.I. Abell and J.D. Chambers, *The Story of Lincoln: An Introduction to the History of the City* (Wakefield, 1971), p. 179.

2 Sir Francis Hill, *Medieval Lincoln* (Stamford, 1990), p. 126. Finally, in 1845 both bailey and close became parishes of the city. Ibid., p. 101.

3 Ibid., pp. 124–7.

4 C.B. Estabrook, 'Ritual, Space, and Authority in Seventeenth-Century English Cathedral Cities', *Journal of Interdisciplinary History*, XXXII:4 (Spring, 2002): 593–620, esp. 593.

5 Abell and Chambers, Lincoln, p. 181.

6 In some instances the roof space behind the triforium of medieval cathedrals was used as a makeshift prison. I am grateful to Professor John Hendrix for this information.

7 Nicholas Bennett, 'The 'Wynd': A Cathedral Prison', in Philip Buckler, Gavin Kirck, Nicholas Bennett, Mary Lucas and Anne Coltman, *Lincoln Cathedral: A Journey from Past to Present* (London, 2010), p. 51.

8 Bennett, 'The Cloister and Chapter House', ibid., pp. 96–109, p. 106. Furthermore, 'Up until the outbreak of the civil war ... sacred and secular authorities appropriated one another's sites and symbols to underscore status and claim legitimacy.' Estabrook, 'Ritual, Space, and Authority in Seventeenth-Century English Cathedral Cities', p. 593.

9 Sir Francis Hill, *Georgian Lincoln* (Cambridge, 1966), p. 22.

10 Ibid.

11 Significantly, this is taken from the 1st of the 63 clauses in the Magna Carta. Quoted in Claire Breay, *Magna Carta: Manuscripts and Myths* (London, 2002), p. 28.

12 Ibid.

13 By the seventeenth century the whereabouts of the Lincolnia was unknown, probably as a result of the turmoil wrought by the Civil War, only to be rediscovered in 1800 by the Public Records Commissioners.

14 Buckler, Kirck, Bennett, Lucas and Coltman, *Lincoln Cathedral*, p. 102.

15 Ibid.

16 In Early Christian tradition the narthex, located at the west end of a basilica, constituted the most 'secular' part of the church, from where the uninitiated or catechumen could witness – but not participate in – the Eucharistic mass. This status of the west end may have contributed to the decision by the clergy to house the prison in the north-west tower at Lincoln.

17 Buckler, Kirk, Bennett, Lucas and Coltman, *Lincoln Cathedral*, pp. 128 and 131.

18 This interpretation was used in a different context, to explain the symbolic intentions for the design of the Palazzo dei Tribunali in Rome by Donato Bramante in the early sixteenth century. Nicholas Temple, *renovatio urbis: Architecture, Urbanism and Ceremony in the Rome of Julius II* (Abingdon, 2011), p. 116. Significantly, the Lincolnia was later moved to the room above the Galilee Porch where it was shown hanging on a wall in an oak frame. The decision to display the parchment document in this room may have been intended to recall its earlier role as a courtroom before the Reformation, where the chapter undertook 'truly to minister the office of stewardship of the Galilee'. Buckler, Kirk, Bennett, Lucas and Coltman, *Lincoln Cathedral*, p. 131.

19 Hill, *Georgian Lincoln*, p. 40.

20 Buckler, Kirck, Bennett, Lucas and Coltman, *Lincoln Cathedral*, p. 18.

21 Quoted in Hill, *Georgian Lincoln*, p. 138. We have accounts, from the early eighteenth century, that testify to the political dimension of the proposed demolition of the spires, which some considered to be an act of vandalism. Ibid, p. 41.

22 Lucas, 'The Close', p. 18.

23 Abell and Chambers, *Lincoln*, p. 166.

24 Hill, *Medieval Lincoln*, p. 91.

25 Ibid., p. 100.

26 Hill, *Georgian Lincoln*, p. 260; Hill, *Medieval Lincoln*, p. 102.

27 Stephen Wade, *Hanging at Lincoln* (Stroud, 2009), p. x. The frequency and extent of hanging as a practice during the late Georgian period is indicated by records; up until 1800 about one third of all prisoners in the castle were hanged in these public settings.

28 Brian Taylor, 'This Disgraceful Thraldom: John Merryweather Keeper of Lincoln Castle 1799–1830' (unpublished dissertation), p. 43.

29 Samuel Bamford, *Passages in the Life of a Radical*, ed. Henry Dunckley (London, 1893), p. 313.

30 Hill, *Georgian Lincoln*, p. 259.

31 A description of Smirke's design can be found in J. Mordaunt Crook, *Lincolnshire Architectural Society Reports*, ix (1962), p. 151.

32 Quoted in Hill, *Georgian Lincoln*, p. 260. Originally published in *Lincolnshire Notes and Queries*, x (1908–1909), p. 19.

33 Bamford, *Passages in the Life of a Radical*, vol. 2, Chapter XXXVII.

34 Ibid.

35 In 1828, the governing body of Lincoln Castle ordered that all the animals be removed from the gaol. Merryweather records in his diary that he complied with this order, 'except for a peacock for which he could not find a satisfactory asylum for a very old pet'. This may explain the presence of a peacock in the illustration, as a kind of testimony to Merryweather's governorship of the gaol. *Lincolnshire Archives Office, Keeper's Journal*, CoC5 1–1 (16 October 1828). For a study of the symbolism of the peacock in Early Christian iconography see Andre Grabar, *Christian Iconography: Study of Its Origins* (London, 1981).

36 Hill, *Georgian Lincoln*, p. 20.

37 Taylor, 'This Disgraceful Thraldom', p. 3.

38 In the event his 'invention' was not successful. Taylor speculates that Merryweather's application for a patent may have been a '... ploy to entice the new steam packets on the River Witham to become more efficient and pay more tolls to the company of which he was a shareholder'. Ibid., p. 20.

39 First introduced by William Marwood in 1872 at Lincoln Gaol, the 'long drop' was regarded as a quicker and more effective method of execution. It was 'designed to dislocate the cervical vertebrae and rupture the spinal cord...' V.A.C. Gatrell, *The Hanging Tree: Execution and the English People 1770–1868* (Oxford, 1994), p. 46.

PART 2
Courthouses and Courtrooms

5

Back to the Future? The Challenge of the Past for Courthouses of Tomorrow

Linda Mulcahy

INTRODUCTION

At the 2009 conference in which the contributors to this book gathered the architect Stephen Quinlan delivered a plenary lecture on the recently built and much discussed Civil Justice Centre in Manchester designed by Denton Corker Marshall.

This new court complex is the largest to have been built in England since the Royal Courts of Justice were completed in 1882. The glass fronted court complex, with its nine storey atrium and gravity defying protruding 'fingers' (Fig. 5.1), could not provide a more stark contrast to George Edmund Street's ornate gothic revival building in the Strand. But what was most significant about Quinlan's presentation for the purposes of this chapter was that the first comment in response to it came from an architectural historian who was concerned that the Manchester civil justice centre was not recognizable as a courthouse. Devoid of the form, signs and symbols associated with this established building type, Quinlan's critic claimed that England's most important new court building rendered the notion of 'courthouse' meaningless.

5.1 Manchester Civil Justice Centre (photo by author)

The idea that courts are, and should be, instantly readable is far from being a controversial one. Whilst recognizing a variety of forms adopted by designers in her authoritative account of the history of the English law court, Clare Graham surmises that one of the key characteristics of modern courthouses is that by 1914 their planning was highly distinctive.[1] In their recent review of historic English courts for English Heritage Brodie *et al.* have also claimed that law courts are designed to be recognized externally and understood internally.[2] In this chapter, I argue that these assertions suggest a certainty about the settled nature of design which is easily disrupted when subjected to closer scrutiny. While it has been suggested that our ideas about what constitute a court are now quite fixed my analysis suggests that the concept of a courthouse to which these authorities allude is actually a very recent invention. Moreover, even if it can be claimed that there is now a recognizable template for courthouse design, I contend that it is one which is in urgent need of review. As reforms of the legal system place increasing emphasis on informality, and the idea of the virtual trial explored by Emma Rowden elsewhere in this collection becomes a reality, I question the legitimacy of confidence in the ongoing relevance of existing templates.

The debate about Manchester Civil Justice alluded to above raises important questions about the very concept of 'courthouse' and the role that the places in which justice is done have played in our civic landscape over time. The topic has been much neglected. Whilst close attention has been paid to public buildings types such as churches, castles, or town halls this has been to the detriment of studies of the courthouse. When justice facilities have been studied the focus has tended to be on prisons as the contributions to this collection make clear. Technical accounts of historic courthouses which focus on aesthetic convention or style such as those provided by English Heritage, the Pevsner guides and the Victorian County Histories are informative but tell us very little about the social or political significance of the buildings described. Contemporary architectural historians have been more interested in going behind an appreciation of technique and style to an understanding of the symbolism and political ideology underpinning design but much of what exists focuses on particular courts of national significance and very few accounts bring the history of court design up to the present.[3] Despite this, there are inherent tensions in design briefs for courthouses which make them particularly ripe for analysis. Their position as democratic spaces in citadels of authority make them an ideal subject for detailed research about the rhetoric and reality of public space in modern societies.[4]

A COMPLEX HISTORY

In contrast to the expectation that we should be able to recognize a courthouse with ease research suggests that for much of the history of court design the idea of a courthouse as a distinct building type was meaningless. For many centuries responsibility and influence on design and build was dispersed amongst a range of people and institutions with different ideals, interests, ambitions and procedures.

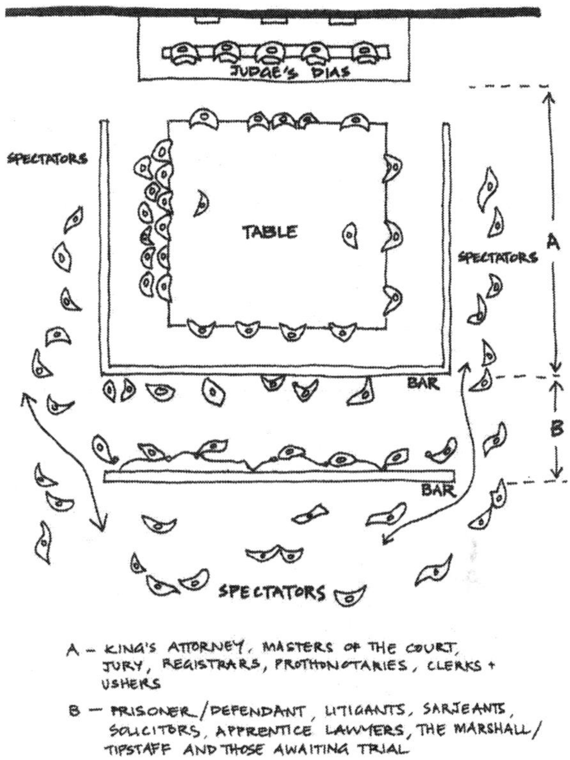

5.2 The layout of the courts at Westminster after the Whaddon manuscripts (courtesy of Emma Rowden)

The presence of a number of parallel legal systems until the late nineteenth century meant that a plethora of bodies such as the church, Chancery, the police, guilds, boroughs and local manors funded and oversaw courtroom design within distinct legal jurisdictions. The fact that courts did not sit permanently, and that the judicial role was frequently combined with political and executive functions, meant there was no call for a sole purpose building for trials.[5]

The result was that for many centuries there were no custom built courthouses, only houses which happened to host courts. Accommodation was makeshift even for the 'national' courts held in Westminster hall. Local trials were held in buildings used for a multitude of purposes such as castles, churches, public houses, manor houses, assembly rooms, county halls and guildhalls depending on their status, jurisdiction and where there happened to be space. When town or county halls were utilized the common practice during the Assizes was to hold the civil court in the first floor chamber and the criminal court in the open market space below.[6] These features of early courts have important implications for courtroom design. Court furniture had to be simple, as well as easy to dismantle and carry and space was commonly sectioned off by little more than simple oak beams or benches. It has been contended that for much of the history of English legal systems it was difficult to find anything other than rudimentary design of the interior of courtrooms.[7] Figure 5.2 shows the organization of a fifteenth century court which provided a model for interior layout for many centuries. This demonstrates that medieval courts were much more sociable than their modern counterpart. The defendant stands shoulder to shoulder with his lawyers and spectators walk freely around three sides of the court.

The trend towards purpose built and sole use courthouses began from the late eighteenth century onwards. As law claimed a more autonomous role in modernity, court business increased, large sections of the population migrated to towns and litigation burgeoned courts were increasingly held in locations designed specifically for the purpose. The proportion of sole use purpose built courthouses remained low in the eighteenth century with early examples including Thomas Rogers Middlesex county sessions house (1779–82); Beverley Sessions Court (1805) and Carlisle Assize courts (1808) but in the nineteenth century 18 of the 40 courts built for the Assizes were built for purpose.[8] The paucity of templates for design, however, meant that architects of the period had very little to guide their planning with the result that new build was born into something of an architectural vacuum.[9] By the beginning of the nineteenth century those few purpose built courthouses and rooms which did exist were not always considered suitable models for the more ambitious projects which began to be envisaged.[10]

Despite the shift towards the purpose built and sole use courthouse it remained debatable whether the buildings which housed the courts during this period were instantly recognizable as having a judicial function. Like all other building types of the nineteenth century, courts became grander and increasingly likely to be seen as major architectural commissions. But as with all public buildings the external design varied with fashion. Preferences for the neo-classical courthouse in the late eighteenth and early part of the nineteenth century gave way to a renewed interest in the gothic courthouse in the nineteenth century. Courthouses often appeared more austere than other public buildings, and architects might argue that a sober Doric or Ionic column was more suitable than a Corinthian, but many of the great symbolic sole purpose courthouses of the nineteenth century such as Alfred Waterhouse's Manchester Assize Courts, the Victoria Law Courts in Birmingham or the Royal Courts of Justice were ostentatious.[11] Stripped of the royal coat or arms or symbols of justice these buildings could be read as fulfilling any one of a number of public functions.

It is to the interior of courthouses that we must look to identify the birth of a new and increasingly sophisticated building type which was distinctive. In the early years of their development the interior of the sole purpose courthouse was dominated by the courtroom. John Carr's elaborate Assize courts at York (1773) and Robert Smirke's more sober courts at Maidstone (1824) demonstrate that early designs for purpose built courts dedicated the bulk of floor space to courtrooms with separate rooms to house administrators and waiting rooms located on the periphery. As the purpose built law court gained in popularity in the nineteenth century the internal configurations of the courthouse changed

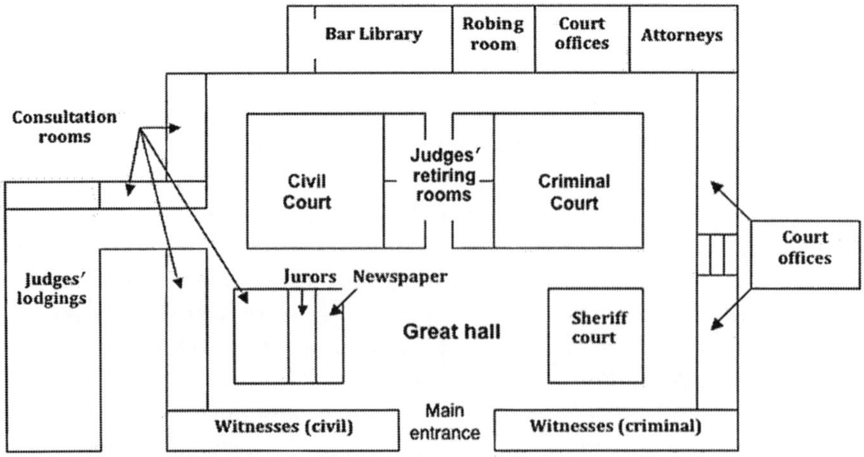

5.3 Final plan for main floor of Manchester Assize Court, after Waterhouse as reproduced in *The Builder*, 25 February 1865, p. 136 (drawn by author)

drastically. New facilities such as waiting rooms, robing rooms, dining facilities and clerks accommodation became common. A new emphasis was also placed on segregating different genders and categories of court users in the environs of the courtroom. With its separate entrances, dedicated circulation routes and range of separate rooms for use by different participants Alfred Waterhouse's Manchester Assize courts (see Fig. 5.3) was to represent the most complex experiment in internal planning of the age and influenced many of the courts built in the latter part of the nineteenth century.[12]

An increasing interest in segregation and segmentation is also evident within the courtroom. The large central table which had dominated the courtroom since medieval times reduced in size during this period to become a small desk for the clerk who sits in front of the judge (see Fig. 5.2). It was replaced by rows of seating for the lawyers. Advocates came to be situated away from their client and with their back to them following John Soane's 'innovation' at the Westminster courts in the early nineteenth century. An increasingly obvious demarcation of the spaces for each category of participant in the trial also became evident. Balconies for spectators became common as did partitioned areas for the judge, jury, witnesses and defendant. The increasing fortification of the dock proved popular as the area set aside for the defendant was transformed from a simple bar in the pre-Victorian era to a high sided wooden enclosure approached from cells underneath the court. What is most interesting about these developments is that, somewhat ironically, as English society moved from feudalism to democracy the courtroom and courthouse became less sociable and evolved into a highly segmented arena in which everyone was given a place which reflected their status (see Figs 5.2 and 5.4). The increasing sophistication and distinctiveness of internal planning was such that Graham has argued that by 1914 it could be characterized as 'fossilized'.[13]

The new purpose built and increasingly grand courthouses which emerged from the late eighteenth century onwards clearly served important political functions which have been explored more fully elsewhere.[14] The trend was certainly encouraged by lawyers and architects as a means of securing public affirmation of their still fragile status.[15] It has also been suggested that there are close links between the reformed legal system of the nineteenth century which increasingly served the interests of a free market and the building programmes which served to aggrandize the role of law in modernity championed by the new mercantile classes. The many symbolic courthouses constructed during this period on which resources were lavished also reflected a desire to imbue a new sense of civic pride. This is particularly evident in the monuments to law constructed in the newly emerging industrial cities of the north and midlands.[16] The new trend towards grander and more prominent courthouses has also been linked to increasingly radical politics of the era and the propensity towards civil unrest. In addition to the glorification of the achievements of industrialists the new monuments to law can be read as being motivated by a desire to instill fear in the working classes who populated the new cities.

CENTRALIZATION OF DESIGN

Confidence about the distinctiveness of court design by 1914 needs to be treated with some caution.[17] Whilst an ideal type might have been recognized by architects and policy makers there is evidence that this was not always reflected in the courthouses constructed. When the Beeching Commission was set up in 1971 to look into the state of the Assize system it reported that many courts continued to share facilities with other public bodies. Indeed, the Commission raised serious concerns about the *lack* of segregation of participants in the trial and absence of a fortified dock in many shared buildings. They were particularly troubled by the 'common practice' of accused, litigants, witnesses, jurors, police officers and even solicitors and counsel having to jostle together in 'embarrassing proximity' in halls and corridors which were often stacked with paraphernalia associated with other uses of the building such as dismantled staging, parts of a boxing ring, or the music stands of a brass band contest.[18] The resulting report demonstrates that not only was the sole use courthouse far from being the norm but that models which Graham suggests were dominant had not been applied across the Crown estate. As a result it could be argued that it was not until the 1970s that design became standardized in the way she anticipates.

Variation in practice as late as the 1970s can be explained by the fact that until the Beeching Report building for the Assizes was largely the responsibility of the County in which courts were held. This inevitably led to considerable variation in design. Historically this had meant that in some areas a rich benefactor might fund the building of an impressive monument to law, money might be raised on the local rate or raised by public subscription and in others still the local populace might find their courts neglected because of lack of funds or political will. Despite the longevity of such arrangements by the late twentieth century these practices were being questioned as outdated and inefficient. This provided policy makers and designers with an opportunity to promote the merits of centralized planning. The result was that the reforms which followed in the wake of the Beeching report led to the birth of the first centralised planning guide and the launch of the largest centrally co-ordinated court building programme in the history of courthouse design.

It was those involved in the construction of the Magistrates courts who pioneered the idea of common design specifications from the 1960s onwards but the shift towards centralized guidance was also fuelled by the need to avoid duplication of work in the design specifications being issued as part of the new court-building programme.[19] Few public building initiatives have been as extensive as the post 1960s court construction programme. Motivated by concerns about overcrowding in the Crown Courts, the programme lasted from 1972 until 1996 and cost in the region of £500million. One hundred and thirty nine schemes were completed in that time and 382 new courts built. In addition, twenty-eight combined court complexes containing up to 20 courtrooms were created.[20] Such was its importance that commentators have referred to it as one of the largest monumental building

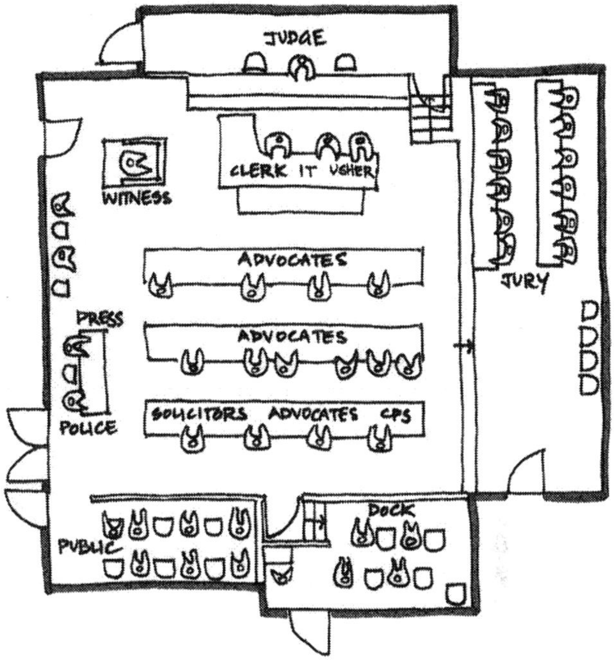

5.4 The prescribed layout of the modern courtroom in a Crown Court (courtesy of Emma Rowden)

programmes since the pyramids or as the last major contribution by central government to Britain's city centres.[21]

The design guide which emerged in parallel with the new building programme also broke new ground. Drawing on the earlier work of the Greater London Council and the Home Office, civil servants, architects and the judiciary were encouraged for the first time to translate their presumptions about court architecture into a set of universal and centralized templates to guide all designers.[22] Whilst recognizing that the law is a 'field well known for strong individualism' and 'strong local judicial tradition' the production of the Guide was a deliberate attempt to provide a standardized and rational base for the rapid compilation of briefs which gave a clear understanding of the design issues to be addressed.[23] Successive editions of the *Court Standards and Design Guide* have been produced over recent decades and it is now keep constantly under review.[24]

The social significance of centralized planning was undoubtedly the challenge it provided for policy makers and designers to consider how a late twentieth courthouse in a democratic society should look and be experienced. The design guide and building programme claimed a desire to break with the past by promoting new visions of the legal system in which the focus was on equality rather than retribution or authority. Practices were certainly ripe for reform. By the time the structure and design of the Assizes came to be reviewed by the Beeching Commission there had been very little new build since the nineteenth century. Seismic shifts in the political and social context in which design of public buildings took place had occurred in the intervening period. The introduction of universal suffrage and post-war shifts in the social contract heralded the birth of an era in which public institutions, including the legal system, were expected to be more accountable to the general public than they had been in earlier eras.

Significantly, the early part of this period corresponded with the highwater mark of penal welfarism in British social policy and there appears to be some reflection of the shift away from the goal of retribution in the new claims being made in the Design Guide. While the architectural ambition and monumentality of Victorian design continued to inspire architects of the period there was also an acceptance that the messages conveyed by sombre hierarchical courthouses of the nineteenth century lacked resonance in the modern age. In particular it was recognised that courthouses of the past had rarely reflected concern for the comfort, convenience or dignity of the working classes. Modern designers began to argue that there was a need for a new approach to court design which reflected the fact that sovereignty was increasingly seen as vested in the masses.[25] In the words of Brown the challenge for court designers of the period was '... the resolution of the dialogue between the individual and State – the rulers and the ruled – and a building which symbolizes the health and viability of such a social contract'.[26] Debates about this 'democratic turn' were highly visible in the field of architecture. The simple undecorated lines, geometric forms and attention to function encouraged by Modernist designs for courthouses provided a stark contrast with the neo-classical or gothic form and deliberately drew on ideas of rupture with the past.

At an international level buildings such as Le Corbusier courts at Chandigarh (1950–57) where the majesty of law is represented by massive concrete pylons proved revolutionary in their subversion of traditional design concepts.[27] In an Australian context Paul Katseiris also names the building of the High Court in Canberra (1975–80) with its use of high ceilings and flat courtrooms as the moment when judicial buildings in the country attained their contemporary voice.[28] In a UK context achievements were more modest but courts such as those built in Plymouth (1961–63) aimed to achieve an appearance of lightness and dignity as a foil to the oppressive mass and solidarity of the adjoining Guildhall which had housed the county and magistrates courts since being opened in 1874. Viewed through such fresh perspectives the Assize system with its many historic buildings which reflected the authority of law were dismissed as antiquated and oppressive. Courts of this era can also be characterized by less pretentious court interiors which consciously resisted the conventional and superficial trappings of pomp and civic dignity.[29] The interior of courtrooms became noticeably simpler and flatter and there was less evidence of hierarchy in the vertical dimensions of the room together with a conscious rejection of the sort of excessive detailing so loved by Victorian architects. The 'wedding cake' interiors of nineteenth century courtrooms with their central well and theatre like qualities were rejected during this period in favour of courtrooms in which additional height was only used for the judicial dais and the back row of jurors. It is clear that contemporary commentators continue to entertain the expectation that architectural programmes for courthouses can strive towards a range of symbolic and spatial functions which engender respect for justice without mystique, intimidation or the exacerbation of conflict.[30]

A DEMOCRATIC TURN?

Despite these changes, shifts in attitudes towards courthouse design in the UK are more apparent than real. Indeed confidence in the design templates for the interiors of courtrooms reproduced in the Court Standards and Design Guide is such that it is asserted:

> *The courtroom layouts are the result of careful consideration by numerous user groups. They incorporate specific and well-defined relationships between the*

various participants by means of carefully arranged sight line, distances and levels. It has been found that attempts by individual's designers to improve on these layouts have rarely been successful and consequently these layouts are to be adopted in all cases.[31]

A closer analysis of the Court Design Guide suggests that the goals of accessibility and equality are more frequently discussed in relation to the exterior of courts than they are the interior. The importance of architectural creativity is recognized by the Design Guide but its aspirations are largely limited to the façade and entrance hall. As regards the courtroom, it makes clear that the expectation is that architects should continue to design courts with an eye to tradition and prescribed order. The government have stressed that whilst always looking for innovative designs the scope for innovation does not extend to the freedom to re-engineer core aspects of design.[32] Viewed in this way the approach suggested by the Design Guide continues to be a nostalgic one in which designers of courtroom interiors should contain aspirations towards progress or change. Courtrooms are seen as having authentic, fixed and unproblematic identities in which the placing of bodies in particular ways is no longer contestable. Is it really the case that the internal design of the courtroom has reached such a peak of perfection?

It could be argued that whilst the building programmes of recent decades have engineered a symbolic break with the past, the opportunity to radically re-think how the design of modern courthouses can best reflect the new respect for egalitarianism, dignity and due process was avoided. Despite a flattening of levels, very little has changed within the courtroom where spatial practices dating back to the medieval era and nineteenth century remain the norm. I argue that this calls for a fresh questioning of much hallowed assumptions about how the relationship between the State and individual should be reflected in the spatial configurations of the trial.

In the limited literature available commentators have suggested that a discourse of potential disorder constantly permeates negotiation about court design and that humanist instincts towards accessibility voiced by designers can all too easily be dismissed as soft progressive yearnings. Brown, who chaired the committees which produced the early design guides, has argued that the presence of articulate high status users of the buildings who veer towards a conservative approach to design made it extremely difficult for architects to suggest fresh ways of thinking about circulation routes or the public interface with officials.[33] Even more evident is the way in which a security agenda poses a potent challenge to the idea of the courthouse as an open, public and readable space. Reflecting on his experiences of consulting with different groups of staff about design he concludes that police, social services and probation staff prefer to draw strict boundaries around their sphere of operations and that unspoken hostilities are discernible in discussions about the spaces where their respective zones meet. Brown has argued that the security advisers, with all their paraphernalia of secrecy, obsession and rigidity of attitude have transformed into modern day 'form makers' alongside architects.[34] Reflecting on such issues Robert Fulford has concluded that the distinction between 'correct' architecture and the architecture of corrections has become increasingly blurred.[35]

A key theme to emerge from the recent history of court design is the desire for complete control over the public space of courthouses. Such is the rise of the centralized planner that in a US context Wong is confident enough to make reference to the 'profession' of judicial space management which he goes on to describe as both an art and science.[36] Seen from this perspective the *Court Standards and Design Guide* can be viewed as evidence of the plethora of techniques employed to stage manage interactions. The Guide is a Foucauldian scholars dream. At over a thousand pages long the document contains a series of illustrations and text which prescribe in minute detail how the internal space of all publicly funded courthouses should be configured. Even the most cursory reading of the text reveals the guide's concern with the minutiae of signifiers in the courtroom which is suggestive of the late twentieth century shift towards cultures of control in penal policy.[37] Much of the Guide is dedicated to discussion of discrete circulation routes within the courthouse and segmentation of space within it. It contains detailed guidance about the materials which should be used to build and fill the court as well as their quality, size and position. It has sections on signs; safety; air; water; acoustics; furniture and furnishings; finishes and materials; alarms; information technology and sustainable development. We are informed of the correct size of the advocate's desk, the appropriate depth of the glass in a secure dock; the positioning of each category of user; recommended floor and ceiling finishes and the type of wallpaper to be used in the court offices. One emerges at the end of reading the guide with a detailed knowledge of such things as the size of the mirror to be positioned in the judges' private toilets and the number of toilet roll holders to be installed there.

Significantly, a new emphasis on 'sightlines' means that modern day surveillance of the public is also facilitated through the detailed prescription of who should be able to see whom within the courtroom. The focus of the Guide is as much on the visibility of spectators as it is the visibility of proceedings and provides a particularly good example of the ways in which law as physical compulsion has been replaced by the simple economic geometry of seamless surveillance. Spectators are expected to have a clear view of the judge but destined to get no more than a 'general view' of the proceedings. Indeed, it is specifically noted that they should have their field of vision restricted. While axial visibility is imposed on them, they suffer from lateral invisibility in ways which clearly associate the public with danger. So for instance, it is prescribed that those sitting in the public gallery should have the minimum possible direct eye contact with the jury in order to reduce the risk of intimidation of jurors. Moreover, a glass screen between the modern dock and public seating area is expected to be obscured to a height of 1525 mm above the floor level so that the public are prevented from seeing the defendant while they are seated. It would seem that design now plays a more pronounced role that ever before in managing the movement and behaviour of participants in the trial in ways which can impact on their ability to participate in it. Observation has become distinct from participation and viewing from accountability.

The spatial configurations of the courthouse have led researchers to argue that design continues to be complicit in the degradation of defendants and spectators in the criminal trial.[38] There is also an emerging jurisprudence on the issue. The 2000 decision of the European Court of Justice in the cases of *T and V v United Kingdom* made clear that the layout of a Crown court in which two youths were tried contributed to the undermining of their right to a fair trial under article 6 of the European Charter of Human Rights. More recently, Justice Bongiorno's decision in the Australian case of *Benbrika 12* to have a secure glass dock dismantled because it undermined the presumption of innocence indicates the direct relationship between how we organized space with notions of due process. These issues become more urgent of consideration still when one considers that in the US, arguably the most security conscious nation in the world, even the most violent of defendants regularly sit next to their counsel immediately in front of the judge and the public sit on the same level with full view of all the other participants in the trial.[39]

Producers of the modern Design Guide can remain confident that they have perfected models of containment unconceived of by their forebears.[40] The complete segregation of clearly defined categories of participant in the trial, the creation of private zones within the courthouse and courtroom, detailed specifications as regards sightlines and the physical separation of the press and jury from the public are all architectural embodiments of control in which notions of 'visibility' could be seen as a ruse. It might also be argued that although the courtroom has become flatter in recent decades with less emphasis on overbearing symbols of power there is also a possibility that discipline and surveillance in the courtroom has become so subtle that these crude symbols of force can now be dispensed with. Contrary to the rhetoric employed by policy makers the architectural apparatus imposed by the Guide can just easily be read as a vehicle for creating and sustaining power relations as it can a site where equality is valued. The sophisticated forms of segregation and surveillance employed allows things to be arranged in such a way that the exercise of power is not added on from the outside but is subtly present in ways which increases its efficiency and transforms 'participants' into docile spectators.

NOTES

1 Clare Graham, *Ordering Law: The Architecture and Social History of the English Law Court to 1914* (Aldershot, 2003).

2 Allan Brodie, Gary Winter, Stephen Porter, *The Law Court 1800–2000: Development in Form and Function* (London, 2001).

3 Graham, *Ordering Law*; David Brownlee, *The Law Courts: The Architecture of George Edmund Street* (New York, 1984); Josef Sharon, *The Supreme Court Building* (Jerusalem, 1993); T. Bürklin, J. Limbach, and M. Wilkens, 'With a touch of Internationality and Modernity', in *The Federal Constitutional Court of Germany: Architecture and Jurisdiction* (Basel, 2004); Katherine Fischer-Taylor, *In the Theater of Criminal Justice: The Palais de Justice in Second Empire Paris* (Princeton NJ, 1993). See

also Linda Mulcahy, 'The Unbearable Lightness of Being? Shifts Towards the Virtual Trial', in *Journal of Law and Society*, vol. 35(4) (2008): 464–89; and Linda Mulcahy, *Legal Architecture: Justice, Due Process and the Place of Law* (London, 2011).

4 David Tait, 'Democratic Spaces in a Citadel of Authority', in *Architecture Australia*, vol. 98(5) (2009).

5 Graham, *Ordering Law*; Mulchay, *Legal Architecture: Justice, Due Process and the Place of Law* (London, 2010).

6 The Assizes were the most senior regional courts and were overseen by judges from Westminster who travelled to the regions for this purpose. The Assize system lasted from the twelfth century until 1972.

7 Graham, *Ordering Law*.

8 Graham, *Ordering Law*.

9 David Watkin, *The Buildings of Britain: Regency – A Guide and Gazetteer* (London, 1982).

10 Christopher Chalklin, *English Counties and Public Building 1650–1830* (London, 1998).

11 Linda Mulcahy, 'Architectural Precedent: Manchester Assize Courts and Monuments to Law in the Mid-Victorian Era', in *Kings Law Journal*, vol. 19 (2008).

12 Mulcahy, 'Architectural Precedent'.

13 Graham, *Ordering Law*, p. 3.

14 Mulcahy, *Legal Architecture*.

15 Martha McNamara, *From Tavern to Courthouse: Architecture and Ritual in American Law 1658–1860* (Baltimore MD, 2004).

16 Graham, *Ordering Law*; Mulchay, 'The Unbearable Lightness of Being'.

17 Graham, *Ordering Law*.

18 Royal Commission on Assizes and Quarter Sessions, *Written evidence submitted to the Commission under the chairmanship of Lord Beeching, Royal Commission on Assizes and Quarter Sessions, 1966–69* (London, 1971), p. 47.

19 Magistrates Court Design Guide 1970. See also Consultative memorandum on the design of the courts, 1970; the Crown and County Courthouse Design Manual 1975. Brown, F. (1977).

20 SAVE Britain's Heritage, *Silence in court: The Future of the UK's Historic Law Courts* (London, 2004).

21 Paul Rock, *The Social World of an English Crown Court* (Oxford, 1993).

22 F. Brown, 'Preface', in *Magistrates Courthouses: Design Study 1977* (London, 1977), p. iii.

23 Not all jurisdictions followed this lead in developing standardized templates for courthouse design although the issue continues to be debated in jurisdictions such as Australia and France. Home Office and Greater London Council, *Magistrates Courthouses: Design Study 1977* (London, 1977), p. 5; J. Brown, 'Design for Law and Order: A general survey', in *Architects Journal*, June 1980.

24 The current version of the guide is the most comprehensive to date and provides standardized templates for all Magistrates, County and Crown Courts. Her Majesty's Courts Service, *Court Standards and Design Guide* (London, 2010).

25 M. Black, 'Representations of justice, A photographic Essay', in JOSCCI, number one, www.uow.edu.au/arts/jiscci. <Last accessed November 2009>.

26 Brown, 'Design for Law and Order', p. 1191.

27 See further <http://www.highcourtchd.gov.in/buildingview1.htm>.

28 A virtual tour of the High court can be taken at: http://www.hcourt.gov.au/about_04.html, P. Katsieris, 'The Design of the Commonwealth Law Courts Building, Melbourne', in *JOSCCI*, number one, www.uow.edu.au/arts/jiscci. Last accessed November 2009.

29 Brown, 'Design for Law and Order', p. 1199.

30 Kim Dovey, and J. Fitzgerald, 'Open court: Transparency and Legitimation in the Courthouse', in *Becoming Places: Urbanism/Architecture/Identity/Power* (London, 2010).

31 Her Majesty's Courts Service, *Court Standards and Design Guide* (London, 2010).

32 Department for Constitutional Affairs, 'Public private partnerships and the PFI', www.dca.gov.uk/courtbuild. Last accessed August 2005.

33 Brown, 'Design for Law and Order'.

34 J. Brown, 'The Law of Architecture: Glasgow Sheriffs Courts', in *Architects Journal,* 11 February (1987): 32.

35 Robert Fulford, 'Correct architecture and the architecture of corrections', *Globe and Mail*, 19 September 1998). See <http://www.robertfulford.com/Courthouses.html>.

36 *Judicial Administration and Space Management: A Guide for Architects, Court Administrators and Planners*, ed. F. Michael Wong (Gainsville, 2001).

37 David Garland, *The Culture of Control: Crime and Social Order in Contemporary Society* (Chicago, 2001).

38 Pat Carlen, 'Remedial Routines for the Maintenance of Control in Magistrates' Courts', in *British Journal of Law and Society*, vol. 1, no. 2 (1974): 111–17; Pat Carlen, *Magistrates' Justice* (London, 1976); Rock, *The Social World of an English Crown Court*; Paul Rock, 'Witnesses and Space in a Crown Court', in *British Journal of Criminology*, vol. 31(3) (1991).

39 Linda Mulcahy, 'Architects of Justice: The Politics of Court House Design', *Social and Legal Studies*, vol. 16(3) (2007).

40 *Court Standards and Design Guide*, 2010.

6

Lecture Theatre: Echoes of the *Palais de Justice* in Legal Education

Keith Crawford

INSTITUTIONAL AUTHORITY AND LEGAL EDUCATION

States rest upon institutions both physical and social such as the Houses of Parliament, the *Arc de Triomphe*, the *Palais de Justice*, the National Health Service, Social Security, or a Court of Appeal; they instil a sense of permanence and stability. The eighteenth century gave rise to the notion that law[1] and architecture[2] could be used as devices for social engineering: 'laws come to the aid of morals: the enlightened temple of justice forms a salutary contrast to the dark lairs of crime.'[3] This revolution in thought climaxed in the French social and political revolution of 1789–99, was internationalised through conquest,[4] and provided 'the issues of liberal and radical-democratic politics for most of the world'.[5] The revolutionary period offers an object lesson in how to use the institution to assert authority.

This paper draws a line between two of the most important physical institutions in French legal methodology; the *Palais de Justice* in France, as an embodiment of the authority of textual law, and the modern day French lecture theatre. It highlights similarities in the techniques used to express authority in the different buildings, and the impact on students of teaching them in spaces that emphasise the supremacy of the speaker and the notion of the law as factual, discoverable truth. It is intended to serve as a warning before we consider using a *Magistral* style education in England to meet the demands of an increasingly large student body, and also to highlight the importance of the choice of the space in which we practice law.

THE FAILURE OF REVOLUTIONARY INSTITUTIONALISATION

The French Revolution is best understood as a series of 'uprisings, purges, coups, and reactions' with each faction, having seized power, striving 'to stop the Revolution, to consolidate it around the ideals and institutions on which the regime rested'.[6] Legal institution was as quick to rise as to fall, with revolutionary regimes 'enacting nearly 15,000 statutes, and then making half a dozen attempts to embody them in a homogenous code'.[7] Architectural institutions also proved easier to destroy than to build. The academies were abolished as 'the last refuge of all the aristocracies',[8] but plans for temples of reason and monuments of the revolution never left the drawing board and the architect found himself, as Jean-Jacques Lequeue once famously scrawled, 'drawing to save myself from the guillotine. Everything for the fatherland!'[9]

The first problem was that architecture requires time and money, and the revolutionary regimes were both short lived and bankrupt: 'throughout the decade successive regimes were too unstable, money was too scarce, and ideology shifted too rapidly for ambitious urban projects.'[10] The second was that architecture requires patronage, which prior to the revolution meant the aristocracy; a fact that led many designers into exile, execution or imprisonment. Institution requires stability before it can maintain it.

Calls for revolution gradually gave way to 'an overwhelming demand for "a Man on Horseback" to restore order, regularity and prosperity'.[11] Napoleon Bonaparte, immortalised as just such a man by the painter Jacques-Louis David, took five years to turn his three man coup into a one man empire, reconciling his 'increasingly monarchical power with the maintenance of the 'social achievements' of the Revolution'[12] by taking advantage of the 'absolute concentration of authority'[13] created by the revolutions extermination of the feudal balance of power.

The institutional legacy he used to create this remains imprinted on France today,[14] from the civil code and the *legion d'honneur*, to the *Arc-de Triomphe*, the *Madeleine*, the *Bourse*, the portico of the *Chambre des Députés* and the *Colonne Vendôme*, all created under the direction and often quite specific guidance of Napoleon himself. He had observed early in life that 'if I were the master of France, I would make Paris … the most beautiful town that could exist',[15] but this says less about his appreciation of the aesthetic than about his understanding of the nature of power: 'A new government needs to dazzle and amaze … . The moment its splendour fails, it falls.'[16] Napoleonic architecture may be 'derivative and monotonous', but it is not art critics he sought to please.[17] He referenced classicism because of the sense of permanence that comes with antiquity; 'I became the arch of the old and new alliance, the natural mediator between the old and new order of things.'[18] He was dazzling his audience with the spectacle of the old to maintain the stability of the new.

THE *PALAIS DE JUSTICE*

Napoleon's greatest legal legacy is the achievement of the centuries old dream of a single code of law for all of France, 'to bring the Revolution to a close while maintaining most of its achievements, to reinforce and reconstruct the fabric of society, and to increase the power of the state by unifying it and centralising the

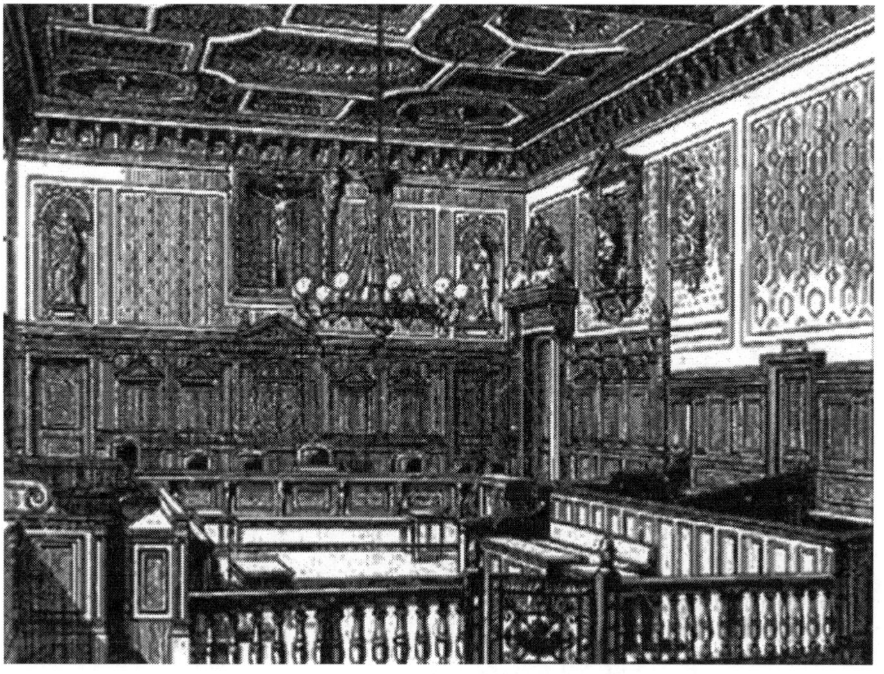

6.1 Salle de Audience 1880. Félix Narjoux, 'Paris: Monuments élevés par la ville 1850–80: Volume 1/Edifices administrif/Edifices Judicaires' Vve A. Morel (Paris, 1883), available online at the BnF website ark:/12148/bpt6k86627r (accessed 25 Jan 2010) – Chapitre Premier – Page 37 – la salle d'audience

administration'.[19] His empire may have fallen at Waterloo but the code endured, physically incarnated in new courts built specifically for 'veneration for the written codes and their unbending application'.[20] The pinnacle of the embodiment of textual law occurred in the 1880 reconstruction of the *Palais de Justice*, part of Napoleon III's Haussemanian redevelopment and still the working supreme court of France. A modern visitor will find that other than for the installation of microphones and bullet proof glass the space is virtually identical to when it was constructed.

HIERARCHICAL AXIS OF POWER

The room is constructed as 'a long rectangle set up like a basilican Catholic church, so as to maximize the longitudinal axis that culminated in the judges' tribune'.[21] While the prosecutor sits elevated alongside the judge, indicating his status as a magistrate and representative of the state, the defence sits in a lower position diametrically opposite the jury.[22] The social structure of the room is a clear expression of state authority, 'physically constructed as a contest between two visibly unequal entities: the individual defendant versus society, represented by the magistrates and, temporarily, by the jury'.[23] The focus of this display is the presiding judge, who leads the inquisitorial trial, conducting, questioning and directing the oral proceedings as a whole.[24] An escalating gradient of grandeur takes us from one end of the room, where the audience sit on plain benches, to the other, where the judges sit on ornate chairs in front of decorated panels. Their

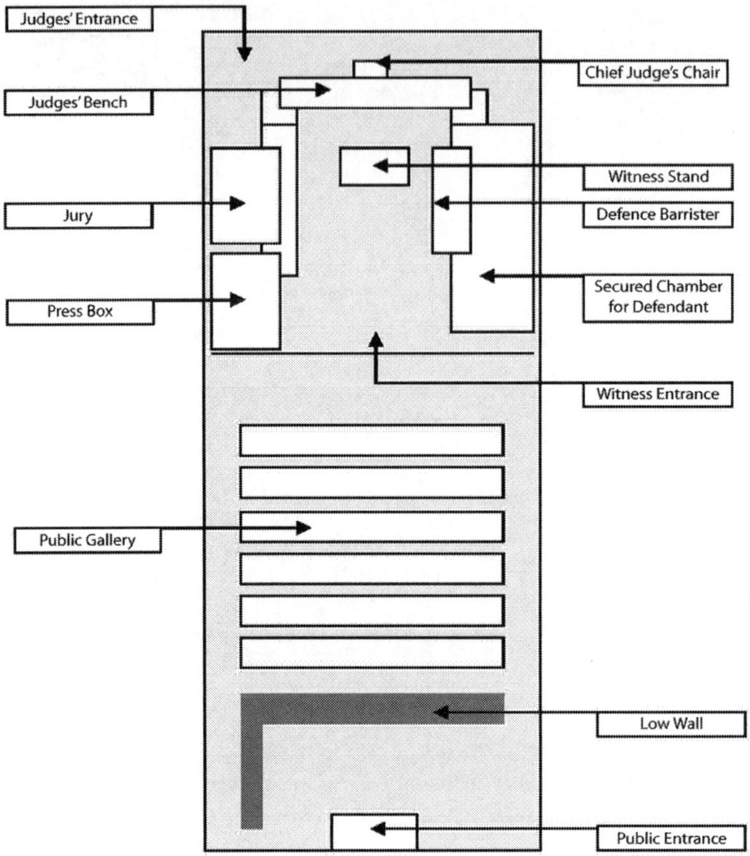

6.2 Diagram of the Layout of the Court (diagram drawn from visit to *Palais de Justice*, 7 October 2009)

costumes evoke the tradition of high ranking magistrates receiving 'their red robes as hand-me-downs from the king … to signify the immortality of sovereignty … In this sense red-robed magistrates made a competing bid for sovereignty not only with lawyers, but also with the spectators and jurors whose public status was signified by their lack of uniform.'[25]

It is hard to believe that this court expresses Abbé Siéyès' notion that all sovereignty 'resides essentially in the nation.'[26] Instead it is brilliant subversion of the principle of publicity, embodying the Enlightenment belief that emotion must be suppressed by rational reflection; that the textual is superior to the oral and gestural.[27] Thus justice must be removed from the public into the hands of a responsible sovereign power for, as Michel Foucault suggests, '"fear of the uproar, shouting and cheering that the people usually indulge in, the fear that there would be disorder, violence and outbursts against the parties, or even the judges." Before the justice of the sovereign, all voices must be still.'[28]

Complaints that the oral trial was too theatrical seem to rest on concerns that 'spectators were treating the trial as an entertainment for themselves, distancing themselves from the debate between the rights of the defendant and those of society and thereby evading application of its stern moral lesson to their own lives'.[29] Viewing the judge from a similar position to that of the witness or defendant when giving testimony, the audience is intended to experience judgment and be chastised through the defendant (and to some extent through the witnesses as well). We are reminded of Foucault's 'regulated mechanism of an ordeal: a physical challenge that must define the truth; if the patient is guilty, the pains that it imposes are not unjust; but it is also a mark of exculpation if he is innocent.'[30] Trials teach 'the public how to apply that general set of principles which constituted the codes in contingent daily life'.[31]

In this sense we see the distinction between the adversarial and the inquisitorial trial is not simply the difference between 'a dramatic thing put to legal use'[32] and a system focussed on 'collegiality, conversation, and consensus – not dramatic confrontation'.[33] The drama of the court of the civil code is lodging sovereignty in a different place: 'the oral, antagonistic courtroom is set up for viewing and hearing a seemingly balanced battle between prosecution and defence. The expert, inquisitorial courtroom is set up to enhance the authority of the judge or the system of justice he enforces.'[34] Inquisitorial justice 'implies a hierarchical axis of power flowing from the knowing judge to his subject';[35] 'the magistrate constituted, in solitary omnipotence, a truth by which he invested the accused; and the judges received this truth ready-made.'[36]

ECHOES IN THE LECTURE THEATRE

This is a picture of the main amphitheatre in the law faculty at the University Paris II Pantheon-Assas, one of the two halls used to deliver both graduate and undergraduate level law courses. Notice the elevated position of the professor's bench, the straight lines flowing from the back of the theatre to the front, and the large flanged structure focusing audience attention to the centre. Amphitheatres have their roots in 'the psychological advantages of assembling people in an enclave where they could see each other and share common emotions', a principle applied by revolutionaries in an effort to 'succeed in bringing back a sense of morals'.[37] Students typically note feeling overwhelmed, intimidated, and small.

> *The lecture theatre is very, almost too big, the quality of the sound is very unequal depending on your place and the distance between seats and the small tables are thin which is pretty uncomfortable to take notes during long or intense classes. (Student, France)*

> *The first thing that strikes me: the theatre of Assas is huge. A multitude of students: it's not very reassuring! (Student, France)*

The second amphitheatre shares major qualities of the first, but with a significant addition. This remarkable fixture is not an anomaly but rather a French university tradition known as *la chaise*. Its presence mimics or even exaggerates that of the judge's bench, creating an unavoidable impression of the superiority of teacher to student. Teachers express the concern that a small table would look ridiculous,

6.3 The French Lecture Theatre and 'La Chaise'

but *La chaise* is so grandiose it actually obscures the view of the speaker; in one interview the teacher spoke of students who would not recognise him outside of the lecture theatre. This is not the only element borrowed from the court that emphasises the alien authority of the speaker:

> *You should know that, until 1968, we would deliver the course in a robe, a red robe; a ceremonial robe. Some of my colleagues still teach in this robe. For some people this perhaps places more authority at their disposal. It is a change from the 1968 revolution that we could come in a suit – but everybody wears a tie, for example. It is out of the question to come to deliver a course, for anyone at our university, which is very traditional, in a T-Shirt or a Polo – it is forbidden. (Teacher, France)*

6.4 A French Law Lecturer in his Formal Robes

The robe is a replica of the one worn by the magistrate, in which the red evoked royal sovereignty and 'consisted of a uniform, which concealed the individuality of the wearer's body and assimilated him to a professional ethos'.[38] We can compare this image of the French lecturer in his robes to that of the English lecturer I observed teaching insolvency law in the UK:

> *Frankly I don't feel as though I should try and generate any sense of authority, I'm just somebody who knows quite a bit about certain given areas. I am there in the first place to tell the students a little bit about those areas, but after that it ought to be a dialogue … this idea of authority, of being the father figure, from whom all knowledge is imparted and is authoritative, is wrong. (Teacher, UK)*

6.5 The French and the English Law Lecturer

6.6 Pictures from the French and the English Law Lecture

Both French and English staff spoke of a need to balance authority and accessibility, the need for students to be prepared to question what the teachers told them. This is much more difficult to communicate for the French teacher, when both the physical and social space him into a position of no longer being an individual but rather being a mouthpiece for the law, and for positivist truth.

STUDENTS IN SMALLER GROUPS

I would have to repeat my course seven times for a group of thirty, which means, I have to repeat my course forty times; I refuse to do it! (Teacher, France)

Many of the practical problems to do with teaching large numbers of students the same course stem from a desire to hold on to these traditional methods of teaching; this teacher's legitimate concern that they would have to repeat the same course forty times would become meaningless if they only had to record it once and post it on a website. A growing number of institutions now do exactly this, allowing students to access lectures at their convenience. If you can resolve the intellectual property issues then the best remaining argument for maintaining the traditional lecture is its value as an authoritative spectacle.

A very different type of teaching of insolvency law can be illustrated at the University of Nottingham. Here, the teacher works in front of a small group. She stands on the same level as the other students, with no barrier between her and them. During the lesson there is dialogue; questions back and forth between staff and students, and at one point she stops and says: 'what I think doesn't matter – what the marker thinks, what the marker's opinion is, makes absolutely no difference to your result and is unimportant regarding what your opinion is.'

6.7 The French Insolvency Law Tutorial or 'TD'

The structure of the room facilitates this sort of interaction, although we should note that the students still scribble down notes intensely, and that the room is still full of laptops. Nottingham has the liberty to teach like this because insolvency law is an optional module with fewer students: what is important is that this difference makes a quantifiable difference to what the students experience as the nature of the law.

Returning to France, the insolvency students from the grand amphitheatre get their opportunity to question a member of staff in what is known as 'TD', with a group of around twenty-five to thirty students. This teacher apologised before the class, explaining that this was a particularly *bavard* or rowdy group. Perhaps I have spent too much time in English secondary schools, but I found them exceedingly well behaved and well mannered! There was a more interactive set of students in the TD session, sitting at the front and centre as is frequently the case with less communication-apprehensive students. The quality of answer and response was telling. A great deal of time was spent reading out sections of the law, questions were answered by reciting pre-prepared responses from the computer, and there was a great deal of frantic tapping at the laptop. This was not a forum for debate; it was a forum for clarification. The teacher's best efforts to encourage debate are limited by the format.

For the French students this is their best opportunity to test their answers, because this is the smallest group and the most interaction they will ever experience. For all modules at the University of Nottingham, both those taught in large lecture theatres and small group sessions, students also receive bi-weekly tutorials. Groups of not more than eight have the opportunity to question the tutor in their office.[39] This sort of space allows the teacher, should they wish, to overcome the student's desire for the right answer and force them into debate. As the students have the opportunity to pose questions in the normal lecture, they can afford to take more risks in the tutorial. It is not that simple; the pressures of the quest for the golden bullet are not abandoned at the door; but the structure of the room certainly makes it easier to achieve.

Another important justification for the limits on debate in the French system is the structure of the course. The style of education radically changes in the final

6.8 The English Insolvency Law Tutorial, in the Tutor's Office

year, the 'M2' year, by which time the size of the student body has been significantly reduced by the rigorous system of testing and examination and teaching is conducted in groups much more like the TD group shown above. The suggestion is that, having provided a solid grounding in the law, students can now be taught to debate and question in this final year.

The argument has some merit, but we must remember that the only students who reach the M2 phases are those who have successfully progressed through the highly competitive stages before it: stages that favour the communication apprehensively, that encourage a linear approach, that prefer accurate reference to creative analysis. Traditionally people with a constructivist learning pattern take longer to establish foundation knowledge but their greater experimentation at an earlier point allows them to develop more thorough and detailed knowledge at a later date. These sorts of people are more likely to be eliminated by early testing that focuses on repetition of fact. Is it credible that upon arrival in the final year of their education, after years of testing and examination, students with more direct learning styles will suddenly abandon techniques that have served them so well?

> *You have to do it in a way that we, the academics, think is appropriate to enhancing the students learning abilities and the students learning experience. So whilst they say 'can we have sample answers to absolutely everything that has been set for the past 25 years, and can we have one to one feedback on our exams with written details,' and so on, we will tend to say no because we don't think that works … . The students, I hope and I actually believe, by the time they actually get into the third year they do tend to appreciate and to come round to our way of thinking, probably because by that time they may have done a little bit of vacation work, so they've seen what they have to do in practice, and*

> *they've seen how what we are trying to do can prepare them for that in a more appropriate way than simply saying 'Right, ok, this is the absolutely cast iron road to the two-one.' (Teacher, UK)*

ENGLISH CONSUMER DEMAND FOR A PALAIS STYLE EDUCATION

English legal education is experiencing significant pressures to adopt more of a *Palais* style system.

> *Higher education typically produces a student who is: curriculum driven; ... used to a classroom setting in which instructors instruct and learners learn; used to working towards pre-set educational objectives; used to being assessed, rewarded, or penalized by external evaluation.*[40]

> *I study law because it opens up numerous opportunities without closing any doors. Lawyer, Jurist, Politician, Entrepreneur, Accountant, Auctioneer; these options interest me. These studies to some extent allow us to access many careers. (Student, France)*

> *I thought it would be useful during my training contract, especially due to the current financial situation. (Student, UK)*

> *The students are paying customers ... [League tables and spoon feeding students] have simply become a part of schooling now. It drives the education agenda below the higher education level. We just have to resist it. (Teacher, UK)*

Having speculated their future incomes on loans to pay tuition fees, students come with expectations they want to be fulfilled. The opinions they give are scored through the National Student Satisfaction Survey, which are incorporated into university league tables that influence student recruitment. Student tutor-feedback forms are taken into account for the promotion and retention of staff. There are significant financial benefits to giving students what they want.

Like Medicine or Teaching, Law is a subject commonly studied with career objectives in mind. After years of education structured around examination, students must become highly proficient in the skills of successfully sitting them in order to reach law school. Their expectation is to be shown how to pass through the next set of exams in order to move on to the world of work:

> *They require more buoying up these days. They require more feedback, more constant reassurance, they like to look very much for rules – rules that are concrete, rules which you can predict and comply with. So they are looking for formulae in relation to legal problems, legal questions, and legal principles. I think that probably comes out of the way they are taught at school – they are taught to look for rules. In law of course there is no such magic bullet. (Teacher, UK)*

Although students will often make requests for more tutor contact, once they are in the room the questions are often along the lines of 'will this be in the exam' or 'what is the right answer?' Studying law is stressful. The students arrive seeking reassurance that there is a right answer. The magistral approach is better for achieving this impression, especially for the sorts of students that have made it this far.

COMMUNICATION APPREHENSION AND LEARNING OUTCOMES

A long standing criticism of examination driven learning is that once they move into employment students 'flounder outside the structured learning environment to which they have been accustomed', that they are 'ill-equipped to deal with aspects of the workplace such as problem-solving, decision making, working in a team, or learning for themselves'.[41] Students are aware of the need to develop these skills, but sitting in the amphitheatre they receive mixed messages:

> *To have a good mark, you must be serious (learn your lessons regularly), to have a good memory and to work on your thinking method. You must also be informed about the current events. Our teachers will want us to think on our own little by little, by using the tools they give us. (Student, France)*
>
> *A good law student must have a 'well made mind rather than a well stocked mind.' Basic knowledge is of course required. But what is important is also to have an ability of thinking, and to make connections between the different areas. In our working life, we'll have to think globally. (Student, France)*
>
> *In business law one must teach that which you practice. If you stay in the books and in the text of the law alone you will miss the meat of the subject. So I try to breathe life into my teaching with some practical examples, but in the exam I don't ask them to speak of practical things, it is necessary to talk of other things. (Teacher, France)*
>
> *It's about instilling strong analytical skills and strong skills of evaluation. Insolvency is highly technical, and then there is this over-arching policy idea; so I'm looking for that . . . , a lively appreciation of the tensions that bedevil this area of law. That's what it's all about; conflict resolution, and how it goes about that, and whether the structures and the regimes are fair. I'm looking for that solid, analytical underpinning, but whatever they write above and beyond that is of great interest to me. (Teacher, UK)*
>
> *To have a good mark: cramming, and sometimes thinking. (Student, France)*

Student participation has long been considered essential to 'learning, motivation, and problem solving ability', but the large lecture theatre renders this virtually impossible:[42]

> *The teaching in France is type we call 'Magistral', the idea being that it is in a great amphitheatre with three or four hundred students, and the professor delivers his course, but no dialogue is possible . . . the students hesitate to come and see us,*

6.9 French law students studiously take dictation onto their laptops

hesitate to discuss, and truly, they have to take their courage in their hands to come ... I have always given good access, amiably discussed and voluntarily responded to their questions, but for them, it is not easy. (Teacher, France)

Students who are communication apprehensive, who would prefer to access knowledge through delivery than debate, have a strong preference for *Magistral* style teaching.[43] While they feel more comfortable in the lecture theatre, more independent students experience a 'negative affect which can interfere with learning'.[44] The combination of dictation, examination, then response to surviving student's preference (where those who have survived are those who profited from the situation we have created), creates an inevitable feedback loop. We should recall this when we look up at the field of students, tapping our dictation into their laptops. It is known that 'information that is not actively processed, but merely "recorded," is harder to retrieve from storage, less available for application to new situations, and more easily forgotten'.[45] The student's poor learning habits are simply the rational response to the educational environment they have been put into. Like the audience at the *Palais*, they have learned the superior morality of repetition and silence.

ALTERNATIVES TO THE PALAIS

The *Palais de Justice* is a living embodiment of Napoleon's distrust of an independent judiciary and the notion of the law as an objectively discoverable truth. A consequence of replicating this in the lecture theatre is it encourages communication apprehension and a linear approach to knowledge unsuited either to academia or practice. The use of magistral lecture theatres is by no means unique to French education but the vivid connection between their legal tradition and their legal education clearly illustrates their impact on the student and upon legal method. The growing pressure to somehow both adopt similar practises in English education, and at the same time promote student interaction, should be resisted. I shall conclude by recommending two alternatives:

1. Bulldoze the lecture theatres and replace them with cafés and study spaces. In the twenty-first century placing all lectures on the internet alongside reading lists is simple and economic, facing up to a reality recognised since the 1960s; 'the professor is too valuable to become a technician, snapping the projector on and off. His class time should be spent imparting special knowledge to his students.'[46] Textual learning can be performed by the student in their own time, making it possible to use the maximum available staff time for interaction.
2. There is evidence supporting the notion that 'statements by teachers, rather than questions, lead to a higher cognitive level of student response'. The lecture theatre is an excellent venue for making statements. Interviews with staff and students tend to reveal that they believe positive feedback and encouragement stimulates discussion and debate, but the evidence in support is mixed.[47] One of the remarkable features of education at Paris II was that a large number of high quality student lead discussion groups; if we don't help them the students learn to help themselves. It would be a bold experiment to remove support, to stop taking questions, to end tutorials and written feedback, and leave the students to challenge what they are being told in the informal spaces where most effective learning occurs.[48]

Both of these alternatives are more cost-effective than the current hybrid, not least due to a reduction of staff time spent reading from a script, and encourage the learner to develop skills of independent inquiry. They are also unlikely to be popular with students, who should be reminded that sooner or later when learning to ride a bike you have to take the stabilisers off; the revolution is over, the state is more than stable enough, and we need lawyers prepared to question what they are being told.

The implications of how we physically institutionalise law are not limited to student pedagogy. Do the courts we use induce communication apprehension in witnesses for a criminal trial? Will holding creditor meetings for an insolvent firm in the courthouse lead to different commercial outcomes than if we hold them in hotel conference rooms? What about if the administrator wears a formal robe? Are lawyers trained in one type of space better suited to certain types of legal task: lecture theatre lawyers for human rights, or Socratic lawyers for commercial arbitration, or vice versa? It is important to be clear that there are likely to be tasks for which the magistral lawyer is better suited! If the law is a tool to achieve targeted outcomes, then the places where law is enacted are as much a part of the law as the words from which it is formed. Those seeking to correct unwanted outcomes must look beyond the letter of the law into the spaces where it comes to life.

NOTES

1 'During the Revolution people were much more interested in using the legislation as a means of social engineering.' Jean-Louis Halperin, *The French Civil Code*, trans. Tony Weir (Oxon, 2006), p. 2.

2 'The objectives of social improvement and social control had to be taken into consideration when laying out ground-plans and dividing up space. There was already on inkling of the twentieth century notion of the architect as a social engineer.' James A. Leith, *Space and Revolution: Projects for Monuments, Squares, and Public Buildings in France 1789–1799* (Québec, 1991), p. 16.

3 Anthony Vidler, *Claude-Nicolas Ledoux: Architecture and Social Reform at the End of the Ancien Régime* (London, 1990), p. 135, citing Claude-Nicolas Ledoux, *L'architecture considérée sous le rapport de l'art, des moeurs et de la legislation* (Paris, 1804), p. 3.

4 See Eric Hobsbawm, *The Age of Revolution 1789–1848* (London, 2008), pp. 115 and 117.

5 Ibid., pp. 73–4.

6 Leith, *Space and Revolution*, p. 308, p. 53.

7 Paul Johnson, *Napoleon* (London, 2003), p. 110.

8 Allan Braham, *The Architecture of the French Enlightenment* (London, 1980), p. 252, quoting Jacques-Louis David.

9 Anthony Vidler, *Claude-Nicolas Ledoux: Architecture and Social Reform at the End of the Ancien Régime* (London, 1990), pp. 373–4.

10 Leith, *Space and Revolution*, pp. 305 and 308.

11 Johnson, *Napoleon*, p. 16.

12 Jean-Louis Halperin, *The French Civil Code*, trans. Tony Weir (Oxon, 2006), p. 19.

13 Johnson, *Napoleon*, p. 31.

14 Hobsbawm, *The Age of Revolution*, p. 98.

15 Allan Braham, *The Architecture of the French Enlightenment* (London, 1980), p. 210.

16 Max Gallo, *The Sun of Austerlitz*, trans. William Hobson (London, 2004), p. 5.

17 Braham, *Architecture of the French Enlightenment*, p. 256.

18 Gallo, *The Immortal of St Helena*, title page, quoting Napoleon at St Helena in the *Memorial*.

19 Halperin, *The French Civil Code*, p. 9.

20 Katherine Fischer Taylor, *In the Theater of Criminal Justice: The Palais de Justice in Second Empire Paris* (Princeton NJ, 1993), pp. 69–70.

21 Fischer Taylor, *In the Theater of Criminal Justice*, p. 13.

22 Ibid., pp. 11–12.

23 Ibid., p. 12.

24 Ibid., p. 12.

25 Ibid., p. 33.

26 Hobsbawm, *The Age of Revolution*, p. 80.

27 Fischer-Taylor, *In the Theater of Criminal* Justice, p. 27.

28 Michel Foucault, *Discipline and Punish: The Birth of the Prison*, trans. Alan Sheridan (London, 1991), pp. 35–6.

29 Fischer Taylor, *In the Theater of Criminal Justice*, p. 28.

30 Foucault, *Discipline and Punish*, p. 41, referencing Ayrault, LIII, chapters LXXII and LXIX.

31 Fischer Taylor, *In the Theater of Criminal Justice*, p. 8.

32 Richard Harbinger, 'Trial by Drama', 55/3, *Judicature* (Oct 1971): 122.

33 Fischer Taylor, *In the Theater of Criminal Justice*, p. 13.

34 Ibid., pp. 10–11.

35 Ibid., p. 6.

36 Foucault, *Discipline and Punish*, p. 35.

37 Leith, *Space and Revolution*, pp. 22, 43.

38 Fischer Taylor, *In the Theater of Criminal Justice*, p. 55.

39 It is worth noting, as an example of the continuing pressures towards increasing class sizes, that [when I started my LLB] in 2004 the maximum size of tutorials was six students, not eight.

40 Candy and Crebert, p. 577.

41 P.C. Candy and R.G. Crebert, 'Ivory Tower to Concrete Jungle: The Difficult Transition from the Academy to the Workplace as Learning Environments', *The Journal of Higher Education*, 62 (1991): 570, 572.

42 Claudia E. Nunn, 'Discussion in the College Classroom: Triangulating Observational and Survey Results', *The Journal of Higher Education*, 67 (1996): 243–66, esp. 243.

43 McCorskey and McVetta, 'Classroom Seating Arrangements: Instructional Communication Theory versus Student Preferences', *Communication Education* 27 (March 1978): 570–92.

44 Ibid., p. 110.

45 Nunn, *Discussions in the College Classroom*, p. 245.

46 Warren L. Hickman, 'Campus Construction for Academic Survival: The Importance of the Curriculum in the College Building Program', *The Journal of Higher Education*, 6 (1965): 322–30, esp. 327.

47 Nunn, *Discussions in the College Classroom*, pp. 246, 258–9.

48 Candy and Crebert, *Ivory Tower to Concrete Jungle*, p. 573.

7

Virtual Courts and Putting 'Summary' back into 'Summary Justice': Merely Brief, or Unjust?

Emma Rowden

INTRODUCTION

The use of videolinks in courts is often heralded as the beginnings of so-called 'virtual' courts, as evident in a recent pilot undertaken in the United Kingdom. While the option to participate in courtroom hearings from remote locations via videolink has been available in many countries for over two decades, the overall effects of this change in procedure on the experience of justice remains relatively unknown. This chapter will argue that existing practices of participating in court processes from a remote location risk proceedings being perceived as procedurally unjust as fundamental aspects of the judicial process are potentially undermined by current 'virtual' – or what might more aptly be termed 'distributed' – courts.

Widespread remote participation in court processes is occurring internationally, often justified through a mix of pragmatic and ethical rationales. Reducing the need for transport which is costly and degrades the environment, improving access to justice for people living in remote areas, attempting to reduce the trauma associated with giving evidence for child and vulnerable witnesses, minimising security risks associated with moving those on remand, enabling access to experts who would otherwise be unavailable – all have been put forward to suggest that videolinks will help create a more efficient and effective justice system.[1] It is generally accepted that the use of videolink technology within the adversarial system has the potential to redress some imbalances, and to improve overall access to justice. However, I argue that the way videolink technology is currently implemented in many jurisdictions – as typified in the Virtual Court pilot discussed below – reveals that the important role of the built environment in supporting successful court processes is grossly underestimated.[2] The chapter ends by discussing alternative ways to conceptualise the role of environmental design within the trend towards what I term '*remote court participation*', in order to address some of these concerns.

THE VIRTUAL COURT PILOT

In May 2009, Justice Secretary Jack Straw announced the arrival of the 'Virtual Court' in the United Kingdom. Established as a pilot, the first instance linked Charing Cross Police Station with Camberwell Green Magistrates' Court in South London, and was proposed in order to speed up the processing of minor offences.[3] Cases under the new system would be heard within hours of the defendant being charged, and a plea of guilty could see sentencing handed down on the same day, all without needing to leave the police station where the person was first taken into custody. Initially a voluntary programme requiring informed consent from the defendant; the pilot became compulsory for all first hearings 'within certain parameters and conditions'.[4] Such moves prompt important questions such as: if a person appearing before a Magistrate in the UK Virtual Court Pilot does not ever physically encounter a courtroom, but only the inside of a police station, is it a problem?

It was obviously important for the Ministry of Justice to prove that the Virtual Court pilot would have no detrimental impact upon the quality of court procedure. According to the official press release from the Ministry of Justice:

> *Virtual Courts are exciting as they have the potential to transform how the justice system deals with crimes. Cases will be resolved more quickly, improving the service given to victims, witnesses and defendants, and justice will be faster and more efficient, without any loss of quality.*[5]

The projected cost savings were not insubstantial.[6] However, one wonders whether people who have appeared in court under this new system would agree with the Ministry's claims of no 'loss of quality'. The implicit assumption underlying this rhetoric is that videoconferencing technology is benign and neutral, and can be easily inserted into existing conditions and used without significantly altering the nature of the experience.

GROWING CONCERNS

It would appear that the assumptions the Ministry of Justice made equating speed with an improved service were not shared by those subject to the new system. Within the first weeks of the pilot going live, there was a large amount of criticism levelled at the Virtual Court pilot by lawyers representing their clients under this new procedure:[7]

> *... solicitor Robin Murray said the system placed lawyers in the impossible position of having to choose between being in court to defend their client or being with them at the police station. He also told the BBC that it left the defendant isolated. 'He won't be able to see his family and friends who normally would turn up for a court hearing if they wanted to support him,' Mr Murray said. 'I think it is an isolating feature – the fact that you are almost taking part in a remote video game. It rather depersonalises the whole process.'*[8]

Roger Smith, Director of legal human rights organisation Justice, expressed concerns that virtual courts could undermine the gravitas of judicial proceedings, commenting:

> ... *I have concerns about it being used to sentence somebody. Being summoned before a TV screen is not the same as being summoned before a court ... Being arrested, taken to a police station and then on to court is a shaming process. It is an extremely unpleasant experience to stand in a dock and be told by a judge that you're going to receive a sentence. There is a danger that this process would be debased by being made to look like a reality TV game.*[9]

Eighteen months after the pilot was initiated, criticism from the legal profession continued unabated, with one solicitor calling the pilot the 'Facebook of the criminal justice system' emphasising the difficulties in establishing empathy over the link and the practical problems in achieving effective advocacy for clients.[10] Concerns raised include the difficulties posed when the lawyer's experience of defending their client is fundamentally altered. With transmission of body language and non-verbal cues less effective over the link, defence lawyers are faced with an 'invidious choice', having to opt either for the ability to have quiet asides with their client, or the advantage of being face-to-face with the Magistrate.[11] More recent commentary questions the ability of virtual courts to adequately create trust and confidence in the criminal justice system given the clear disadvantages that the pilot imposes on the defendant and their counsel.[12]

The idea that the Virtual Court is potentially unfair towards the remote defendant was picked up by the recently published official evaluation of the pilot.[13] The evaluation identified that the physical separation of defendants (and sometimes their solicitors) made it harder for communication before and during hearings, raising some concerns for practitioners. Furthermore, the report found that some judicial officers found it more difficult to impose their authority 'remotely', and: 'perceived that defendants took the process less seriously than they would if they appeared in person.'[14] Recently expressed concerns hinted that many defendants who appeared under this system were confused and uncertain about what exactly it was that they were taking part in. In the words of one UK lawyer describing the experience of some of their clients: 'a couple of them haven't even realised that they're in court at all; they just haven't taken it in.'[15]

Economic questions aside, the key question now facing the Ministry of Justice is how many of the above concerns can be ironed out and addressed by changes to the way in which the pilot has been designed and operates, and what aspects, if any, are perceived to be inherent to remote participation, and potentially unresolvable? For instance, one reason for the criticism of virtual courts as 'isolating' is that the technology at present is only focused on conveying official court business. Contact with 'family and friends', as simple as an encouraging smile or nod, are significant social interactions that the court as a public setting affords, but which are not necessarily a high priority for court administrators consumed with providing an efficient and expedient system for handling a busy Magistrate's caseload. The opportunity for dialogue between others involved in the process is also missed, as unplanned encounters in lifts, corridors and waiting areas, where money saving negotiations can take place, are lost.[16] While it is clear that concerns such as these might be addressed with improved design of videolinks to encompass a wider range of verbal and nonverbal communication and more interactions between different types of participants, associations with an experience that is unreal, 'depersonalised' and like a video game – are perhaps less easily reconciled.

VIRTUAL – OR MERELY DISPERSED?

In some ways the tag 'virtual court' that has been ascribed to the pilot seems to be a misnomer. This procedure is not substantially different from how a court that currently uses videolinks might operate and hardly involves the immersive avatar-filled cyber-environments that the term virtual court might imply. Perhaps apprehensions expressed about virtual courts have more to do with the term 'virtual' itself. In many ways – perhaps mistakenly – the virtual is seen as tightly linked to the relatively recent advances in computer technology, yet as many authors point out, the virtual as a concept is really nothing new.[17] The ubiquitous acts of writing, reading, or looking in a mirror have all variously been described as ways in which virtual spaces have long been a part of our embodied existence. By contrast, the terms virtual reality and virtual environments emerged recently, and are closely tied to the computer technologies that allow them to occur.[18]

Virtual, by definition, seems inevitably to connote lack. Our associations with the word are such that when we describe something as 'virtual', it seems to involve a level of trickery in regards to perception, or, that while the end result may be the same there was something different or lost in the process. Some have argued that when speaking of the virtual in its current application to describe technologically mediated communications distinctions between the terms real, actual and virtual need to be made, and that we need to create a clearer understanding about the relationships between them.[19] For most people, the real is strongly associated with concreteness, tangibility and reliability, whereas the virtual is seen as insubstantial, intangible and unreliable. However, the actual (concrete) and the virtual (insubstantial) can both be real and constitute a person's reality. As such, the virtual in this context, needs to be seen as being opposite to 'actual' (concrete) rather than 'real'. Perhaps until the term 'virtual' reaches this semantic shift, and shakes itself from associations with fiction (the simulated, the fake, and the unreal), the term virtual court will always imply something is lacking, and infer unauthenticity. Perhaps in some ways the term 'distributed court' is more apt to describe what is actually achieved both in the United Kingdom pilot, and in other so-named operational 'virtual courts', to avoid these unwanted associations.[20]

In order for a virtual – or distributed – court to work effectively, a level of trust in the mechanism by which justice is dispensed and a confidence that all participants are being treated equally and with respect, whether appearing in person or remotely, needs to be established. Associations with fiction then may be seen to undermine the role of the court as a symbolic entity, and may in turn unsettle its authority. Authenticity implies legitimacy, and establishing legitimate authority is of critical importance to generate public trust that court processes are fair and just.[21] Feelings of remoteness and alienation, coupled with difficulties in communication and engagement between participants described by critics of the United Kingdom's pilot would seem to foster distrust, rather than a belief in the legitimacy of the authority of the court.

NEW WAYS OF UNDERSTANDING THE IMPACT OF REMOTE PARTICIPATION

The widespread use of videoconferencing technology has facilitated a major shift in what we see as the boundary of the physical court and the place for conducting legal procedure, mirroring more closely our experience of 'court' not as a single, discrete object or process, but as a 'multi-faceted entity'.[22] Courts, it may be said, operate simultaneously on a symbolic, a structural and an embodied level, and in combination they contribute to our collective notions of justice.[23] They are experienced by the citizen as the locus of law, by the members of the courtroom as a communally performed ritual, and individually as a participant with a specific role to perform (as witness, defendant, lawyer, judge, as court officer, as jury member, or as a representative of the press or of the public, family or friends of the parties and so forth).

An initial analysis would suggest that there are significant implications that the current use of videolink technology has on all three levels of experiencing the court. The question we then need to ask is does the adoption of technology in this way improve things? And to obtain an adequate answer, we really need to ask the question in different ways: *how* has the introduction of video mediated communication altered the *experience* of being a participant and can each participant adequately perform their role in court? Can the participants still understand the social context and the court rituals in which they are partaking? And does widespread use of video-mediated communications in this way affect our collective understanding of the symbolic function of the court within society?

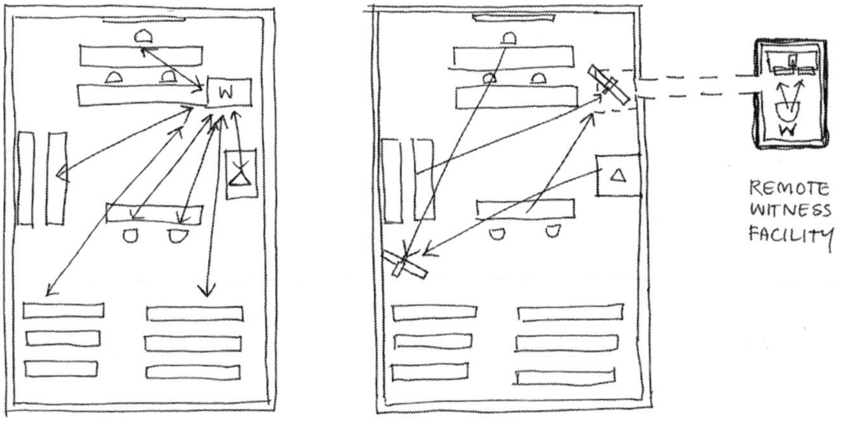

7.1 Remote Court Participation, and the shift from the court operating on a single site, to multiple sites, significantly alters the structural dynamic of court interactions (drawn by author)

There are a number of issues raised in the Virtual Court pilot discourse with regards to what is perceived to happen when a court process is altered by the use of video-mediated communication. Firstly, the technology allows for a splitting of place – the highly-structured performance setting of the court is now effectively operating simultaneously in two discrete locations: the courtroom in the courthouse, and the remote room which in this instance is in a police station. From an architectural perspective, a major concern with current videolinks is that the environment remote participants find themselves in is often at odds with that of the courtroom itself. Remote participation spaces are often described as extensions of the courtroom – and yet, more often than not, the places in which remote participants are located are small, windowless, bland, with only a chair and the video-technology itself; and it would seem the virtual court pilot is no exception. Perhaps if the design of the remote space achieved a similar sense of import and dignity evident in a courtroom, the sense of gravitas might not be as muddied, nor the sense of 'unreality' as sharp, as when court proceedings are perceived through the frame of an anonymous remote space. Linda Mulcahy further questions the lack of attention paid to spaces in which remote participants are linked to court, stating: 'the importance of architecture and design is marginalized if not completely denied'.[24] In one study that included opinions of remote participants about the environment in which they participated, 27 per cent disliked the videolink room, most often likening it to a box or a cupboard.[25]

An interesting feature of the discourse to date is the way that communication technologies allowing remote participation in court processes are being conceived of, and discussed. Audio-visual technology is often revealed as merely another tool but not as something that is an integral or active part of the interaction itself. This is a view contrary to recent work undertaken by Actor-Network and assemblage theorists who re-conceptualise the interaction between human and nonhuman actants, attempting to dismantle previous notions of nonhuman parts of the assemblage as passive or inactive.[26] According to Actor-Network Theory, videoconferencing technology – with its cameras, screens and audio-visual equipment – as nonhuman elements have a capacity equal to humans to influence the nature of connections, meanings and processes. In light of these perspectives, two recent studies stand out as identifying potential ways forward in the analysis of the effects of communication technologies on court processes and the role of the built environment in the enactment of justice.

Lanzara and Patriotta examined six courtrooms that piloted the use of video-cassette recorders (VCR) to document proceedings as a supplement to transcription, seeking to understand the impact of introducing this technology on the behavioural response of courtroom actors.[27] They viewed these videotaped court proceedings through the lens of assemblage theories that conceived of the activities of the courtroom as a kind of knowledge-creation, whereby knowledge is always performed and negotiated.[28] Lanzara and Patriotta found that judges and other relevant actors had to redesign their habitual routines, which abruptly displaced them from established ways of thinking and acting in the court.[29] In order to create a successful record of the event on the VCR, the judicial officers needed 'to develop the kind of sensitivity and skill that belongs to a film-maker rather than a man of law'.[30] Lanzara and Patriotta noted that some were better than others at adjusting to the new media, suggesting that where the VCR was ignored or where experimentation was inadequate, matching the real and recorded events were rarely an issue, compared to when there were no interruptions nor detection and correction of errors during the recording process, the quality of the video as a result was very low.[31] When these interventions were successful and an accurate VCR recording was achieved, however, they were identified by the researchers as instances of making and remaking organisational knowledge in the courtroom setting.[32]

Most relevant for the study of videolink use in courts, Lanzara and Patriotta highlight the effects of the screen and cameras in terms of its capacity to make explicit the fabricated nature of the trial, as an event 'fashioned by and within a medium'.[33] For them, the VCR disrupts traditional practices and challenges the existential fixedness of the scene.[34] By describing the activities of the courtroom as an assemblage, Lanzara and Patriotta enable a different perspective on the insertion of new technologies – the VCR, cameras and screens – into the existing phenomenology and everyday practices of the court. This approach is useful as it provokes a rethinking of how those parts problematise existing relationships and activities in the performance of justice, which – rather than being fixed, pre-determined and certain, are exposed as already contingent, performative and emergent. Ultimately, such a perspective is dependant on how the technology itself is viewed – not as an inert and unbiased medium through which justice is enacted (as it ever was), but as actively transforming the court's performance of justice-in-the-making.

Such a perspective of new communication technologies is not, however, common amongst court regulars. In Christian Licoppe and Laurence Dumoulin's research for instance, they observed the way in which the court participants of their study considered videoconferencing as 'relatively transparent with respect to courtroom interaction', commenting that:

> *... interviewees repeatedly claimed that as long as the audio and video technology was working, and that the participants could see and hear one another through the screen, manage next-speaker selection, and ask questions that elicit relevant answers, judicial business could proceed as usual – irrespective of how strange the scene of distributed hearing might appear to courtroom professionals.*[35]

The reported views of their participants – that the technology is unproblematic – are refuted by Licoppe and Dumoulin, who state that: 'communication technology is not transparent. It makes a difference'.[36] This is a conclusion reached by the researchers after a careful analysis of a particular instance of a distributed, videolinked hearing, where the familiar ritualistic opening of: '[T]he hearing is now open. [Y]ou may be seated,' was unceremoniously omitted.[37] Its absence went – rather surprisingly – unnoticed by participants, so much so that in posthearing interviews, even when confronted with the videorecording of the hearing in question, participants failed to identify anything as different or amiss unless heavily prompted by the researchers.[38] In their analysis, Licoppe and Dumoulin revealed that the task of the opening line, to signal to all participants that the hearing itself had started – was being achieved by other means. A 'roll call' of relevant participants performed at the beginning of the videolink by the judge functioned in a similar way to the conventional opening statement in the discrete court setting – so much so that to utter it at the point where it would have seemed appropriate to do so, would achieve little more than what verbal and nonverbal resources had already accomplished.[39] For Licoppe and Dumoulin, then, technology makes a difference 'as it is part of a network of social and material, linguistic and non-linguistic agencies, which shapes the activity setting and the relevance and force of the linguistic performances occurring within it'.[40] The utility of certain phrases, under the new videolinked court regime, render them no longer useful, so they are dropped without comment.

Communication technologies in the courtroom are not conceived of here as a transparent force, but a transformative one. Such readings compel us to pose the following questions: are we aware of how the use of these technologies transforms the interactions taking place? Do we think these changes are positive and lead to fair proceedings? And if not, how might other parts of the network be manipulated or employed to enable the performance of hearings and trials that are procedurally fair? I argue that the built environment – as nonhuman parts of the network, or, as integral components of the assemblage – need to be viewed as having a similar capacity as the inserted communication technologies to influence perceptions of procedural fairness in both distributed and discrete court proceedings. As such, more attention needs to be paid to the effects of changing the environment of remote court participants. The advantage of Actor-Network and Assemblage theories for this task is that they not only try to account for the influence of nonhuman entities – in this context, *both* the built environment and audio-visual technologies – but that they account for them in a non-deterministic way.[41]

CONCLUSIONS

Inserting audio-visual technology into the courtroom involves disrupting long-established and complex social and physical relationships. In some instances, such as for vulnerable or child witnesses, it has been well documented as a positive disruption, for others, unless there is serious consideration as to what these disruptions imply, it is possible that this results in a step backwards. Seemingly trivial decisions such as the location and décor of a remote room, the size of the screen, the angle of a camera and the position of a participant, may nonetheless prove to be critically important to perceptions of fairness. Particularly, the important role of the built environment to provide social information, by way of 'behavioural cues' has been overlooked in the design of remote court environments.[42] An unstudied approach to the design of remote court spaces and the insertion of audio-visual technologies into existing courtrooms that does not take into account these subtle but accumulative ways in which video-mediation alters the dynamics of the interactions taking place and the individual's experience of court, then 'no loss of quality' may well be impossible to achieve.[43]

The court is not then, a transparent space in which adjudication happens and in which form does not impact upon either process or outcome. Court spaces are not only an intrinsic part of the enactment of justice being done and 'being seen to be done', but they can also be seen as a reflection of the socio-political context. By simple shifts of place, location or ornamentation, a person's position within the space can transform them from the margins to being at the centre of the action taking place, it can enlarge or curtail their voice and it can convey respect and dignify a person, or alternatively, degrade them. As Pierre Bourdieu claims: '... the feeling of injustice or the ability to perceive an experience as unjust is not distributed in a uniform way; it depends closely upon the position one occupies in the social space'.[44] As such, any account of spatial changes to court practices must take into account the diversity of perspectives from within the social space. If we are focused on analysing the impact of altering the setting of the court on perceptions of justice and procedural fairness – a key question we need to ask before we proceed is: how can we adequately capture the myriad ways in which the setting of the court can influence the way the court is perceived by the individual, by the group and by society as a whole? How can we view the court in a way that encompasses the courtroom acting as a performative space, the hearing as a symbolic event, or the way in which the court space can help to define roles, mark boundaries and transform status?

The Virtual Courts pilot was portrayed at the time of its implementation by the Chair of the London Criminal Justice Board as a major advance in court procedure, helping face the challenge to put 'summary' back into 'summary justice'.[45] The major risk, however, is that brevity might be sought at the expense of fairness, and that the right to a fair process – inherent in the true legal use of the term 'summary justice' – may in fact be subverted by the bureaucracy's attempt to save time and money. While such issues are perhaps more acutely felt in the context of lower courts with their high volume caseloads, such questions are pertinent for remote participation throughout the judicial system. How we measure whether remote participation is occurring in a satisfactory manner is important, and needs to engage with the complex ways in which we relate to our courtrooms and courthouses, and the actions that take place within them. Clearly, in some instances, the ability to participate in court processes remotely has redressed pre-existing imbalances within the system – such as its use for vulnerable and child witnesses to give evidence – and its use has no doubt eased the trauma of court participation for many people in these groups.[46] But while 'access to justice' is often cited as the key reason for implementing videoconferencing technology and promoting the concept of virtual courts, *real* access to justice will only be achieved when remote participation does not equate to diminished participation.

NOTES

This research was funded by the Australian Research Council Linkage Project *Gateways to Justice: Improving Video-mediated Communications for Justice Participants (2008–2010).*

1 Joyce Plotnikoff and Richard Woolfson, *Preliminary Hearings: Video Links Evaluation of Pilot Projects* (London: The Home Office, 1999), pp. 54–8; Plotnikoff and Woolfson, *Evaluation of Video Link Pilot at Manchester Crown Court* (London: The Home Office, 2000), pp. 47–8; Michael D. Roth, 'Laissez-faire Videoconferencing: Remote Witness Testimony and Adversarial Truth', *UCLA Law Review*, 48/1 (2000–2001): 190–91; Anne Wallace, 'Virtual Justice in the Bush: The use of court technology in remote and regional Australia', Paper presented at the 3rd Conference on Law & Technology, Malaysia (11–12 November 2008); EU Council Working Party on e-Justice, *Guide on Videoconferencing in Cross-border Proceedings* (Brussels: Council of the European Union, 2009); Reid Howie Associates, *Vulnerable and Intimidated Witnesses: Review of Provisions in Other Jurisdictions* (Edinburgh: Scottish Executive Central Research Unit, 2002), accessed 12/11/09: http://www.scotland.gov.uk/Publications/2002/07/14989/8012; Anne Wallace and Emma Rowden, 'Gateways to Justice: The use of videoconferencing technology to take evidence in Australian courts', *Proceedings of the 9th European Conference on eGovernment* (London, 2009); Adam Brett and Lawrence Blumberg, 'Video-linked court liaison services: forging new frontiers in psychiatry in Western Australia', *Australasian Psychiatry*, 14/1 (2006). In Australia it has even been suggested that videolinks may save lives. See: Nicholas Perpitch, 'Bail videolink could have saved life', *The Australian*, 15 June 2009, 4; Coroner's Court of WA, *Inquest into the Death of Mr Ward (File No 8008/08)*, no. 70–71 (2008).

2 It is generally accepted that use of videolinks has improved the quality of justice by providing access to evidence that would otherwise be unavailable. In a recent study, 39 per cent of young witnesses interviewed would not have given evidence at all, had remote participation not been available. Plotnikoff and Woolfson, *Measuring Up? Evaluating Implementation of Government Commitments to Young Witnesses in Criminal Proceedings* (London: NSPCC, 2009), p. 9.

3 BBC News, 'London hosts first virtual court' (27 May 2009). Minor offences can result in a two year prison term.

4 Ministry of Justice (UK), *News Release: Jack Straw: New Virtual Courts Launched and Intensive Community Payback Extended* (12 May 2009); Catherine Baksi, 'Solicitors Raise Confidentiality Concerns in Virtual Court Pilot', *The Law Gazette* (24 September 2009). As at 16 December 2009, the pilot became compulsory in all pilot areas. Baksi, 'Chaos Predicted Over Virtual Court Pilot'. *The Law Gazette* (16 December 2009); Criminal Justice Board (UK), *The Virtual Court* [promotional DVD] (undated, *c.* 2008); Rowden, Wallace, and Goodman-Delahunty, 'Sentencing by videolink: Up in the Air?', *Criminal Law Journal*, 34/6 (2010): 366.

5 Ministry of Justice (UK), *News Release*.

6 Prior to the establishment of the pilot, it was estimated that the change in procedure could deliver benefits in excess of £10 million a year if rolled-out nationwide. See: Ministry of Justice (UK) *News Release*. The official evaluation of the pilot reveals the cost-benefit scenario to be overstated. Ministry of Justice (UK), *Virtual Court Pilot: Outcome Evaluation*, Ministry of Justice Research Series 21/10 (2010).

7 Baksi, 'Defence solicitors shun pilots of virtual court', *The Law Gazette* (4 June 2009).

8 BBC News, 'Solicitors boycott virtual courts', 31 July 2009.

9 Roger Smith, as quoted in the *London Evening Standard* (2007).

10 Bruce Reid, solicitor advocate quoted in Michael Peel, 'Jury still out on 'virtual courts'. *Financial Times*, 3 November 2010.

11 Michael Peel, 'Jury still out'; Rowden, Wallace and Goodman-Delahunty, 'Sentencing by videolink'.

12 Frances Ridout, 'Virtual Courts – Virtual Justice?', *Criminal Law & Justice Weekly* 174 (25 September 2010): 603.

13 One of the four main objectives of the *Virtual Court Pilot: Outcome Evaluation* was to assess 'whether the Virtual Court process was no less fair than a traditional court'. Ministry of Justice (UK), *Virtual Court Pilot: Outcome Evaluation*, p. iii.

14 Ministry of Justice (UK), *Virtual Court Pilot: Outcome Evaluation*, p. vi.

15 Bruce Reid speaking on ABC Radio National, 'Virtual Courts and the Technological Revolution', *The Law Report*, Broadcast 12 April 2011. Reid further explained of his clients' difficulties in understanding the Virtual Court process: 'I would estimate at least ten per cent of my clients have mental health difficulties, and at least another 20 per cent will be recovering from overindulgence in alcohol, or withdrawing from various forms of narcotics, drugs and sometimes both.'

16 Julienne Hanson, 'The architecture of justice: iconography and space configuration in the English law court building' *arq: Architectural Research Quarterly*, 1/04 (1996): 59.

17 Elizabeth Grosz, *Architecture From the Outside: Essays on Virtual and Real Space* (Cambridge MA: MIT Press, 2001), p. 79; Ali Yakhlef, 'We Have Always Been Virtual: Writing, Institutions, and Technology!', *Space and Culture*, 12/1 (2009).

18 The term virtual, as it is applied to computing, emerged according to the Oxford English Dictionary around 1959, and in relation to virtual reality, around 1987. See: OED definition of 'virtual' adj. (and n.) Second edition, 1989; online version November 2010. Accessed 3/01/11: http://www.oed.com:80/Entry/223829. Earlier version first published in *New English Dictionary*, 1917; Yakhlef, 'We Have Always Been Virtual', p. 81.

19 Edward Castronova, *Synthetic Worlds: The Business and Culture of Online Games* (Chicago, University of Chicago Press, 2006), pp. 285–94; Rob Shields, *The Virtual* (New York: Routledge, 2003), pp. 34–5.

20 The term distributed court is preferred over 'virtual court' as it implies the distribution of the court space over several locations, without the implied 'insubstantial' or 'fake' connotations of the term 'virtual'. While I came to the term distributed court independently, it seems that the phrase has already gained currency in academic circles. For instance, a variation of the term was applied recently in a French study of videoconferencing use in courts to describe a 'distributed hearing (see Christian Licoppe and Laurence Dumoulin, 'The "Curious Case" of an Unspoken Opening Speech Act: A Video-Ethnography of the Use of Video Communication in Courtroom Activities', *Research on Language & Social Interaction*, 43/3 (2010): 211–31, and the phrase 'distributed courts of law' appears on Professor Licoppe's research website). My use of the term refers to the phrase adopted by Sherry Turkle from marketing discourse 'distributed presence', or how one can be 'in several contexts at the same time', in Anne Friedberg, *The Virtual Window: From Alberti to Microsoft* (Cambridge MA: MIT Press, 2006), p. 235. 'Distributed presence' also appears in William J. Mitchell, *Me++: The Cyborg Self and the Networked City* (Cambridge MA: MIT Press, 2003), pp. 143–241. A term that might also be used is 'dispersed space', see Kazys Varnelis and Anne Friedberg, 'Place: The Networking of Public Space', in *Networked Publics*, ed. Varnelis (Cambridge MA: MIT Press, 2008), pp. 15–42. In my definition, the distributed court has one sitting judge, as distinct from the example given in the Australian Family Law Act that defines a court constituted by two or more judges sitting at the same time

but in different places linked by audio-visual technologies as a 'split court', stating: 'for the purposes of determining which law to apply in proceedings in which a split court is sitting, the Court is taken to be sitting at the place at which the presiding Judge is sitting.' Family Law Act (1975), s27/3.

21 Kim Dovey, *Becoming Places* (London; New York: Routledge, 2010), p. 125.

22 Stephen Parker, *Courts and The Public* (Melbourne: Australian Institute of Judicial Administration Incorporated, 1998), p. 23.

23 For a similar description of the tripartite nature in which we encounter architecture see Thomas A. Markus, *Buildings and Power: Freedom and Control in the Origin of Modern Building Types* (London: Routledge, 1993), pp. 21–2.

24 Linda Mulcahy, 'The Unbearable Lightness of Being? Shifts Towards the Virtual Trial', *Journal of Law and Society*, 35/4 (2008): 480.

25 Plotnikoff and Woolfson, *In Their Own Words: The Experiences of 50 Young Witnesses in Criminal Proceedings* (London, 2004), p. 38.

26 Jonathan Murdoch, 'Inhuman/nonhuman/human: actor-network theory and prospects for a nondualistic and symmetrical perspective on nature and society', *Environment and Planning D: Society and Space*, 15 (1997).

27 Giovan Francesco Lanzara and Gerardo Patriotta, 'Technology and the Courtroom: An Inquiry into Knowledge Making in Organisations', *Journal of Management Studies*, 38/7 (2001): 943.

28 Ibid., pp. 944–6.

29 Ibid., pp. 945–6.

30 Ibid., p. 953.

31 Ibid., p. 954.

32 Ibid., p. 954.

33 Ibid., p. 965.

34 Ibid., p. 965.

35 Licoppe and Dumoulin, 'The "Curious Case"', p. 212.

36 Ibid., p. 230.

37 The opening is a judicial convention rather than prescribed by law. However it also performs two specific functions: it establishes the beginning of the hearing in question (a performative utterance that marks everything subsequent as legally relevant), then the second turn 'you may be seated' resolves the practical problem that arose with the judge's entrance (Licoppe and Dumoulin, 'The "Curious Case"', pp. 214–16).

38 Ibid., p. 227.

39 Ibid., p. 221, 227. Ironically, the 'roll call' is uttered as a way of re-establishing the order that was previously performed by the court space – in essence, 'the spatial arrangement of persons and artifacts', the symbols that indicate roles, hierarchy and deference – are being performed verbally instead by the judge (Licoppe and Dumoulin, 'The "Curious Case"', p. 219).

40 Ibid., p. 229.

41 Scott McQuire, Personal Communication, 7 August 2011.

42 For further discussion on this point, see: Rowden, Wallace and Goodman-Delahunty, 'Sentencing by videolink'.

43 A.B. Poulin, 'Criminal justice and video conferencing technology: The remote defendant', *Tulane Law Review,* 78 (2004): 1089–167.

44 Pierre Bourdieu, 'The Force of Law: Toward a Sociology of the Juridical Field', trans. R. Terdiman, *The Hastings Law Journal,* 38 (1987): 833.

45 Tim Godwin (Chair, London Criminal Justice Board), in London Criminal Justice Board, *The Virtual Court.*

46 No doubt improvements could be made here also. See Mulcahy, 'The Unbearable Lightness of Being?'; Wallace and Rowden, 'Gateways to Justice'.

8

Constitution Hill: Just Space or Space of Justice?

Zarina Patel and Clinton David van der Merwe

> *It is 'architecture' that drives the development of this site [Constitution Hill]: it will be a place that embodies the Constitution and its possibilities – and perhaps also its frailties.*[1]

INTRODUCTION

South Africa's post-1994 period of legislative and policy reform has been shaped by the objective of democratising society with an explicit commitment to reversing injustices. Theorising and testing the limits and potential of social justice in a post-apartheid context remains an underexplored area in urban studies.[2] Here, we engage with the relationship between the spatial form and symbolism of Constitution Hill and conceptions of social justice. As urban geographers, we assume that spatial changes in the urban fabric of the post-apartheid city landscape cannot be understood purely in physical terms. Whilst addressing a history of socio-economic exclusion has physical dimensions, 'becoming a city that all citizens can feel part of'[3] must engage with what it means for citizens to belong; as well as the values and intentions of the planners and architects designing spaces for citizens to 'be' in. We have argued that spatial change in a city landscape[4] is underpinned by particular motivations and values that inform the pattern of development and redistribution of resources: human, social, economic and environmental capital.[5] The relationship between spatial change, accessibility and sustainability are therefore dependent on how discourses of justice inform design as well as the extent to which society can identify with these elite-led designs.

We respond to Parnell and Pieterse's[6] claim that the challenge of the post-apartheid city is one of physically as well as psychologically incorporating marginalised groups into the city.[7] In promoting justice, urban regeneration projects, including the development of the Constitution Hill precinct, are based on these objectives.[8] Decreasing visitor numbers,[9] the under-utilised public space, and the alienation from the site expressed by neighbouring residents[10] indicate that Constitution Hill is failing to provide a space that socially and psychologically resonates with the public or even spatially integrates the city. These trends are contrary to both the development vision for the site, and to the social justice ethos of the Court. We question the extent to which the re-design, form and function of Constitution Hill are framed by notions of justice; the accessibility of this framing for visitors to the site; and the potential this might have for the social and psychological integration of citizens into transformed urban spaces. These three questions then lead to conclusions regarding the relationship between the spatial attributes of design and form in the theorisation of social justice in urban regeneration.

We interviewed visitors to Constitution Hill,[11] to assess the extent to which they were able to identify signifiers of justice in the design of the precinct. Justice and sustainability were found to have purchase at the policy level, with limited public resonance, furthermore interviews with architects, social historians and heritage specialists, with an interest in inner city Johannesburg generally, and Constitution Hill specifically were held – to assess the extent to which they consider it possible for justice to be reflected through the physical design, and the effect that this might have on people using and interacting with such value-driven spaces.

THEORISING SOCIAL JUSTICE

Understanding the social injustice of apartheid is a straightforward task,[12] however, theorising justice in a post-apartheid context is less clear-cut. Visser identifies three strands of social justice theory having a key influence on South African policy.[13] Firstly, the policy emphasis on the satisfaction of basic human needs, and in particular the poorest and most marginalised members in society ('Rawlsian Justice'). The prioritisation of the prospects of the least advantaged, with the rider that there should be no losers, is a central feature of the theory of justice expounded by John Rawls.[14] Whilst South African policy sectors including housing and the delivery of key basic services have a clear Rawlsian approach, policy areas such as land restitution are interpreted as adopting a process-based Nozickian understanding of justice.[15]

Robert Nozick[16] supported the entitlement of persons to benefit from their 'holdings', which might have been historical. With the rectification of historically unjust land transfers then, the second expression of justice interprets the mere equalisation of resource inputs to be inadequate; redress through positive discrimination is required to achieve justice (as opposed to equality). The third key strand relates to a number of forms of empowerment, the development of a culture of human rights and inclusion of difference as principles enshrined in the Constitution, and hence pervading all policy, are reminiscent of Iris Marion Young's focus on the politics of difference.[17]

Young therefore shifts the focus from the material and physical effects of political economy in a cultural direction, where social justice involves 'equality among groups who recognize and affirm one another in their specificity'.[18] The extent to which previously marginalised groups are able to feel psychologically and physically integrated into a development would resonate with Young's politics of difference approach to justice. In summary, the common concerns that characterise these approaches include: the distribution of the means of human well-being; (in) equality; and the structure of society and its institutions.[19] Social Justice is therefore concerned with distribution of resources, power relations and equitable access to decision-making.

HISTORY OF CONSTITUTION HILL

The development of the 95000m^2 Constitution Hill Precinct in the early 1990s, chosen as the site for the new Constitutional Court, was a unique collaboration between national, provincial and local government. The call for the development of the new constitutional court[20] saw the Johannesburg Development Agency (JDA) (within its broader urban regeneration strategy for the City of Johannesburg), conceptualise and develop the precinct. The symbolic, political and historical significance of the site has been preserved as a museum and 'campus for human rights' with the Fort, Number 4 (the African Jail) and the women's prison as national heritage sites. The women's prison houses the Commission on Gender Equality, whilst the Human Rights and Youth Commissions of South Africa are also based at the precinct. The symbolism of being the site of the highest court of the land is made more poignant in the context of its historical role in upholding systems of injustice, and the physical or spatial role the site played in racially dividing the city and its peoples.

Originally a military garrison, built in 1892 by Paul Kruger's Boer Republic, the Old Fort was ultimately a place of surveillance, control and defiance,[21] an Afrikaner garrison against the threat of British access to the gold reefs. The outside of the Fort was camouflaged as an impenetrable hill, within which secretive activities were carried out, with the façade and its grand Zuid-Afrikaansche Republiek coat of arms facing inwards. The Fort soon became a jail in 1893 for petty criminals and traitors to 'Afrikaanerdom'. In the early 1900s, the Fort became a British bastion and a place where Afrikaners were humiliated and forced to surrender arms.[22] Spaces of incarceration burgeoned under the British with the building of Section 4 and 5 (the 'native gaol') in 1904, and the women's prison in 1910.[23]

In 1964, the prison complex became a National Monument which was used to house criminals and political prisoners until 1987, in contrast to Robben Island, which was used to incarcerate political prisoners, the Fort held all sorts of people – political prisoners including Mandela (1958 and 1963) and Gandhi (1906 to 1913), and most political activists opposing the state.[24] However, the majority of people held on the site through the last century were common criminals without any 'iconic value' in the freedom struggle, criminalised under the colonial and apartheid race laws, including pass offenders, curfew breakers, beer brewers, and people arrested under the Immorality Act:[25] people who in a just society, would never have been imprisoned.[26] The prisoner profile and the injustice of their incarceration set the scene for the Constitutional rights that the Court now

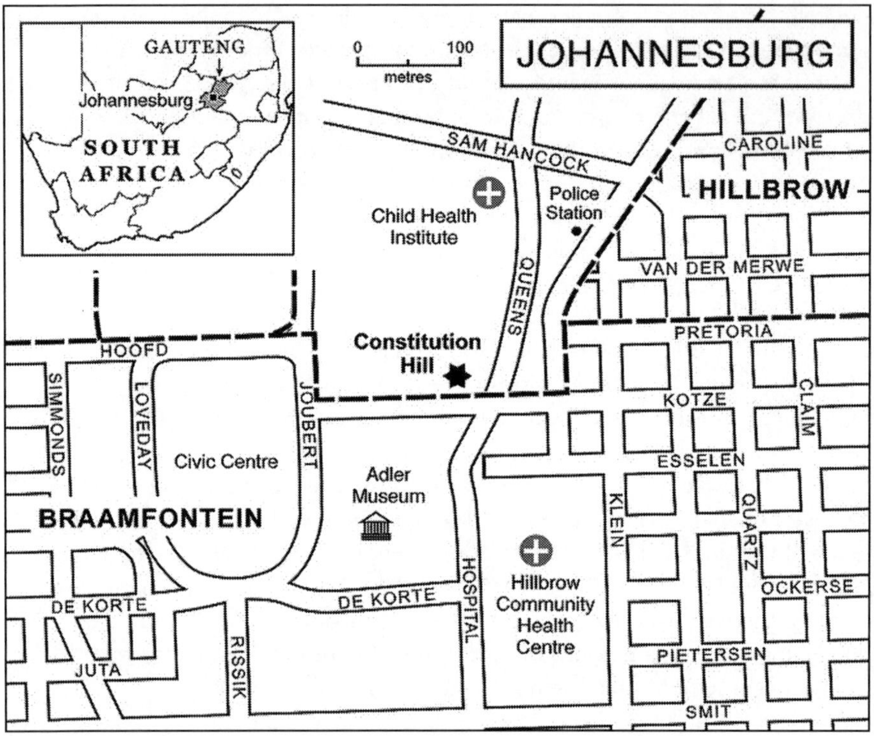

8.1 Plan indicating location of Constitution Hill (map by Wendy Job)

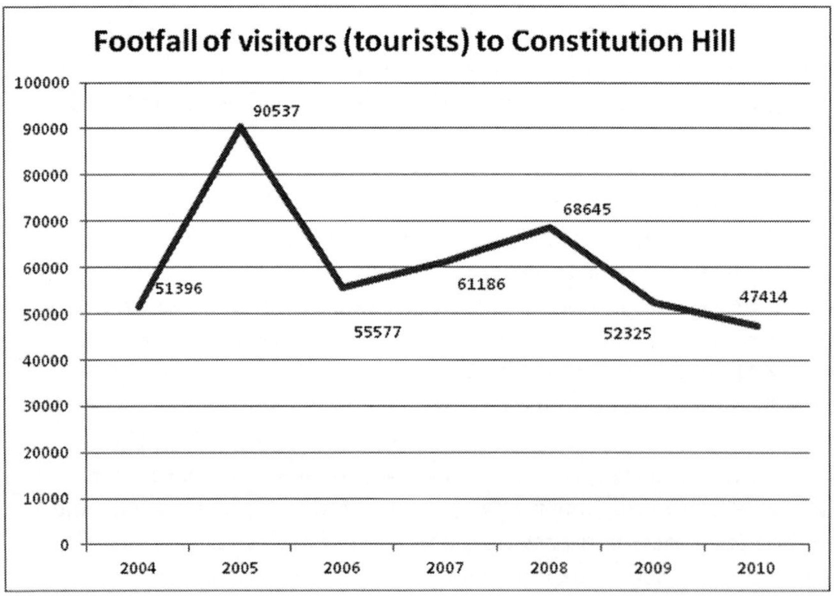

8.2 Graph indicating declining visitor numbers to Constitution Hill (graph by Clinton van der Merwe)

upholds. R460-million[27] was invested in the development of this site to produce buildings and spaces dedicated to upholding justice, opened on Human Rights Day, 21 March 2004 by President Thabo Mbeki. The precinct is located northeast of the CBD of Johannesburg (Fig. 8.1). The high-rise apartment blocks of Hillbrow constitute a neighbourhood of over one hundred thousand people, 'most of whom are immigrants from other parts of Africa'.[28] This neighbourhood is currently served with only one library with twenty seats in it,[29] with other public services being similarly inadequate. Although once prosperous, these neighbourhoods are now neglected sights of social malaise. Constitution Hill is therefore an island in a sea of social and economic inequality.

Since its inception, the precinct has had thousands of both local and international visitors; however numbers have been decreasing (Fig. 8.2). Many reasons account for this decrease in visitor numbers (as will be discussed below), although experts flag poor marketing and lack of advertising, as chief causes for this concerning trend.[30]

SPACES OF JUSTICE?

The focus on a historical site of injustice, and its transformation both in terms of its 'practice' and 'inhabiting'[31] allows for an analysis of space as a medium of power.[32] Constitution Hill is regarded as a site of South Africa's emancipation, with the Constitutional Court giving effect to the rights and freedoms of all citizens. The extent to which the values underpinning justice are reflected at the site are analysed by: The physical accessibility of Constitution Hill to be a thoroughfare that would integrate the city as public space for people to use and interact with on a daily basis, is discussed, and we reflect on the broader planning context that shapes the distribution of resources that have a direct bearing on the effectiveness of Constitution Hill as an integrating node.

POWER RELATIONS

Here we examine the extent to which a narrative of justice is being reflected in the physical design of the Constitution Hill precinct. The symbolism of cases and justice performed under a tree, an African expression of justice in action (Fig. 8.3), is reflected in the architecture of the foyer to the court, with its wire and bead tree sculptures suspended from the ceiling. This powerful symbol is followed through and captured in the identity of the court. The walkway through the art gallery to the Court is a majestic stairwell, the height and openness suggests *transparency*, a fundamental constitutional value. The journey to democracy and freedom is captured in the various art forms that are exhibited to articulate and represent South Africa's varied heritage. These art forms were selected from a range of local artists, not biasing any specific genre, medium or group of artists, to ensure that the diversity of South African society and histories are reflected.

8.3 View of the Constitutional Court's Foyer (photo by David Viljoen)

8.4 View of the doors to the Court Building (photo by David Viljoen)

8.5 View of the human rights inscribed on the entrance wall (photo by David Viljoen)

The 27 human rights, cornerstones of the Bill of Rights, are carved into the 9-m timber doors of the Court in sign language, Braille, as well as South Africa's eleven official languages (Fig. 8.4).

The basic human rights (*Human Dignity, Equality and Freedom*) were handwritten into the concrete (Fig. 8.5) by each of the eleven Constitutional Court Judges (including Justice Yacoob who is blind), thereby reinforcing the consultative and public feel of justice as well as embracing the politics of diversity. The decision to locate the Court in the inner city reflects the dual role of the court – activist and evangelical.[33] The intention was for the Court to be 'of the people, with the people and for the people'.[34] In designing a Court that is approachable and accessible, the design team has ensured that they did not use typical state dominating and power-based architecture. Some architects[35] argued that in ensuring that the Constitutional Court has not taken on the proportions and symbolism of buildings such as the Reichstadt, they have created a space that lacks in the 'reverence' that is required for the highest Court of the country. The extent to which understandings of 'reverence' are shaped by the pervasiveness of Colonial Victorian architectural style typical of other state buildings is unclear here.

Nonetheless, Constitution Hill has been described as 'whimsical',[36] 'sentimental', 'theatrical',[37] 'a spectacle and a tourist attraction'.[38] One architect describes the space as being 'contrived' and 'over designed'.[39] This architect went on to argue that the mixed postmodern narrative serves to dilute its effectiveness. Striking the balance then between mechanisms to reflect diversity and confusing the message, are a clear challenge. The interior design of the Court Chamber embraces several aspects of South African heritage through the use of cowhides as the upholstery for

8.6 View of the cow hides that embellish the Judges' bench (photo by David Viljoen)

the judges' bench and seats, which reflect African culture and endemic notions of justice (Fig. 8.6). The bricks that make-up the chamber were taken from dismantling the previous Awaiting Trial Block. Within the walls of this site's past oppressive and hurtful history, people's pleas are today being heard, their rights protected and justice served.[40]

Keeping the old alongside the new is evidenced on the 'plaza' where sections of the Awaiting Trial Block have been preserved to reflect its historical significance. The remains of the Block have been renamed the 'Towers of Justice', 'reflecting the ying yang of oppression and freedom'.[41] Section 4 is kept in its original form, although the Awaiting Trial block was removed (to create the Constitutional Square or plaza), with sections of the Awaiting Trial block's stairwell being kept as reminders of the grim past. The women's prison is now open as a museum reflecting the oppressive aspects of Apartheid on women.

Intersecting the Court buildings on one side and Section 4 (the Prison) on the other are the 'Great African Stairs', juxtaposing the old oppressive past against the new Democracy and freedom of the present. Built using the original bricks from the Awaiting Trial Block, visitors walk through the suffering of people imprisoned at this site. The tower of the Constitutional Court building can be seen through the restrictive and entrapping mesh of the solitary confinement. Sections 4 and 5 have been kept in their original form as much as possible, so that the brutality of prison life is reflected on the walls of cells – through such mediums as the graffiti of prisoners.

The research found that in an attempt to reflect the diversity of society, the design (including architecture, use of symbols and function of spaces) reflects a range of narratives. The approach to the design of Constitution Hill resonates with Young's approach to justice, with a focus on the politics of difference being a central factor shaping design decisions. Here historical, cultural, political, economic and even difference in relation to disabilities is consciously reflected in the art and architecture of the site. In comparing Robben Island to Constitution Hill, Gevisser makes the following observation: 'this site [Constitution Hill] is more messy, ambiguous, less clear-cut in terms of the psychic and political terrains it seems to take us into ...'[42] The dominant narratives that are reflected include: the tree; low key architecture, re-use of old materials, the art gallery housing a diverse range of genres, political struggle, and the use of and marketing of the iconic political prisoners. Although the objective of the mixed narrative is to ensure that there are elements that could resonate with all in society, respondents have identified the lack of a clear story line as a factor distracting the public from the use of and purpose of the space.

THE RE-FORTIFICATION OF CONSTITUTION HILL

One of the key objectives of the design of the precinct is to ensure the integration of the city and its citizens. The frontage of the court building suggests that everyone's heritage in South Africa is equal by acknowledging (in the various colours of the flag) all eleven official South African languages. Constitution Square is open and expansive, indicating that all people have the right to space and opportunity, simultaneously celebrating diversity. The symbolism of opening up this historically impenetrable space and providing the public with access to the highest court of the country is significant. However, despite claims of Constitution Hill having become an 'integrated, multipurpose and multidimensional space'[43] a visit here reveals a barren space, devoid of any public life. In effect, the site has not fulfilled the objective of being a 'place of pilgrimage, the place where you touch the holy stone of the "South African miracle"'.[44]

Respondents put forward a number of explanations for the low and decreasing public interest in the site. Firstly, high levels of crime in South Africa together with the notorious reputation of the areas adjoining Constitution Hill result in car-bound middle class South Africans visiting the site only to attend a function or to bring international visitors. Dirsuweit confirms that the citizens of Johannesburg fear public spaces as arenas of crime.[45] Visitors have a dual purpose of visiting the court, but also to get a sense – from the safe distance of the ramparts – of life in inner city Johannesburg.[46] Furthermore, for the people living around Constitution Hill, fear about personal safety prevents them changing their known commuting patterns. Connectivity and access points into the precinct are not considered to be serving the needs of pedestrians in the area.[47]

A significant point raised by architects interviewed is that the South African public is largely 'illiterate' with regards to architecture.[48] The architects argued that visiting Constitution Hill to reflect on the symbolism in the architecture and the narratives presented is consequently not an area of interest for the majority of South Africans. 'If asked to stereotype what the typical South African valued about their country, seldom will the built environment and urban centres feature as key identifiers. Natural landscapes, wildlife and open spaces are more likely to be listed as valued attributes.'[49] As one interviewee stated: 'Of course the public is architecturally illiterate. Not only is architecture a specialist discipline with its own history and values, its own forms of knowledge, expensive to train for, buildings are also the product of design, a highly subjective, creative process.'[50] The discussion on 'architectural literacy' does however raise questions about the extent to which the autonomous architect is in touch with the diversity of points of resonance within a varied public, as well as the responsibility of the architect to engage with these diverse publics in the design phases.

Whilst the arguments presented by respondents above reflect on factors affecting the physical accessibility of the site, of significance too is the psychological access to the site.[51] The focus on the historical injustice of this site is perhaps of diminishing interest and significance to the youth of South Africa, who share an optimistic future filled with the promise of opportunity from the hosting of the FIFA Soccer World Cup in 2010.[52] For older South Africans who do still have memories of the Old Fort and who indeed were incarcerated there, those painful memories and experiences need a different form of healing. The re-fortification of the site and the failure to psychologically incorporate the public into this space therefore has as much to do with physical design, as it has to do with symbolic accessibility and memory.

The fact that Constitution Hill is an elite island surrounded by a sea of immigrant communities, many of whom do not have legal standing in Johannesburg, and who were subject to violent xenophobic attacks provides a further example of non-physical barriers in accessing the site. Observations that the site serves the interests of the elite, to the exclusion of the poor resonates with a Rawlsian understanding of (in)justice. The focus on history and redress with respect to the themes reflected in the museum and art installations, as well as the principles informing the broader urban regeneration programme that this precinct falls within, reflect a Nozickian approach to justice. Dirsuweit and Schattauer characterise urban regeneration projects such as this one as being shaped by neoliberal strategies that serve to further entrench the divides between the rich and the poor.[53] Dirsuweit describes Johannesburg as a 'fortress city' where urban developments exclude a cross section of classes.[54] In discussing the accessibility of Constitution Hill, it is clear that this site too has become re-fortified.

PLANNING CONTEXT

Decisions about how resources are allocated must be considered in the context of the broader planning environment. Here, the planners and architects have an important role to play in determining the limits and interpretations of justice. Whilst a number of architects are sympathetic to the need to knit the physical and social aspects of the city together, the participants argue that 'a building is only as good as the client'.[55] Whilst an architect described the Court as an 'architectural masterpiece', she cautions against the notion of an architect having agency in shaping the values of society. Instead she highlights that 'architects provide services to clients, who commission them and determine what will or will not be built. ... It is all about power and money. The extent to which it reflects social values is the extent to which (a) those values are well formulated and (b) those with power and money are prepared to invest in them.'[56]

The architects all agreed that the vast expenditure of public funds on the development of the precinct is appropriate and in keeping with the stature of the Constitutional Court. However, all participants argued that although the development is based on laudable sentiments and objectives, it fails to integrate the city, or to shape the values and aspirations of society. One of the architects argued against attributing a causal relationship between designed space and the shaping of social values.[57] 'More needs to be invested in the site to make it more viable and to complete the subsequent phases of the development which have a greater potential to create and sustain positive public spaces'.[58] Simultaneously, more needs to be invested in the surrounding neighbourhoods to assist the integration from the outside.[59] Gevisser has shown that the people of Hillbrow are not interested in the values of the Constitution per se, but in 'how those values are going to improve their lives'.[60] Their experience is one of living in an under-resourced city, with negative public spaces. A key challenge for the site therefore is to 'ensure that it does not fade, that it remains relevant and alive in people's minds'.[61]

To remain relevant, he argues, the site must respond to what's happening in the society around it rather than ossifying a particular moment of liberation. Three factors were identified as limiting the potential of Constitution Hill: criminality, zoning restrictions,[62] and lack of an ethic of developing public open spaces.[63] Firstly, concern (and perhaps paranoia) about personal safety and dealing with crime through the creation of barriers has resulted in 'South Africa having more linear meters of fencing than the rest of the world put together'.[64] In order for integration to occur, fences must come down, and cannot form the basis of design. Given this history, innovative ways of increasing accessibility to the site and transparency regarding its function need to be integrated into the design, if the site is to function as part of the city.

One of the ways in which accessibility could be enhanced is through the creation of mixed-use zones. However, the zoning restrictions and land-rights inhibit the creation of mixed zones. Women who were previously incarcerated in the Women's Jail have requested space on the square from which they can sell crafts informally. Despite the potential of this proposal for re-dress and its tourist potential, this proposal was turned down by the City Council, as informal trading on the site is prohibited through the zoning restrictions of bylaws.[65] South Africa, unlike Europe, does not have a tradition of creating open, positive public urban spaces that provide places where people can interact. The City's vision for public spaces is restricted to soft interventions including the development of pavements and lighting, which alone do not provide a magnet to attract the public. Participants indicated that activities such as coffee shops, bookshops, exhibitions, sale of local crafts, etc, would serve to attract public on an ongoing basis, as opposed to exhibitions based on prison life.[66] However, the activities identified for the creation of viable public spaces will serve to favour and attract middle-class visitors, which could reinforce the alienation of the neighbouring communities from the site.

In addition, Gevisser raises some pertinent questions: 'In a place like inner-city Johannesburg, can public space be secure and accessible at the same time? Can it be attractive to tourists without being removed from the city by security booms and white-gloved officials ...?'[67] This reinforces the need for a holistic strategy that looks beyond the site (physically, psychologically and symbolically) in its efforts to address questions of accessibility. One of the architects argued that 'space cannot bring parties together ... assembly is a political matter.'[68] The responsibility for increasing accessibility and integration cannot be the sole responsibility of architects, but must be prioritised as part of a bigger strategic plan for the site and its surrounds involving a range of stakeholders. The discussion on the planning context reveals the multiple objectives being expressed by architects, clients, the city authorities and planners' informing what is possible with regards to the spatial layout and design of the site. This is juxtaposed with the objective of providing a space for all citizens to interact, with the reality of having developed public spaces for elite and South African consumption, to the exclusion of the immigrant communities surrounding the site.

CONCLUSION

The relationship between the potential of the site to physically and psychologically integrate the city at Constitution Hill has been shown to defy a linear causal progression. The postmodern mix of narratives and symbols is perhaps a reflection of the lack of commitment at both the levels of policy and practice to any one theoretical interpretation of justice. This is not to argue that there should be a single interpretation of justice – how can there be, in a diverse society? Although Constitution Hill can provide a just space, it cannot serve as an icon of justice, as justice cannot be embodied in a static entity, it must be practised. It is the practice of the Court itself therefore that will have a greater potential to shape the values of society. The vision for Constitution Hill at its inception was to create a space of emancipation, and to re-dress an unjust history. However, in its actualisation, it is experienced as a 'whimsical tourist attraction', from which neighbouring communities feel alienated. In the progression from vision to implementation, the influences of power and money have served to dilute and deflect from the intentions of the site. The study shows that architects are having to perform under a number of restrictions that work against shaping developments that can influence the public's values, some of which are historical, and others that require attitudinal shifts within institutions of government (as the client). Whilst the architectural literacy of the public was identified as a further factor inhibiting the public's appreciation of this 'architectural masterpiece', the study raises questions regarding architects understandings of the public(s) they are designing for.

We argue therefore that architects and planners need to take on a more activist role and greater responsibility for shaping just futures in a post-apartheid context. Neighbouring communities have been shown to feel excluded from the space – whilst access points, crime and zoning restrictions play a role in deterring visitors to Constitution Hill, we argue the inaccessibility of this monument to justice is both psychological and physical. Theorising justice therefore must engage with questions dealing with history, memory and aspirations for alternate futures. Given that politics plays a key role in determining peoples' engagement with space, the sustainability of the site rests with developing a detailed understanding of the values, needs, expectations and aspirations of a diverse public.

ACKNOWLEDGEMENTS

Thank you to our interviewees. Earlier versions of this chapter were presented at the Architecture and Justice Conference (University of Lincoln in 2009); the Planning Africa Conference (Durban, 2010), as well as departmental seminars at the School of Education, University of the Witwatersrand and the Geography Department at the University of Sheffield. Funders who have supported these conferences, and who supported Zarina Patel during her sabbatical from the School of Geography, Archaeology and Environmental Sciences at the University of Witwatersrand to the University of Sheffield include: The National Research Foundation, The Carnegie Corporation of New York, The Oppenheimer Trust and the British Academy. The University of Witwatersrand, Faculty of Humanities is gratefully acknowledged. Thanks to Wendy Job (UJ Cartographic Unit) for the map and David Viljoen (photographs). Any errors or omissions remain our own.

NOTES

1 M. Gevisser, 'From the Ruins: The Constitution Hill Project', *Public Culture*, 16 (2004): 507–19.

2 D.M. Smith, 'Social Justice and the (South African) City: Retrospect and Prospect', *South African Geographical Journal*, 86 (2004): 1–6.

3 L. Bremner, 'Reinventing the Johannesburg Inner City', *Cities*, 17/3 (2000): 185–93.

4 Zarina Patel, 'Understanding environmental change in South African Cities: A landscape approach', *Transformation*, 57 (2005): 24–40 and C.D. van der Merwe and Z. Patel, 'Understandings of urban regeneration, heritage and environmental justice at Constitution Hill, Johannesburg', *Urban Forum*, 16 (2005): 244–58.

5 W.J.T. Mitchell (ed.), *Landscape and Power* (Chicago and London, 1994) and C. Nash, 'Landscapes', in P. Cloke, P. Crang and M. Goodwin (eds), *Introducing Human Geographies* (London, 1999), pp. 217–25.

6 S. Parnell and E. Pieterse, 'Developmental Local Government: The Second Wave of post-apartheid urban reconstruction', *Dark Roast Occasional paper Series No. 1* (Cape Town, 1998).

7 D. Hallows and M. Butler, 'Power, Poverty and Marginalised Environments: A conceptual framework', in D.A. McDonald (ed.), *Environmental Justice in South Africa* (Cape Town, 2002).

8 Constitution Hill, *Constitution Hill Development Company: Business Plan (2012–2013)* (Johannesburg, 2011).

9 Constitution Hill, interview held at the CH Precinct, Johannesburg, South Africa, June 2009 and Constitution Hill (2011).

10 Gevisser (2004).

11 C.D. van der Merwe and Z. Patel, 'Understandings of Urban Regeneration, Heritage and Environmental Justice at Constitution Hill, Johannesburg', in C.M. Rogerson and G.E. Visser (eds), *Urban Tourism in the Developing World: The South African Experience* (Piscataway NJ, 2007), pp. 293–306.

12 Smith (2004).

13 G.E. Visser, 'Social justice and post-apartheid development planning: reflections on moral progress in South Africa', *International Development Planning Review*, 26(4) (2004): 359–76.

14 As cited in Smith (2004).

15 Visser (2004).

16 As cited in Visser (2004).

17 Ibid.

18 As cited in Smith (2004), 2.

19 Smith (2004), 2.

20 Constitution Hill (2011), 2.

21 Gevisser (2004).

22 Ibid.

23 J.R. Shorten, *Die Verhaal van Johannesburg (The Story of Johannesburg)* (Johannesburg, 1970).

24 Gevisser (2004), 514.

25 In 1949, the Prohibition of Mixed Marriages Act had previously banned interracial marriages.

26 Gevisser (2004).

27 £37,313,575.00 in 2012.

28 Gevisser (2004), 517.

29 Ibid., 517.

30 E. Naude, personal communication during a meeting at BLUE IQ, Johannesburg, South Africa, 27 September 2011.

31 J.M. Jacobs and P. Merriman, 'Editorial: Practicing Architectures', *Social & Cultural Geography*, 12/3 (2011): 211–22.

32 A. Stanley, 'Just space or spatial justice? Difference, discourse and environmental justice', *Local Environment*, 14/10 (2009): 999–1014.

33 Gevisser (2004).

34 Ibid., 511.

35 Architect Interview, 10 November 2009.

36 Heritage Specialist Interview, 19 October 2009.

37 Historian Interview, 9 November 2009.

38 Architect Interview, 24 February 2010.

39 Architect Interview, 12 November 2009.

40 Heritage Specialist Interview, 16 October 2009.

41 Architect Interview, 12 November 2009.

42 Gevisser (2004), 514.

43 JDA (2009).

44 Gevisser (2004), 518.

45 T. Dirsuweit, 'From Fortress City to Creative City: Developing Culture and the Information-based Sectors in the Regeneration and Reconstruction of the Greater Johannesburg Area', *Urban Forum*, 10/2 (1999): 183–213.

46 Historian Interview, 9 November 2009.

47 Architect Interview, 9 November 2009.

48 Ibid.

49 Architect Interview, 10 November 2009.

50 Architect Interview, 24 February 2010.

51 Parnell and Pieterse (1998) and Parnell (2005).

52 Heritage Specialist Interview, 16 October 2009.

53 T. Dirsuweit and F. Schattauer, 'Fortresses of desire: Melrose Arch and the emergence of urban tourist spectacles', *Geoforum*, 60 (2004): 239–247.

54 Dirsuweit (1999).

55 Architect Interviews, 9 and 10 November 2009.

56 Architect Interview, 24 February 2010.

57 Ibid.

58 Architect Interview, 9 November 2009.

59 Architect Interview, 10 November 2009.

60 Gevisser (2004), 511.

61 Ibid., 512.

62 Architect Interview, 10 November 2009.

63 Architect Interview, 9 November 2009.

64 Architect Interview, 10 November 2009.

65 Heritage Specialist Interview, 9 November 2009.

66 Architect Interview, 12 November 2009.

67 Gevisser (2004), 517.

68 Architect Interview, 24 February 2010.

9

The Architecture and Operation of the Imperial Chinese Yamen*

Peter Blundell Jones

This investigation began as one of a series of case studies exploring the links between architecture and ritual, looking at the way meanings are established and perpetuated through use and custom, with the aim of discovering the extent to which the process is universal as opposed to specific to period and culture. The topic of the Chinese yamen or law court was instigated by discovery of Liuhong Huang's *Complete Book Concerning Happiness and Benevolence* published in 1694.[1] This detailed account of the role and duties of the seventeenth century Chinese magistrate, the effective ruler of a provincial city, provides a wealth of information about the ritual operation of the yamen, his official residence and seat of government.[2] Although we cannot fit Huang's descriptions to precisely the buildings and cities in which he operated, the architectural form of the yamen was relatively standardised. Djang Chu, translator of Huang's English edition published in 1984, chose to include a map of Ping Xiang (see Figure 9.1) to show a yamen in its city.[3]

This shows the city as conventionally viewed from the south, in the ideal feng-shui position with mountains behind to the north and a river flowing around its south edge. City wall and gates could hardly be more prominent, and right at the centre bounded by its rectangular wall is the yamen, presented as a gate and a couple of halls straddling the centre line or axis,[4] with a screen wall in front, and a connection to the south city gate. This depiction reveals not only the central axial position and hierarchical importance of the yamen in relation to other public buildings, but also the way it exists as a city within a city like the Forbidden City in Beijing, the grand model it imitates. The resemblance is not only spatial and architectural but political, since the magistrate was the agent of the Emperor, and in some crucial ways he was regarded as invested with the Emperor's quasi-divine power.

In contrast with Chinese temples and palaces, the architectural importance of yamens seems to have been little recognised. After the collapse of the empire in 1911 many were demolished or converted for other uses, while later under Mao they were reminders of a defunct and hated regime. Relatively few have survived

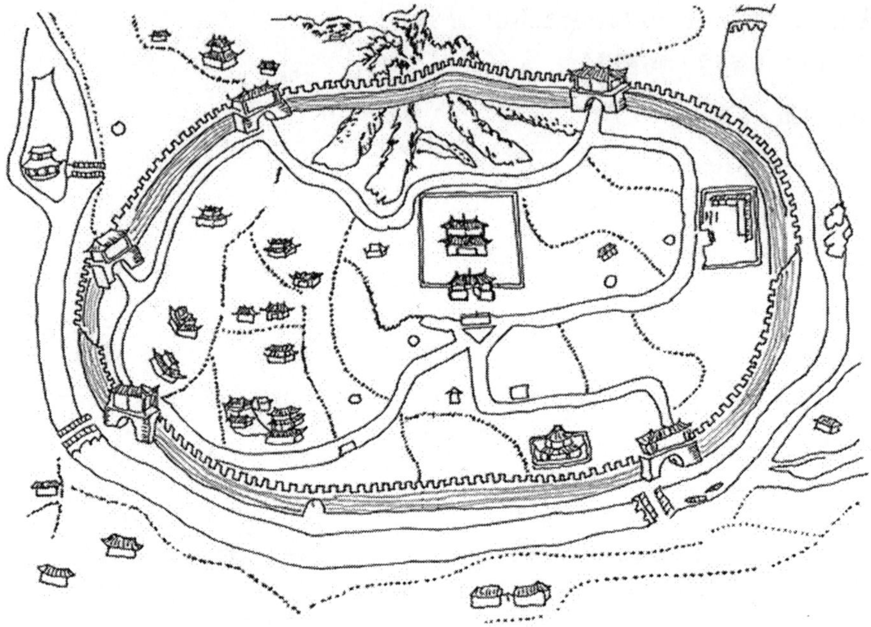

9.1 Ping Xiang and its Yamen 1872. Redrawn by author from a traditional Chinese map reproduced in Huang 1984 as note 1 below

9.2 *Left*: original Chinese version of Neixiang Yamen as redrawn by Pengjin Liu 1998
Right: Author's diagram picking out the main spatial progression

1. Main gate
2. Paifang (a purely ceremonial timber structure)
3. Screen wall at the other side of the street
4. First court
5. Place to tie up horses
6. Prison
7. Gate of Death
8. Hostel for eminent guests
9. Temples of Earth God (right) and of Yamen God
10. Second gate
11. Principal court
12. Paifang
13. First hall and seat of judgement
14. Liberal departments: Civil Office, Revenue, and Rites
15. Martial departments: Punishment, Military, and Works
16. Gate to second court
17. Second court
18. Magistrate's seat
19. Intermediate court
20. Gatehouse to residence
21. Third court
22. Third Hall and residence
23. Private garden entered to west of hall
24. East hall for magistrate's family
25. Revenue Department
26. House of the Guards
27. Houses of Magistrate's Assistants
28. House of the secretaries
29. Police Department

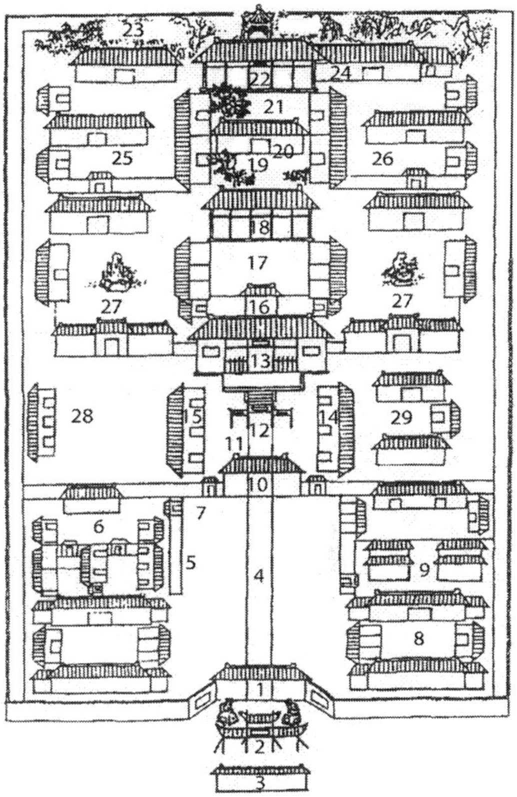

9.3 Keyed plan of the Neixiang Yamen

and some have even been rebuilt recently as a cultural record. One of the best preserved is at Neixiang in central China, and is here taken as the primary object of study, relying on a plan redrawn by Chinese scholars following traditional conventions, and on photographs taken on a visit in 2009. The proviso should be added that the buildings were restored according to what remained and could be reconstructed, but are presented as a museum as if in a constant and static state.

A preserved drawing from around 1700 reveals that there have been changes, for example in the progression of roof types, so the restored version does not show Neixiang yamen quite as it was in the late seventeenth century. But it had been in existence at least since 1300, and was broadly similar in organisation for planning was strictly standardised. Written records suggest that some aspects of the ritual use of space date back as far as Confucius at 500 BCE,[5] for it followed a longstanding tradition reflecting the long established centralised state even if every dynasty also saw changes.

The plan drawing (see Figs 9.2 and 9.3) which in the Chinese style includes elevations, gives a convenient overview. The yamen occupies a rectangular enclosure orientated north-south and divides into three bands vertically, the central band containing the principal courtyards with the main functions. My added diagram (see Fig. 9.2 *Right*) picks out the centre line crossed by the gatehouses and main halls depicted in black. These constitute the primary spatial

9.4 View outside the main gate (photo by author)

progression, starting from south at the bottom. The sequence of photographs permits a visual journey up the axis (see Figs 9.4–9.13).

We start with the gatehouse, but this is already set behind an open ceremonial wooden *paifang* and complemented by a screen wall across the street, so its impact would have been greater than just the building shown, the combined elements forming a public square as a point of transition between general public space and the territory of the yamen. Here the magistrate could make declarations and administer punishments. The first gate is a three-bay building with central passage, and as the entrance is approached, one sees through to the first courtyard beyond. To left are inscribed stones declaring the virtue of justice, to right a ceremonial drum, memory of the real drum which used to gather the townsfolk in emergencies. The gate provides the public face for the whole institution and has a large roof with a swinging ridge, the gables decorated with a series of ornamental animals. The inscription declares the importance of the administration, likening it both to a pillar supporting the sky and to having feet firmly on the ground.

As we pass through, we encounter the first court with stables and prison on the left, temples to local gods and hospitality buildings on the right. Important visitors can tie up their horses at the series of carved posts to left: nobody would ride on through the second gate. The central path is paved with special marble raising it above the surrounding court. It is slightly convex to cast the water to the sides and to prioritise the central line of pavers as the magistrate's ritual route. Continuing on axis, we approach the second gate, and we see that the paved route continues unabated beyond it. The second gatehouse is much like the first, again its roof decorated with ornamental animals.

There are side gates as well as the central one, and that to left is called the gate of death because this is where condemned criminals left the court for the

9.5 View northward along the main axis taken just inside the first gate (photo by author)

9.6 View outside the second gate (photo by author)

9.7 View inside the second gate, facing the paifang with the hall beyond (photo by author)

9.8 View of the main hall where judgements are given (photo by author)

prison, whose entrance is signalled by the flank wall just visible at the left edge. The second gate marks the entrance to the central and most important courtyard where trials were held and other political business conducted. It was at this gate that the magistrate, on first arrival, was obliged to swear a solemn oath that he would perform his duties honestly and correctly, an oath made in the presence of all his assistants and the important people of the town, but addressed to the God of the Inner gate. It is described by Huang as a key ritual of taking office.

Passing through the second gate we see that the axis progresses to the steps of the first hall, the first five bay wide building in the series, but before reaching that point it must pass through a stone *paifang*, a kind of purely ceremonial gate common in China for tombs and memorials, using the dead material stone as opposed to the once live wood. It is inscribed with characters meaning 'justice brings clarity and light', and carries an admonishment to the magistrate to behave in an honourable manner. This element does not appear in Huang's description and may belong to a later era. The paifang initially obscures the view of the main hall, which is revealed as we proceed.

The axial route leads up six steps onto a stone platform beyond which is the seat of judgement. This is the largest hall with the highest roof, placed at the very centre of the whole complex. Here the magistrate presides as defendants and witnesses are brought before him, and here also many other public duties are carried out. We reach what seems to be the termination of the main axis with his desk. He sits at the centre on a raised dais, before a painting of sun and water which represents the yang energy of the emperor as the son of heaven and the wholeness of his empire stretched out between the four seas. The inscriptions translate 'Cheating people is cheating God. Don't cheat yourself. Betraying people is betraying your country. How can you do this?'

9.9 View of the magistrate's seat completes the first part of the axis (photo by author)

This sequence of pictures along the centre line gives some idea of the scale of the spatial progression, but only covers so far the front half of the complex, and only the middle one of three progressions of courts. Referring to the plans, other elements can be identified. Flanking the central court to right and left are the administrative offices for the six departments of government bureaucracy, the martial ones on the left (west) and the liberal ones to right (east). Moving from gate to hall, those on the left are Punishment, Military Affairs, and Works, while on the right are the Civil Office (appointments), Revenue, and Rites (including the examination system). The presence of these offices surrounding the court indicates how inseparable administration was from law-keeping, the magistrate being the governor, as used to be the case with the Lord Mayor of London. Apart from his role as judge of the local court he was also the organiser of the constables and militia, the collector of taxes, and the head of the local bureaucracy. He was responsible for public works and maintenance, disaster relief, and for the local part of the horse-based postal system. He was also the supplicant in public worship, making regular observances at various temples, particularly those of Confucius and the City God where he had to perform rites on the 1st and 15th of each month.[6] The Emperor, as Son of Heaven, was considered responsible for natural forces and undertook calendrical rituals to assure the fertility of the crops. As his agent, the magistrate assumed local responsibility, and Huang sincerely believed that his actions during his period of office had averted climatic disaster. This was not disconnected from the keeping of the law, as lawbreaking was regarded as a disruption not merely of human but of cosmic harmony.

The magistrate was both judge and detective, and a large part of Huang's book is given over to questions of detection, motives for crime, dealing with forensic evidence, and so on. There were no lawyers to argue cases adversarially, and witnesses were given a surprisingly uncomfortable time, sometimes even tortured. On the other hand there was a high moral ideal of probity for magistrates, as people who by their own merit reached a very high level in the national civil service examinations. These were not concerned with law and administration, but expected an intimate knowledge of the Confucian classics and an ability to compose appropriately elegant poems, just as Oxford and Cambridge used to be based on Greek, Latin and theology. Huang, having climbed this scholarly ladder, comes across as a moral and humane person full of advice about how to deal with corruption and moral degradation of all kinds, determined to maintain both social and cosmic order. Although his powers over his own locality were great, even permitting summary executions in certain cases, he was constantly answerable to his superiors, obliged to pass capital cases to the superior yamen and to report on many kinds of issues. He suffered a full and merciless inspection of his books and premises every three years. He was expected both to preserve the peace and to keep the local economy in balance. Huang's book is full of cautionary tales not only about detecting and preventing sharp practice among inferiors but also about dealing tactfully and cautiously with superiors.

Everyday court proceedings were held primarily in the courtyard and were something of an ordeal for the litigants and witnesses, as all were expected to kneel for long periods in the open air.[7] For sessions held at noon, after lunch, the magistrate's dais was brought to the front of the hall so that he could more directly overlook the courtyard. Occupying his position of power on the axis and sitting in his grand chair on the dais, he not only enjoyed the advantage of height but also the full enclosure of the hall and the elaborate protection of its main roof, as opposed to the persons brought before him. Cases were listed strictly in order, and waiting litigants lined up at the front gate, the magistrate having examined the paperwork in advance and marked up for himself the pertinent points. Within the hall he was accompanied by a scribe to document proceedings and two runners standing at attention in the left side, one of whose duties was to handle tallies, the other to prepare ink. A further runner in the courtyard organised the participants and set labelled tablets on the ground within the court to mark the places where litigants should kneel: plaintiffs at the east corner, defendants at the west corner, and witnesses centrally inside the inner gate on a raised area of pavement. When a case was set to proceed, the runner would report the presence of the parties to the magistrate, and on gaining his approval would call them to take their places. Lictors were instructed to stand by and to bring in and display instruments of torture if necessary, as a useful threat against reluctant defendants and lying witnesses.[8] The magistrate himself carried out the interrogation using a series of seven tactics of detection, called the hook, the raid, the attack, intimidation, browbeating, comparison, and compelling. His essential aim was to determine the truth before imposing judgement, and a substantial portion of Huang's text concerns how to achieve this while disarming the various kinds of subterfuges and stratagems regularly attempted by lawbreakers.

The main hall and its court were used for many other things besides trials. Tax prompters and payers were expected to assemble there, and Huang devised a system of reward and punishment, giving early payers special rosettes and letting them march out accompanied by music, while those in arrears were made to kneel alongside the central path in the court and were even flogged.[9] Taxes were counted in the hall, the silver chests being brought in and set behind the dais, with chest clerks and revenue clerks on hand to weigh contributions and report them in a book, which was finally signed in red by the magistrate himself.[10] The twice monthly roll call of rural police was carried out in the courtyard,[11] and also that of escaped slaves about to be sent elsewhere.[12] The prison where they were kept awaiting deportation was in the corner to the right of the hall, close by.[13] The magistrate could use his hall and court also as the site of munificence, handing out food to the poor on the first day of the month and winter clothing in the tenth month.[14] It was the place where the people met the government, and they were constantly expected to show the magistrate the greatest respect. Huang advises that interviews of militia heads – locally important people – should be carried out not in the main hall but more tactfully at the entrance gate 'so that the candidates need not kneel before the magistrate'.[15]

It was crucial to the power of the magistrate that he lived on the premises and in a secret zone seen only by a few privileged people. He must have appeared in

9.10 View of door to the inner realms, back on axis but behind the magistrate's seat (photo by author)

public quite frequently, but only on official business always accompanied by his many minions, and treated with great deference. For his court appearances he could slip into his place in the hall from behind, for the axis of the yamen extends beyond the first hall into increasingly private realms.

Immediately behind the magistrate's desk is another door and raised paving carries through to the elaborate gateway of the second court and hall, this time with a threshold to step over followed by double doors which can be closed to enforce passage around the side. It seems likely that the double doors were opened only for the passage of the magistrate and his peers, while lesser persons stepped to right or left. Within the court the axial path continues, still raised and defined with special paving, but diminished in width.

At the end is a second desk at which the magistrate can preside, again facing south. This court was used for cases of a more special character and meetings with important persons. Again the magistrate could slip in from behind, and again the axis continues. After a narrow cross street linking the lateral parts of the complex comes another small court but this time with a building across it as a doorway to the residence. The building fills the court with a roof returning along the sides, in contrast with previous roofs which were treated as independent.

9.11 View of the second court, for meetings and special cases (photo by author)

9.12 View of the small court leading through to the magistrate's residence, again on axis (photo by author)

9.13 View of the courtyard of the magistrate's house leading to the final hall (photo by author)

9.14 View of the way through to the garden, again facing north but to the west side (photo by author)

The inscription translates 'Rectitude, Discretion, Diligence'. This door leads to the third and final court and the third hall opposite which is the magistrate's house. Here only family and friends were admitted – apart from servants. The middle room was used for everyday life and private meetings, the end rooms as bedrooms. The magistrate's family had further accommodation in the side pavilion to east. Even here there are inscriptions encouraging probity, such as 'Even family members have to face the law', and 'Even old friends have to obey the rules'. Progress on axis is arrested here, with no rear exit from the third hall, but there is a garden behind reached by walking around the west side and passing through an octagonal doorway. The typical Chinese garden was treated in an informal way like a scaled-down landscape, its irregularity contrasted with the strict orthogonal layout of the rest of the complex. As it was enclosed by a continuous high wall with no openings, the magistrate and his family could only reach the outside world by finding their way back southward through the entire complex. This must have made it all seem very deep and well protected.

The entire complex was both surrounded by a masonry wall with protective capping and subdivided by such walls. The contrast between the protective character of the freestanding masonry wall and the open building, all roof and columns with no lateral enclosure, epitomises the special quality of Chinese architectural space. Their primary building tradition was carpentry, in which timber columns support a complex layered roof and any partitions are secondary. This leaves the building comparatively open, freestanding away from the enclosing wall, which belongs instead to the ground. Chinese architecture has therefore always been very much about the roof and the logic of its assembled structure, with elegant interlocking joints avoiding nails. Lacking diagonal bracing, they relied on the joints for stiffness, piling timber on timber rather than triangulating with trusses as in the West. Dependence on timber meant rectangular buildings, division into bays, a discipline of progressive assembly, and a strict sizing and numbering of parts. The treatment and shaping of the roof was paramount, and the connection between column and roof gave rise to bracketing as the main ornamental treatment. This priority of the roof also meant that each roof was treated as an entity and given separate form even when they were placed close to one another. The open nature of the columns meant also that a hall tended to be used in tandem with its outdoor room, the courtyard. In central and southern China this suited the hot and humid climate, while by contrast the hearth and chimney were absent.

Looking again at the general plan (Fig. 9.3), the whole complex has a structured character in which each element finds its place according to principles of concentricity, progression, opposition, and adjacency. Consider first centre and periphery. The court lies at the centre of the yamen as the yamen lies at the centre of the town and the town in its region, a nesting series. This parallels many cases in pre-modern Europe and clearly has a defensive as well as a hierarchical role. Added to this is a linear principle: the south-north axis as centre, which is stressed by the progression of buildings, by the bilateral symmetry, and by differentiation of height and material in the ground plane. The centre line or axis could hardly be more strongly stated or be more clearly differentiated from the treatment of the east-west connections. We have seen how effectively it allows development of a sense of progression, acting as a route along which increasing layers signal increasing importance as well as entry into more private and exclusive realms, and where going forward is much more important than returning. Here again there are comparable European precedents, but the orientation is more crucial. It might seem at first only common sense to face south to enjoy the sun, but there is much more. The Emperor, as Son of Heaven, had a special connection with the sun and in consequence was expected to face south, an ancient custom, for which there are at least two references in the Analects of Confucius from 500 BC.[16] Some idea of the continuing significance of this connection in Huang's time is his advice that a newly arriving magistrate must never make his first entry to the town by the south gate, lest this cause too great a concentration of yang energy, bringing about a major fire in the city during his period of office.[17] Orientation was important enough in China for nearly all building complexes to be orientated south and for the siting of settlements, graves and temples always to be considered in relation to the cardinal points, still reflected in the various practices of feng-shui.[18] They derive from ancient Daoist cosmology and its founding diagrams, Ho tu and Lo shu, which interconnect phenomena through the universal polarity of yin yang and the cycle of the five agents (wood, fire, earth, metal, water), sometimes called elements. Without straying too far into this very complex subject, it suffices to say that the cardinal points are tied into the space of the diagram as an essential fourness with five as centre, and that therefore connections are implied between them and many other phenomena, such as seasons, numbers, animals, tastes and sounds.[19] Colours also correspond with them, so north is black, south is red, east is blue and west is white. In Huang's book these are precisely the colours of the caps of the militia who guard the respective gates to the city.[20]

9.15 Author's diagram of the Yamen plan to indicate the three parallel bands, north to top. The asterisk marks the centre and the seat of judgement, the square bottom left is the prison, and the double rectangle bottom right the temples. B indicates symmetry, whilst A/C indicates less symmetry'

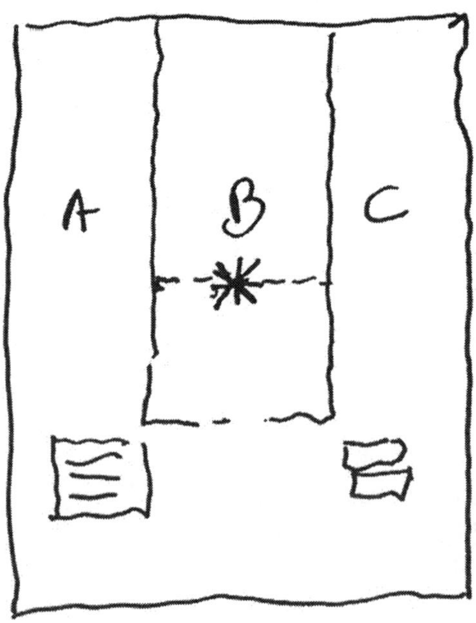

B symmetry
A/C less symmetry

If the centre line produces the sense of progression and layering south to north, it also creates a tripartite field laterally. This has echoes of the magic square as ideal city plan, and it is easy to read the yamen's court as the central square of nine. The tripartite division also creates a clear hierarchy between centre and side, so central band B has the major functions while side bands A and C are given to subordinate ones, the courts at the north end for the houses of the magistrate's deputies, for example. But there is also a hierarchical difference between east and west. East, which is the right hand when proceeding up the axis, is more propitious and important, so the treasury was on the east side of the main hall balancing the records room on the west, while next to the entrance the temples to the Yamen God and Earth God to east stood opposite the prison to west. The symmetrical relationship of A and C tends to throw things into pairs, but the propitious east and unpropitious west, perhaps related to the rising and setting of the sun – a widespread if not cross-cultural symbolism – differentiate them again. A telling cultural detail, again going back to the Analects of Confucius, is that a man in mourning for his father must not use the eastern steps to his hall for three years out of respect, but must instead take those on the west normally reserved for guests. Precedence for east over west is also reflected in many rituals described by Huang.

The above discussion has been concerned largely with space in plan, but relative height is clearly important as platforms step up and down throughout the yamen. It seems to be a cross-cultural principle that the magistrate sits on the highest seat and at the end of the axis like European judges and monarchs: I have yet to find a contradiction to this rule. Because the yamen complex is a chain of courtyards the gates and thresholds punctuating them are extremely well-differentiated, and there is both a great variety and highly specific designation of threshold types. The architecture gains in colour and decoration where it gets more important, and sinks to its most banal and basic form with the prison, though even there gates are important, including that for those facing execution. There is a prison god in a south-facing temple in the prison's first court, and he should be treated with respect. All this might be considered a very highly developed and effective *architecture parlante* at a time when European architects only dreamed and theorised about such a thing. Far from the Chinese having little architecture worthy of note, as James Fergusson so naively claimed in the 1880s,[21] they had an immensely sophisticated architecture, rich in meaning. There was a standardised set of building types defined by two interlocking disciplines: that of the carpenters who had elaborately prescribed rules, even defined in written manuals, about bay sizes, number of bays, elaboration of roof and jointing, propitious dimensions etc. On the other hand there was the department of rites which prescribed colours and ornaments, and even how many nails you were allowed to show in the face of your door. With rules like that, and the possibility of prosecution and disgrace, you would certainly have counted them. Such order and discipline in architecture bring coherence and shared meaning, but they also reflect the oppression of a dominant cosmology to which citizens were obliged to subscribe, accepting their places in the hierarchy. Shared social order and its spatial manifestations can be both a comfort and a tyranny.

NOTES

* With special thanks to Jianyu Chen for information, translations and arranging our Neixiang visit.

1 Huang Liuhong, *Complete Book Concerning Happiness and Benevolence* published in 1694. English edition Tucson 1984, 655 pages, translated by Djang Chu and subtitled *A Manual for Local Magistrates in Seventeenth-Century China*. It is the social source for most of this chapter.

2 Ibid. Each magistrate was responsible for around 150,000 people: translator's introduction, p. 17.

3 Maps of this kind, following official conventions of representation, are preserved in Chinese local records or gazetteers.

4 Peter Carl objected at the conference that 'axis' is a western and relatively modern word, and I agree that this case needs distinguishing both from Cartesian axes and Beaux Arts ones. The Chinese centre line, consistently orientated north-south, is both an axis of symmetry and a register of progression, while the ancient Chinese character for centre is an oblong horizontal body bisected by a longer vertical stroke. The word axis remains nonetheless a convenient and familiar term of reference.

5 Several mentions of spaces and spatial transitions in the Analects of Confucius accord with later buildings. In Book III section 22 a screen wall is mentioned as a mark of status; in Book VI, section 1 the Emperor is equated with facing south; Book IX, section 3 mentions the hierarchical importance of the dais; Book X, section 4 includes a long description about how to behave correctly on entering the palace; and in Book XIX, section 23, the height of the boundary wall is revealed as an index of status. See Arthur Waley, *The Analects of Confucius* (London, 1964).

6 He was obliged to burn incense and say prayers on the first and fifteenth of each month in the temple of Confucius and that of the City God, as well as at larger seasonal observances: Huang, *Complete Book Concerning Happiness and Benevolence*, p. 29.

7 That this was uncomfortable and humiliating is confirmed by further advice to spare both the elderly and young women, and to keep them in a corridor or a secluded place until required to give evidence, ibid., p. 272.

8 Ibid., p. 269. He tells of a case where the threat of torture proved effective in producing a confession, but elsewhere admits (p. 278) the reduced value of false confessions.

9 Ibid., pp. 194–8.

10 Ibid., p. 99.

11 Ibid., p. 414.

12 Ibid., p. 430. The slaves were a hangover from the military conquest by the Manchus who had gained power half a century earlier, as explained in the translator's preface, pp. 12–15.

13 Right in this case presumably in relation to the sitting magistrate facing south, as prisons were generally on the west side.

14 Huang, *Complete Book Concerning Happiness and Benevolence*, p. 553.

15 Ibid., p. 469.

16 Analects Book VI, section 1 translates 'I should not mind setting him with his face to the south' which refers to making someone ruler. See Arthur Waley, *The Analects of Confucius* (London, 1964), p. 115.

17 Huang, *Complete Book Concerning Happiness and Benevolence*, p. 85.

18 Much nonsense and many half truths have been published on this subject: for a reliable and concise summary see Alfred Schinz, *The Magic Square: Cities in Ancient China* (Stuttgart, 1999), pp. 416–19.

19 Much on this in Joseph Needham, 'The *Tao Chia* (Taoists) and Taoism', *Science and Civilisation in China*, vol. 2 (Cambridge, 1956), pp. 33–164. See also Paul U. Unschuld, *Huang Di Nei Jing Su Wen: Nature, Knowledge, Imagery in an Ancient Chinese Medical Text* (Berkeley CA, 2003); especially the appendix 'The Doctrine of the Five Periods and Six Qi in the *Huang Di nei jing su wen*', pp. 393–488.

20 Huang, *Complete Book Concerning Happiness and Benevolence*, p. 476.

21 James Fergusson, *History of Indian and Eastern Architecture, Forming the Third Volume of the New Edition 'History of Architecture'* (London, 1899); see preface to the Chinese part, pp. 685–90.

PART 3
Civic and Societal Order

10

Violent Stone: The City of Dialectical Justice – Three Tales from Court

Jonathan Charley

The history of nineteenth century urban Europe is scarred and deformed by its relationship with imperialism, slavery and colonial exploitation. This chapter tells three interconnected stories about the pivotal role that Glasgow, Liverpool, Brussels and their respective law courts played in this history, a dialectical history in which reason was shadowed by ignorance, civilisation by barbarism and monumental institutions by diseased hovels.

GLASGOW – SUGAR, TOBACCO, AND THE OLD COURT

> *Legally, government by bureaucracy is government by decree, and this means that power, which in constitutional government only enforces the law, becomes the direct source of all legislation. Decrees moreover remain anonymous (while laws can always be traced to specific men or assemblies), and therefore seem to flow from some over-all ruling power that needs no justification.*[1]

Like an unstoppable storm of creative destruction the bourgeois revolution tore through the familiar terrain of town and country, spitting out the space-time certainties of old lives and reassembling them in unrecognisable forms. Vast new landscapes of production emerged out of ancient commons and felled forests, whilst terrifying institutions crept out of the smog to categorise and discipline the unruly and unwilling. And at the epi-centre of this urban revolution were buildings devoted to the rule of law and the circulation of money and commodities. In an unprecedented pageant of judicial and pecuniary imagination, all manner of banks, trading houses, notary and lawyer's offices filled the streets of rapidly expanding cities, and in the midst of all this sat the emblematic monarchs of modern political economy, the Stock Exchange and Law Court.

Law and Money became inseparable twins and with their institutional merging all the economic endeavours that financed the construction of the nineteenth

10.1 View of the County Court, Glasgow (photo by author)

century city, whether it was reaping tobacco, cutting sugar cane, manufacturing cloth, building ships or smelting pig iron, in a flash of a quill pen and a wax seal were objectified as legal documents and commodities. Contracts were signed, property rights were assured, tobacco smoked, sugar eaten, a wage paid, and slowly but surely the real social origins of commodities became clouded in the mysteries of the fetish world.

The monumental architecture of the nineteenth century played a crucial role in this process of camouflage. Every city competing to become a fully-fledged capitalist metropolis was required to elevate the houses of legal contract and money to a status hitherto reserved for Cardinals and Royalty. 'City Fathers' accomplished this task with varying degrees of success measured by how well such institutions dominated the city. For money they built temples to Mammon. And for the law, no expense was spared. The bigger the better, for it was the job of the new courts fashioned in glorious antiquity to confer the grandeur, authority, and legitimacy that the bourgeoisie so desperately craved. It was also the court's task to silence incendiary talk about self-regulating communes and workers' rights, and to approve the legislation necessary to ensure the smooth progress of capital accumulation.

One of the first examples in Glasgow of this new architecture of legal might was William Stark's sombre judiciary court and gaol built at the Saltmarket in 1809. Its foundation was opportune because it coincided with a marked increase in threats to civic order. Indeed a year after its inauguration the Glasgow Commission of Police issued an alarm about roaming gangs of 'Thieves, Rogues, and Vagabonds' who were posing a threat to both persons and property.[2] Exacerbated by repeated outbreaks of labour militancy, typhus and cholera, Stark's court and gaol soon proved inadequate to the task of meeting the disciplinary and punitive demands of a rapidly expanding capitalist economy and metropolis. The solution was to commission the construction of the monumental County Buildings and Court Houses. Built nearby in the Merchant city in the 1840s at the height of the Irish famine and the attack on Chartism, this old centre of government, itself superseded by the City Chambers forty years later, bears few signs of its original function and now houses boutique flats, up market shops, restaurants, and the Scottish youth theatre. It is still surrounded by old merchant warehouses, but these too have changed their use and are no longer scented with the odour of tobacco and boiling molasses, but by perfumed real estate. Like many of the city's nineteenth century institutions, it is a neo-classical building dressed with giant Corinthian and Ionic columns. Such facsimiles of the architecture of the ancient world reflected the deeply held bourgeois conceit that they were somehow the legitimate heirs to a democratic tradition that could be traced back to classical antiquity.

Reaping the rewards of plantation and proletarian labour, the early nineteenth century bourgeoisie liked nothing more than to imagine themselves dressed in togas, defending private property and upholding laws of contract that declared the capitalist and the labourer as 'free' and equal traders in commodities.[3] Accordingly, carved into the blond sandstone wall on its southern elevation that sits beneath a raised portico of fluted columns, is a mixed up allegory of classical Greece and the death of Jesus that represents bourgeois law and government as high-minded, honourable and in tune with *universal* laws of nature and history.[4] To reinforce this vision of the timeless qualities of bourgeois justice, the sculpture features an impressive cast of characters judging and dispensing wisdom that includes disciples, sages, jailors, executioners, manacled prisoners, a prostrate man and a mourning woman.

There is however a far more insidious connection between Glasgow's merchant class and the ancient world to which they aspired. Much of the wealth of the Athenian Republic came from agricultural slavery. Plato even barred artisans from the polis considering such labour to be the antithesis of what it meant to be human.[5] Similarly cognitively displaced in an unknown hinterland, the source of much of the finance needed to construct the grand streets and mansions of the merchant city came from the slave economy of the New World. In 1807, a group of prominent merchants gathered in a local meetinghouse to discuss the foundation of the West Indian Association to defend their commercial interests. Like their Liverpool counterparts they were opposed to the abolition of slavery, expressing both concern over the 'comfort, health, and happiness of the negro population' if abolition was passed, and anxiety over 'the effects of emancipation on a race prone to indolence and idleness'.[6]

The pivotal role slavery and the plantation economy played in the development of capitalism in Scotland have yet to be fully acknowledged. But the evidence of Glasgow's relationship is strewn across the city. One part of the city atlas is composed of prominent family names. There is Buchanan of Buchanan Street, owner of vast plantations in Virginia, who later became Lord Provost, along with Ingram, Glassford, Dennistoun, Oswald, Mitchell, Speirs and Wilson, all of them either tobacco, sugar or cotton merchants who saw no moral contradiction between their belief in Calvinism and laissez faire economics and their activities in the plantation economies of the southern United States and Caribbean. Dissecting the urban grid are other names that without conscience commemorate the locations of their estates. It is a roll call of colonial interests – Jamaica, Kingston, Virginia, Plantation Quay, and the ghostly apparition of vanished Antigua. Together they scatter the pink coloured streets with soap, fine cigars, chocolate, sweetened tea and coffee; a culinary and confectionary mix of 'sugar and spice and all things nice'. That is what Empire was made of.

LIVERPOOL – FEVER SHEDS, FAMINE AND ST GEORGE'S HALL

> *By taking the form of law, right steps into a determinate mode of being. It is then something on its own account, and in contrast with particular willing and opining of the right, it is self-subsistent and has to vindicate itself as something universal. This is achieved by recognising it and making it actual in a particular case without the subjective feeling of private interest; and this is the business of a public authority – the court of justice.*[7]

It is 1838, a mere eight years after the abolition of slavery. It is a momentous period in British political history. Working class militants, bitterly disappointed by the failure of the Reform Act of 1832 to introduce universal suffrage had turned to revolutionary syndicalism. Owenite building workers in Birmingham had drafted a plan to reorganise society along cooperative communist lines, and the People's Charter was about to be launched.[8] And it is in the midst of this proto-revolutionary shift in English political sensibilities, in spitting distance of smokestack and dockyard chains that the Liverpool bourgeoisie embark on their own quest to build their belief in the eternal nature of capitalist morality and justice. Glaswegians claim their city as the second city of Empire. Bengalis claim Kolkata. Scousers insist it is Liverpool. All of them have good reason. I stepped out of Lime Street station in the low autumnal sun and was dazzled by what was once the biggest and strangest civic building in Britain, a combination of concert hall and court of law.[9]

It is true that when I visit medieval cathedrals, my mind jams with a cacophony of sheep, indentured serfs, fearful labourers, maniac priests, and tyrannical landowners. But I also see extraordinary spatial engineering, delicate craftsmanship, and the building labour of love and devotion. Similarly here in front of this homage to Athens the landscape glitters with the trowels of heroic stonemasons whilst nostrils contract with the odour of choleric fever sheds.[10] And as the city fathers sought immortality in the foundation of St George's, they commissioned the construction of prison cell and workhouse dormitory that were planned with the same attention to detail as the hold of a slave ship. Here

10.2 View of St George's Hall, Liverpool (photo by author)

capitalist reason is stripped bare. Planning the distribution of bodies on bunks as preparation for labour in sweatshop or plantation becomes a question of maximising the number of human commodities that can be crammed into every cubic metre.

Simply obeying instructions in the same way that two hundred years later they would plan housing estates and office blocks, architects and engineers drew meticulous plans and sections in which individuals become abstract blobs between lines. Meanwhile in a subterranean world of gloomy and banal offices hidden up back streets and alleyways, armies of accountants, solicitors and bank clerks compile inventories of every conceivable kind. Bureaucratic administration is elevated in importance and becomes the essential modus operandi of the 'great game of expansion', both domestically and abroad. In a blink of the eye capital accumulation and conquest become logistical operations that can be precisely detailed in leather bound ledgers and legal documents. Neutralised in words and numbers, the administrators' archives conceal a rule which 'out of sight and out of mind', and therefore unrestricted by social and ethical values, 'exploded with the suddenness of a short circuit in the phantom world of colonial adventure'.[11]

Confident that they were conducting God's work and reassured by the classical economist's vision of a bourgeois utopia founded on the notion of 'free' wage labour, the Liverpool merchant class and bourgeoisie embraced Hegel's idea that law should be made universal and inviolate in the foundation of a 'court of justice'. Their conceit was breathtakingly audacious. With the exception of Roscoe, all of Liverpool's MPs at the turn of the nineteenth century were either slave traders in their own right or defenders of the trade in Parliament.[12] Like Glasgow, Manchester and Bristol, Liverpool's street names and architecture heap praise upon the triangular trade and plantation system, inadvertently reinforcing the argument that such economic activities provided up to fifty per cent of the capital that propelled the industrial revolution and funded the construction of the nineteenth century city.[13] Only eight years before the foundations for St George's Hall were laid, civic leaders, merchants and politicians drank a toast on the King's birthday. Attired in the finest Egyptian cotton and Syrian mohair, glasses brimming with Portuguese wine and Jamaican rum, they clouded the drawing room with flumes of Cuban tobacco. Staring through the window at the profiles of African children neatly embossed in the entrance to a bank, they announced: 'Prosperity to the African Trade, and may it always be conducted with humanity.'[14]

Forty years later without malice or irony they carved their governing ideals into the east elevation. In a burst of utopian delusion they declared the foundation of a new 'World supported by knowledge and right', and of a society in which 'Justice is relieved of her sword by virtue and the scales of concord.' Their ideal of a natural and God-given justice knew of no limits, for it was born out of 'righteousness and the crown of immortality'. Drunk on ideology they proselytised from pulpits a concept of justice that was to be pure and untainted by the trappings of 'wealth and fame'. But words of 'conscience and wisdom' were not enough. The Greek goddess of blind justice, Dikē, and a supporting cast of angels are summoned to command this cosmic ambition to plant the kingdom of divine law on earth. Swaying in the folds of Grecian gowns, they sport wreaths, wings, weapons, globes and scales. In a brilliant combination of sculpture and text, the city fathers feminised and eternalised their concept of law and justice as if such demonstrations of state power were in time with history and at one with the universe.

Whilst the friezes of St George's were unveiled to the public, Marx was dying in London. His first writings on alienation and estrangement marked the inception of St George's, and the development of his critique of political economy coincided with its opening. As discipline and punishment were meted out to the sound of choirs and violins, Marx unleashed his concept of the 'fetishism of commodities' in which he describes a spectacularly upside down world where the social relations between human beings assume the 'fantastic form' of a relation between objects seemingly imbued with mystical powers.[15]

Fantastic indeed was the form of St George's and its sister institutions, and between law court where property was defended, and the stock exchange where it was traded, there emerged 'an enchanted, perverted topsy-turvy world, in which Monsieur Le Capital and Madame La Terre did their ghost walking as social characters and at the same time as mere things'.[16] As they performed their spectral dance they whispered the words 'capital, land and labour', a semantic trilogy in which 'the secrets of the social production process', profit, rent and wages were hidden.[17] It was an ingenious act of camouflage reinforced by the sacred words that decorated St George's. The magician completes his trick, 'Legal fetishism complements commodity fetishism.'[18] The result was a new and mysterious vocabulary of economic and juridical categories constructed from 'distorted, mystified mental images', in which the reality of capitalist exploitation was obscured in fog.[19]

And it was the same fog that provided much of the cover for dubious acts of exchange in the sea ports of Britain, nowhere more so than in the Albert Docks. During the 1890s, long after the 'formal' abolition of slavery, Liverpool had a monopoly on all shipping to the Congo, and it was a clerk for one of the shipping companies, despatched to Antwerp, that came across a horrible secret. The ships being filled with commodities, were not listing in the water with the weight of textiles and copper pans, but with guns and armaments. I too was on my way from Liverpool to a Belgian city that reminds me of a 'whited sepulchre'.[20] Joseph Conrad's Marlowe in *Heart of Darkness* does not mention the city's name, but we know where it is, because he looks at a giant map on the wall in the Company's offices and realises, 'I am going into the Yellow dead in the centre.' How the foreign secretaries must have argued over the colour to mark their possessions, a grotesque parlour game in which the scramble for Africa became a board game with dice and gun. Pink for the British, purple for the Germans, Orange for the Portuguese, Green for the Italians, Blue for the French, and Yellow for the Belgians.

BRUSSELS – RUBBER, OIL AND THE *PALAIS DE JUSTICE*

> *The bourgeoisie has stripped of its halo every occupation hitherto honoured and looked up to with reverent awe. It has converted the physician, the lawyer, the priest, the poet, the man of science into its paid wage-labourers . . . . It has been the first to show what man's activity can bring about. It has accomplished wonders far surpassing Egyptian pyramids, Roman aqueducts, and Gothic cathedrals; it has conducted expeditions that put in the shade all former Exoduses of nations and crusades.*[21]

Still early on a damp morning the Grand Place was almost empty of the steady stream of tourists who arrive throughout the day to admire the gothic *Hôtel de Ville* and the opulent baroque homes of the merchants and guilds that laid the foundations for Belgium's claim to be the first industrialised economy in continental Europe.[22] Tucked away in a corner there is a bar where Marx, following his expulsion from Paris, met Friedrich Engels. Peering at the framed views of the guild houses that flank the square, Karl Marx puts pen to paper, and begins to draft one of history's most influential documents, the Communist Manifesto. As his infectious and lyrically political narrative grows, the legacy of his youthful commitment to legal struggle fades. By now he is convinced that the battle will not be won by the rhetoric of courtroom gowns, but by the class struggle. He flippantly depicts the law as an epiphenomenon of capitalist society's superstructure, and the lawyer, which was once his intended profession, as little more than a paid wage labourer.[23]

10.3 View of *Palais de Justice*, Brussels (photo by author)

One hundred and fifty years later and I am standing in front of a small plaque on the wall of the *Maison de Cygne* that commemorates his stay, pondering the irony of predicting world revolution whilst surrounded by the extravagant architectural display of capitalist economic and political invention.

A short walk from the Grand Place will take you past the *Bourse* and Opera House, a convenient arrangement so that having first secured the deal and traded on it, the bourgeoisie could relax to the sound of Richard Wagner and Giuseppe Verdi. But my route proceeds down the hill to the old working class district of Marolles with its terraces of red brick housing named after professions like cooper, carpenter and sweep. Once out of the narrow streets linked by arched tunnels you have to creep furtively lest you are spotted. Even then, there is little chance of remaining concealed.

I stole a glance up an alley in the shadow of a modern council housing scheme with an advert for David Lynch's film *Eraserhead* (1977) glued to the lamppost. But the *Palais* had seen me.[24] It glowers with the same sepulchral silence with which the *Sacre Coeur* in Paris sends shivers through the descendants of the communards.[25] It is a grey and unforgiving monument to cruelty and murder. Inaugurated by Leopold the II in 1883 at the very moment when his expeditionary forces delivered gun and sword justice to the indigenous peoples of the Congo, it was the biggest building constructed in the nineteenth century. It was even larger than St Peter's Basilica in Rome. As an unambiguous ideological expression of state power, it is no surprise that Hitler admired the *Palais* and he instructed Albert Speer to draw it in detail as a candidate for the new Germania plan for Berlin.[26]

As he dreamt of Brussels acquiring an Imperial crown, Leopold could rely on Belgian taxpayers to foot the bill for civic buildings like the *Palais*. But to furnish his private universe, the lavishness of which rivalled that of absolutist monarchs and embarrassed visiting dignitaries, he required a source of revenue that was unrestrained by the demands for political reform sweeping Europe.[27] The Belgian working class, that lived and laboured in some of the most miserable conditions on the continent, were becoming increasingly militant and organised a wave of strikes and riots in support of universal suffrage in 1886 and 1893. Both uprisings were met with military force, mass arrest, and mounted gendarmes wielding sabres. It was the same Belgian sabre that would glint and sparkle in the African sun as Leopold II's mercenaries' dispensed punishment, severing the hands of recalcitrant Africans who ignored demands to increase the production of rubber and who refused to accept European authority over their lands. From the very beginning, extraordinary levels of violence marked the European invasion of the Congo delta led by Leopold's adventurer agent Morton Stanley who boasted to having in no time at all 'attacked and destroyed twenty eight large towns and four score villages'.[28] In contrast to Stanley's moral ambivalence, other stories filtered back of unspeakable horror.[29] It was Casement, soon to be executed by the British who met Joseph Conrad and warned him of things 'I have tried to forget, (of) things I never did know.' One of these was the story of Van Kerckhoven, the collector of African heads, the inspiration for Conrad's Kurtz (and Frances Ford Coppola's version of Kurtz, as played by Marlon Brando), who was said to have surrounded his compound with a palisade of human skulls, and whose expeditions were described by a contemporary as a hurricane that passed through the countryside leaving nothing but devastation behind it.[30] Meanwhile back in Belgium unperturbed by any of these tales, Leopold prepared for the grand opening of the *Palais de Justice*. In the background his ministers and propaganda department hastily set about building his reputation as a philanthropist king, friend of the African and anti-slavery crusader.

During the construction of Imperial Brussels, the population of the Congo delta declined by a half, with an estimated ten million people dying through the combined effects of murder, starvation, exhaustion and disease.[31] The violence, speed, and scale of the Congo conquest along with all the other crimes that litter the history of the colonisation of Africa, India and the Americas are almost impossible to grasp. But by inventing concepts of race and bureaucracy the European managed to create a 'refined atmosphere' through which the tragedy of this real history became geographically and historically displaced.[32] Whether it is possible through a plaque on a wall or a piece of public art to evoke the memory of imperial crimes and the suspension of the rule of law is an open question. But unlike the attempt to objectify the memory of the holocaust in camp museums and commemorative landscapes, there is no trace in Brussels of the African genocide, and very little – it should be added – in British cities that speak of the crimes of Empire.

Whether Leopold had ever seen St George's Hall, I am not sure. But Lord Leverhulme, MP for the Wirral, philanthropist and founder of the model worker's village at Port Sunlight, certainly visited the Congo where he followed in the footsteps of the Belgian monarch and set up his own private kingdom based in Leverville that was reliant on forced labour to provide palm oil for his soap business.[33] There was however to be no model philanthropic village for the Africans.

The public career of the soon to be Lord Lever of Hulme survived his Congo expedition as did the *Palais de Justice*. Nowadays the *Palais* performs a number of civic duties. But there is no hiding its origins in the megalomaniac vanity of one man who was oblivious to the idea that justice might have anything to do with Wallonian miners, let alone native Africans.

The prosperous merchants and wealthy bankers of the Belgian bourgeoisie had urged Leopold to build the *Palais*' one million cubic metres of corridors and staircases, and were delighted with the citadel of secrets in which to defend their property and provide their profits with a legal foundation. The *Palais* like St George's seemed to prove Evgeny Pashukanis' contention that bourgeois-capitalist property need no longer be contested weapon in hand for it had been 'transformed into an absolute, fixed right … and which, ever since bourgeois civilisation extended its rule to encompass the whole globe, had been protected the world over by laws, police and law courts'.[34] But others were less than impressed with Leopold's gift to justice, particularly the local proletarians shuffling in the streets below and the former inhabitants of the area who had been forcibly evicted to make way for the *Palais*. Incandescent with rage they ran to the Swan bar where under the watchful eye of the ghost of Marx they joined the recently formed Belgian Worker's Party.

By the general strike of 1902 Brussels was shaking with the tremors of insurrection. Socialists fought running battles with police as they paraded the streets, 'smashing the windows of churches and cafes, firing revolvers and singing revolutionary songs'.[35] They retreated to the *Maison du Peuple*, the art nouveau masterpiece designed by Victor Horta where they tore up tramlines and constructed barricades. But other residents resorted to more macabre acts of revenge and if the legend is to be believed there was a witch who could be seen at dusk wandering the back streets busily sticking needles into an effigy of the *Palais*' architect Joseph Poelaert with a relentless ferocity that greatly hastened his descent into terminal insanity.

THE WITHERING OF THE COURT OF LAW

> *The state is not 'abolished'. It dies out. This gives the measure of the value of the phrase 'a free state', both as to its justifiable use at times of agitators, and as to its ultimate scientific insufficiency; and also of the demands of so-called anarchists for the abolition of the state out of hand.*[36]

Engels wrote that the 'The central link in civilised society is the state', of which one of the central institutions is the Law Court. Indeed, Glasgow's Old Court like St George's and the *Palais* ostensibly captures the idea of a civilised society governed

10.4 Marx in Brussels (photo by author)

by law. But he added, that the State, 'in all typical periods is without exception the state of the ruling class and in all cases continues to be essentially a machine for holding down the oppressed, exploited class'.[37] For those that dream of the parliamentary reform of capitalism, the idea of the State and the legal system as little more than a weapon designed to maintain the hegemony of the ruling class is too crude and unsophisticated. They will point to evidence that shows that although courts can be places where draconian judgements are delivered or indeed where the rule of law is abandoned altogether, they have also been the forum where progressive legislation has been passed. By necessity they cling to the belief that however terrifying a court may be when controlled by political criminals, however intimidating its scale and size, and however grim its origins as the legal face of a repressive and exploitative system, changing the regime that resides within can alter its metaphorical associations. However in the latter half of the nineteenth century, before universal suffrage, when the courtrooms of Glasgow, Liverpool and Brussels echoed with black skins, tubercular workers and wigged rhetoric, Engel's depiction of the State and its legal machinery as an adjunct of capital made absolute sense.

The meanings we attach to buildings are unstable and transitory. Transformations in use, ingenious forms of camouflage, and the distortion of memory, have softened and fundamentally altered the significance of old buildings like the courts of the nineteenth century city. Glasgow's County Court becomes a chic place to live. St George's doubles up as a dance hall and cultural centre, and the *Palais de Justice* becomes a picture postcard … . Meanwhile, light years away from faith in courtly dialogue or civilian changes in use, the anarchists of the Spanish Civil War dreamt of a society in which all forms of authority, discrimination, and punishment would be abolished.[38] In this Stateless world there would be no need for such things as a court of law, a prison or the headquarters of the secret police. Such institutions would simply be allowed to disintegrate until they were indistinguishable from a ruined garden.

NOTES

1 Hannah Arendt, *The Origins of Totalitarianism, Ideology and Terror* (London, 1976), p. 243.

2 See Tom Devine, *The Scottish Nation, 1700–2000* (London, 2000), p. 224.

3 'The slave is exactly subservient to his master. This is why this exploitative relationship requires no specifically legal formulation. The wage worker on the contrary, enters the market as a free vendor of his labour power, which is why the relation of capitalist exploitation is mediated through the form of contract.' Evgeny, Pashukanis, *Law and Marxism: A General Theory* (London, 1989), pp. 110–13.

4 See Arendt, *The Origins of Totalitarianism*, pp. 461–5.

5 See Perry Anderson, *Passages from Antiquity to Feudalism* (London, 1974), pp. 18–28.

6 For the statements of Glasgow Merchants see, MacLehose, J, *Memoirs and portraits of 100 Glasgow men* (Glasgow, 1886), p. 130 and other entries. For a brief snapshot of the West Indian Association and black history in Glasgow see David Dabydeen, John Gilmore and Cecily Jones (eds), *The Oxford Companion to Black British History* (Oxford, 2008), pp. 189–91.

7 Georg W.F. Hegel, *Philosophy of Right* (Oxford, 1967), p. 140.

8 For general commentary on the European and British dimensions of political militancy, see Eric Hobsbawm, *Age of Revolution* (London, 1997). For a history of labour in the nineteenth century construction industry, see Raymond Postgate, *The Builder's History* (London: The National Federation of Building Trade Operatives, 1923).

9 Architectural historians like Niklaus Pevsner claim St George's as one of the finest and important examples of neo-classicism in the world. See for instance Quentin Hughes, *Liverpool-City of Architecture* (Liverpool, 1999), p. 59.

10 For first hand details of living conditions in Liverpool in the mid-nineteenth century see the Liverpool Journal, November 24th, 1849, <www.old-merseytimes.co.uk>.

11 Arendt, *The Origins of Totalitarianism*, p. 190.

12 See for instance Gail Cameron and Stan Crooke, *Liverpool – Capital of the Slave Trade* (Liverpool, 1992), p. 44.

13 See Robin Blackburn, *The Making of New World Slavery: From the Baroque to the Modern, 1492–1800* (London, 1998), pp. 517–18.

14 See Cameron and Cooke, *Liverpool*, p. 72. See also Marika Sherwood and Kim Sherwood, *Britain, the Slave Trade and Slavery from 1562 to the 1880s* (Liverpool, 2007), pp. 73–7.

15 See Karl Marx, *Capital, Volume I* (London, 1990), pp. 163–7.

16 Karl Marx, *Capital, Volume III* (London, 1984), p. 830.

17 Ibid., p. 814.

18 Evgeny Pashukanis, *Law and Marxism; A General Theory* (London, 1989), p. 117.

19 Ibid., p. 73.

20 'I was crossing the Channel to show myself to my employers, and sign the contract. In a very few hours I arrived in a city that always makes me think of a whited sepulchre. Prejudice no doubt. I had no difficulty in finding the company's offices. It was the biggest thing in town, and everybody I met was full of it. They were going to run an overseas empire, and make no end of coin by trade.'

Joseph Conrad, *Heart of Darkness* (Oxford, 2002), p. 110.

21 Karl Marx and Friedrich Engels, *The Communist Manifesto* (London, 2002), p. 222.

22 Eric Hobsbawm, *Age of Empire* (London, 1987), pp. 41–2.

23 Karl Marx and Friedrich Engels, *The Communist Manifesto* (London, 2002), p. 82. See also the infamous and often misunderstood passage that begins: 'The totality of these relations of production constitutes the economic structure of society, the real foundation, on which arises a legal and political superstructure ...' Karl Marx, *A Contribution to the Critique of Political Economy* (London, 1981), p. 20.

24 For a description of the *Palais*, see Walter Sebald, *Austerlitz* (London, 2001), pp. 38–9.

25 See David Harvey, *Paris, Capital of Modernity* (London, 2006), p. 311.

26 See Albert Speer, *Inside the Third Reich* (London, 1997), pp. 78–9.

27 Adam Hochschild, *King Leopold's Ghost: A Story of Greed, Terror, and Heroism in Colonial Africa* (London, 1998), pp. 293–4.

28 Stanley added that 'The blacks give an immense amount of trouble; they are too ungrateful to suit my fancy.' Hochschild, *King Leopold's Ghost*, p. 49.

29 Reports relayed by Roger Casement, Morel the Liverpool shipping clerk and Williams the African American journalist. 'This officer's ... method ... was to arrive in canoes at a village, the inhabitants of which invariably bolted on their arrival; the soldiers were then landed, and commenced looting ... after this they attacked the natives until able to seize their women; these women were then kept as hostages until the Chief of the District brought in the required number of kilogram's of rubber.' Hochschild, *King Leopold's Ghost*, p. 161.

30 Ibid., pp. 196–8. Francis Ford Coppola, dir. *Apocalypse Now*, 1979.

31 That took place between 1880–1920. Ibid., pp. 225–34.

32 The ability to forget about Africa, to 'create a vicious, refined atmosphere' around such crimes was institutionalised within the European mind through what Arendt suggests were the concept of race, a mechanism to explain 'other' human beings 'who no civilised European could understand', and through the great game of bureaucratic administration, the essential *modus operandi* of the 'great game of expansion'. Arendt, *The Origins of Totalitarianism*, pp. 185–90.

33 See Jules Marchal, *Lord Leverhulme's Ghosts: Colonial Exploitation in the Congo* (London, 2008).

34 Pashukanis, *Law and Marxism*, p. 115.

35 *New York Times*, April 11, 1902.

36 Friedrich Engels, *Anti-Duhring* (Moscow, 1978), p. 341.

37 Friedrich Engels, *The Origin of the Family, Private Property, and the State* (London, 1981), p. 235.

38 See for instance, Murray Bookchin, *The Spanish Anarchists: The Heroic Years 1868–1936* (Edinburgh, 1998), pp. 269–70. In addition for reprints of various libertarian manifestos from the Iberian anarchist tradition see Daniel Guerin, *No Gods No Masters*, vol. 2 (Edinburgh, 1998).

11

The Spatial Registers of Justice

Richard Patterson

In the 'Introduction' to *Social Justice and the City*, David Harvey stated his ambition as that of 'healing the breach in our thought in what appear to be two distinctive and irreconcilable modes of analysis', that is, of social process and spatial form. He also referred to certain unsustainable dichotomies, including for example 'fact/value', 'subject/object', 'public/private', and to what he considered to be the methodological error of treating 'things' as possessing 'an identity independent of human perception and action' located in (a thing called) space.[1] But this 'space', Harvey argued, is of two types, sociological and geographical, each with its own exclusive methodological precepts and structure, such that it was methodological exclusivity that prevented sociological analysis from recognising the 'profound effect (of spatial configuration) upon spatial processes on the one hand, and the inability of geographers, architects, and urban planners, on the other, to inform their formal manipulation of space with anything other than mere intuition', on the other. As such, it was his view, the implementation of social control through the agency of planning and other forms of spatial development, was not subject to critical analysis of the competing social factors it concerned, nor of the varying lived experiences it effected. Harvey proposed that conceptions of geographical space were in fact themselves constituted in social process and were not therefore objective, universal conditions, independent of human perception and action, etc, but intrinsically interest laden and not neutral grounds against which to measure 'objective' social truths. This led to his declared intention, to establish a new 'ontology' of space, one encompassing the sociological and geographical, one that provided a basis for just social actions.

The question of identity between spatial form and social form or process was part of a more general debate questioning principles of objectivity and transference of methodologies from the physical to the human sciences. The functionalism that had previously been accepted as the ground of an objective analysis of space was challenged by Claude Lévi-Strauss in such essays 'Do Dual Organisations Exist?', where he sought to explore the proposal that certain traditional or autogenous societies were organized according to parallel, yet 'dual' or mutually exclusive organisational 'structures'.[2] It was his contention that this exclusivity was based around opposing moities, and that its conceptualisation and expression differed not simply in terms of nominal affiliation, but in terms of contrary and incompatible discourses that were reconciled temporally through cyclical reciprocal ritual obligations. Central to the examples given were the divergent renderings by informants of spatial concepts with specific reference to village form, and the meanings attached to its various components. It is noteworthy that this particular piece was cited by Roland Barthes as constituting an introduction to an 'essentially semantic' urban semiology, potentially offering a direction for overcoming a methodological inadequacy of then contemporary urban theory.[3] But he also pointed to the limitations of Lévi-Strauss's proposals, specifically concerning how we come to infer or impose meaning on space more generally. Barthes raised the following point that would in essence differentiate the requirements of an urban semiology from the epistemological terms of the structural model proposed by Lévi-Strauss. Barthes held that there exist contradictions in modern urban space arising between functionality on the one hand and the semantic charge of history as a non-cyclical temporal development, which lead to an absence of 'definitive signifieds'. For Barthes, this clearly pointed to a multi-valent structure relating concepts, perceptions, and the use of space with its various correspondent social and cultural processes, a multi-valent structure which he described as an urban 'erotic'.

Contemporaneously Henri Lefebvre also had the ambition in *The Construction of Space* to articulate a 'theoretical unity between "fields" which are apprehended separately ... [as] the *physical* – nature, the Cosmos; secondly, the *mental*, including logical and formal abstraction; and, thirdly, the *social*'.[4] Lefebvre is interesting in this context as, although he approached the matter with similar methodological and epistemological concerns, his objectives were more along the lines of the alignment of a spatial taxonomy with modes of production, than with issues of justice *per se*. Thus, he proposed a tripartite process of spatial development leading from *spatial practice* (acts of production and reproduction), codified signs as *representations of space* and 'complex' symbolic *representational space*. This highly complex structure appears to embed a number of otherwise more familiar models. Initially, for example, his characterisation of activities of spatial practice were modelled principles drawn from Noam Chomsky's linguistics, namely on the principles of 'performance' and 'competence'.[5] For Lefebvre, the linguistic analogy was significant in that it offered an example according to which operative mechanisms and regulatory structure, like grammar, only became conscious upon reflection. As he put it 'spatial practice is lived directly before it is conceptualized'.[6] Equally interesting is the way he considered this conceptualisation to fall into two categories modelled on the opposition of 'sign' and 'symbol' as, respectively, the 'representations of space' and as 'representational space'. The representation of space is the more straightforward of the two, and is based on commonly understood codified systems, which he claimed had emerged from habitual spatial practice. In the case of the hegemony of abstract, Euclidean and perspectival space, for the period extending from the Renaissance to the nineteenth century, the spatial practice from which he claimed the codes had emerged from capitalist mode of production. His articulation of 'representational space' is, however, more difficult to summarize. Initially, he claimed that through imagistic associations it 'serves to maintain social relations in a state of coexistence and cohesion', as a result of the fact that it is what is 'directly "lived" through associated images and symbols'. But then he introduced a caveat, that it 'conceals as much as it reveals'.[7] 'Representational space' or, as he put it the 'historical space' of religious origin, in contrast to the *abstractions* of 'representations of space', must in some significant way be an illusion, an *imaginary* object of some kind. Indeed, a significant part of Lefebvre's argument about representation and space concerns the function of illusion (transparent or realistic) in obscuring the real conditions of social, spatial practice.[8]

The target of the critiques raised by Harvey, Lévi-Strauss and Barthes was the putative objectivity of standard spatial constructs of the day, as typified in the work of geographers, urban planners, and architects, a model that was essentially Euclidean and abstract, epitomized by linear perspective, objective, scientific and Cartesian. In all three cases, there is at least an implicit intention to move beyond methodological limitations, towards a fuller, more complex understanding of space, in Harvey's case explicitly with the objective of developing an 'ontology' that would ground implementation of a more socially just policy through regarding the use of 'spatial' resource. Lefebvre's approach, on the other hand, reduced the term 'space' to that of metaphor, critically accessible through a tripartite structure, according to which *Spatial practice* (material/social) precedes conceptualisation and, crucially, is as such inaccessible to conceptualisation other than through *representations of space* or as *representational space*. These latter 'conceptual' spaces are differentiated according to standard linguistic models, the former – representations of space – 'syntactically' through formally ordered, visual codes, the latter – representational space – 'semantically' through associations of meaning, imaginary, and naturalized relationships based on specular identification, etc. As such they propose a structure of modes of spatial experience that translates across a spectrum including and reconciling material, empirical practice, conceptual experience and Imaginative potential. It may be worth noting that this tripartite structure bears a strong similarity (albeit with a contrary terminology) to Jacques Lacan's registers of the psyche: the Real (the ineffable), the Symbolic (signifier) and the Imaginary (signified/signification), suggesting that while there may be no linear mediating sequence between the abstract and the concrete, between material/social practice and our means of conceptualising it, we may nonetheless recognize the varied and often internally conflictual manner of our occupation of the world.[9] Secondly, the model that these studies propose implies that space, as we conceive and experience it, is a form of projection mirroring our innermost desires and anxieties, for which environmental manipulation is the form of a therapeutic construction of our self.

In each of the cases summarized above there has been the ambition to critique the principle of space as an objective given in favour of the use of spatial concepts and perceptions instantiations of social and cultural meaning. This paper is concerned with the particular process through which the absolute or Cartesian space that was the object of their critique came into being. It will not propose a linear generative model as, say, from base to superstructure, except perhaps in a more nuanced, recursive version. In this context, it will propose that absolute space emerged from discourse through the medium of pedagogical method and that it functioned, through the reductive process of orthogonal measurement and diagrammatic representation, as the putatively neutral ground of judgement between opposing and conflictual patterns of occupation, use and location. The introduction of the regulating properties of discourse in this instance provides a link between the requirements of objectivity and universality (initially with reference to commerce and the terms of contracts) and (latterly) principles of spatial description, exploitation, and control.

HABITS OF MIND

Long before Michel Foucault's *Le mots et les choses*, Walter Ong had proposed an historical taxonomy mapping the sequence of change in discursive practice, albeit on material rather than structural grounds, that he qualified as follows: 1) the Classical world, in which learning and memory were functions of listening; 2) the Middle Ages, when they were functions of reading; and 3) the post-Gutenberg age, in which the relative proliferation of texts had created special problems for teaching, leading to simplification and diagrammatic forms of representation. What is of particular importance for our purposes is the emergence of the third phase, the technology for the dissemination of which Ong located in transformations in the teaching of 'dialectic' (or logic) in the later Middle Ages.[10] The initial conceptual element, trope, or mental reflex he was concerned to articulate began in what he described as the scholastic 'passion for fixity and exactitude' derived from the material base of reliance on books – books containing the written and formalized words of iconic authors, a memorized canon – rather than on spontaneous and dynamic language of live oratory or speech. One may speak therefore of Ong's work initially as one of the history of this reifying/hypostasizing influence on Western thought.[11]

Ong was concerned with the changes in objectives resulting from the extension of education to wider sectors of the population after the middle of the thirteenth century. The vehicle of this transformation, he claimed to be the *Summulae logicales* (1246) of Peter of Spain, a textbook for use in the training of university students, that came to constitute the first year or one-third of the arts faculties' programme throughout Europe.[12] In contrast to previous practice it was highly technical and formal, in line with the Scholastic focus on the use of logic for strength of argument rather than as an agent of enquiry or a means for revealing truth. It provided a skeletal version of logic in comparison with its Classical antecedents, and although this was cited by its humanist critics in their battle to overcome its malignant effect through a return to fundamentals (and to epistemological and metaphysical questions), there were several modes of thinking it had initiated – which became so engrained, automatic, natural, and to a degree unconscious – that they were not subject to this Humanist reformist zeal. These included 1) the practical application of probable claim as a form of certainty, 2) the use of reification as a dominant trope, and 3) a tendency to quantification which resulted, crucially for arguments presented here, in the use of spatialisation as a mode of pedagogical delivery.

Whereas Aristotle presented language as an open system enabling dialogue, Peter of Spain set out a system for regulating and controlling discourse by way of reference to quantity, in that the component elements to which he referred were comparable by way of reference to the standardized surrogates of suppositional logic, themselves weighed against each other, and which were most effectively taught through images, 'diagrammatically', in ways which Aristotle's logic could not have been. Yet although this visual and quantified method of thinking was inculcated through a European-wide curriculum, it was less apparent initially because of the difficulty in the publication of handwritten manuscripts, and of reproducing images. But with the advent of printing, including the possibility of employing complex visual imagery through the use of woodcuts, charts, illustrations, and geometric diagrams, a complex visual pedagogy began to appear with great regularity. An early example of this can be found in Jean Lefèvre d'Etaples's (1455–1537) *Grammatographia*, in which he developed a schematisation of grammar in a particularly visual way, that is, rather than in a traditionally 'discursive' format.

Such pedagogical strategies were universally taken up across Europe with a profound effect on normative thought processes, not to mention on the re-framing of objectives in the transformation of the Latin heritage that latterly came to be called the Renaissance. To reiterate, this included an enhanced sense of abstraction through the formal properties of substitution in suppositional logic with its inherent and subtle turns of reification and quantification.

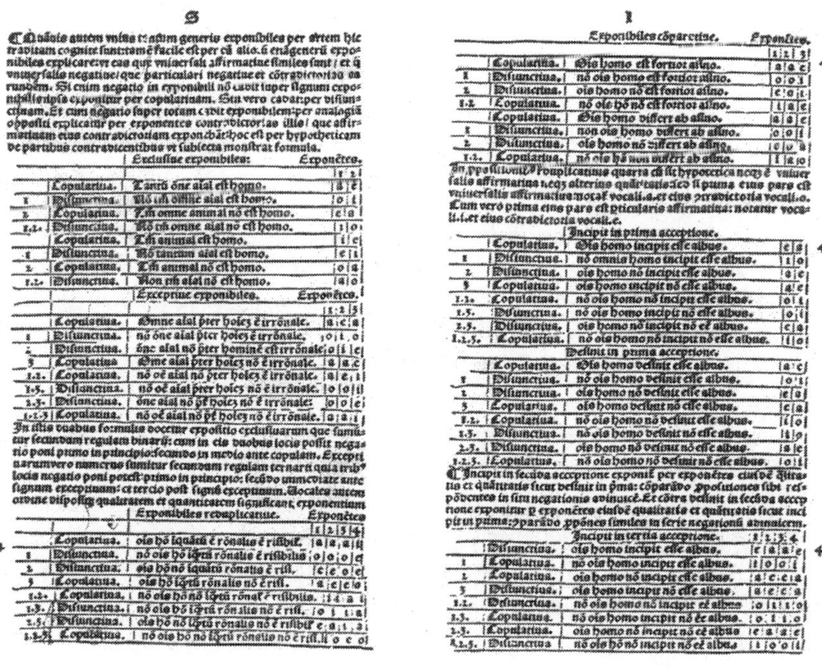

11.1 Demonstration of an attempt to schematize grammar. From Jean Lefèvre d'Etaples, *Grammatographia* (Paris, 1529)

Secondly, the development of knowledge as formally complete, multi-dimensional paradigmatic sets superseded aural, temporal, or linear narrative (especially after the advent of print in 1450–55), when, through the development of tables and diagrams, its inherently visual and spatial potential was realized. These formally complete spatial constructs and diagrams are thus reifications of what had been contingent, allusive, figured or dynamic modes of understanding, communication, and conceptualisation, implication and inference. Thirdly, conventions for differentiating classes of discourse according to their putative objects were simplified and blurred in this process of abstraction and simplification, such that 'thought' itself was universalized – no longer dependent on context-specific narrative – and 'reified', made into a thing of fixed, formal constancy.[13] This had the effect, not only of reorganising the business of teaching and learning, and not only of specifying what was taught and learned, but of shifting the status of the learning or teaching 'subject', namely to place the 'subject' or individual consciousness at the root and focal point of a universal paradigm of conceptual order, giving the subject a clear perspective on the objects of knowledge, so to speak, as opposed to a polar location in discursive reciprocity.

OBJECTIVITY

The spatialisation of knowledge was not, however, just limited to such paradigmatic grammatical and logical sets, but was extended to subject matter itself, as can be seen in the idea of the memory theatre, and in the many diagrammatic taxonomies proposed for the study of nature.[14] Again significantly, what we read and interpret as 'space' in these representations were projections of discursive structure, to be exact, projections of pedagogical practice. Where these developments can most clearly be seen to engage with issues of representation and aesthetics is in the theoretical writings of Leone Battista Alberti (1404–72), particularly in *De pictura,* where, in the text of the third book, he advises artists that in order to construct a proper narrative structure in a painting, they should:

> *take pleasure in poets and orators, for these have many ornaments in common with the painter. Literary men, who are full of information about many subjects, will be of great assistance in preparing the composition of an 'historia'.*

This was the focal point, so to speak, of Michael Baxandall's discussion of the background to *De pictura*, with particular reference to the term *compositio,* which he believed to have been drawn directly from the rhetorical treatises.[15] Both Vitruvius[16] and Cicero[17] had used the term, but by '... *compositio*', wrote Baxandall, 'Alberti means a four-level hierarchy of forms within the framework of which one assesses the role of each element in the total effect of a picture; planes go to make up members, members go to make up bodies, bodies go to make up the coherent scene of the narrative paintings ... .'[18] With this theoretical demand, pictorial imagery was to be submitted to the same criteria as a well-constructed

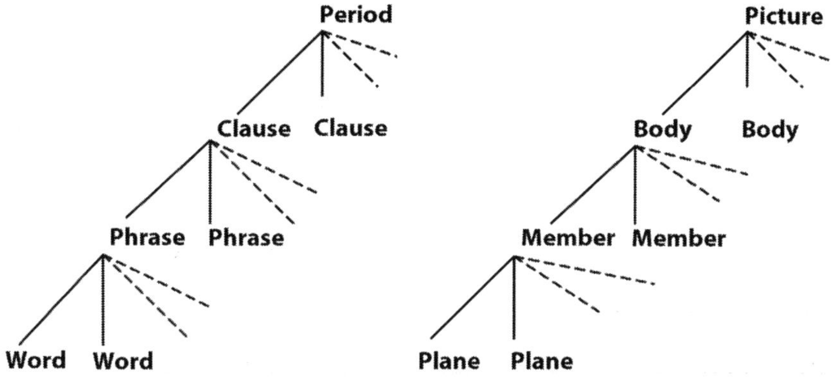

11.2 Alberti's translation of the arborescent structure of rhetorical composition to that of painting as 'compositio' (after Baxandall)

text: a hierarchy of component elements were to be regulated so as to focus in a clear and unambiguous way on the theme, argument or plot, in Alberti's terms, on a generic 'historia'. Elsewhere, Baxandall noted that the term *compositio* was used metaphorically 'transferring to painting a model of organisation derived from rhetoric itself. *Compositio* was a technical concept every schoolboy in a humanist school had been taught to apply to language. It did not mean what we mean by literary composition, but rather the putting together of the single evolved sentence or period, this being done within the framework of a four-level hierarchy of elements: words go to make up phrases, phrases to make clauses, clauses to make sentences.[19]

Seeking to impose an organisational framework on painting Alberti (1404–72), according to Baxandall's argument, did not attempt to seek out a visual principle *de novo*, but utilized the compositional commonplace of this arborescent structure in a new application. This had the benefit of enabling him to articulate a radically new principle in the development of visual practice by organisational means that were already entirely and generally familiar to anyone with an education. What we shall now attempt to demonstrate is the way in which this same formal structure came to dominate the seminal organisation of 'space' in the church architecture of Filippo Brunelleschi (1337–1446).

ARCHITECTURE

Unity in the architecture of Brunelleschi is achieved by two associated means, initially through the resolution of geometry in the composition of volumes, and latterly by the submission of all geometric form to a single underlying system, by which visual rigour was developed through a consistent, unbroken geometric resolution of volumetric composition. At San Lorenzo, the plan of which he inherited (and which recapitulates a fourteenth century Florentine tradition), Brunelleschi's innovations were largely syntactical and limited to controlling the progression of scale from aisle chapels to nave to crossing to the dome as a unified composition.

11.3 San Lorenzo, Florence. View showing progression of scale from side chapels to nave (photo by author)

11.4 San Lorenzo, Florence. View showing culmination of scaled progression to the dome crossing (photo by author)

At the most intimate scale of the chapels, a motif of order-plus-arch is established as an arch inscribed within pilasters and entablature. This motif is projected across the aisles to determine the nave colonnade, as the form and dimension of the pilasters and the 'stylobate' on which they stand. But whereas the side chapel pilasters support an entablature, the nave columns are capped with 'dosserets' (three dimensional derivatives of an entablature), similar to those of the Portico of Pompey. In a similar projected 'movement', the vaults capping the aisles above these the pilasters and entablature determine the form and dimension of arches rising above the dosserets. In this way, to summarize so far, Brunelleschi has created the first stage of the overall compositional structure of the church, initially in two dimensional format along the chapel arcade, and projected to three dimensions by means of sail vaults as the colonnade separating the nave from the aisles.

The next stage in the composition involves further development of the established motif, through two interlocked scales through the positioning of a second entablature, resting on/tangential to the architraves of the colonnade arches. This establishes visual continuity along the length of the nave. A third magnitude of scale is achieved in the culmination of the nave entablature on a projected 'double height' pilaster defining the corner of the transept. From this pilaster springs elliptical arches that mark the end of the nave and determine the geometry of the transept and the pendentives of the crossing.

Brunelleschi's innovation was twofold in the introduction of Classical ornament to a traditional Christian *parti*, along with the elaboration with an ordination or compositional principle as an unbroken hierarchy, in this instance of three traditional volumetric entities and scales, bound into a single narrative unity, into a single reified proto-space. Like the arborescent order elicited by Baxandall's in his analysis of Alberti's theory of painting, there is an arborescent order, again a simple commonplace of contemporary pedagogical method, to be found in the ordinating, compositional principles of Brunelleschi's work.

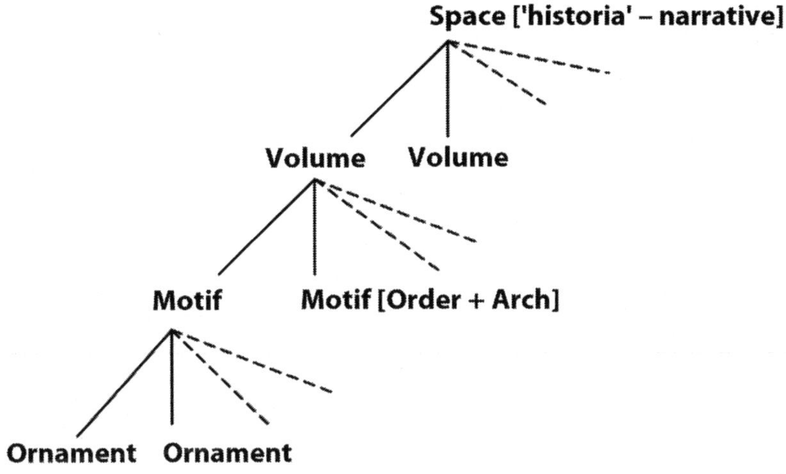

11.5 Brunelleschi's 'compositio'

Ornaments, or surfaces, severally go to make up motifs; motifs together structure volumes; volumes together when so continuously ordinated adumbrate a concept of space. Previous buildings had been composed of volumes, frequently allowing for variation in the use of ornament and motif and certainly producing wonder in contemplation of their drama and light. But it is only in the work of Brunelleschi that the totality of the whole is submitted to and defined by an overarching ordinating structure, an ordinating structure that is derived from language and provided a signified for the signifier '*compositio*'.

Sto. Spirito represents the submission of the compositional idea of arborescent form to a single underlying system, that fundamentally alters the building's semiotic. The forms of Sto. Spirito do not articulate elements of varied liturgical practice, accumulated special interest or patronage in the provision of large-scale ostentatious family chapels as had existed in San Lorenzo. There is a similar refocus in its lighting, in that whereas the light entering through windows in the lunettes over the aisle chapels of San Lorenzo in a sense balances that of the clerestory, at Sto Spirito, the dominant source of light is from above. In these two parallel, yet distinct compositional principles, uniform hierarchy and clear direction from relative darkness to light, there is no confusion, disruption, interruption, or insertion in the gradual development of dimension and clarity of direction from the level of human occupation to that of the divine.

On the one hand, there is an architectural-historical theme that leads from this point, specifically through the work of Bramante, towards the development of a universal, hierarchical, arborescent compositional system based on interlocking proportions, constituting the basis of what would become known as 'space'. The history of this development is extensively documented, largely in the context of analogies with musical harmonies, none of which in the era prior to 'well temperament' provided any basis for the comprehensive structures discussed here. What did carry this development beyond metaphors of universal harmony was the drive, initiated by late-mediaeval and Renaissance pedagogy, towards arborescent order and classification according to three-dimensional visual diagrams. And it was the mental habits involved in these practices that led to a predominance of truth criteria that were metonymic, qualitatively uniform, quantitative and universally applicable.

Correspondingly, this ordering system, developed by architecture in ever more overt, rigorous and all-encompassing forms, generated a context of human actions that was neutral and abstract, and against which, significantly, those actions became above all measurable. As such, a progressively more ordered, ultimately universal environment came to constitute an external baseline against which registers of value with reference to ownership and behaviour were referenced to a common standard and not subject to symbolically or qualitatively distinct, local and historically contingent standards of judgement.

The critiques of 'space' discussed above were variously concerned with the ways we describe and change the world as we perceive it and in which we live. Specifically, these critiques were focused on the judgement of objectivity arising through the reifications of absolute or Cartesian space. Architecture, in so much as it has been grounded in these reifications and claims to objectivity since the Renaissance, has served to naturalize and treat as objective that set of socially derived, historically contingent principles of order based on measurement and calculation, specifically with reference to the calculation of value. Also, at the very base of the drive for objectivity was the desire to overcome dispute and confusion arising out of the context of historically contingent events and material conditions. Architecture's role has been to order and measure buildings and cities, such that through the embodiment of calculation and the determination of value, those principles – putatively external, objective and value neutral with reference to dispute resolution and the allocation of resources – are rendered 'objectively'. Architecture and its allied professions have represented and manipulated the material basis for the social contract in a way that Harvey has judged to be socially unjust. Yet it is not at all clear that principles of spatial order based on interest or culturally singular forms of practice would amount to anything more than a precipitous politicisation of all areas of material opposition – not to mention conflict – as a relentless discourse of power.

Alternatives to arborescent structure, with its principles of single, 'root' genesis, progressive bifurcation and causal chronologies, have been proposed by Gilles Deleuze and Félix Guattari in their concept of the rhizome.[20] Utilising language including geological metaphors and heterogeneous semiotic chains in place of linear semantic continuities, the rhizome has been proposed in architectural practice as a principle means of superseding hierarchical, perspectival (univocal) space.[21] As an historical phenomenon, however, the Deleuzian rhizome is of very recent origin, without the comprehensive impact on discourse that was the case of arborescence. What the rhizome has provided in the reconceptualization of space is a permissiveness, a lack of hierarchy, and a multiplicity. Despite the distinctive and ahistorical content of cultural practice reflecting rhizomatic principle, it is effectively a phenomenon of Postmodernism. Without the establishment of a common context, point of reference or frame of meaning, the rhizome does not constitute the grounds for judgements regarding the deployment of urban resources or social justice, but it may serve to represent the variety and power of contesting forces.[22]

NOTES

1 David Harvey, *Social Justice and the City* (Baltimore MD, 1973).

2 Claude Lévi-Strauss, *Structural Anthropology* (Harmondsworth, 1968), pp. 132–63.

3 Roland Barthes, 'Semiology and the Urban', in Neil Leach (ed.), *Rethinking Architecture: A Reader in Cultural Theory* (London, 1997), p. 166 (first given as a lecture to the *Institute of the History of Architecture at the University of Naples* on 16 May 1967).

4 Henri Lefebvre, *La Production de l'espace* (Paris, 1974), trans. Donald Nicolson Smith, *The Production of Space* (Oxford, 1991), p. 11.

5 Noam Chomsky, *Aspects of the Theory of Syntax* (Cambridge MA, 1966).

6 Lefebvre, *Production,* p. 34.

7 Lefebvre, *Production,* pp. 32 and 39.

8 Lefebvre, *Production,* p. 27ff.

9 Jacques Lacan, trans. Alan Sheridan, *Ecrits: A Selection* (London, 1977), p. 87.

10 Walter Ong, *Ramus Method, and the Decay of Dialogue* (Cambridge MA, 1958).

11 See Walter Ong, *Orality and Literacy: The Technologization of the Word* (London, 1982) for a discussion on the development of print and the shift from aural to visual thought as a result of reading. Cf. Ivan Illich, *In the Vineyard of the Text: A Commentary to Hugh's Didascalion* (Chicago and London, 1993), p. 99: '*Ordinatio*: visible patterns'...(on the use of visual signs identifying the function of a particular section within the argument) 'These signs ... shift the task of perceiving the authors ordinatio from the inner ear to the eye.'

12 Ong, *Ramus,* p. 55ff.

13 Baxandall provides another example of this phenomenon in his citation of the use of proportion in Renaissance commercial discourse. Universality in the application of proportional laws in architecture, painting, sculpture and music is obviously well known, but what is interesting in Baxandall's commentary is the citation of Piero della Francesca's use of a marketplace anecdote to explain the Rule of Three. Michael Baxandall, *Painting and Experience in Fifteenth-Century Italy* (Oxford and New York, 1988), pp. 94ff.

14 Frances Yates, *The Art of Memory* (London, 1966); Richard Patterson, 'The Hortus Palatinus and the Reformation of the World', *Journal of Garden History*, vol. 1, nos. 1 and 2 (1982): 67–104, 179–202.

15 Michael Baxandall, *Giotto and the Orators* (Oxford, 1971), pp. 130–31; for a discussion of the Vitruvian basis via Barbaro, of a 'linguistic' basis for the visual tradition, see Oskar Bätschmann, 'Diskurs der Architektur im Bild', in Carlpeter Braegger (ed.), *Architektur und Sprache* (Munich, 1982), pp. 11–48; Alberti, *De statua* 'Dedication to Brunelleschi'; Alberti, *De pictura,* 21; Baxandall, *Giotto,* pp. 130–31; Alberti, *De pictura*, ii 35; Vitruvius II 36 on members and modules.

16 Vitruvius III I, 1.

17 Cicero, *De officiis* I xxviii, 98.

18 Alberti, *De pictura* ii, 33–35.

19 Baxandall, *Giotto,* p. 131: quoting Isidore of Seville, *Etymologiae* ii, 18.

20 Gilles Deleuze and Félix Guattari, *A Thousand Plateaus,* trans. Brian Massumi (London and New York, 2004); volume 2 of *Capitalism and Schizophrenia*, trans. of *Mille Plateaux* (2 vols, Paris: Les Editions de Minuit,1972–80).

21 Deleuze and Guattari propose a distinction between two types of space, which they name 'smooth' and 'striated'.

22 For an introduction to this topic, see Andrew Ballantyne, *Deleuze and Guattari for Architects* (Abingdon, 2007).

12

Gimme Shelter: Mass Incarceration and the Criminology of the Housing Boom

Jonathan Simon

INTRODUCTION: BUILDING A CULTURE OF CONTROL

Mostly when we think about the intersection of architecture and justice we think of the connections between buildings, like courts, prisons, jails, and the ideas, ideologies, and policies that shape both the scale and aspirations of these buildings.[1] Here I want to propose a different kind of connection. Just as buildings belong to a 'built environment',[2] and policies emerge not directly from interest groups but out of broader 'political rationalities',[3] we can learn something by reflecting on how these influence each other.

My example in this chapter is 'mass incarceration'. Between the 1970s and the end of the twentieth century, the rate of imprisonment more than quadrupled in the US (reflecting wide variations in states but in degrees of rapid growth).[4] This departure from a long term pattern of around 100 prisoners per 100 thousand adults to more than 400 by 1999, was a product not of a sustained wave of crime, but of policies that promoted the building of many new prisons and shifted imprisonment from a penalty for individuals to one directed at whole categories of criminal offenses with little regard for the individual circumstances or prospects.[5] There is much to be said about mass incarceration in terms of the growth in the number of and architectural qualities of prisons, as well as in the laws and public policies enacted to address crime by sending more people to prison for longer periods of time, but here I propose to reflect on the relationship between the broader built environment and mass incarceration as a political rationality.

As geographer Mike Davis suggested some years ago, the rapid build up of prisons should be understood as integral to a broader reconfiguration of metropolitan areas in which different segments of society once located in fairly tight proximity in the great industrial cities were now distributed in class segregated bands in a dispersed metropolis. In Robert Park and Ernest Burgess's influential sociological model of cities (published in their 1925 book, *The City*) neighbourhoods were distributed in concentric zones of different kinds of housing and business. Crime and other outcomes, according to their pioneering urban sociology of Chicago and its neighbourhoods, reflected these enduring social and economic functions, rather than the morals of the often shifting populations that occupied them. In Davis's revision of the model for post-industrial cities like Los Angeles, prisons alternate with bands of gated suburbs in the outer peripheries of the metropolis as a kind of 'gulag rim'.[6] Likewise, mass incarceration is not simply a criminal justice policy but part of a broad reframing of approaches to governing social problems through incapacitating a demographically substantial and economically expendable portion of the population.

If mass incarceration is situated at the intersection of the reterritorialization[7] of the American urban built environment and a new framework of governing anchored in fear of crime, as I will suggest, there is both bad and good news. On the bad news front, this account helps explain why mass incarceration prisons have been largely immune from popular criticism of their internal environments or external outcomes despite clear and substantial evidence that they are seriously failing.[8] If the public legitimacy of mass incarceration is protected by a precautionary mentality toward criminal offenders anchored in the economic and moral economy of the new metropolitan spatial order, prisons and the policies that keep people locked up will tend to become and remain a common denominator of partisan politics and thus subject to little innovation or risk taking by political leaders. We can talk about evidence based crime policies or the folly of building prisons that cannot support rehabilitative programming or even adequate health care, but no one will be listening much.

On the good news front, when we consider the alternative accounts of mass incarceration – its constitutive role in contemporary racial formation and stratification, and its utility to managing the disorders and instabilities engendered by neoliberal economic governance – the claims made here about the built environment and the political rationality behind mass incarceration may suggest reason for optimism about change in the short to medium term. While change in racialized fears or inequalities can be expected to be a slow and relatively continuous process and the grip of neoliberalism seems tight (notwithstanding the Great Recession), the metropolitan spacial order that dominated in the US from the 1950s through the present, with its emphasis on home ownership, class segregated suburbs (with greater distance from the city center associated with higher prices and prestige), and heavy reliance on automobility, now appears to be unsustainable as the price of energy goes up.

MASS INCARCERATION AND THE CRIMINOLOGY OF THE HOUSING BOOM

In seeking to explain the dramatic shift in the scale and nature of US imprisonment, social scientists have identified several links between transformations in the built environment, the reterritorialization of the American metropolitan areas toward sprawling 'edge cities'[9] and mass private property (homeowner association controlled residential subdivisions, shopping malls, office parks, etc.),[10] and the formation of a political rationality in which incarceration was a central tool of governance. These are not inconsistent but highlight different behavioral and institutional connections.

THE PRISON AS A SOLUTION TO SURPLUSES OF MARGINAL LAND AND PEOPLE

Geographer Ruth Gilmore's spatial and economic study of California's prison boom documents the importance of a new economic ascendancy of finance, construction, and real estate interests.[11] The prison as a site of state investment and legal power served to resolve several challenges to California's economy and existing spatial arrangement, posed by the restructuring of the national manufacturing economy that began at the start of the 1980s. That restructuring left a number of significant mismatches all over the US including California. In cities that had enjoyed strong manufacturing economies the closure of many factories left large amounts of urban real estate vacant and large numbers of surplus industrial workers (soon followed by young people who had never been industrial workers but lacked the education to move into higher paid service sector jobs). The decade also saw considerable surplus in agricultural land as the state's water scarcity (itself a product of the state's failure to invest in more water infrastructure) forced more marginal agricultural land out of production. At the same time, the political ascendance of anti-tax politics created a surplus of public finance capital that could not be tapped for the kind of infrastructure projects that the state had long indebted itself to build like universities, dams, and highways.

Gilmore suggests that mass incarceration was perfectly situated to resolve the disequilibriums created by deindustrialization. Land devalued for its agricultural uses, but too far out from population centers to have residential real estate value, was used for prisons financed by public borrowing, to house surplus urban (non) workers whose race made them relatively easy to demonize into a dangerous class. New political alliances helped transform sentencing laws to facilitate a ramping up of imprisonment. New debt strategies permitted the state to finance construction without committing to new taxes to pay them off. The overall result has been a powerful engine of imprisonment.

THE HAUNTED SUBURBS

In his early and pioneering study of mass incarceration and the broader transformations in understandings of and approaches toward crime that produced it, David Garland gives a prominent role to the intersection of two long term social trends in both countries, suburbanization and the rise of female labour force participation.[12] Suburbanization, the movement of families with means from urban neighbourhoods proximate to employment, to more remote 'bedroom' communities of housing, began under the ascendance of a single earner family in which the higher wages of male workers allowed by post-World War Two affluence, permitted their female spouses to 'stay home'. But a generation afterwards as suburbanization continued and intensified, the wage squeeze on middle class jobs (particularly those without high education requirements) made it increasingly common for women to join their spouses in full time employment. But as female work force participation climbed the suburban residential communities, which were supposed to be an anchor of security in the lives middle class families, became empty and insecure feeling during the day when both parents might be at work and children either in formal after-school care or minding themselves (another source of insecurity).

In Garland's complex and subtle account, the new residential and employment context of middle class families made them highly sensitive to the rises in reported crime that occurred in both the US and the UK beginning in the 1960s. According to Garland, the formation of a new 'common sense of high crime societies' quickly forged a new politics in which modern correctionalism and its relatively optimistic presumptions about the capacity of penal treatment to rehabilitate citizens who commit crime and 'reintegrate' them into society, became an anathema, and the prison came to represent a consistently 'tough' approach to crime.

HOMEOWNERSHIP AND REFLEXIVE RISK

One could contrast Gilmore's and Garland's accounts as economic and cultural respectively, although each deals carefully with both economic and cultural issues. Gilmore identifies the prison with macros flows of investment in land and buildings while Garland focuses on the phenomenology of crime as it becomes part of the everyday experience of home owners. In recent work I've suggested that homeownership as a legal relationship played an important role in mediating between the sensibilities of citizens on the one hand, and investment flows on the other.[13]

When violent crime in the big cities became a national problem because of the nationwide ban on alcoholic beverages known as 'Prohibition' beginning in 1920, it generated a sustained political and media mobilization that bears clear comparison to our more recent 'war on crime';[14] yet this original crime war had relatively little impact on the routines of American life or on the structures of political power. At least part of the reason, I would suggest, may lie in the fact that Americans in the 1920s were overwhelmingly renters, but by when violent crime in the cities returned as a national political issue in the 1960s Americans were on their way to being a super-majority of homeowners.

There is nothing new, of course, in the political importance of this watershed in economic life. Historians and political scientists have long recognized the potency of homeownership as a pull to the right for many Americans whose labour market role might suggest a left of center set of policy preferences, but whose identity as a homeowner has made taxes, schools, and yes, violent crime important. As compared to renters, homeowners face a non-transferrable economic risk in the price of their home. Outside of periods of great financial calamity, the value of homes has generally advanced (and in recent history quite considerably) but specific properties are subject to local conditions that can pull them out of the general trend, including taxes, school decline, and violence, but also of course, the loss of a major nearby employer, an environmental exposure (in real time or the revealing of historic toxicity).

Home ownership in the twentieth century moved from being a reflection of economic security to a platform for building it. In the 1920s, when real estate boomed along with the new financial and corporate economy, the average homeowner was a middle aged or even older person for whom the privately owned home was a form of comfort and a way of saving for retirement. By the 1950s, the average homeowner was becoming a young family, for whom the privately owned home was a vehicle for building wealth and a form of debt. In between the New Deal forged new legal instruments, like the 30 year fixed rate mortgage, and the tax deduction for mortgage interest, designed to socialize some of the cost of homeownership, and make it possible for young families to borrow the private money to buy in the expectation that growing earnings would allow them to pay it off while building equity and enjoying the autonomy of owning their residence.

Much of this new investment went into new suburban housing rather than recuperating blighted central city housing. Historians have shown that fear of racial integration and its effects on housing prices was one driving factor, but so likely were the economic benefits of driving new home building which by the 1970s had become the major motor driving American economic recoveries following recessions.

While the privately owned home was promoted as a form of security for both homeowners and their communities, the new arrangement came with a built in risk. Should local conditions make the value of the home go down, the money owed on the home through the mortgage could quickly become much more than the house was actually worth. Threats to home values came from many sources, from plant closures (especially in smaller towns), to new urban infrastructures (like freeways), changes in the racial demography of the neighbourhood in segregated societies, and environmental disasters.[15]

One of the most prominent threats to property values comes from crime which inevitably occurs in a specific locale and when publicized, which the most serious crimes frequently are, can often leave a 'reputational stain' on the vicinity. Crime has long been linked in both elite and popular discourse to neighbourhoods and their character. Crime diminishes the value of a house if it suggests that a neighbourhood is at risk for crime. This creates a distinct risk sensitivity to crime for the homeowner as compared to renters. Both may share a concern with being an actual victim, but only the homeowner is exposed to risk of the neighbourhood's reputation for crime getting worse.

Fear of crime began to go up in the United States during the 1950s, even before reported crime rates began to rise steadily, due to the increase in home ownership experienced in that decade after the long break in the real estate market from the Depression to World War Two. Returning World War Two veterans were particularly favoured for loans for new suburban housing. This surplus crime risk sensitivity in homeowners becomes more acute once crime has become particularly salient to government and media. The rise of reported crime in the 1960s and 1970s, amplified by politicians and the media, resulted in a securitization of new real estate, so that housing was increasingly marketed through its security. But the securitization of housing, by promising more security, also made the value of the house even more vulnerable to value loss through crime risk. Perversely the more the value of the house was tied up in its security, the lower the threshold at which signs of crime risk could diminish its value. Not just actual crime, but signs of disorder could damage the value of the house. By the 1980s and 1990s, new housing estates almost everywhere, but particularly in the hot real estate markets of the sunbelt, were taking forms that visibly manifested their security attributes, especially the ubiquitous gated entryway. This in-security dynamic also helps to explain why housing growth has pushed relentlessly toward the urban periphery. It is not only that land is cheap, but green fields come without a reputation for crime.

LEARNING FROM THE CRIMINOLOGY OF THE HOUSING BOOM

Whatever account one might favor for why America in the era of mass home owning affluence became committed to mass incarceration, and indeed all of them might play some role in explaining not only the general trend but the enormous variation we see across the United States, several general observations can be made. They start with the place that the home, owned (mostly on borrowed money), now plays (or at least did until the great financial crisis of 2008) in the lives of middle class Americans. It is supposed to provide not only shelter against the elements, but shelter against financial instabilities and shelter against criminal violence. It is endangered by anything that makes it, the home, less valuable to potential buyers, or less affordable by its present owners. Thus the privately owned home in the current political economy anchors a whole approach to citizenship.

First, the respatialization of Americans from urban renters to suburban homeowners has increased the level of crime based insecurity and the role it plays in public life. Irony abounds here, naturally. People were encouraged to buy homes and move to the suburbs (and national policy tended to merge the two in any event) precisely so they could enjoy more security, but whatever gain in real or even imagined everyday security they or their children experienced in their new homes came along with a permanent adjustment in the level of overall commitment to the project of security from crime that made itself felt in the way many Americans organized their daily routines.

As architecture and film scholar Renée Tobe has noted specifically about the US investment in the home:

> *In the postwar period, media and advertising spread the notion that all Americans should and could own their own homes. House owners desired communities and felt nostalgia for the past. Reliance on reason and rationality in all things formed part of the creation of America and the development of the 'American way.' The ultimate mode of dwelling came to represent the ultimate mode of living.*

But as Tobe argues, the idealized security of the home constantly invites the invasion of insecurity and even terror, a theme worked and reworked in the popular film and television creations of US auteur David Lynch.[16]

Nowhere has this been more visible than in the policing of childhood, which has moved in slightly over a generation from a tradition of essentially free-range childhood (as author and anti-fear activist Lenore Skenazy calls it)[17] for all but the children of the most wealthy or famous, to a gated childhood of varying enrichment and pleasure for children of virtually all classes. It also goes along, with a more general gating of public and private spaces, including work places which have become a maze of secured access spaces and 'smart cards'.

Second, in ways that architects can help us to define more precisely, reversing this securitization of American could expand enormously the degrees of freedom available to architects and builders to realize other objectives in the built environment generally and in many of our most important and beleaguered institutions.

The gated community, which has been the gold standard of residential security in the United States (the kind of place where Tiger Woods lives, but cheaper knock offs exist for many), is a design configuration that deliberately frustrates many features that would be otherwise desirable, for example the ability to walk to stores and other business, or even, public transportation. The huge costs to our national health care budget (disguised because of our hodgepodge of public and private insurance schemes) of obesity and obesity related chronic illness created by gating gets some discussion today, and almost everybody agrees that integrated use walkable cities would be better, but almost nobody connects it to the gating of the contemporary urban landscape and the mandate that security requires complete physical segregation from public access. However to question what Garland usefully described as the 'common sense' of high crime societies is to stop being heard altogether even if your point is just a step away from the current consensus.[18]

Schools, designed to maximize security by locking down campuses make it difficult for students to resolve their own disputes as well as pursue many of the learning experiences that accompany formal education.[19] Security in schools often sucks priority, funding, staff, and attention from the educational mission. Furthermore, by reducing the distance between schools and criminal justice agencies, indeed in many schools placing law enforcement officials directly into the school campus, schools have increased the risk that students will end up being recruited into deeper engagement with criminal justice and ultimately incarceration. Nor is it clear that this kind of securitization even protects young people from becoming victims of violence.[20]

Of course prisons, and to a lesser extent courts, which are more commonly the focus at the intersection of architecture and justice, would also benefit enormously from a downscaling of mass incarceration. California is the nation's most extreme example but its pathologies are broadly present in America's distended penal systems. In California despite building twice as many prisons in the past thirty years than in the previous 120 years of statehood, California entered this decade with prisons at over 200 per cent of capacity, inside of which long term deficit of medical and mental health care had created a humanitarian crisis that required federal court intervention.[21] Among the many reasons for California's terrible overcrowding was the practice of returning tens of thousands of released prisoners for relatively minor violations, underscoring the utter failure of imprisonment to either deter or rehabilitate as currently practiced. The failure to rehabilitate is not surprising given the priority given to physically segregating prisoners from the community. A system unable to keep track or respond to even florid symptoms of mental and physical illness could hardly be expected to employ contemporary techniques of behavioral therapy or education. Once hyper-overcrowding becomes an acceptable norm even the pretense to providing an opportunity at self betterment for those prisoners willing was dropped. Moreover, once people are sent to prison with little consideration for their individual condition, prison populations begin to concentrate individuals with high levels of chronic illness (often linked to drugs and other life-style choices).

While California's degree of overcrowding and the background level of chronic illness are at the high end of American states, these widely shared traits are an expensive little noted feature of the US prison model. California's crisis, ironically, gives it an important opportunity to rethink what prison and jail spaces should look like and do. Much of the action is already taking place at the county level where new jails in some communities have emphasized treatment and education in their very design as well as facilitating the engagement of the community, all features expelled from the prisons of mass incarceration.

Third, as costly as mass incarceration has been and as powerfully rooted in American life as it has become, the relationship criminologists have drawn between the built environment and mass incarceration is one that may be less intractable than other sources of insecurity and imprisonment. The other way of looking at the sources of US mass incarceration emphasizes the significance of racial stratification. Mass incarceration is, on this account, a political tool kit for managing racial hierarchy and subordinating non-white and especially African American citizens. Evidence abounds that the effects of mass incarceration are heavily shaping racial stratification and reproducing the disadvantages of the racialized past. It is also clear that the political origins of the war on crime lie in the complex politics of party competition around race in the 1960s and 1970s.

If mass incarceration is the 'new Jim Crow' in Michelle Alexander's compelling thesis, an updated version of the legal framework that kept African Americans in separate and unequal lives in the South until the Civil Rights movement broke its back in the 1960s, it is difficult to see any powerful obstacles to its continued grip on American life given that racial justice movements are even weaker today than they were a generation ago.[22] The same is true with Neoliberalism, the other structural source generally pointed to as a source of mass incarceration.[23] To the extent that the embrace of prisons is driven by deregulated labour markets and increasingly pro-business governments (whether in pursuit of legitimacy or social control) there is little reason to expect any near term change and indeed unless the present economic crisis dictates new commitments to regulation (rather than a marginal increase in some sectors like banking) and to collective risk institutions, we would expect the prison to spread to regions that remain relatively ambivalent (such as Europe, Asia, and Latin America).

Finally, if mass incarceration is dependent, through various mechanisms, on the peculiar model of residential development aimed at homeownership increasingly dispersed in expanding metropolitan regions, there is good reason to believe that it has reached its natural limits and is in the process of reversing (to some extent). The current economic crisis is unlikely to rewrite the rules of economic management in the US, but the long pause it has hit on sprawl and the retraction of homeownership as hundreds of thousands have lost homes due to inability to pay mortgages on loans now worth more than the property they were made on, has placed this model under new scrutiny. The economic uncertainty also underscores the benefits of renting which seems to be making a comeback after shrinking for decades.

Long term, government policies aimed at reducing carbon emissions and market prices driven by energy shortages may align to shift the American built environment away from the current dominance of sprawl and physical segregation of uses. More reliance on high density housing accessible to public transportation and schools will drive some families back to central cities, or at least inner ring suburbs, while the advantages of flexibility may quickly turn the necessity of renting (due to the still tight lending market in the US and UK, Scotland, and Ireland) into a virtue.

If the criminology of the housing boom is correct the US should be entering a period where violent crime (which conveniently remains at levels substantially lower than in the last decades of the previous century), has less resonance in the built environment. That does not mean of course, that mass incarceration, or the legal and social policies that promote it will disappear quickly, or that fear of crime will easily loosen its grip on American identities and routines. Both of those will require positive action by active citizens, including criminologists, lawyers, and architects, ready to challenge received common sense when it comes to building, dwelling, raising our children, running our organizations, etc.

CONCLUSION

Looking mostly at the United States, one can draw a relationship between the built environment associated with the long boom in residential housing and the epic expansion of imprisonment that punishment and society scholars call 'mass incarceration'. This chapter lays out alternative accounts, or criminologies of the housing boom. The forces for change in our built environment, especially the shift toward lower carbon life styles for the middle class and the corollary high prices of energy, could also open the door to rethinking what seem to be entrenched commitments to mass incarceration as a form of security.

This pattern is not limited to the United States. Some European countries show signs of a similar affinity between housing booms and prison booms (especially the UK, and Ireland, but also the Netherlands, Spain, and Greece). Going forward, architects, lawyers, and criminologists have a role in warning societies about the consequences of promoting American style home ownership and suburban sprawl. Indeed, even in countries where housing expansion has been less vigorous (before the collapse) we see populist pressures to respond to broad insecurities with harsh punishment and treatment for those demonized as criminal threats (for example, the Roma).

Indeed, architects, lawyers and criminologists have a distinctive mission in addressing the lingering fear of crime, which even if it is losing much of its motive force, will remain capable of defining expectations for change as well as active opposition from powerful interest groups in a position to defend the old ideas of security. If fear remains highly salient to middle class routines, we can expect that the new metropolitan terrain, even as it conforms to pressures for greater density and lower energy consumption, will remain gated and exclusionary. Ideas about how to reinvigorate the self ordering and reassuring capacity of neighbourhoods have been circulating since Jane Jacobs's classic polemic against 1960s urban redevelopment planning.[24] Since the early 1990s police strategies in New York and a few other cities appear to have resulted in drops in reported crime even more dramatic than the general crime decline recorded across the United States.[25] If the mass incarceration prison figured as the dark anchor of the valorized safe and gated residential community of the 1980s and 1990s, defining the model of public safety to go along with reinvigorated urban neighbourhoods with high density and high mobility is the challenge we face.

NOTES

1 See John Bender, *Imagining the Penitentiary: Fiction and the Architecture of the Mind in 18th Century England* (Chicago, 1987).

2 See Denise L. Lawrence and Setha M. Low, 'The Built Environment and Spatial Form', *Annual Review of Anthropology*, vol. 19 (1990): 453–505.

3 The term comes from Michel Foucault who uses it to describe the discursive formations that can productively shape and seed public policies. See, Foucault, *Omnes et Singulatun: Towards a Criticism of 'Political Reason'*, Tanner Lecture, Stanford University (Stanford, 1978).

4 The data since the 1980s is available here: <http://www.albany.edu/sourcebook/pdf/t6292009.pdf>.

5 David Garland, *The Culture of Control: Crime and Social Order in Contemporary Society* (Chicago, 2001); Bruce Western, *Punishment and Inequality* (New York, 2006).

6 Mike Davis, *Ecology of Fear: Los Angeles and the Imagination of Disaster* (London, 1998).

7 I draw on this term from cultural studies to capture the way built environment, legal authority, and social norms are all embodied in 'territory' as a spatial order. The term was used by Gilles Deleuze and Félix Guattari to describe the process by which a particular order of power is broken down and replaced by another, for example in the process of colonization or conquest (picture American troops pulling down the statue of Sadam Hussein in Baghdad during the American occupation of that city). See Deleuze and Guattari, *Anti-Oedipus: Capitalism an Schizophrenia*, trans. Robert Hurley, Mark See and Helen Lane (New York, 1972).

8 The literature on the criminological failings of prisons, often and problematically summarized through 'recividivism', or the rate at which released prisoners return to prison within a standard period after release, is now significant an excellent and reasonably recent summary can be provided in Joan Petersilia, *When Prisoners Come Home: Parole and Prisoner Reentry* (New York, 2003). The failings of prison design have been brought out by recent litigation in California which has documented both catastrophic failures to provide safe, secure, and healthy environments for prisoners, and a failure to reduce the potential criminal risk posed by those released from prison, see *Plata v. Schwarzenegger*, 3 Judge Court final opinion and order, upheld, *Brown v. Plata*, 09–1233.

9 Joel Garreau, *Edge City: Life on the New Frontier* (New York, 1991).

10 Clifford D. Shearing and Phillip C. Stenning, 'From the Panopticon to Disney World', *Perspectives in Criminal Law: Essays in Honour of John LL.J. Edwards*, edited by Anthony N. Doob and Edward L. Greenspan, Q.C. (Toronto, 1984); Evan MacKenzie, *Privatopia: Homeowners Associations and the Rise of Residential Private Government* (New York, 1996).

11 Ruth Wilson Gilmore, *Golden Gulag: Prisons, Surplus, Crises, and Opposition in Globalizing California* (Berkeley CA, 2007).

12 Garland, *The Culture of Control*, p. 130.

13 Jonathan Simon, 'Consuming Obsessions: Housing, Homicide and Mass Incarceration 1950–1980', *The University of Chicago Legal Forum*, vol. 2010, p. 140.

14 Marie Gottschalk, *The Prison and the Gallows: The Politics of Mass Incarceration in America* (Cambridge, 2006)

15 It was this local risk that, in part, mortgage securitization was intended to eliminate. Historically, other than in the Great Depression, national real estate values had risen, with local declines out paced by local gains. Mortgage instruments mix bits of mortgage payment streams from all over the nation together in one instrument. As compared with holding the actual mortgages from a single area (which could be quite risky), these instruments promised gain with far less risk. Unfortunately the same instruments came with a bevy of new risks because of the moral hazards built into the model (i.e., the opportunities for some participants to pass off risks at no price), some of which proved catastrophic.

16 Renée Tobe, 'Frightening and Familiar: David Lynch's *Twin Peaks* and the North American Suburb', in *Visual Culture and Tourism*, ed. David Crouch and Nina Lubbren (Berg, 2003), pp. 241–58.

17 See, Lenore Skenazy, *Free Range Kids: Giving Our Kids the Childhood We Had Without Going Nuts with Worry* (New York, 2009).

18 Garland, *Culture of Control*, p. 163.

19 Calvin Morrill and Michael Musheno, *Youth Conflict: Culture and Control in a Multiethnic High School* (forthcoming).

20 In January 2012 the shooting of an eigth grade boy named Jamie Gonzalez inside his school in Brownsville, Texas, by police officers after he brandished what turned out to be a pellet gun raised the question of whether police were protecting anyone but themselves. William Welch and Carolyn Pesce, 'Parents question lethal force on 8th grader with pellet gun', *USA Today*, 5 January 2012, <http://www.usatoday.com/news/nation/story/2012-01-04/texas-student-shot/52379064/1>.

21 In 2009 a special three-judge federal court ordered California to reduce its prison population by as many as 40,000 prisoners in order to achieve overcrowding that was only 137% of capacity. This order was upheld by the US Supreme Court in *Brown v. Plata*, 09–1233 (2011).

22 Michelle Alexander, *The New Jim Crow: Mass Incarceration in an Age of Colorblindness* (New York, 2009).

23 Bernard Harcourt, *The Illusion of Free Markets: Punishment and the Myth of Natural Order* (Cambridge MA, 2011).

24 Jane Jacobs, *The Death and Life of Great American Cities* (New York, 1961).

25 Franklin Zimring, *The City that Became Safe: New York's Lessons for Urban Crime and its Control* (New York, 2011).

13

Drawing Conclusions: Fort Rupert, British Columbia in 1863

John Bass

INTRODUCTION

Colonial settlement in British Columbia was built on its share of broken promises and the province of today bears a legacy of contested space. On BC's Vancouver Island, where the Hudson's Bay Company (HBC) settled on land long used by the region's First Nations' peoples for their own settlements, property rights treaties between the HBC and fourteen Vancouver Island First Nations were signed to defuse turf tensions. However, the colonial, and later, provincial obligations to their First Nations co-signatories were ignored or deferred. Settlers continued to settle and, in the eyes of those judging land claims through the lens of British property law, their settlements made scores of subsequent Native land claims moot.

Using archival photographs and other documents as a source of data and architectural documentation and analysis as a tool of enquiry, we will examine one such contested space – Fort Rupert, British Columbia – a coastal outpost of the HBC's Pacific Coast operations in the mid-nineteenth century, and home to the Fort Rupert Kwakiutl Band, members of the Kwakwaka'wakw First Nation.[1] The data strongly suggests an act of injustice (first by the Colonial, and later, the Provincial, governments of British Columbia) was perpetrated on this community. This research uses the agency of architectural analysis and representation directed at events that unfold in time to provide new knowledge and methods of communication to the Fort Rupert Kwakiutl, who continue to seek redress.

To summarize: In 1851, representatives of the HBC and two families of the Kwakiutl people who settled adjacent to the fort signed a treaty establishing the property claims of Colonial and Kwakiutl groups, temporarily defusing growing tensions between the two. Twelve years later, a property survey that ignores this treaty is approved and private land is created, or 'preempted'.[2] Within a few years plus or minus of this pivotal year, several graphic documents are produced describing the spatial organization of fort and Kwakiutl village. These documents are the central pieces of evidence that we have studied in support of 'specific claims' cases made by the descendants of the Kwakiutl people who signed the two treaties. The work is similar to the methods of context building employed by art historians and archaeologists – a search for circumstantial evidence concealed within the portrayal and artifacts of everyday events – methods that produce arguments fusing interpretation and fact.[3]

In the context of the Fort Rupert research, photographers began to make images there as early as the 1860s. These include several extraordinary images that portray the early years of its colonial and Kwakiutl settlement. An archive of photographs taken over six decades describes the gradual processes of spatial, material, and social assimilation that occurred there. An analysis of the spatial dissolution and social assimilation of the paired colonial and Kwakiutl settlements at Fort Rupert led to a set of specific legal issues that originated in the 1851 treaty and are as yet unresolved.[4] This unresolved legal status of territory became the real question of project described here.

FORT RUPERT, 1849–86

> *Thirty years after its invention in 1839, the camera was no longer 'a gadget for an elite', but instead was being used for police filing, war reporting, military reconnaissance … anthropological records (often, as with the Indians in the United States, accompanied by genocide) …*[5]

The historical context of this research is set in the mid-nineteenth century, when the British began to occupy the aboriginal territories along the Pacific Coast of Canada. The early colonists were vastly outnumbered.[6] Tensions inevitably developed between the two groups. Among them were spatial conflicts that arose as the colonists settled, built cabins, farms, cities and forts on land used for millennia by Native people for settlements and food harvesting. Where the proximity of the two groups was especially close, the Colonial government defused tense situations by negotiating fourteen separate but identical treaties with their Native neighbours. The treaty was representative of British property law, of which the Native people would have had little understanding since their practices of ownership were seasonal, and not absolutely fixed to pieces of land. In addition to this fundamental problem, the language of the treaties is confusing, and two of the treaty's clauses are key in this regard. In the first, the Native people agreed

> *… to surrender, entirely and for ever (sic), to James Douglas, the agent of the Hudson's Bay Company in Vancouver Island, that is to say, for the Governor, Deputy Governor, and Committee of the same, the whole of the lands situated and lying between McNeill's Harbour and Hardy Bay, inclusive of these ports, and extending two miles into the interior of the Island.*

For surrendering their land to the HBC, the treaty assured that

> *... our village sites and enclosed fields are to be kept for our own use, for the use of our children, and for those who may follow after us and the land shall be properly surveyed hereafter. It is understood, however, that the land itself, with these small exceptions, becomes the entire property of the white people for ever (sic); it is also understood that we are at liberty to hunt over the unoccupied lands, and to carry on our fisheries as formerly.*[7]

That the colonial government did not follow through on their agreement to survey the 'village sites and enclosed fields' is the basic fact from which this research emanates. If they had done so immediately, many Kwakiutl 'properties' that were lost to preemption would have been preserved. While the Fort Rupert Douglas Treaty was signed in 1851, it wasn't until nearly twenty years later that their first village site was surveyed, and it took another decade and a half before it was reserved. By that time, their key settlements – level ground near river inlets or shorelines, the most desirable and accessible space in this remote and mountainous area – had become the private property of white settlers through the preemption process.[8]

What follows here is a micro-analysis aimed at helping to make the case for reclaiming a small but important piece of land taken by this nineteenth and early twentieth century policy. This geography is limited to the space of the Fort Rupert Kwakiutl Band, and more still to just one of their many specific land claims – that of the southern shore of Beaver Harbour, where one hundred acres of their land was preempted by an occupant that demonstrably settled only eight acres, subsuming a Kwakiutl village in the process.

TIMELINE OF FORT RUPERT'S EARLY SPATIAL EVOLUTION

Described below are the key events in a seventeen year period beginning in 1849. The timeline identifies key data in the form of maps, sketches, surveys, charts and images. Supported by narrative accounts, these visual documents made it possible to develop a graphic analysis of the configuration of and change over time to the Fort Rupert's Hudson's Bay Company fort and surrounding Kwakiutl village.

1849–55: The Hudson's Bay Company builds Fort Rupert. By 1855, staff at the fort is reduced to 'a dozen men and their dependents'.[9]

1850: Magistrate Dr. John Sebastian Helmcken describes the Kwakiutl settlement at Fort Rupert: 'This Rupert village contained at least two thousand five hundred bodies, i.e. men, women and children ...' 'The Quocholds ... occupied the north side of the fort.' And 'The Queechars ... occupied the south side.'[10]

1851: The HBC signs two separate but identical treaties (so-called Douglas Treaties) with 16 'Quakeolth' [Kwakiutl] and 12 'Queackar' [K'umuyoyi] chiefs. The Royal Navy surveys Beaver Harbour (Fig. 13.1), and depicts in some detail the Kwakiutl settlement flanking the fort to the east and west, corroborating Helmcken's narrative account.

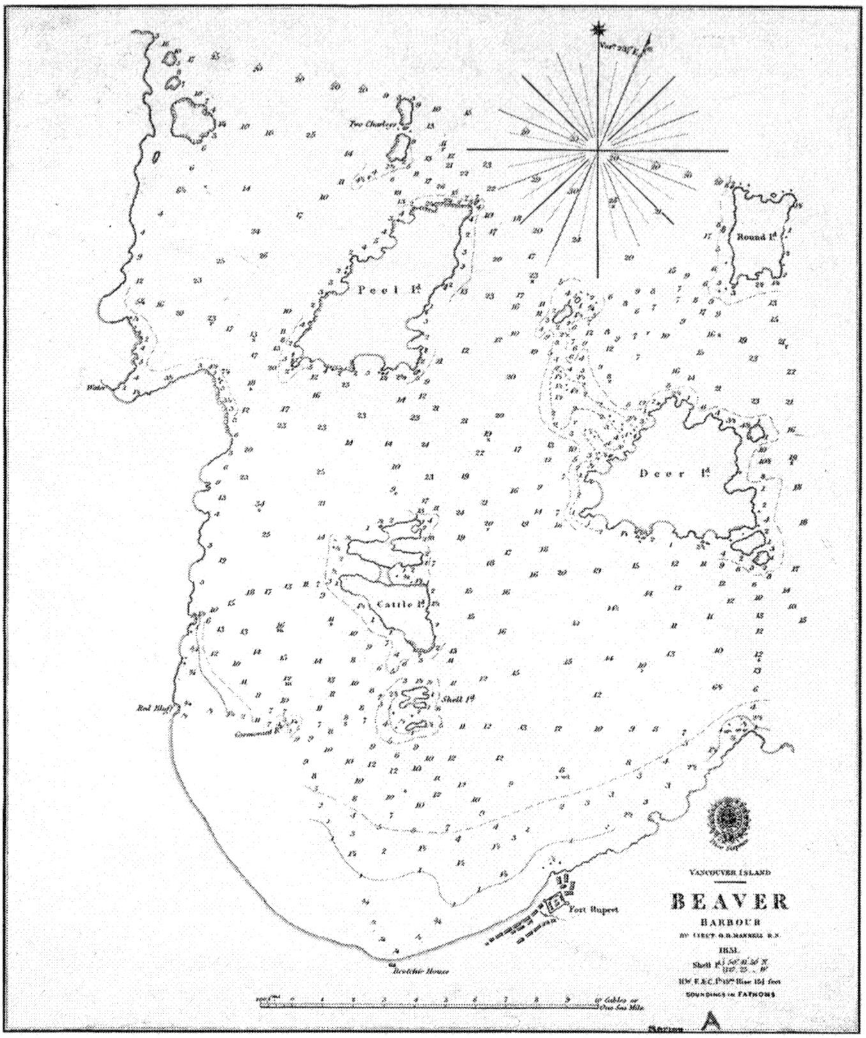

13.1 1851 Admiralty Chart of Beaver Harbour, by GH Mansell RN UKHO Admiralty Chart 2153 series A1 (1851) (courtesy of the UK Hydrographic Office)

1857: The HBC takes stock of its Fort Rupert holdings. A valuation produces detailed graphic descriptions of the locations and functions of the fort's physical elements, including a plan of the fort with dimensions.

1860: HMS *Plumper* Captain Richards estimates the Kwakiutl population at Fort Rupert to be 700 to 800.[11]

1862: HBC Chief Trader Finlayson requests 'preemption' of 100 acres at Fort Rupert.

1863: A fire destroys four K'umuyoyi houses and threatens the fort. These houses were located very near to the northeast walls of the fort's coal yard.[12] Surveyors complete a 'Plan, One Hundred Acres of Land, Preempted for The Honourable Hudson's Bay Company, at Fort Rupert V.I.' (Fig. 13.3)[13]

Two Fathers from the Catholic Missionary Oblates of Mary Immaculate build a mission church and school at Fort Rupert. Originally called the Mission of Assumption, it was renamed St Michael's after the mission moved to nearby Harbledown Island in 1865. Father Fouquet, who said that the Kwakiutl 'were very far from heaven', perhaps best summed up underlying causes motivating the move.[14]

c. 1864: A panoramic image of the fort and Kwakiutl village and two group portraits of British Naval offices and Fort Rupert Kwakiutl people are made (Figs 13.5 and 13.6).

December 1865: The HMS *Clio* shells the Fort Rupert Kwakiutl village. 'I told him he should have a certain time to give the men up, and if they were not then forthcoming, we should open fire from the ship and destroy the village. At the expiration of the time appointed we fired upon the Ranch, and totally destroyed it, with 50, or 60 large Canoes …'[15]

May 1866: Captain Edwin Porcher of the HMS *Sparrowhawk* makes several watercolour paintings of Fort Rupert, two of which depict the fort and a destroyed village. Porcher's account of the visit indicates that the village was in great disrepair. '(o)n the West side there was an Indian Ranch, but the greater number of the Indians were at the time away fishing. Only a few of the houses had been rebuilt since they were destroyed by the Clio in December last for refusing to give up some murderers, and the marks of the hatchets on the canoes were still visible.'[16]

1879–80: A survey of land allotted for the first Fort Rupert reserves is produced for Indian Reserve Commissioner Gilbert Sproat. The survey again confirms the presence of Kwakiutl houses on land preempted by the HBC in 1863. According to Robert Galois: 'The reserves allotted by Sproat covered: 1) the area between Fort Rupert and the eastern limit of the section of land sold by the HBC to the Oblate and here identified as R.C. Mission, and 2) the area west of the limit of the HBC pre-emption and the aforementioned Oblate mission land. The first reserve covered the majority of Tsaxis village, however the houses east of the Fort buildings remained on land owned by the HBC.'[17]

1881: Edward Dossetter takes a panoramic photograph of fort and village, the first photograph of Fort Rupert with an unassailable provenance and attribution. Houses rebuilt after the 1863 fire are evident, as are many significant differences in the material and technology of the Kwakiutl settlement.[18]

1886: Land transfer survey completed, making Robert Hunt the owner of land preempted by the HBC. The resulting survey contains several new and important pieces of programmatic and spatial information that can be correlated to other graphic documents.

1888: The last of the early Fort Rupert Kwakiutl Band's reserves are surveyed and formalized, and do not include land occupied by the 'old houses' referred to in the 1886 Hunt survey.

1914: The Provincial government's MacKinnon-McBride Commission hears the land claims of representatives of the Fort Rupert Kwakiutl. Only one of their 24 land claims petitions was honored, either due to the request being 'unreasonable' or because the land in question had become private property.

1919: George Hunt, son of Robert Hunt and Franz Boas's collaborator, makes a census and illustrates it with a plan diagram he titles 'as Fort Rupert was in the year 1866.' (Fig. 13.7)

COLLECTING, SIFTING AND SEEING

The narrative implicit in this timeline was distilled by a review of hundreds of texts, images, and other documents produced over more than seventy years. The first work we undertook was to derive from the images a body of precise measured drawings of changes over time to the settlement at Fort Rupert. To do this, we began by constructing more than two-dozen plates that correlate buildings and time across the photographic record.[19] The plates describe the position of the camera, significant built elements and image provenance. The images traced changes to the HBC fort and Kwakiutl village – changes to and disappearance of buildings, and the construction of new buildings, fortifications and fences, bridges, platforms, public spaces and house poles.

The images led to the creation of phased site plans and other detailed drawings that trace the gradual dissolution of the space of the fort and its merger with the space of the Kwakiutl settlement (Fig. 13.2). All of this

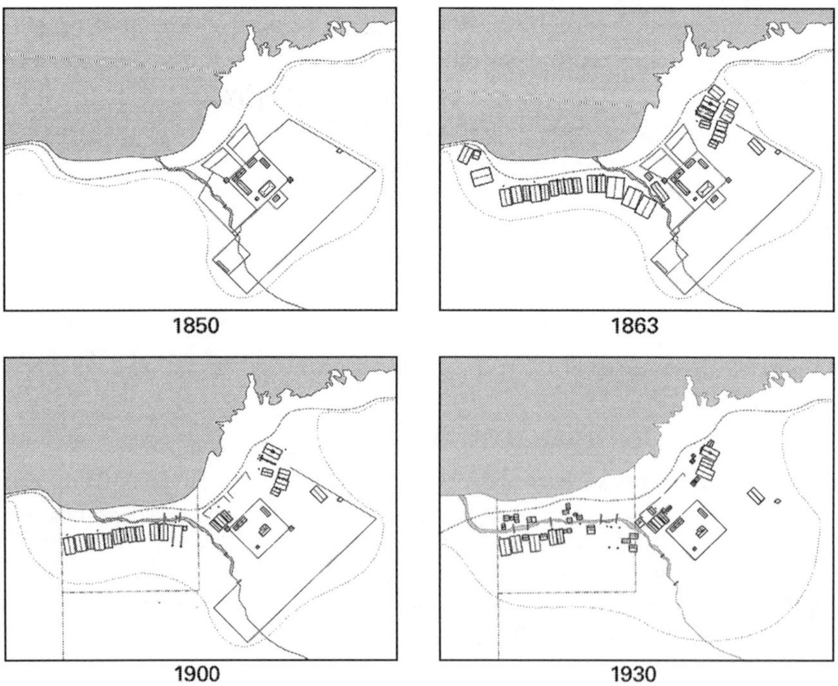

13.2 Diagrams of the settlement at Fort Rupert in 1850, 1863, 1900 and 1930 (drawing by Jenny Xu, Heather Maxwell and author)

work was formatted in a book entitled *Naming and Claiming: The Fort Rupert Reconstruction Project*.[20] The spatial dissolution of fort and village was occurring simultaneously to the hardening of legal distinctions regarding ownership. That photographs by the year 1900 give the appearance of an amalgamated community is therefore very misleading.

As the reconstruction project progressed visual evidence emerged that seemed to support the 'specific claims' litigation of the present-day Band and its legal agents. The reconstruction project led to the explicit question of whether it would be possible to make a case, primarily through precise drawing, that the terms of the Douglas Treaties were not met by the colonial and provincial governments.

'AS FORT RUPERT WAS IN 1866': PREEMPTION, PANORAMA, PORTRAITS, DIAGRAM

Our extended observation of images and other graphic documents allowed us to see change. The problem was how to precisely situate and scale the gradual evolution of the artifacts depicted in the images. Luckily, we had a few vital bits of dimensional information that gave us a scale of comparison, including the dimensions of an important big house, the dimensions of the fort and its buildings and the location of the only extant artifact of the original fort, a large masonry chimney.

Out of the meditative process of simple description, several images emerged that were particularly loaded and potentially open to comparative analysis. Particularly fruitful was comparing the 1863 HBC preemption survey (Fig. 13.3),

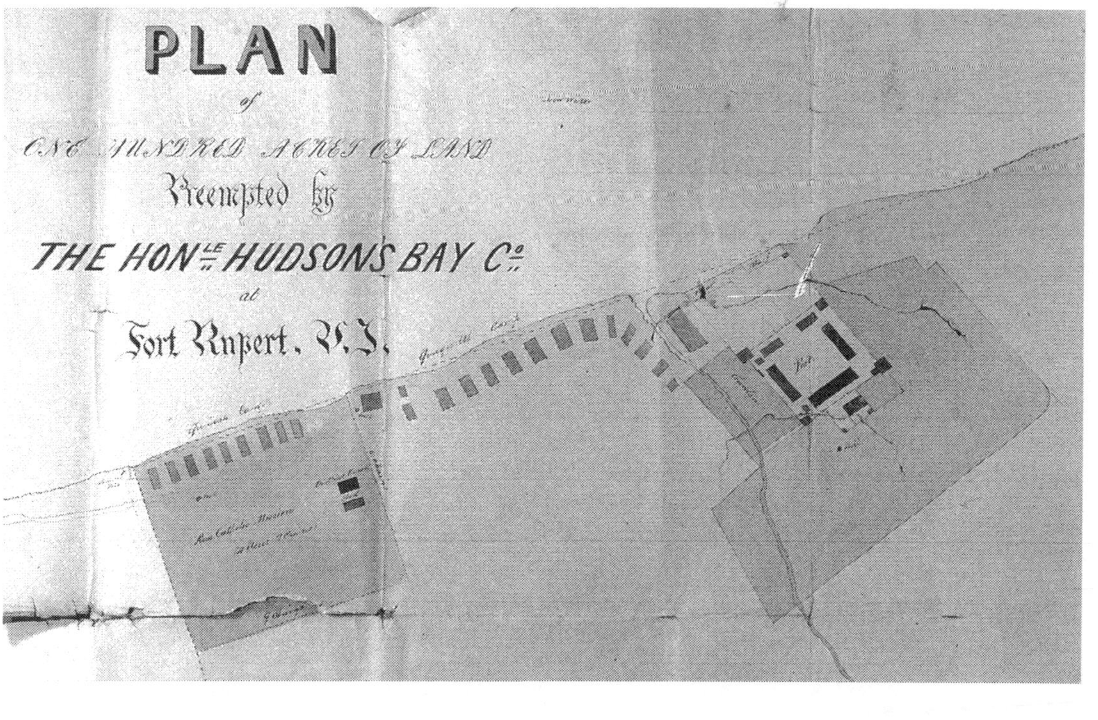

13.3 Plan of One Hundred Acres. Survey by Pym Nevins Compton, 1863 HBCA G.1/231, detail (courtesy of the Hudson's Bay Company Archives, Winnipeg, MB)

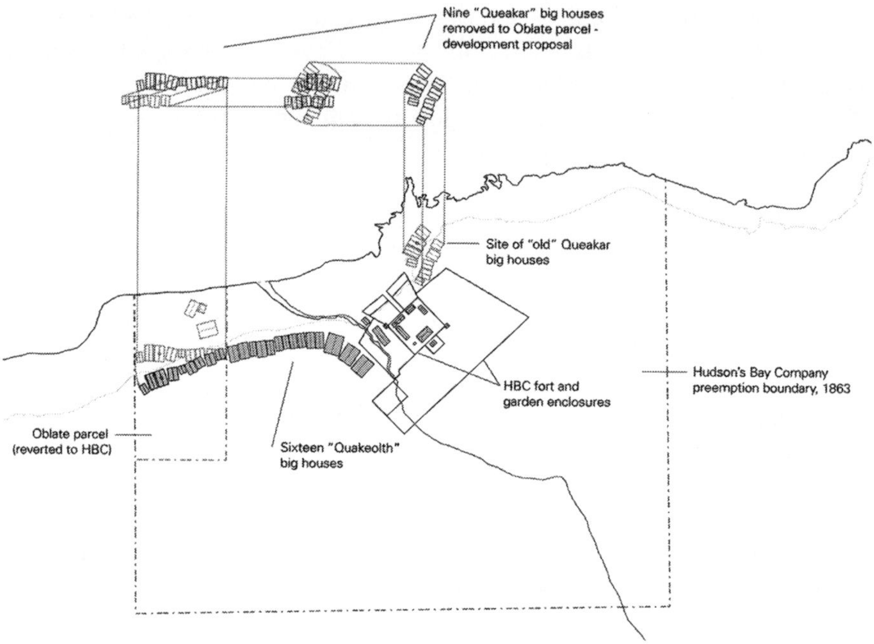

13.4 Diagram of preemption survey and Queackar house relocation (drawing by author)

the *c.* 1864 panorama and group portraits (Figs 13.4 and 13.5), and perhaps most importantly, the 1919 George Hunt sketch 'As Fort Rupert was in 1866' (Fig. 13.6). We will further inspect these images in order of creation, and use Hunt's sketch to bind them together.

The 1863 survey is titled 'Plan, One Hundred Acres of Land, Preempted for The Honourable Hudson's Bay Company, at Fort Rupert V.I.', and indeed, it is a Plan – a plan of action. Without a doubt the graphic data it contains is much more than a simple boundary survey. In addition to describing the dimensions and boundaries of the HBC preemption, the Kwakiutl houses, shoreline, river, wells and other elements of the landscape, the drawing stakes out a four-acre parcel called 'R. C. Mission' that was to become the property of the Catholic Church. Within that parcel are nine houses of the Queackar sept, one of the two Kwakiutl Band Douglas Treaty signatories.

The presence of the nine Queackar houses on the preemption survey begs several questions: Were these houses being relocated, and if so, why? Were the treaty rights of the Queacker family to move with their houses? And regardless of the answer to those questions, why was their proposed relocation integrated into a preemption survey?

That the 1863 survey indicates nine houses were to be relocated to the Roman Catholic mission site sheds light on where in the Kwakiutl village the houses once were. The 1851 Hydrographic Survey shows a long strip of houses to the west of the fort, and five houses to the northeast of the fort (Fig. 13.1). While the line of buildings to the west is represented in the preemption survey, none of the buildings to the northeast are indicated. Their absence suggests that it was these houses that were being relocated to the mission site.

As noted in the timeline, in 1863, a fire destroyed four Queackar houses. No doubt the HBC considered this a serious threat due to the close proximity of the houses to the fort's enclosing wooden walls. The fire occurred just months before the preemption survey was completed, but after HBC officer Finlayson requested it.

This description of *c.* 1863 events suggests that at the time of the preemption the HBC was attempting to relocate the K'umuyoyi to the Roman Catholic parcel as a way to accomplish three things: 1/ Provide a place for those who had lost their homes to rebuild; 2/ Remove the threat of fire to the HBC property; 3/ Increase the distance between the fort and the Kwakiutl houses, reinforcing the 100-acre preemption claim. The so-called preemption survey was really more a proposal for a land exchange, without Queackar property rights part of the bargain.

The *c.* 1864 panorama taken by Frederick Dally (Fig. 13.5) is an extraordinary image, and makes an important contribution to understanding the spatial organization of Fort Rupert at the time of the preemption. The panorama, composed of three separate photographs, is a very early image, taken before the evident use of Western building materials and technologies, and is striking in the contrast of the two cultures it documents.

Seemingly, this image is simply a description of the quotidian – some people sitting or walking along the foreshore escarpment, some preparing food or heating their houses, using fire and creating smoke in the process – a depiction of a day in the life of a Fort Rupert Kwakiutl person. But the image also is a document of a political event – the arrival of a woman in a hoop skirt, welcomed by a group of Kwakiutl who sit on the wharf above her, watched by two guards who stand behind the fort's fenced yard enclosure – a tableau staged for a camera that required its subjects to remain still for half a minute during exposure of the glass plate negative.

But in order to focus on the known facts of the image, coming to understand the motivations for creating such a tableau must unfortunately be left for another

13.5 Panorama of Fort Rupert, V.I., Frederick Dally, *c.* 1864 (courtesy of the Toronto Public Library)

day. Near the centre of the panorama is a large Christian cross, perhaps twenty feet high, located just outside the fort's protective stockade. As described in the timeline, Robert Hunt, the English father of George and an HBC employee, had given Catholic Oblate missionaries, and later, the Anglicans who followed them, a space where the missionaries could educate his children.[21] The Oblates had left in 1865, and were, as discussed above, part of the abandoned three-way development proposition described in the 1863 preemption survey. It is significant that in another image, taken slightly later (*c.* 1869–70) than the panorama and from a similar position, the cross is nowhere to be found.[22]

The foreground of the panorama provides little information, but it is worthy of note. In the foreground, there appear to be piles of earth and light material, probably shells cast off as part of the process of food processing. The earth is certainly disturbed, turned over, but not cultivated. The camera that took the panoramic images is positioned at the place where four houses had recently been destroyed by fire, the place where the K'umuyoyi lived. What we see in the foreground is quite likely the trace of a past fire, and possibly the site of new construction.

REVERSE CAMERA: DALLY'S GROUP PORTRAITS

Two group portraits provide additional facts to bolster the argument that there was a Kwakiutl village on land that was preempted by the HBC. In the background of both (and in the foreground of panorama) is an intact Fort Rupert. This is unlike the state of the fort in Dossetter's 1881 image, by which time much of the fort's enclosure had been removed.[23]

13.6 Group portrait of Fort Rupert Indians and Officers From HMS Scout, Frederick Dally, *c.* 1864 (Image PN 2554 courtesy of the Royal BC Museum, BC Archives)

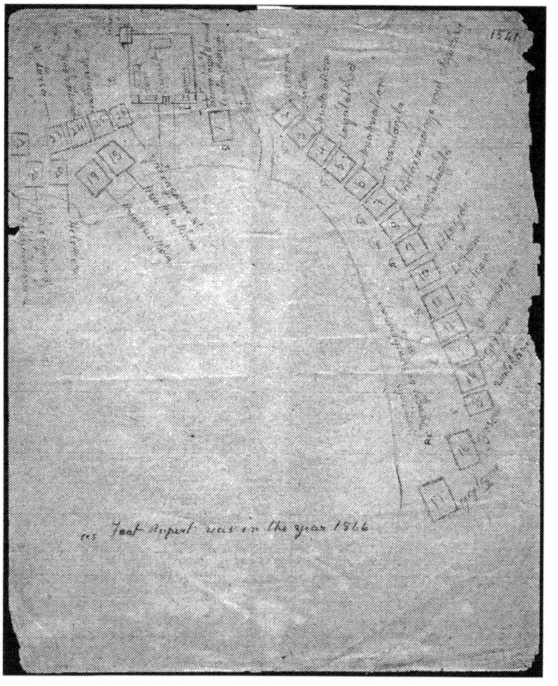

13.7 *As Fort Rupert Was in 1866*, Sketch by George Hunt, 1919 (courtesy of the American Philosophical Society Library, Philadelphia)

To the left of the fort, four light-coloured poles rise. In the second of the group portraits,[24] which is taken from a slightly different vantage point, only a single pole is visible, but in this one a notch is clearly discernible at the top of the pole. These are large posts, perhaps three feet in diameter. The notches are being made to accept very large beams. A big house is being built during the time that this image was taken.

The other notable element in the second of the group portraits appears at the right edge of the image, in the foreground. Visible there are the large-scale planks and binding poles typical of all but one of the row of buildings seen in the panorama. By the time of Dossetter's image, planks and binding poles had been replaced by milled siding. In these earlier images, none of the territory-marking poles evident in the Dossetter image are visible. The fact that the vertical binding poles and large planks are visible in both the panorama and the second group portrait strongly suggest that the three images were taken before the HMS *Clio* shelling.

George Hunt's 1919 census and diagram 'As Fort Rupert Was in 1866' will serve as a coda to the analysis made in this essay. Hunt, who was 65 when he made the drawing in 1919, generated the data from his memory and from information he gathered from others who, like himself, had lived in Fort Rupert in 1866.[25] The census describes in great detail the number and hierarchical structure of Fort Rupert's families in that year as well as the position of their houses relative to other houses and geographical features.

Hunt's diagram is keyed to some twenty pages of notes that Hunt produced for ethnologist Franz Boas that described what Boas called the 'social organization of the Kwakiutl' of Fort Rupert in 1866.[26] In these notes, Hunt identifies nine families, one each for the nine houses he locates northeast of the fort. These families are all of the 'Queackar' (K'umuyoyi) sept.

Despite the fact that Hunt's sketch diagram was made 53 years after the date to which it refers, it is clearly a more accurate description of the physical settlement of fort and Kwakiutl village than is the 1863 preemption survey. Fig. 13.8 illustrates this correlation by superimposing Hunt's numaym (family descent group) data onto the buildings visible in the panorama. Hunt's diagram is not to scale, but it is carefully drawn, and full of demographic information that can be linked to other data. Indeed, the ability to seamlessly map Hunt's data onto the *c.* 1864 panorama gives Hunt's inclusion in his survey of the family houses not seen in the panorama legitimacy, and gives legitimacy to the conclusion that this area of Kwakiutl Fort Rupert was illegally preempted.

13.8 Numayms of Fort Rupert, 1866, detail (photomontage by author)

While this analysis may prove nothing, it implicates a great many acts and people in events of the period of time it addresses. Before, after and during the Hudson's Bay Company preemption in 1863, Kwakiutl signatories of the Fort Rupert Douglas Treaties had built and occupied a settlement at the northeastern flank of a fort. This settlement was erased, and its occupants denied title to property ensured to them by treaty. Whether this violation of the terms of a living treaty will be emended remains to be seen.

This work draws from the forensic, observational methods of art historians and archaeologists to uncover circumstances and the graphic, representational methods of architectural documentation and analysis to visualize them. At the disciplinary core of architecture is the necessity to synthesize socioeconomic structures, technical systems, and physical processes into drawings. But this ability need not be limited to design and building. One may also apply these skills to other aspects of the production of space. Looking comparatively at these photographs and other visual documents has provided just such an alternative – and a way to act on John Berger's thesis about the early use of the camera – that images may conceal acts of injustice through their attempts at recording, reconnaissance and control.

NOTES

1 A note on names: The HBC's Fort Rupert was built within the Kwakwaka'wakw First Nation's traditional territory. Kwakwaka'wakw is the name of an aboriginal 'First Nation' of which the Fort Rupert Kwakiutl Band is a part. The four Kwakwaka'wakw families (septs) who settled at Fort Rupert became known as the Fort Rupert Kwakiutl Band. I will refer to the local Native people as the Kwakiutl when in the context of the people of this community. When referring to a larger scale of territory, I will refer to this group as the Kwakwaka'wakw. Two other key Anglicizations are: Kwaguhl (Quakeolth) and K'umuyo'l (Queackar).

2 Preemption, the word used in the British system for converting land into privately owned property, required the settler to clear land, fence it, to build a house and cultivate a garden before ownership was granted.

3 I owe a methodological debt to Michael Baxandall, whose *Patterns of Intention* (Yale, 1985) taught me to respect the limits of interpretation, to John Berger, whose many works taught me the importance of pushing up against those limits, and to both, for teaching me the pleasure of looking closely at pictures.

4 The contents of this paper have been made available to lawyers representing the Fort Rupert Kwakiutl Band.

5 John Berger, *About Looking* (New York: Pantheon Books, 1980).

6 See Barry Gough, *Gunboat Frontier: British Maritime Authority and Northwest Coast Indians, 1846–90* (Vancouver: UBC Press, 1984), p. 9.

7 The Aboriginal and Northern Affairs Development Canada website maintains a comprehensive record of the 14 Douglas Treaties. This includes a transcription of the 'Conveyance of Land to Hudson's Bay Company by Indian Tribes' document for the Fort Rupert's two treaties. The website URL is http://www.aadnc-aandc.gc.ca/eng/1100100029049/1100100029050.

8 The starkest impact of this difference in conceptualizing property was recorded during the 1914 MacKinnon-McBride Commission's hearing adjudicating Native land claims. At the hearings, the Fort Rupert Kwakiutl petitioned to have 31 (settlement, food harvesting, and burial) sites reserved. By 1914, all of these had been preempted, leading the commission to deny the Kwakiutl petition on all claims.

9 Ibid., p. 75, footnote 266 (BC Archives, HMS *Driver* Correspondence, O/A/D83J, Johnson to Hornby, 21 Jun, 1850. Copy in UBCA, Akrigg Papers, Box 1, file 55, original in NMM; HBCA, B 226/b/7, f 83, Douglas to Blenkinsop, 22 March 1853).

10 Dorothy Blakely Smith (ed.), *The Reminiscences of Doctor John Sebastian Helmcken* (Vancouver: UBC Press, 1975), p. 300.

11 Robert Galois, *The Fort Rupert Band and the Fort Rupert Treaties: A Report Prepared for Mandell Pinder,* April 2009, footnote 453. Galois is also author of *Kwakwaka'wakw Settlements, 1775–1920: A Geographical Analysis and Gazetteer* (Seattle: University of

Washington Press, 1994), widely considered the definitive geographical history of the Kwakwaka'wakw Nation.

12 Galois (2009): 'Four Indian houses were burnt to the ground … [and] A great deal of property was consumed.' *Victoria Daily Colonist,* 14 Sept, 1863.

13 An 1857 survey, done to inventory HBC assets at Fort Rupert, indicated that the entire fort and grounds comprised only 8 acres, not 100, as requested by Finlayson.

14 A.G. Morice, *History of the Catholic Church in Western Canada: from Lake Superior to the Pacific (1659–1895)* (Toronto: Musson Book Co., 1910), p. 330.

15 Transcript, Statement of Lieutenant Carey, R.N. H.M.S. *Clio*. BC Archives Microfilm #B1349, F1208a.

16 From Dwight L. Smith (ed.), *A Tour of Duty in the Pacific Northwest: E.A. Porcher and H.M.S. Sparrowhawk, 1865–1868* (Fairbanks: University of Alaska Press, 2000), p. 50.

17 Galois (2009), p. 140.

18 The image (BC Archives call no. B-03566) may be viewed online at the Royal British Columbia Museum's BC Archives.

19 I would like to thank my research assistants, James Eidse, Amaury Greig, Aaron Knorr, Heather Maxwell, Ouri Scott, and especially Jenny Xu, who provided valuable insights and produced much of the graphic work of the reconstruction project.

20 This work was produced under a Memorandum of Understanding with the Band, stipulating that any work produced would be the property of the Band. Several copies of the manuscript are now in the possession of the Band's elders and teachers, as are copies of this paper.

21 See note 12.

22 This later image is in the collection of the Alexander Turnbull Library, Wellington, NZ. Cat. No. PA1-f-021-071-8.

23 See note 15.

24 This image (BC Archives call no. C-05561) may be viewed online at the Royal British Columbia Museum's BC Archives.

25 Judith Berman, 'The Collectors: Hunt and Boas', in *Gateways: Exploring the Legacy of the Jesup North Pacific Expedition, 1897–1902*, ed. Igor Krupnik and William W. Fitzhugh, Contributions to Circumpolar Anthropology, No. 1 (Washington DC: Smithsonian Institution, 2001), pp. 190–95.

26 Franz Boas, *The Social Organization and the Secret Societies of the Kwakiutl Indians* (New York: Johnson Reprint Corp., 1970), pp. 330–32.

14

Repurposing With A Vengeance: A Dance of Restrained Acts Towards Justice

Catherine Hamel

A CALL TO JUSTICE. A CALL THAT IS ALWAYS WOUNDED.[1]

Justice is a complex topic with numerous incisions into space. This paper explores the potential for justice through subtle disturbances. It is a potential to instigate change, not by altering existing systems, but the attitudes towards them. They are intrusions that impact the spaces we inhabit but do not define themselves by it. Unlike the built forms that generally define architecture, these intrusions allow themselves to be diluted in their endeavor to reposition justice in the public realm. The framing narrative stems from the meeting of a Rwandan journalist and the narrator. A fleeting and slight occurrence, insubstantial in the public history of genocide and ensuing attempts of justice through acts such as the Gacaca Courts, it nevertheless allows the attitude to seep into a different stance. Personal contact and personal forgiveness invite considerations beyond the more overt retributive justice that the context can propel.

A series of examples, intentionally subtle in the face of the overwhelming violent narrative are proposed as possible ways into negotiations of justice in space. Classified, the examples are a vessel of conversation; a receiving surface; a vessel of condensation; and a bridging surface. They are not limited to war and the environment but relate to the context of crossing borders of imposed political segregation and setting boundaries of social consideration. These examples are fragile, for many perhaps too quiet to be heard, or merely a drone of background noise. The initial narrative and its turbulent context directed the examples through contrast and provide the opportunity for a form of spatial exploration in which justice might be negotiated in space.

VIOLENCE, A HOME IS TAKEN BRICK BY BRICK
A TREATY, A HOME IS RETURNED BRICK BY BRICK

In an apartment embedded in a concrete and glass city where the only soil that is exposed is quickly removed for the untidiness it represents, a sole painting hangs.

The importance of the selection of this solitary image is undermined by the casual slant that defies the right angles of its hosting wall. The brush strokes are rough and betray the attempt of a novice who painstakingly tried. There is beauty in its raw quality. The image as a composition is simple. The picture displays a hill covered in green vegetation with a gouge revealing red soil. In the vicinity lays a chaotic pile of bricks – clay, compressed and torched. There is no title. There is no hint of location. The fleeting voice of the painting's owner discloses, *this is my home in Rwanda.*[2]

The appropriation of homes in war is a thread in the bolder appropriation of land. Structures undergo varying levels of destruction. Some structures are razed while others have their decay accelerated to evict the owners then halted for their eroded space to be occupied by uninvited guests. These guests appear and disappear as the lines of confrontation shift engulfing them in one enemy territory or another. In cases where the lines of confrontation recede and the houses are returned, a destroyed version or at least a foundation remains. Often a trace remains. What strikes one in this painting is the full erasure of the original home. There is but a gouge revealing red soil and in the vicinity the chaotic pile of bricks. This had been a large homestead, not a small structure easily moved. In violence, the home was taken brick by brick. A treaty was signed after agreement at the conclusion of political negotiations. It attempted to guarantee the security of the people and their property. This included the return of what was taken.[3] A home was returned brick by brick.

The return of the home as a pile of bricks! Though the scale differs, though the actors differ, there is commonality in the scripts with the contamination of water that flows; the discarding of deforested land; the abandonment of depleted soil; the return of carcasses where once was flesh. There is commonality in the violence of material profitability and its indifference to how it affects certain social realities. This story and its wounded space expose acts of violence and material repurposing. It is not war and the relentless assault on humans that is of interest, but the parallel with material appropriation in the environment in the judicial systems at play. Environmental repurposing with a vengeance, less blunt but not necessarily less barbaric. These words attempt to build a mental stepping-stone in a torrent of survival, of greed, of appropriation. A stepping stone that often sinks (an argument lost) and resurfaces (an incoherent island). It is a way of knowledge formation towards the hope to collaborate, to provoke towards a reflective understanding that will lead to actions that instill the quest for justice.

LESS A QUESTION THAN A SERIES OF QUESTIONS LESS AN ARGUMENT THAN A STRING OF OBSERVATIONS THE SUBJECT OF THESE WORDS IS A CONFESSION OF BEWILDERMENT[4]

The act of hanging this painting instigates an interest in restrained acts towards justice. The term justice is used with a conscious awareness of a limited understanding of its connotations. The structure of this act gives form to something that has not been distilled enough and still difficult to narrate clearly should all its implications be considered. A line is drawn and a dance occurs within its confines: a home taken and the implications of the form in which it is returned.

The structure of the story is used to give form to the search into the potential role of the spaces we build as facilitators of justice. The acts within the story itself expand the dialogue to include spaces shaped by people, not just architects. This also serves as a way to constrain the scale, to give freedom to the time frame of the existence of these spaces and the process in whish they come to be. Architecture, in its most generic understanding, is too often framed with lines that are rigid, aggressive, imposing. Large in scale and pretentiously even larger in intent, it tends to be planned to respond to the magnitude of the investment and the needs of the multifaceted collaborations. Its claim to concepts such as human rights, ethics, and justice exist fluidly in the realm of words but are not easily given form. Certain possibilities remain outside the conversations that consume architecture and dwell in the silences of its peripheral and underlying implications – in the spaces that may not be intended or precise. It is in imprecision that sometimes promise lies.

The act of painting, hanging and repeatedly viewing this painting charts vulnerable lines that exhale and are not afraid to dissipate to allow for their repercussions to emerge. Lines that can be subtle, delicate wondering. Working towards a potential consequence of justice not a defined space for justice, the words that follow emerge from silence and end in silence with no claim to offer solutions through architecture to reach a just society. The potential for justice stems from Walter Benjamin's premise in 'Critique of Violence',[5] that generalizations are contradicted in issues of justice and the possibility that law could be viewed as a series of negotiations. The context of a possible justice arises and justice as law is replaced by a call for justice.[6] The answer to this call is studied in moments and acts that demonstrate these negotiations in space, infectious subtle spatial and material intrusions that disperse and affect the quest for justice. It is a dance in that shapes appear and disappear. Concepts are confronted momentarily only to be escaped as they become too near. It is a dance as there is something to listen to as a way to respond, and something to escape as a way to survive.

I SPEAK OF THE HOUSE, A HOME TODAY, AND TOMORROW, STOLEN, RESURRECTED AS A RUIN[7]

Repurposing with a vengeance. Why vengeance? Has something been violently taken away and given new purpose that inflicts punishment or retribution for an injury by someone? Repurposing is a form of recycling that is focused on finding new uses for items that are already present rather than discarding them. The idea of repurposing can include making modifications to the items or simply finding new use without changing any of the physical aspects. A brick still remains a brick, a unit, multiplied and mortared, still makes a wall. New use has not been specified. The variation lives in the space the walls enclose. It is the life that inhabits that suffers the inflictions. There is an obvious violence in the act of taking, and an ever more poignant brutality in the act of the return. Some humans have an aptitude for ferocity. Others retain tremendous patience in vulnerability. If justice is a series of negotiations, where do conversations occur between the fangs of the wolf and the sumptuous flesh of the sheep? In the silence that follows the conversations…

There is a saying in the French language that rivals dwell on opposite banks. They do not run around in the open countryside. They are cautiously separated by water.[8] While, we can by treaty, seek a process of justice and restoration; it seldom speaks for those who know the experience of the painful assault. A pile of bricks on the land, it is that place, it is that material but it is not that fabrication that was lived in and shared. A brick, a unit in a wall, it held a unit in a life. In speaking of bringing to justice the wolf that has eaten the sheep, there is a betrayal of sides being chosen. Was not the sheep a wolf in disguise? Had they not been in such desperation and limited means, they would not have taken the brick. Is their desperation a justification for their act? And so the river flows, and separation is imposed with a succession of dams and a complicated arrangement of wickets and the gap between the different categories prohibits crossings.[9]

When blood has flown and its stain remains visible, negotiations are too easily hindered by the reactionary blame. It is not justice but bitter anger that often speaks. Distance dilutes the immediacy of blame.[10] Yet it is the warmth of the spilled blood and the threat of more that brings rivals to the table. Past violence rests in forged peace. It is a forgetfulness that leads to stagnation, the kind that war propels. It festers enough to erupt more violence but not enough to instigate action. *A relevant interlude*: After the treaty was signed, the brick was not the only material returned. People speak of instances where strangers disrobed in public as enforcers of law walked by. A parallel story lingers of the man who received his wife's dress as another woman unclothed in fear in front of him, running in skin, nothing but her pure skin sewn by Mother Nature. She was leaving the dress she had repurposed behind. I spoke of the return of carcasses where once was flesh. A story also lingers in the return of the dress that disrobed the carcass. Is it not worth considering such moments in the way we toil the land? Who is taking, what is the violence inflicted, not in the taking, but in the giving back? What is the relevance of skinning the land for the architect? The underlying question is the relevance and role of the architect when the land is being skinned. What can be done should they acknowledge their complicity in the situation that propels pillaging of some for the profit of others? The architect, a mere builder with good intentions, can be the wolf that knows he can devour the lamb and chooses not to. What space can move us towards justice through negotiations that occur outside political grounds in the simple and chaotic, the quiet and the vocal, acts of people?

IVAR AND ASTRID RAISE ARCHITECTURES, CUBES OF ECHOES, WEIGHTLESS FORMS. SOME THEY CALL POEMS, OTHERS DRAWINGS, OTHERS, CONVERSATIONS[11]

Spatial conversations, some might rant about the inaccuracy of these words. Space does not speak and conversations need language. Yet in their imprecision they provoke the idea of a dialogue between fissures that might receive subtle intrusions that allow justice to be negotiated in space. Is it not the intrusion that causes the crack? It is perhaps too violent a consequence for the negotiation that leans towards collaboration. Patient and doubtful acts that navigate but do not propel the action of others; acts in space that question; acts in space that provoke; acts in space that invite. They often dissolve into the oblivion of a forgotten past and do not need to shriek to be heard. Four such voices are temporary observed. They are generous invitations for another to respond. Subtle, they claim space as they harden into surfaces, defy fear even at the threat of death, break a silence they choose to hear. It is the quality of the interaction between the act and its consequence that is of interest.

The emphasis in these examples is on the character of the act or the interaction, not the physical object. It takes on the character of a performance in that context, no content provided. The more traditional way of making in which a creator deposits an expressive content into a physical object to be withdrawn later by a consumer, is replaced with a process of dialogue and collaboration. It is a means to encourage the ability to speak and listen outside the tensions that surround the typical interactions.[12] These examples, an art project, and three people propelled spaces, range and are not limited to war and the environment. Two of the examples speak of vessels, one anchored, the other moving. The other two speak of surfaces, one bridging, and the other receiving. One vessel and one surface relate to the context of continuously crossing borders and boundaries of imposed political segregation. The other two halt intrusions to allow transformation. They all quietly endeavor to reposition justice in the public realm.

TO BE A TRESPASSER IN A WORD OF SYSTEMS

This first example is a receiving surface on which footprints dissolve into dust. They are feet that move across lines of confrontation in Beirut, Lebanon. Based on vernacular hearsay of the aunt who knew the sister who heard of the daughter who dared, this is an instance that speaks of a leak in the divide of the city of Beirut, Lebanon, during the 1975–90 war. It was a context where fighting shifted for years and mapping the city was a daily exercise for its inhabitants. Among these fluid allegiances and violence, the cut of the 'Green Line', the largest divider that tore the city remained a constant. The neutrality of the subdivided ideological territories relied on the non-porous nature of their containment. There were leaks, as individuals vary in their viscosity. The main road next to the National Museum came to be called the 'museum passage' because it was the main communication route between both parts of the city. People crossed for many reasons: to work, to visit, to get married. The passage was also crossed as an act of defiance by the few, mostly women, who refused to fall prey to the situation. They crossed just because they could. Back and forth, they went behind enemy territory, an act of will to defy the forced political segregation. These trespassers seeped in and contaminated the hatred with their humanity. Unstable links, there was faith in their persistence even though their acts left faint traces that could easily be erased. They were markers in the space of the city, moving targets that refused to be anchored on a map. Their footsteps agitated the dust, temporarily.[13]

The vessel of condensation refers to the moving buses that drone across sectarian lines in Ireland. Known as The Route Project, it was organized over a series of exchanges between those seeking to record through words, film, objects and the people driving the buses across that country's lines of confrontation. The initial exchange occurs between the bus drivers recounting the experiences of driving across sectarian lines and the writers, filmmakers, and artists who heard and recorded. Though each bus driver had different loyalties, their professional identification reconciled their differences. The dilution of rejection towards acceptance was embodied in the spatial movement of their buses across the dividing lines of the city. The project set out to preserve and valorize the historical culture of reconciliation among drivers, but it also sought to 're-purpose' this accumulated knowledge, to learn from it, and to apply its lessons in the context of present day struggles to mediate the nascent peace process.[14]

The wind blew and the footprints were erased. The bus crossed but for an instance and disappeared into the other side. The negotiations exist in the stories, in the defiance, in the courage, in the myth. They inhabit the single body that can be an effective obstruction against the rage of military imposition. Knowledge arises from the threat of these 'trespassers without visas, anomalies, mistakes, deviations of the imagination'.[15] In receding behind enemy territory and returning alive, these periodic crossers of the borders of segregation show that the beast that had been demonized could be touched, conversed with, humanized. The motion of their bodies, raw or armored in metal, cut a connection in space. It is an exchange of values carved out with their defiance. A transfer occurs from objectified information to contact, from a common public heritage to individual exchange. Opposition takes the form of resistance to the systems of knowledge and the institutions that regulate the population. It displaces the cultural memory by contaminating, an impurity in the war order of the city.

DO NOT TRESPASS

Whereas the receiving surface in Beirut offers possibility in the memory engrained in each grain of sand, the tenacity of dust lingers in the bridging surface of YWCA Police Station Desk in Peru. The goal of the project was to teach women their rights and not accept discrimination. This was promoted through the creation of a desk in a police station. The women's desk in the police station was to help guarantee that the women who came with a complaint when abused would be heard and legally advised. By knowing that they will have a sympathetic ear as opposed to one that will reject and mock them, women are able to denounce domestic violence and if necessary get shelter.

The police station, an emblem of security is the fraught space of potential mockery for the feminine body in some cultures. Injustice imposed. Abused, she might seek shelter only to be further vilified by the very face of authority she sought shelter with. A thought, a space receives a designated table for a designated user. A man who can receive the possible reality of the abused feminine body mans a table. The simple guarantee that the policeman behind that surface will not mock; will believe; will question him who has violated; not her who was violated. A seemingly small gesture, an opening allowed in a conversation where words are received and potential equilibrium is restored. It is a fragile equilibrium, or merely the hope of it as no words heal the bruises. A negotiation towards, not a solution. A subtle but stubborn contamination. The one who used to receive the cries and mock them has been withdrawn.

Minute, small, even seemingly insignificant and fragile gestures can erode larger systems. A few conversations and housing policy is altered. Not architectural style, but space inhabited. Such was the outcome of the vessel of conversation, a boat used in the project by the Austrian Art collective WochenKlausur entitled Intervention To Aid Drug Addicted Women in Switzerland. The task of this project was simple: to have a conversation as an intervention in drug policy. The topic of this conversation was the difficult situation faced by drug addicts who had turned to prostitution to support their habits. A boat on Lake Zurich, a series of three hour cruises, and a sign that spelled the command: do not trespass, conversation in progress. This was its most aggressive order. These floating dialogues were organized between key political figures and some of the women who suffered the predicament. In the ritualistic context of an art event, with their statements insulated from media scrutiny, a new communication emerged.[16] One of the outcomes was a change in housing policy and the creation of a boarding house where these young women could seek refuge away from the violent attacks of their clients. Justice? Some might argue that this merely enables the wolf disguised as a sheep to prosper. Where does the blame begin, and hence the injustice? Justice cannot be calculated but momentarily. They are prostitutes, many said. They are women, others responded. They are human. Do not trespass. A space of protection is architecture.

WHY DOES HE MAKE ME SPEAK WITH YOUR TONGUE?

These acts create turbulence in the order imposed. Turbulence is intermittent, in its very definition and in its presence, in its nature and in its distribution. It is multiplicity before reaching unity. It has gaps. It has margins. It is riddled with exceptions.[17] Turbulence is created between the state of tolerance and its counterpart. Too subtle for most, the potential nevertheless persists. In their act, rather than accepting the closure of identity, these acts sought to open up the boundaries of conformity. With resolve they exposed the possibilities contained in diversity. It is a knowledge that dislodges people from their false sense of security. These acts open up the possibilities of indeterminacy. Indeterminacy as an expressive achievement rather than blind chaos, an achievement in experience requiring will, resolve and judgment.[18] It is not the number of bodies that follow these passages that matter. One, two, a hundred, none. The idea of an imaginary trespasser or the stopping of an aggressive intruder, is enough to dissolve the aggressive container. It is possibility that perpetuates knowledge. It is knowledge that perpetuates the possibility of negotiation.[19]

PAINTING HAS ONE FOOT IN ARCHITECTURE AND THE OTHER IN DREAMS[20]

Act one: a man lives the consequences of human horror, paints a piece of his testimony and hangs the painting to remember. He does not seek revenge. Act two: the woman asks, listens to his testimony and imagines the story. She retells the story already told, in a new language, to learn from the translation. She does not seek to solve a problem. She does not pretend to offer a solution. They both bear witness, hanging fully neither to tragedy nor paralysis, but the impossible bravery and willingness to live and listen with a courageous hope in a tragic world. The task is rife with failure. It is in that very moment of failure that the act of translation occurs, and hence possibly understanding.[21]

Does this recourse to performing testimony, of telling and witnessing, imply that we are in danger of contemplation that somehow betrays the urgency to act on the depicted horror? 'Why do you keep watch, while the human tribe sleeps across the earth, indifferent to misfortunes, to wars, to joys, to massacres? Asked the watcher. There has to be someone, Kafka answers, watchers, prophets of the present, agents for the most arduous, most dangerous cause.'[22]

What does it mean to do this in concrete terms: to give more than to take, to listen more than to speak; to speak to start a dialogue, not just to be heard; to intervene in places of fear and horror? To witness, bravely and merely to witness though the possibility of being a savior is nowhere near. 'In the task of living these things, where is the dignity in failure, the beauty in a ridiculous hope?'[23]

THOUGHT WITH A GUN AND A HUMAN AIM

In the face of an overwhelming sense of impossibility, sometimes it takes a doubt, to trace and retrace what cannot be captured. To attempt to envision a shift outside the boundaries within which we exist. To still be able to be thrilled by inquiry, not certitude within the systems that allow no variation. To envision a shift from the series of events, of policies, of laws that work to hold our system within a defined, bounded reality.[24]

A brick, multiplied and mortared and then there is a life that is enclosed. The spaces we inhabit are not neutral. They offer possibilities. They betray prejudices. They segregate by imposing division. They liberate by allowing their transformation. Negotiations in space can occur regardless of the space. They can occur despite of the space. They can occur precisely because of the nature of the space. They start in words and convert to form. It is sometimes the form that creates the words. If justice cannot be calculated, but is always sought, the environment we build and inhabit converses in seeking it. An aggressive context can be sedated. A serene situation aroused. A painting hangs. Not merely to be viewed. A painting on the wall, it is a story. It did not know it was a story to be told.

NOTES

1 Jacques Derrida, 'Force of Law: The Mystical Foundation of Authority', in Gil Anidjar (ed.), *Acts of Religion* (London, 2002), p. 257.

2 The conflict in Rwanda is not the theme of this paper and the specific reasons and details are beyond its scope. Experts differ as to the relative importance of different causes for the disputes. Poverty, land scarcity, population growth, environmental trends, unequal land distribution, are debated as factors at varying degrees. The common thread recognized by all is the important role that was played by competition for land and resources in fuelling the conflict.

3 The treaty referred to is the Peace Agreement between the Government of the Republic of Rwanda and the Rwandese Patriotic Front. It notes the Protocol of Agreement on the Rule of Law signed at Arusha in 1992 to repatriate and reintegrate all Rwandese refugees who may wish to go back home guaranteeing the security of all the people and their property.

4 Alberto Manguel, *The City Of Words* (Toronto, 2007), p. 3.

5 Walter Benjamin, 'Critique of Violence', in *Selected Writing*, vol. 1, 1913–26 (Cambridge MA, 1996), p. 247.

6 Derrida, 'Force of Law', p. 257.

7 The phrase is an adaptation of Paz's poem 'I speak of the city,' in Octavio Paz, in Eliot Weinberger (ed.), *The Collected Poems of Octavio Paz: 1957–1987* (New York, 1987), p. 511.

8 Michel Serres, *Genesis*, trans. James, G. and Nielson (Ann Arbor MI, 1995), p. 94.

9 Serres, *Genesis*, p. 94. 'Classing is a succession of dams, a complicated arrangement of wickets, hierarchy is semi conductive, the gap between subsets prohibits crossings, classing is there to disarm, to slow momentum, be it creative or destructive, who can tell, to cool down its heatedness or slacken its celerity, complex classing encumbers the bed of violence, or else, I can't choose, classing is formed by violence and the disorderly course of its flux, violence deposits it as a river lays down in passing its heavy or final alluvial deposits, it deposits it, codes it structures it, makes it, it looses some of its virulence along the circuitous route of its products. The gravel comes to a standstill in the flux and in return, the flux comes to a standstill amidst the gravel. Violence makes the classes and the classes unmake violence.'

10 This concept for the need for distance is based on Slavoj Zizek's discussion of subjective and objective violence, and the 'systemic' violence of the catastrophic consequences of the functioning of the economic political systems, in Slavoj Zizek *Violence: Six Sideways Reflections* (New York, 2008).

11 Octavio Paz, in Weinberger, *The Collected Poems of Octavio Paz*, p. 531.

12 Grant Kester, *Conversation Pieces: Community and Communication in Modern Art* (California, 2004), p. 3.

13 Catherine Hamel, 'The National Museum of Beirut: Crossing into a Border', in Andreas Broeckmann and Gunalan Nadarajan (eds), *Place Studies in Art, Media, Science and*

Technology: Historical Investigations on the Sites and the Migration of Knowledge (Germany, 2009), p. 260.

14 Kester, *Conversation Pieces*, p. 8.

15 Hélêne Cixous, *Stigmata: Escaping Texts* (London, 1998), p. 177.

16 Kester, *Conversation Pieces*, p. 3.

17 Serres, *Genesis*, p. 111.

18 Richard Sennett, *The Conscience of the Eye: The Design and Social Life of Cities* (New York, 1990), p. 173.

19 Hamel, 'The National Museum of Beirut', p. 260.

20 Paz, *The Collected Poems*, p. 591.

21 Julie Salversons, 'Taking liberties: a theatre class of foolish witnesses', *Research in Drama Education*, vol. 13, no. 2 (June 2008): 246.

22 Cixous, *Stigmata*, p. 177.

23 Salversons, 'Taking Liberties', p. 245.

24 Frances Westley, Brenda Zimmerman and Michael Quinn Patton, *Getting To Maybe: How the World is Changed* (Toronto, 2006).

PART 4
Philosophical Questions of Propriety

15

Architecture, Justice, Conflict, Measure

Peter Carl

In the simplest possible terms, justice refers to fairness, equity, balance among people and between people and reality as a whole. Accordingly it appears at the opposite extremes of human existence. On the one hand, it appears as a principle of order, as the nature of order itself, as that which names the working-out of reality's infinite processes on behalf of a (usually beneficent) higher purpose or destiny. On the other hand, justice appears to be at the disposal of our freedom, appealing to our altruism, generosity, sense of fairness.

It is not obvious that architecture and justice are related to each other. Buildings or settings devoted to judgement or punishment, however important or richly symbolic in their own right, would seem to be secondary interpretations of the promise that architecture itself might somehow embody a theme as grand as justice. The more recent concern for social justice, inevitably derived from John Rawls, would seek to establish a reasonable (rational) basis for ensuring that the disadvantaged or disenfranchised are not excluded from, for example, adequate housing.[1] This would seem to imply an urban organism which might embody social justice, perhaps to be called a eu-topia; but I am not aware of such a speculation (although all projects make claims in this direction). A bit like the disembodied world in which Jurgen Habermas's intersubjective communication takes place,[2] debates within social justice seem to concentrate on laws, or theories of just action.[3]

However, it does appear that what might be termed 'the spatialisation of justice' was of some significance during the emergence of the Greek polis. Within the struggle to find a just democratic order, the theme of order became attracted to geometric and spatial metaphors derived from the practico-symbolic inheritance, as part of the style of reflection on the nature of reality that became philosophy. With the advent of the Hellenistic culture radiating from Alexandria, and the establishment of geometry as an internally-consistent apodictic discipline, the earlier speculation became flattened to the instrumentalisation of geometry in mechanics, statics, perspective, as it is seen in Vitruvius.

THE PRACTICO-SYMBOLIC INHERITANCE

The emergence of law within cities in the late third millennium BCE represents a proto-philosophic understanding rooted in an evolving urban praxis. Growing out of such phenomena as custom elevated to ceremony and ritual, personal contracts, trade agreements, the standardisation of weights and measures, and supported by the elaborate ritual and administrative apparatus of the temple-palace, the establishment of law requires thematizing the city, or kingdom, as a whole, at a level that transcends, and claims, all particular individuals. This degree of objectivity is most succinctly represented in an elaborate *kudurru*, or boundary stone, from the Kassite period.[4] A *kudurru* is a stone inscribed with an invocation to preserve the boundary which it marks, although this example is missing its inscription, having only the preparatory guide-lines. Between what appear to be the two halves of the serpent Tiamat (cleft in two by Marduk in the Babylonian version of the cosmogony recounted in the *enuma elish*) is a crenelated city-wall with towers and above that, two rings of images: the lower depicts animals and musicians, probably a festival, whereas the upper is symbolic, depicting altars and deities. The *kudurru* is evidently stratified from temporal to eternal, with an emphasis upon motifs, like the wall and the (missing) legal text, that invoke permanence. Between the two halves of Tiamat, one moves upwards from the contingent temporality of the city (and legal text) to festival time, repeatable and offering communication between gods and humans, to the eternal domain of gods; and at the very top are the remains of a solar bull, as if to invoke the entire cosmic order.[5] This indicates that such an order was possible to conceive at this time,[6] although 'cosmos' as a concept, referring to all of reality (not just astronomy, as at present), will emerge only a millennium later, legendarily with Pythagoras.

An explicit relation between architecture and justice is to be found in the investiture scene atop the Stele of Hammurabi,[7] whose general formulation follows the Code of Ur-Nammu, of approximately 250 years earlier. About half a millennium before Moses received the commandments from Yahweh on Mt. Sinai, Hammurabi was depicted receiving a measuring-rod and knotted chord from the solar deity, Shamash. Hammurabi's sculptor drew upon a Mesopotamian topos that appears in reliefs, cylinder seals and even murals.[8] The prologue to the code serves as a caption to this image, in which the structure of a just kingdom is outlined: Hammurabi is appointed by Shamash to protect the meek, serve the gods, defend the peace. The primary motif is that of measure, evident in the economy of infringements and punishments. For example, item 228 specifies that the architect of a house for a noble shall recompense a collapse causing death with his own.

The measuring-rod appears to be about two cubits in length and the cord is assumed to be knotted to produce a right angled triangle; the belatedly-named Pythagorean Triangle was well known in Babylonia and Egypt, but as discrete cases, not as a theorem.[9] These implements produce 'right' measure distributed spatially. The knotted cord implies an emphasis upon right-angled corners, and indeed one finds that corners are symbolically important, where votive deposits are regularly found (including set-squares and plaques depicting the ruler as hod-carrier). The use of 'four corners' to describe the full extent of an empire or of reality seems to have been interchangeable with 'four quarters', Christ is characterised as cornerstone in the New Testament,[10] and of course we still have cornerstone-laying ceremonies. Finally, 'architecture' in these contexts comprises mostly city-walls (and gates, where justice would be enacted), and, with the exception of the ziggurat, the *interiors* of temples and temple-palace compounds (the less ceremonial buildings would be constructed by developers and builders). The importance of these principal edifices is evident in their sheer scale (the main temples and the palace compound at Ur occupy nearly 40 per cent of the area within the walls), in the amount of resources, both human and material, devoted to their construction, in the precision, lavishness and subtlety of their design and ornamentation and in the rich metaphors in the texts which fuse the concrete and divine milieux.[11] Too often written off as manifestations of prestige and power (as if corporate headquarters), these configurations may be understood as pre-conceptual interpretations, rooted entirely in the practico-symbolic domain, of the order of reality. The Giparku at Ur,[12] for example, shows a structured hierarchy of parts within a whole that will not appear conceptually, and certainly not thematised as 'geometry', for a millennium and a half.

'Measure' in such contexts connotes not only precision, but also decorum (as in the right size of a door for a god, for a king, for a lesser person), rightness of relationships (which, much later, will become the analogical structure of geometry), practical efficacy in building, and, in varying degrees depending on local circumstances, resonance with weights and measures, with the rhythmic aspects of poetry, ritual, music and dance – echoed in writing and its discipline as well as in bureaucratic and military protocol – and, ultimately, with the regular (cyclic) temporalities of celestial phenomena. The knotted cord and staff do not 'represent' this cluster of phenomena (no contemporary text joins them all in this way) so much as they participate in it, and have the additional value of joining authority/responsibility with making/ordering the contexts propitious for communication between gods and humans. In other words, what is most important is the identification of the space between Shamash and Hammurabi with instruments of just measure that are themselves concerned with spatial ordering. It implies that the order of reality is a gift bestowed by a highest (celestial) god, which contains within it the basis for communication between finite humans and the eternal order (of Being), and that this lies at the heart of any conception of a 'just' world or realm.

THE GREEK POLIS, THE AMBIGUITY OF 'GEOMETRY'

It is only in the post-Hellenistic, and particularly post-Renaissance, conditions of perspectivity that this group of themes might be generalised as geometry and inspire the plans and elevations of buildings. As already hinted, there are many proto-geometric phenomena, particularly in ritual/ceremonial settings, the sizes and dimensions of customary use, ornament, architecture, construction, surveying, taxation/tithes, astronomy, etc. in the millennia prior to the advent of proper geometry with Euclid, in the fourth century BCE.[13] Accordingly, any attempt to discover geometric orders in architecture prior to the generation of Euclid must be treated with extreme scepticism, and the ready association of geometry with 'order' still deployed by architects deserves similar qualification. Indeed, it is probably safe to say that the conceptual power of geometry as a framework for a particular kind of ordering has so captivated the imagination as to invert the proper understanding – for most people, it is a question of what the geometry 'represents'; and for such people, the geometry is secure and all other meanings are contingent. Under these conditions, any profound relation to justice has been reduced to iconography.

In order to appreciate how this conceptual flattening was achieved, it is necessary to recall the famous Anaximander Fragment, from about a millennium after Hammurabi, at the beginning of the period in which 'cosmos' attains conceptual status. This arises within the Ionian speculations on *physis*, which already with Anaximander attracts geometrical and mathematical motifs. Here 'origin' is meant ontologically (not historically) and is endowed with a 'where', anticipating the Heideggerian interpretation of *Dasein*, 'there-being':

> *The origin from which things/beings come-to-be,*
> *must be also where they pass away*
> *according to necessity [kata to chreon];*
> *for they must do justice [dike] and pay recompense [tisis]*
> *to each other for their injustice [adikia]*
> *according to the order [taxin] of time.*[14]

One way to 'translate' this dense passage is as follows: the Being of beings exhibits a necessity manifest in the temporal reciprocity of justice and injustice.[15] The two phrases prefaced by 'according to' establish temporal necessity as an order which is enacted as a paying of recompense (justice) between coming-into-being and passing-away. The fragment preserves no mention of a deity, rather order itself is characterised according to the temporal measure of justice. However, the temporal character of justice may reflect Hesiod's *Theogony*, from a century and a half earlier, in which the goddess Dikē (human justice) appears among the Horai (hours), alongside Eunomia (good law) and Irene (peace), who were the daughters of Zeus and Themis (divine justice/custom and prophecy).[16] A struggle between two female figures labelled '*dikē*' and '*adikia*' (the latter tattooed like a barbarian), appears on both the Chest of Kypselos[17] and a red-figured amphora in the Kunsthistorisches Museum in Vienna, dated to a few decades after the Anaximander Fragment. The two women are obviously personifications, or types;[18] and an *agon* of opposites is not only preliminary to full conceptual determination but also fundamental to the order of the still-emerging polis. It is as if Anaximander had characterised reality in terms of a (just) polis. At about the same date, Solon's poem conventionally called, 'Eunomia' says of Dikē:

the silent one, knows what is and has been done
and comes with certainty to claim the payment due
this aims an inescapable blow at the whole community[19]

In other words, within the evolving democracy of the polis, the practico-symbolic style of understanding persists alongside, or underneath, alternative styles of analogy and concept (indeed, it still does, although usually under the conceptual rubric of 'the' sacred). In the few examples we have considered, justice retains an affiliation with the order of reality as a whole (cosmos), but is no longer channelled through the institutions of palace and temple.[20] More significantly, the polis-culture represents an emancipation from the tensional network of analogies,[21] the referential continuum of nature, gods and humans characteristic of the Bronze-Age kingdoms. For Sophocles, '... language and winged thought and the city's instituting passions were self-taught ... '[22] The assumption of responsibility by the body of citizens for its own order – executed across a spectrum that includes political reason, religion/myth as a framework for concepts, and tragic drama – seems to correlate historically with the experience of reality as a reciprocity between the claims of the parts (open to discovery) and the nature of the whole (also open to discovery), which in turn requires finding a voice, or way of speaking, with respect to the reciprocity, rather than only from concrete circumstances. When Parmenides asserts the proximity of being and thinking, he also expects the former to protect the latter from delusion.[23]

When, therefore, I suggest that Anaximander is using, as it were, his polis-imagination to help him think the nature of reality as temporal justice, there can be no hint of a direct correlation of his Fragment with the contemporary composition of the polis of Miletus. Indeed, architecture is less necessary to participation in the order of reality than it was in the Mesopotamian cities, or rather more institutions are involved (even the houses of citizens) and their distribution about the polis means that the structures of connectivity or relation endow the polis as a whole with the importance once reserved for a few institutions. Within this, the institutional typicalities of praxis such as addressing, propitiating, hosting or gift-giving, which had been elevated to ritual and ceremonial status in Bronze Age cities, retain a ceremonial importance in the new conditions. However, the most important typicality of this kind, the agon, is new to the polis (although not new to cosmogonies), as is a formalised language – Rhetoric – to support it. Varieties of agon appear in all the important collective institutions of the polis – religious sacrifice, the making of laws (*bouleterion*), judging (*heliaia*), tragic drama, symposium (house), and of course competitive games and combat. The agon is significant as an institution because it makes conflict the vehicle of order. It matters only to the litigant who wins or loses a law case; what matters to the polis as a whole is that justice is institutionally situated. This institutionalisation of for-and-against represents a removed level of self-understanding analogous to the 'reciprocity' mentioned above, and invokes a level of objectivity that inspires not only personifications of justice and injustice but, more fundamentally, such principles as the coincidence of opposites cultivated by Heraclitus, Empedocles and Pythagoras, putative student of, among others, Anaximander.[24] In Heraclitus' famous 'all things happen by strife (*eris*) and necessity' and in Empedocles' cycles of all things coming together through love (*philotes*) and apart through strife (*neikos*), we again see the thematising of reality in terms of the life of the polis.

If the advent of law with which we began allows the city to understand its diverse praxes as part of a continuum with the order of the gods, the collective claim of the law, its transcendence with respect to any individual, is retained in the polis, even though the laws are 'made' – debated for-and-against – by the citizens. Accordingly, the most important structure of connectivity in the polis is the logos. The *heliaia* exemplifies the degree of concreteness constituted in this new investment in logos.[25] The *heliaia* is extracted (supposedly by Solon) from the *ecclesia*, or full assembly of representatives of all ten demes (this division of the polis into ten, as part of the Cleisthenic reforms, itself represents a conceptual structuring of wholeness that cancels out the influence of particular families, wealth, status, etc.). The jurors witness the debate of the litigants (the central section of a Rhetorical speech is known as *agones* because it rehearses both sides of the debate) in an open-air setting that is bounded like a *temenos* (perhaps *helios*, sun, is heard in *heliaia*, recalling the role of Shamash in Babylonia). This boundary acts like a horizon with respect to the common ground of disagreement. The configuration recurs in the other agonic settings; and it appears that the structure agon > common ground > horizon constitutes a paradigmatic, quasi-ritualised setting. The ground and its horizon establish the conditions for the for-and-against debate, which claims both disputants, within the Rhetorical formality that claims all civic discourse.

The famous Socratic dialogue recapitulates this situation; and in Plato's dialectical logos, we find the motif of measure reconstituted in terms of the participation of the soul in the movement that ascends and descends the four levels of the stratification of Being, articulated through the analogical structure of the Divided Line.[26] This stratification is a primary insight, derived from the paradigmatic setting of agonic debate, in which the horizon is effectively recalled at each level of participation/understanding, with the primary division between *doxaston* (opinion) and *noeton* (intellection) marking the movement from ambiguous involvement in the life of the polis (corresponding to the shadowed cave of the 'myth' that explicates the Divided Line) to structured reflection (corresponding to the luminosity outside the cave). This movement back and forth between the Many of the fractious polis and the One of the Highest Good is rendered in terms of Dikē. Placing this configuration alongside the harmonic cosmic order depicted in the *Timaeus* (which takes place the night after the dialogue of the *Republic*, and is therefore paired with it[27]), it is evident that we are in the presence of a reformulation of the situation depicted in Hammurabi's investiture. The communicative gap between Hammurabi and Shamash, identified with the measuring-implements connoting justice, is recapitulated in that between the two disputants (dialogue) and the proportional ascent to intellectual understanding (dialectic).

The Latin *proportio* translates the Greek *analogia*, which emerges as the principle underlying the several concrete involvements with 'measure' outlined above, and allows the several styles of embodiment (actual things, depictions of things, personification, types, oppositional pairs, geometric figures, ideas, etc.) to communicate with each other within logos (which itself comprises word, discourse, reason, a proposition, account, ratio, analogy). Within the idea of ratio (well-known to Bronze Age cultures, but as discrete ratios, worked out as routines and used for particular purposes) lies the heart of the communication between measure and justice – the null-point of equality between differences.

Geometry and arithmetic occupy the second-highest level, *dianoia*, of Plato's stratification, whose figures, *eikones*, 'seek mental realities';[28] that is, these disciplines have a preparatory function with regard to dialectic. The great division in the stratification between *doxaston* and *noeton*[29] corresponds to a distinction Plato regularly draws regarding geometry and arithmetic that are practical, 'drawn in the sand' or used for building or music (*doxaston*), versus those that are philosophical, conducted wholly mentally (*noeton*), where the latter participate most closely in the Good.[30] There is therefore nothing to derive from Plato regarding geometric figures in buildings as being more true or beautiful or just.

Aristotle preserved the motif of stratification in his description of praxis in Book VI of the *Nichomachean Ethics* (*technē* underlies *phronesis*, and, above them, *episteme* underlies *sophia*), despite having little respect for Plato's Ideas and in particular for a vision of ethics that involved participation of individual choice with a pre-existing, eternal harmonic order. Indeed, Aristotle began the discipline that is rooted in *ethos*, a species of communal commitment to what is held in common. For him, the practical life was the receptacle of order in the polis; and, for example, he proposed to decant dialectics from the exalted position it held in Plato's *VIIth Letter* to the concrete debates of the polis.[31] Although not approved by Aristotle,[32] one might see the planning principles of Hippodamos of Miletus in similar terms – for it is evident that Hippodamus' *diaresis*, division, of the polis, popularly associated with the actually very ancient grid of streets (not least familiar from the planning of Greek colonies, from the eighth century), was intended to provide the framework for a more general *isonomia* involving recurrent threes (e.g. division of the land into sacred, public, private). One might say the result is a physical approximation of the logos, and of distributive justice (therefore a species of 'eu-topia', as against the tendency to classify his proposition as an 'ideal city' or utopia).

One must place Hippodamus in a much longer history of attempting to place the civic order in relation to spatial metaphors,[33] which originates with the generation of Thales and Anaximander, and turns on several key terms – *kosmos, isonomia, geometria, arithmos, physis, logos, democratia* – and the (often violent) efforts to discover *dikē* in the actual governance of the polis. This trajectory of thinking is summarised in its complete form by Plato: '... heaven and earth and gods and men [Heidegger's four-fold] are held together by community and friendship, by orderliness and temperance and justice and for this reason they call the cosmos an order, not disorder ... geometric equality has great power among men and gods ... .'[34] The speculation in Plato's *Republic* represents the most profound interpretation of this tradition, and he contrasts this with such 'magical' cities as the concentric circles of Atlantis.[35] However, the radial city of his last dialogue, *Laws*, appears to share in this style of thought (despite obvious differences), reverting also to the Ionian twelve under a cosmic god, instead of the expected secular ten, of the generation of Cleisthenes and Pythagoras. This period also corresponds to the transformation of geometry from practico-symbolic routines into a domain of internal coherence (autonomy). However, once the nature of geometry as an axiomatic discipline is clarified by Euclid, and Plato has clarified the ontological movement across the four horizons of participation in the Good [or Being], any consideration of uniting practical with speculative geometry requires either leaving this aspect of Plato's thinking to one side, as did Aristotle, or deploying a mixed – or corrupt – ontology, as did the Hellenistic culture originating in Alexandria.

THE ALEXANDRIAN TRANSFORMATION

Whether or not Euclid developed his geometry in Plato's Academy (Proclus has him synthesising and improving the work of his predecessors in the Academy, declaring he 'belonged to the persuasion of Plato'[36]), it is generally agreed he was in Alexandria shortly after its founding. Alexandria was a cosmopolitan city rich in syncretism, including the notions of divine kingship of its namesake, the late Egyptian dynasties as well as an influential population of Jews, and, most importantly for us, an interest in 'knowledge' (supported by the famous library and the Museion) giving rise to the systematic communication between speculative geometry and practical making, in machines, architecture, and illusionistic painting.[37] After the period of quite rigorous speculation, beginning in the mid-fourth century BCE, was stifled by the Roman conquest, in the mid-second century BCE, the discoveries were simply put to use (like the water-wheel), forgotten completely, or partially remembered in fragmentary form. In the fluid syncretism of late Republican and Imperial Roman culture, the combination of intrinsic certainty of geometric relations and their (largely Platonic-Pythagorean) meanings attracted numerous analogies and speculative possibilities. It is to this post-conquest Hellenistic culture that Vitruvius is indebted when he thinks the theatre not as a setting for tragedy or comedy but as an arrangement of triangles/squares recalling the zodiac,[38] replete with literal Pythagorean harmonies,[39] or the city as a harmony of four winds, four humours, and so forth, or architecture as an interdisciplinary synthesis of knowledge.[40]

A good example of this style of 'interdisciplinary' knowledge – or syncretism – is Plutarch's *Isis and Osiris*,[41] in which one finds the Platonic movement between mythos and logos elevated to a synthesis with Osiride and Dionysian myths.[42] For anyone not prepared to research Plutarch's elaborate Platonism, the impression is given of a composite milieu whereby philosophy communicates easily with Egyptian and Greek cults reduced to referential motifs. Similarly, the archaic conception of *harmonium mundi* becomes flattened to the epicycles[43] corresponding to chains of ratios (of revolution), by which the various proposals were in fact calculated, as if the heavens were a giant algorithm as well as the paradigm of divine movement (because heavenly bodies were luminous, precisely regular and self-moving, they articulated celestial temporality). One suspects that Hadrian, who served a year as archon in Athens, had himself inducted into the Academy and appointed Plutarch procurator of Achaea in 119, drew upon a similar composite of concepts in his Villa, both literally, in terms of the Egyptian themes connected with Antinous and more generally, with respect to the geometric sophistication and solar 'games' of some of the buildings within his Villa.

For Plato and Aristotle, architecture hardly mattered, except for the manner in which the *technē*, craft, arrived at its results; indeed Aristotle uses the term '*architectonikes*' to characterise politics as the most authoritative master-craft.[44] By contrast, in the Hellenistic Roman milieu, architecture achieved a level of elaboration and sophistication never before seen; and we might say that it was possible to 'philosophise' in or through architecture. With the exceptions of the Stoics Cicero and Marcus Aurelius and the Epicurean Lucretius, philosophy was less important to Roman culture than were Rhetoric, law and religion. Accordingly one finds in the developed perspectivism that animates, for example, Vitruvius' text, Pompeiian houses, Tiberius' twelve villas on Capri (one for each of the gods) or Nero's Golden House, such a close co-ordination between domestic custom and mythic themes, supported by the ubiquitous scenae-frons, that it is possible to suggest that these configurations are among the principal vehicles for speculation on the individual's relation to the cosmos, beings in their Being. The philosopher-poet-architect-general-statesman Hadrian therefore has at his disposal a well-developed iconographic typology dependent upon layers of practice and geometric reasoning brought to a high conceptual synthesis then re-embedded in practice, endowed with 'cosmological' significance. One might argue his Villa, supposedly a representation of the Roman ecumene over which he ruled,[45] falls within the millennia-old tradition of the semi-sacred palace; but this does not account for the presence of these techniques in houses, villas, tombs, even markets. The enchanted quality of the Imperial Campus Martius, apparently devoted to affairs of the spirit and dubbed 'most sacred' by Strabo,[46] derived less from the range of activities – worship and commemoration, tragic and comic drama, bathing, races and athletics, politics, gossip, discussion, reading – than from the great scale and the persistence of shrine-like motifs and ornament in the edifices and in the great colonnades, disposed about a huge artificial lake (the Stagnum Aggrippae) and rendered in gardens and exotic marbles. The resulting conflation of secular and sacred in a vague theatricality enabled Augustus to see the city as a receptacle for cosmic, historical and personal symbolism. Three centuries later, this iconographic typology enabled Christian architects to assemble churches and palaces as symbolic configurations, and indeed the central area of medieval Constantinople must have seemed like one extensive temple. Eventually it provided the Renaissance with its leading representational strategy.

Against the distinction between divine and human still present in Plato and Aristotle, the Stoics and subsequent Neo-Platonists both argued for a continuum, evident particularly in the Neo-Platonist Proclus' four-level 'geometric ontology'.[47] As Hans-Georg Gadamer rightly declares, for most of European history, Plato was effectively Plotinus.[48] This of course made such composite configurations easier to imagine and to achieve; and the Christian addition of soteriology to the received ontology put an even greater emphasis upon concreteness, particularly after the Reformation and Counter-Reformation. The culmination of this procedure is to be found in the sequence that leads from Michelangelo to the post-Tridentine Baroque of Francesco Borromini and Guarino Guarini, thence to South Germany and Central Europe. Tracing the dialogue between the motives of corporeality with those of Jesuit mathematics and geometry (whose two chief characteristics for these purposes were the survival of medieval light-ontology and geometric projection, continuity through transformation), Dalibor Vesely argues that the principal desideratum is the 'embodiment (Incarnation) of divine presence in the human world ... a problem of embodiment of culture as a whole' ... which he summarises in the phrase 'luminous flesh'.[49]

ONTOLOGY AND SOTERIOLOGY

An example from the very beginning of the Renaissance recovery of Hellenistic procedures which still preserves a reciprocity of justice and architecture is the Sala dei Nove in Siena, as ornamented in the early fourteenth century by Ambrogio Lorenzetti's famous frescoes.[50] The nascent perspectivity – the entire argument is delivered to visibility as views and texts, distributed across three walls of the simple box of a room – is still rooted in the concrete *agon* of the deliberations of the Nine, and their relation to the adjacent Major Council and to the Chapel, which together occupy the piano nobile of the Palazzo Pubblico, which in turn is the focus of the fractious – even dangerous – civic life of the medieval Roman Catholic republic. The lateral walls of the Sala dei Nove depict the Evil and the Good cities, and each of these views is divided in half by a city wall, since each *contrada* included both an urban and rural component. From south to north there is a progression from literal to symbolic representation: from actual fields visible from the single window in the south wall to the painted fields outside the Good and Evil city walls to the cities *intra muros* to the allegorical judgement scene on the main, north, wall (paired with its negative in the Evil city, on the left [west] wall). Solomon, dressed in the colours of Siena, is enthroned in the company of the Virtues and personifications of Distributive and Retributive Justice. The Judgement of Solomon embodies both distributive and retributive justice. Following the south-north transformation from literal to symbolic, the Judgement Scene fulfils an eschatological movement from the Edenic themes of the southern half of the room, and foreshadows the Last Judgement. Like the *heliaia*, the four walls establish a horizon for the common ground of disagreement, the tension between the *sic et non* of good and evil always alive in human finitude, and helps us realise that, from the inside, the four walls of the *heliaia* too are, as it were, façades to the polis.

The Last Judgement – with Christ as judge – is of course characteristic of the west wall of churches.[51] In churches, God's Justice and His Mercy framed the worship of all Christians, indeed temporality itself. On this basis, one might imagine Christian Churches to be the most comprehensive architectural embodiment of dwelling with justice. To the gathering of Christians in the promise of Heavenly Jerusalem could be added the response to Job,[52] in which the universe is characterised as a temple made by God, as well as the preservation of 'measure, number, weight',[53] which Augustine develops as 'measure fixes the mode of everything, number gives it its species, and weight gives it rest and stability'[54] and which Thomas Aquinas qualifies in turn as 'these three follow upon being, only so far as it is perfect and according to this perfection it is good'.[55] This style of theology forms part of the background to such motifs as the famous manuscript illustration of 'God the Geometer',[56] or the depiction of creation in the Genesis cycle in the nave mosaics of Monreale Cathedral, or the generative geometric mediation presented in the *Büchlein von der Fialen Gerechtigkeit*, 1486, of Mathes Roriczer. The persistent Neo-Platonism in Christianity implicated light in ontological order; and Aquinas anticipates Grosseteste (*De Luce*) when he says:

> *[T]he nature of light is spoken of[57] as being without number weight and measure, not absolutely, but in comparison with corporeal things, because the power of light extends to all corporeal things inasmuch as it is an active quality of the first body that causes change, that is, the heavens.*[58]

However, light was also implicated in soteriology, based on such passages as Psalm 27:1–6 ('The Lord is my light and my salvation'), and John 8:12 ('I am the light of the world: he that follows me walks not in darkness, but shall have the light of life'). These are among the ways that medieval Christian churches preserved the traditional attributes of the symbolism of justice – the interval between human and divine orders marked by measure/ratio/analogy – but turned toward the promise of salvation.

Although virtually interchangeable in texts, there is an important difference between redemption, the style of exchange of which the Anaximander Fragment speaks, and salvation, in which, as Augustine conceived it,[59] finitude is overcome and those who are saved will enjoy silent and eternal communication with God in heaven. On this basis, the Sala dei Nove sits between the *heliaia* (or, more accurately, the *bouleterion*), where the communicative interval/*agon* takes place between citizens, and a church, where the communicative interval is between humans and God (who is also Judge at the end of time). If, similarly, the tension between Lorenzetti's Good and Evil cities recalls Anaximander's contest/*agon* between *Dikē* and *Adikia*, this clearly prevails in a different register from salvation. The Sala dei Nove is one civic institution among many which has this character, and, in manifold ways the urban order of such towns (street, arcade, *cortile*, *salone*, etc.) comprises the continuity between settings for this situation.

Conversely, when Renaissance architects, dramatists and painters recovered Vitruvius' Tragic and Comic *scenae*,[60] they saw them not only as reciprocal forms of drama, but also in terms of good and evil. The 'Tragic' centre of the town held all the attributes of nobility, beauty, harmony, profundity of meanings whilst the 'Comic' periphery of artisans and merchants held the opposite qualities. *Renovatio urbis* arrived to the expectations behind our term 'urban renewal' by a gradual progression from a rich ensemble of theatres of renewal (poetry, charities, defence-works, etc.) to the simple process of replacing what was inevitably deemed a version of 'Comic' set with the latest version of 'Tragic' set. After five centuries of refinement of this procedure – largely obtained through transforming civic life and topography into concepts through theory – it was possible for Le Corbusier to present his Plan Voisin as the luminous ('Tragic') renewal of what he deemed the dark and crooked 'slum' ('Comic') of central Paris. Like the several aspects of the Christian tradition smuggled into Enlightenment culture (progress, the absolute, the sublime, etc.), we are in the presence of a species of secular salvation.

Of course Le Corbusier also attempted to recover something from the remains of the western tradition; and with respect to the theme of justice, his most notable effort was the exploitation of the pun on '*droit*' in his *Poème de l'angle droit*.[61] This work takes its overall ethos from Symbolist poetics and their gnostic interest in secret meanings. Advocating a Dionysian/Orphic combination of creativity and insight that owes more to Nietzsche than to the originals, it also draws upon Plato's *Symposium* and Aeschylus' *Prometheus*. Architecture is subsumed within Le Corbusier's vision of world-order, a milieu of *coincidentiae oppositorum* (for example a contest between creative darkness and luminous struggle), signs (mostly of his own creation), and a desire to reconcile moments of intense clarity with a chaotic, even violent, context. The French term *droit* connotes a legal or moral claim, moral rectitude (*droiture*), uprightness and straightness (both physical and moral) as well as the right angle. Combining motifs of conflict with a vaguely Neo-Platonic harmony, the *Poème* develops seven levels of meaning which are deemed to be held in his symbol for the right angle: the visual cross placed within a squared circle broken on one side. With regard to measure, it deserves remarking that his Modulor is less interested in all the magical properties usually associated with the Golden Section, than it is the leading figure in a numerological and geometric symbolism that emphasises continuity across differences (even if only as a matter of dimension) and mimesis of certain natural forms. Neither a philosopher nor a theologian, but a 'practical man', Le Corbusier only alludes to the transcendent conditions for justice which are common to our other examples. The *Poème* is an effort to move between the extremes of justice, between morality and cosmological order, even inadvertently recalling Anaximander when he attempts to develop a sequence from orbital periods of the earth and moon about the sun to figured matter to personal identity.

Although such themes were a preoccupation of architects of his generation, Le Corbusier's insights bear more prolonged scrutiny and respect than do those of others. After the revival of interest during post-modernism derailed into linguistics and historicism, few architects presently concern themselves with these matters. It must be admitted that 'symbolism' (usually just iconography) is part of the problem, fostering the hope that facile references, excised from any plausible living context, might save the case for practices otherwise indistinguishable from the production of 'form'. As it was with Le Corbusier, we are much better at designing small to medium-sized buildings than we are at cities, or urban nuclei, where the phenomenon of justice manifests itself most prominently. Despite the regular critiques of the CIAM city even before Jane Jacobs, its principles persist in the cities we now make. The continuity of agonic settings has evaporated into statistics and 'space', more recently into 'information' (we have no idea what constitutes 'local' or how to do a proper 'Comic' topography). Any reference to distributive justice has been reduced to raw economics. The meaning of a town – why to have it – has become subsumed under planning: the ever more desperate management of resources weirdly metabolised into an aesthetics of ethereal form.

The drama of technological change seems still to dominate our sense of history; and it is true that cell phones enable otherwise disenfranchised urban immigrants to construct international supply-chains or that digital monitoring of energy-systems enables efficiency savings. However, it bears remembering that all of the important human situations have remained quite constant – face-to-face discourse, cycles of wake/sleep, use of language, and so forth. It is these which are the receptacle of 'meaning' and therefore of any concrete sense of 'justice'. It is the regrettable tendency of the social sciences and particularly of economics to characterise the whole as statistical distributions of 'subjects' or 'agents', helping to support such pseudo-phenomena as 'human consciousness'. Against this, the common feature of the apparently archaic examples studied here is to have taken collective life – comprising the horizons of commonality of people, things, nature – as the primary assumption, with respect to which only does individual freedom have meaning.

Of the three themes that comprise global sustainability – resource depletion/competition, climate change and connectivity – the first two incite an orientation to justice that takes account of our natural/fundamental conditions, which the third has so far failed to deliver. We may simply fulfil the UK Met Office prediction of a chaotic migration northwards from rapidly desertifying middle latitudes.[62] Even if such predictions are inaccurate, the eventual necessity of discovering an ethos of mutual commitment at very high densities may result in vast high-rise barrios, and/or may inspire topographies and civic cultures as rich, differentiated and profound as fourteenth-century Cairo, Siena or Prague. In our post symbolic culture, the initial emphasis will necessarily be rooted in city making as agonic praxis, in the form of local transformations of the existing late-capitalist topographies. We may eventually recover ways of understanding our relation to the whole, not as a matter of hyper-efficient resource-allocation, but as an opportunity granted to finite humans. As Anaximander understood, however, this will inevitably involve trying to name the place where beings, temporality, justice are allowed a 'measure' of hope.

NOTES

1 John Rawls, *A Theory of Justice* (Cambridge MA, 1971, 1999).

2 Jurgen Habermas, *On the Pragmatics of Social Interaction* (Polity, 2001), and *The Theory of Communicative Action*, 2 vols (Cambridge, 1984).

3 For example, see P. Marcuse *et al.*, *Searching for the Just City* (London, 2009); David Harvey, *Social Justice and the City* (London, 1973) uses motifs like 'spatial form' and 'land use' in order to make the city available to his Marxian economic analysis. Henri Lefebvre's inconsistency seems to have made him attractive to all persuasions.

4 Late second millennium, Louvre, Sb 25, the so-called 'Unfinished' Kudurru.

5 For a slightly different reading, and detailed photographs, see Anton Moortgat, *The Art of Ancient Mesopotamia* (London, 1969), p. 102.

6 A similar stratification is evident on the vase from Uruk, *c.* 3000 BCE, National Museum of Iraq, IM19606.

7 Early eighteenth century BCE, Louvre, Sb8.

8 At Mari, where Hammurabi's contemporary, Zim-ri-lim, substitutes Ashtarte for Shamash, Louvre AO 19825.

9 See Moortgat, *Art of Ancient Mesopotamia*, Plate 201, for a detail from the Stele of Ur Nammu, which clearly shows the chord and staff, often mistakenly called a ring and staff because of the more summary representation in later reliefs and paintings. On the status of 'geometry' in the Ancient Near East, see Otto Neugebauer, *The Exact Sciences in Antiquity* (Princeton NJ, 1952) and Corinna Rossi, *Architecture and Mathematics in Ancient Egypt* (Cambridge, 2003).

10 For example, see Ephesians 2:20; all New Testament references devolve from Psalm 18:22.

11 Cited in Samuel Noah Kramer, *History Begins at Sumer* (New York, 1959), pp. 85–96.

12 Leonard Wooley, *Ur Excavations, Vol. VI, The Buildings of the Third Dynasty* (Philadelphia PA, 1974), plate 57.

13 Peter Carl, 'City-Image versus Topography of Praxis', *Cambridge Archaeological Journal*, vol. 10, no. 2 (October 2000): 328–35.

14 Anaximander, *Peri Physeos* (early VIth BCE), via Theophrastos (IVth BCE), via Simplicius (early VIth AD). See, *inter alia*, G.S. Kirk and J.E. Raven, *The Presocratic Philosophers* (Cambridge, 1957), pp. 117 ff.; Charles H. Kahn, *Anaximander and the Origins of Greek Cosmology* (London, 1994); Friedrich Nietzsche, *Philosophy in the Tragic Age of the Greeks* (Washington, 1962); M. Heidegger, *Early Greek Thinking* (New York, 1984), pp. 13 ff.

15 Anaximander's fragment precedes Parmenides' advocacy of being; Simplicius/ Theophrastus placed the fragment in the context of the Ionian speculation on exchange among elements, and declared that Anaximander argued the principle/ origin, *arche*, of existing things to be *apeiron*, the boundless, which I have elevated to Being. See Kahn, *Anaximander*, p. 168ff., 193ff., 231ff.

16 Hesiod, *Theogony* II. 901–6.

17 Pausanius, *Guide to Greece* V.17.5–19.10; H.S. Jones offers a reconstruction in 'The Chest of Kypselos', *The Journal of Hellenic Studies*, vol. 14, 1894, pp. 30–80; see more recently, Anthony Snodgrass, *Homer and the Artists: Text and Picture in Early Greek Art* (Cambridge, 1998), pp. 109 *et. seq.*

18 T.B.L. Webster, 'Personification as a mode of Greek Thought', *Journal of the Warburg and Courtauld Institutes*, vol. 17, nos. 1, 2 (1954): 10–21.

19 Solon, 'Eunomia', ll. 15–17; see K.A. Rauflaub, 'Political Thought, Civic Responsibility, and the Greek Polis', in Jóhann Páll Arnason, and Peter Murphy (eds), *Agon, Logos, Polis* (Stuttgart, 2001), pp. 72–117.

20 Jean-Pièrre Vernant, *The Origins of Greek Thought* (London, 1982).

21 Eric Voegelin, *The Ecumenic Age* (Baton Rouge LA, 1974), p. 77.

22 Sophocles, *Antigone*, 354–6; Jan Patocka insists that history is possible only with the advent of politics and philosophy in the polis; Jan Patocka, *Heretical Essays in the Philosophy of History*, trans. Erazim Kohak (Chicago, 1996), Lecture Two and p. 143. In general see Eric Voegelin, *The World of the Polis* (Baton Rouge LA, 1957).

23 *Proclus: Commentary on Plato's Timaeus*, I, 345 ff., Kirk and Raven, *The Presocratic Philosophers*, p. 269.

24 Walter Burkert, *Lore and Science in Ancient Pythagoreanism* (Cambridge MA, 1972); Charles Kahn, *The Art and Thought of Heraclitus* (Cambridge, 1974); see also Anne Michelini, 'Political Themes in Euripides' *Suppliants*', *The American Journal of Philology*, vol. 115, no. 2 (Summer, 1994): 219–52.

25 The *heliaia*, originally the name of a particular court, became a general name for law courts, otherwise known as *dikasteria* (a juror was a *dikast*, both words made from *dikē*). In general, see Mogens Herman Hansen, *The Athenian Democracy in the Age of Demosthenes: Structure, Principles, and Ideology* (Oxford, 1991), Chapter 8. The edifice in the South East corner of the Agora in Athens is now considered a grain store; but the group under the North West end of the Stoa of Attalos lays fair claim to being the remains of fifth-century law courts. Richard Ernest Wycherley, *The Stones of Athens* (Princeton NJ, 1978), p. 56, fig. 18.

26 Plato, *Republic* 504a–540b; Hans-Georg Gadamer, *Dialogue and Dialectic: Eight Hermeneutic Studies on Plato*, trans. P. Christopher Smith (New Haven CT, 1984) and *Plato's Dialectical Ethics* (New Haven CT, 1991).

27 Plato, *Timaeus*, 17c.

28 Plato, *Republic*, 510e.

29 This is undoubtedly inspired by Parmenides' similar division in his poem, but the so-called 'Way of Opinion/Seeming' is mostly lost.

30 Plato, *Statesman*, 284e; *Philebus*, 55d ff., 64b.

31 Aristotle, *Topica*, VIII.

32 Aristotle, *Politics* 1267b22 ff. and 1330b24.

33 Pierre Lévéque and Pierre Vidal-Naquet, *Cleisthenes the Athenian: An Essay on the Representation of Space and Time in Greek Political Thought from the End of the Sixth Century to the Death of Plato*, trans. and ed. David Ames Curtis (Amherst NY, 1996).

34 Plato, *Gorgias* 508a, ff.

35 Plato, *Timaeus* 25a, ff.

36 Proclus, *Commentary on the First Book of Euclid's Elements*, trans. G. Morrow, II.iii.68 (New Haven CT, 1970), p. 57.

37 P.M. Fraser, *Ptolemaic Alexandria*, 3 vols (Oxford, 1972); Judith McKenzie, *The Architecture of Alexandria and Egypt 300BC-700AD* (New Haven CT, 2007); Lucio Russo, *The Forgotten Revolution* (Berlin, 2003).

38 Mark Wilson Jones argues this is an adaptation of building-practice to the 'standard of *symmetria*', *Principles of Roman Architecture* (New Haven CT, 2000), pp. 58–9.

39 Sounding-vessels are attested in a few theatres.

40 Vitruvius, *De re aedificatoria* (in order of mention): Book V, vi, vii; Book V, iv, v; Book I, vi; Book I, i.

41 *Moralia V.*

42 On the similarity of the latter two Plutarch was preceded by Herodotus.

43 This was first proposed by Apollonius of Perga a century after Euclid, perhaps inspired by the circular metaphors of elemental change, sometimes seen as stratified cosmic rings and compared to the phases of the moon in Empedocles B 26, from which Plato, *Phaedo* 72b and Aristotle, *de Generatione et Corruptione*. 337a1–7.

44 Aristotle, *Nichomachean Ethics,* 1094a28.

45 *Historiae Augustae*, 'Hadrian', 26.5.

46 For the full passage, see Strabo, *Geographica* (London, 1917), 5.3.8.

47 Proclus, *Commentary on the First Book of Euclid's Elements,* II.iii.62, op. cit., p. 50.

48 Hans-Georg Gadamer, 'Thinking as Redemption: Plotinus between Plato and Augustine', in *Hermeneutics, Religion, and Ethics*, trans. Joel Weinsheimer (New Haven CT: Yale University Press, 1999), Chapter 5.

49 Dalibor Vesely, 'Corporeality of Baroque Art and the Mystery of Incarnation', paper delivered at Werner Oechslin Stiftung, Einsiedeln, July 2011.

50 Randolph Starn and Loren Partridge, *Arts of Power* (Berkeley CA, 1992), Chapter 1; Chiara Frugoni, *A Distant City: Images of Urban Experience in the Medieval World*, trans. William McCuaig (Princeton NJ: Princeton University Press, 1991), Chapter 6; Diana Norman (ed.), *Siena, Florence and Padua; Art, Society, and Religion 1280–1400* (New Haven CT: Yale University Press, 1995), vol. II, Chapter 7; Alan Dundes, and Alessandro Falassi, *La Terra in Piazza; an interpretation of the Palio in Siena* (Berkeley CA: University of California Press, 1975).

51 However, the fifth century apse mosaic in Sta. Pudenziana in Rome would appear to include a reference to judgement along with the evident regal, blessing and teaching Christ, set in a vision of Jerusalem fusing Golgotha with the end-time framed by the Tetramorph. See Wendy Pullan, 'Jerusalem from alpha to omega in the Santa Pudenziana mosaic', *Jewish Art*, vols 23–4 (1997/98): 405–17; and Frugoni, *A Distant City*, Chapter 1.

52 *Job* 38.

53 *Wisdom* 11:21.

54 Augustine, *De Genesis ad Litteram*, trans. J.H. Taylor (New York: Paulist Press, 1982), IV.3.

55 Thomas Aquinas, *Summa Theologica,* Pt. 1, Q. 5, reply objection 1.

56 *Codex Vindobonensis* 2554, frontispiece.

57 Ambrose, *Hexaemeron* I.9.

58 Aquinas, *Summa Theologica,* Pt. 1, Q. 5, reply objection 5.

59 Augustine, *De Civitate Dei*, Book XIX.11,13; Book XX.1, 16, 17; Book XXII.1, 30.

60 Vitruvius, *De Architectura*, V.vi.9; Sebastiano Serlio, *Tutte l'opere d'architettura et prospetiva,* Book II.3.

61 Le Corbusier, *Poème de l'angle droit,* 155 lithographs, boxed (Alec Tiranti, 1953).

62 Interactive Google Earth map from Met Office at: <www.fco.gov.uk/google-earth-4degrees.kml>.

16

Politikē Aretē: Or the Origins of Civic Justice

Renée Tobe

In the dialogue of his name, Protagoras professes to teach *aretē* and in particular *politikē aretē*. Plato's exposition of how a skill becomes an excellence through the giving of justice and good sense demonstrates the relation of *politikē* and polis and the relation of justice to both. The linguistic origins of *politikē technē* conceal whether it is a craft relating to city building and planning in terms of architecture, and reveal the role it plays in how to plan a city as a society of justice. Different translations of *politikē aretē* and *politikē technē* shed light on our received notions of civic justice and the complexities of urban co-existence, that is, the means by which millions of individuals from diverse strata all live together in cities. Translations of *Protagoras* render *politikē aretē* variously as: 'running the city'; 'civic art'; 'political excellence or virtue'; 'political excellence' or 'good citizenship', and *politikē technē* as: 'art of running a city'; 'civic art'; 'the art of government'; 'city craft'; or 'the art of politics'.[1]

Table 16.1
Table of Plato's *Protagoras*. Different translations of *Politikē Technē* and *Politikē Aretē*

line	Taylor (1889)	Lamb (1924)	Ostwald (1956)	Hubbard and Karnofsky (1982)	Griffith (2010)
ton de politikon (321d)	skill in running a city	civic wisdom	political wisdom	city craft	political knowledge
politiken technē (322b)	art of running a city	civic art	art of government	city craft	art of politics
politikē aretē (322d)	running the city	civic art	political excellence or virtue	political excellence	good citizenship
politikē aretē (323b)	excellence as a citizen	civic virtue	political virtue	political excellence	good citizenship

Politikē aretē is both running the city and excellence as a citizen.[2] Civic art, good citizenship, political excellence, and running the city have various interpretations, although in Plato's era this may have been far less ambiguous when all public discourse was both influenced by and sought to influence the socio-political life of the polis.[3] Refinement and maturation of political concepts may be understood only through connecting them to historical events that include social and economic developments. In current interpretations, citycraft and skill in running a city are worlds apart, and political knowledge and civic wisdom also have differing connotations.

PROTAGORAS

It is not known how familiar Plato (427–347 BCE) was with Protagoras' (490–420 BCE) actual writings, and he may have relied on secondary sources for his dialogue.[4] The *Protagoras* begins with Protagoras the Sophist's arrival in Athens and features historic characters who were politicians, other Sophists, and wealthy aristocrats. The nature of the Platonic dialogue helps the reader gain 'critical acquaintance' with the general character of Protagoras. He is a bit proud, or vain, likes to promote himself, doesn't like being shown up, is intellectually evasive, but essentially well intentioned as a Sophist.[5] Socrates describes Protagoras as a foreigner of Abdera, an outsider to Athens quite distracting with his wisdom. In Classical Greece Sophists taught rhetoric as an intellectual practice and advised on public policy. In this period architects Callicrates and Ictinos built the Temple of Athena Nike and the Parthenon on the Athens Acropolis (447–432 BCE). During this era of Hellenic expansion military leader and statesman Pericles (495–429 BCE), who wished to set up a new colony at Thurii, entrusted the design to the foremost city-planner of his day, Hippodamus of Miletes, but the job of drafting the laws to Protagoras.

Towards the end of the fourth century BCE, Plato wrote the *Republic* delineating the structure and philosophy of an ideal citystate where political justice has great value and provides moral guidance for both rulers and for the ruled.[6] In Plato's *Republic,* justice is found through doing one's own work, that is, doing what one does best must be just. Public discourse both cast and reflected light on the social political life of the polis. Ancient Athens did not discriminate between political, philosophical and dramatic discourse. Just as Plato's *Symposium* satirises comic playwright Aristophanes, Aristophanes' *Birds* lampoons Sophists like Protagoras and Plato's *Republic* with Cloudcuckooland, a city for birds designed in the clouds whose tiered system reflects Plato's *Republic* and his *Clouds* ridicules Plato's Academy itself with the satirical Thinkery.

So called 'Older Sophists', such as Protagoras were known for their cleverness and ability to impart knowledge to pupils willing to learn. The abandonment of kingships raised the question of who should rule in a democracy since leaders were granted authority on the basis of their excellence. At a time of increasing prosperity, it was important that the sons of wealthy men, and not just those of the nobility or traditionally prominent in politics could learn *aretē*, not just inherit it, and become leaders in the Assembly.[7] With the increasing prevalence of oratory and the need to 'win arguments' Sophists became known for teaching rhetoric, which is both positive in that it helps politicians to influence citizens to good and responsible behaviour, and negative since it makes a weaker argument appear strong. In other words, it can promote both justice and injustice.

Only fragments of Protagoras' writing remain. According to Plato he also wrote a treatise entitled Truth, *Aletheia*, that contained his statement that 'man is the measure of all things' explained by Protagoras in the *Thaeatetus* where he states 'that individual things are for me such as they appear to me, and for you in turn such as they appear to you – you and I being 'man'?'[8] This dictum suggests our everyday experience and understanding are the means or standard by which we measure or assess social values, basic human needs and responsibilities. It weighs the art of measurement against the power of appearances and suggests that we perceive the existence and qualities of things only in so far as they come into contact with our senses.[9] Protagoras' principle of the individual being the measure of all things means judgement and knowledge are relative to the one judging and that correction of one's own perceptions is impossible, for one is as true as another. What our senses perceive is true, for us. Appearances can confuse, they are different for you than they are for me. What feels right to me may not be what feels right to you, and, in fact, what feels right to me at one point, may seem wrong later on, and judgements are made on facts presented.[10]

WHAT IS *ARETĒ* AND CAN IT BE TAUGHT

The question of 'what is *aretē'* and is it teachable runs as a familiar motif in Plato's dialogues. Protagoras professes to teach excellence. When asked excellence in what, he responds somewhat evasively. Protagoras explains that it is the ability to manage ones household in the best way, good judgement in one's own affairs and in public life and how best to exercise political power whether through actions or words.[11] As listeners gather around him, Protagoras promises to teach the art of running a city, described as *ten politikēn technēn* and to be a good citizen that translates as *agathoi politas* and suggests that this is a *technē* at which individuals can improve to the point of excellence.[12] Socrates suggests this is not something that can be taught, that is, *aretē* may not be *didacton*.[13] For this reason Protagoras describes *politikē* as a *technē*, a skill at which, with practice, study and learning, we may improve.

As a master rhetorician, Plato attacks Protagoras' theory of *aretē* in the style of the Sophist himself and presents both sides of the argument, both what Protagoras states, and the refutation.[14] Protagoras argument seems to be:

> *First: A student who studies with Protagoras will become better.*
>
> *Next: A student who studies with Protagoras will become a better citizen and able to administer civic affairs.*

> *Then: Protagoras professes to teach skill in civic management.*
>
> *Finally: A student who studies* politikē technē *with Protagoras learns* politikē aretē.

Protagoras purposefully builds on ambiguities between *aretē* and *technē* to show that although all may possess these skills, he, Protagoras the Sophist, being more skilled than others, may teach them and that not just noble born but all citizens, can be political leaders. But what is *politikē technē*? Different translators had different ideas. More than just 'hands on' knowledge, *technē* is an art, a skill, an ability to know, or learn through practice.[15] A special kind of *technē* is required for the polis as illuminated by the different translations below:

> *You seem to me to be talking about the art of running a city, and to be promising to make men into good citizens.*
>
> *It seems that the technical subject of which you speak is citycraft and that you are promising to make men good members of their city.*
>
> *You seem to me to be talking about the art of politics, and promising to turn men into good citizens.*[16]

Protagoras thesis seems to be that a student who studies *politikē technē* with him, will learn *politikē aretē*. In order to understand what this means, we insert different translation into the premise:

> *A student who studies the art of running a city with Protagoras learns excellence as a citizen.*
>
> *A student who studies civic art with Protagoras learns civic virtue.*
>
> *A student who studies the art of government with Protagoras learns political excellence or virtue.*
>
> *A student who studies citycraft with Protagoras learns political excellence.*
>
> *A student who studies the art of politics with Protagoras learns good citizenship.*[17]

Politikē aretē suggests good citizens, skilled in politics. Citycraft connotes the activities of the professional politician and the operations of modern political institutions. Socrates suggests that this is not a skill that can be taught since, unlike medicine, for example, where one consults an expert, with *politikē aretē* everyone has an equal voice on civic matters, since, in the polis being a citizen qualifies each to speak to the assembly.

PROTAGORAS GREAT OR LONG SPEECH

Classic Greek scholars describe the passage of dialogue where Protagoras explains that he will teach *aretē* as a 'confused and confusing piece of Greek' that forms the philosophical introduction to 'one of Plato's most baffling dialogues'.[18] In his Great

Speech, described as a 'tremendous display of eloquence' that leaves his listeners entranced, Protagoras illuminates the means by which this *technē* becomes an *aretē*.[19] These confusions are present in the Greek text although an Athenian of Plato's era might be less perplexed by both *technē* and *aretē* than current readers with our centuries of philosophy.[20]

Contemporary language and thought distinguishes on far more levels between 'being a citizen' and 'running a city' than in the time of Classic Greece. For ancient Athenians, 'teaching the city' meant instructing its citizens; teaching citycraft is the same as teaching a person to be a good citizen.[21] Protagoras, identified as the one who knows the measure of all things, is most appropriate to be able to instruct on how to act correctly in all things. The language of political philosophy is 'linguistically mediated' and the definition of citycraft, that is, being a good citizen, may vary in relation to the qualities people happen to regard as important at a particular time.[22] This definition of *aretē*, as a kind of self-consciousness and self-realisation, may not be formally teachable, but developed as a skill, or learned as a language.

When asked to explain how *aretē* may be taught, Protagoras suggests he can do this equally with fable or *muthos* as reasoned argument or *logos*. Here, as in the *Republic*, *muthos* and *logos* are juxtaposed. Plato often uses myth or parable to convey truth where literal truth is not possible. While *muthos* is often subsumed under *logos*, parables need not be logically proven arguments but judged by the inherent values they convey and the evaluation of their shifting layers of meaning.[23] Plato pokes fun gently at his character Protagoras; the suggestion that the Sophist can teach as easily with a fable as factual argument clearly expresses Plato's scepticism of Sophistry that treats accuracy and rigour in detail somewhat disdainfully. He uses the myth to persuade, and *logos* to demonstrate. Plato's emphasis on the artistry rather than the veracity of the Sophistry weakens the point itself. Using both fable and logical argument demonstrates his power as a Sophist, but undermines the validity of his line of reasoning. Although representing him as upright and respectable, throughout the dialogue Plato uses Protagoras' rhetoric and style of Sophistry to destabilise Protagoras' case that *arete* is teachable.

THE MYTH

Protagoras relays a creation myth that features brothers Prometheus and Epimetheus. Prometheus is known for stealing fire from the gods, and being punished for it by having his liver pecked out by an eagle each day, while it grows back each night. Epimetheus, his younger brother, was also punished through a hapless marriage with Pandora who opened the box that released evil spirits to the world. The myth draws from the *Prometheus Bound* trilogy of Aeschylus.[24] Both Epimetheus and Prometheus also appear in Hesiod's writings where Prometheus is described as having a 'labyrinthine mind' and Epimetheus as 'foolish'.[25] Hesiod's writings promoted the combination of justice as a moral force of a higher order and the social values necessary for the emergence and prosperity of the polis, the civilized and law-abiding city. Hesiod presents justice as an essential condition for peace and prosperity and distinguishes between concrete manifestations of justice and justice itself as a requisite for the civilised society, which is the polis. Justice is, above all, a civic virtue. Protagoras' interpretation of his myth shows this clearly:[26]

> *In the beginning, (as all myths begin) Zeus commissioned Prometheus (Forethought) to hand out qualities to all living creatures as they were brought forth from where they were formed within the earth. His brother Epimetheus (Afterthought) begged to be allowed to distribute the qualities himself. He suggested that when the qualities had been distributed to all creatures, Prometheus might survey them to see that they are all fine. With surprising lack of forethought, Prometheus acquiesced.*

Plato is unusually lyrical, using poetic language to describe the bestowing of weapons and armatures on some, and on others mechanisms for safety such as an ability to fly, or to run fast or hide:

> *Epimetheus distributed the provisions such that all species were ensured of survival. They were given fur or feather to keep them warm, the ability to burrow for shelter or build nests. Each had food, from plants, fruit, roots, or flesh. Those creatures destined to be the victims of others were made small, given more offspring, able to fun fast to escape, or to fly away, while those who preyed on them were given teeth, claws, greater strength and cunning. Humans, however, Epimetheus had forgotten and Prometheus found them naked, unshod, unbedded and without weapons. Searching for some quality to give to humans, Prometheus headed for Olympus, the citadel of the gods, but, frightened by Power and Violence, the sentinels at Zeus' gate, went to the lower city where he stole fire from Hephaestus and knowledge of the arts from Athena for one is useless without the other.*[27]

When the theft was discovered, Prometheus was punished. The final line to the myth, in the original language, sounds like a rhyme, or clanging of a gate: 'Prometheus through Epimetheus fault, later on (so the story goes) stood his trial for theft.'[28] Plato uses a technical term, *klopeis dikē*, meaning stood his trial for, from the Attic criminal process; 'a prosecution for theft' pursued Prometheus.[29] The story continues, and engages with our discussion:

> *Their skill at making things afforded them adequate protection and they were able to build cities, but humans found themselves unable to live together peacefully in them as they lacked the art of politics. Using his messenger Hermes, Zeus distributed respect and justice, so that all share equally in justice and good citizenship generally that there might be order in cities, and bonds to hold people together in friendship.*[30]

While they are given *technē* and fire by Prometheus, the divine qualities humans receive are *dikē* and *eidos* translated as: 'justice and conscience'; 'right and respect'; 'justice and reverence'; 'justice and a sense of shame'; and 'justice and respect'.[31]

line	Taylor (1889)	Lamb (1924)	Ostwald (1956)	Hubbard and Karnofsky (1982)	Griffith (2010)
sophian anthropos (321d)	practical skill	wisdom of daily life	wisdom necessary to the support of life	wisdom for his [man's] sustanance	knowledge needed to stay alive
aidos dikē (322c)	conscience and justice	respect and right	reverence and justice	justice and a sense of shame	respect and justice
dikē aidos (322c)	conscience and justice	right and respect	justice and reverence	justice and a sense of shame	justice and respect
dikē aidos (322d)	justice and conscience	right and respect	justice and reverence	justice and a sense of shame	justice and respect
aidos dikē (322d)	conscience and justice	respect and right	reverence and justice	justice and a sense of shame	respect and justice
dikaison sophrosone (323a)	justice and soundness of mind	justice and good sense	justice and self-control	justice and moderation	justice and prudence

Table 16.2 Table of Plato's *Protagoras*. Different translations of *Aidos* and *Dikē*

These are gifts not just of the gods, but of the greatest god, Zeus, therefore they are the greatest gifts. When Protagoras describes the precarious condition of people before the foundation of cities, able to practice the arts and crafts but unable to defend themselves he adds: 'for they had not the art of politics, of which the art of war is a part'.[32] *Politikē aretē* helps us overcome our tendency for *polemike technē*.[33] We make our way through life guided throughout by justice and common sense and these along with *politikē technē* and *aretē*, constitute the socialisation that enable us to live in the polis. Aristotle develops this further in his discussion of *eudaimonia*, in which he suggests that the polis is necessary not just for life but exists for the good life. Political expertise is introduced in the story as an extra endowment that humans, already in possession of technical skill, required to enable them to live in organised communities. *Eidos* is the good will to put this practical wisdom at the service of the larger community.

And with the giving of *aidos* and *dikē*, *politikē technē*, develops into *politikē aretē* and civic art becomes civic virtue; the art of politics becomes good citizenship, the art of government becomes political excellence or political virtue; citycraft becomes political excellence; and finally, the art of running a city becomes excellence as a citizen. With the art of Sophistry Protagoras sneaks political skill into the argument as an excellence.

Since it is the divine gifts or qualities of justice and common sense that allow humans to live in cities, we try once again to follow the logic of Protagoras' claim that he can teach excellence, which has somehow become more complicated rather than otherwise:

1. I can teach excellence.
2. I teach excellence in managing a city and how to be a good citizen.
3. This requires *politikē technē*.

4. Every one has justice and good sense/respect otherwise we could not live in cities.
5. Therefore I teach political excellence.

   Or

6. There are cities. Cities require justice and good sense. We use our justice and good sense to live in cities. Therefore I can teach excellence.

Protagoras speaks as a Sophist; using both the structure of rhetoric and the paradoxical argument. The nature of a paradox is that it doesn't make sense, although there is usually something to learn from it. The argument situated on an ambiguity is often the most effective. There is a paradox between *politikē technē* and *politikē aretē* that Protagoras, and Plato, emphasise: Is it given or can it be taught? And how does a *technē* become an *aretē*? With the giving of *eidos* and *dikē*, *politikē technē* develops into *politikē aretē*.

The Sophist's argument employs an analogy in which one thing resembles another. The word analogy itself derives from the term *logos*, giving the impression of a logical conclusion. When Plato moves from *muthos* to logos he shifts from divine gifts personified as *aidos* and *dikē* to qualities of human behaviour, the human capacity for justice or *dikaiosune*, and instead of *aidos* uses *sophrosune*. This word has a large elusive semantic range, whose core meaning is 'soundness of mind' or 'good sense' but then in different contexts 'self control' or 'moderation' or 'prudence', conditions that underly all necessities of social and civilised life and enable the polis to exist.

The main argument of the section is the sentence stating that all must share in *dikē* and *aidos* or there would be no cities at all.[34] While all different kinds of *aretē* may not be distributed equally, the example being that a doctor may be more excellent at medicine while a carpenter is excellent at working with wood, since all share in *eidos* and *dikē*, all share equally in *politikē aretē*.

PLATO'S INTENTIONAL AMBIGUITY

Plato uses mythical language personifying *dikē* and *aidos*, while in the logos, more contemporary language is used, *dikaosune*, and *sophrosune*. Justice (a quality we all possess equally) is not the same as 'being just' that implies action.

The main argument of this section is that without respect, common sense, and a sense of justice we could not live together in cities. Plato sums this up when he states 'all men must possess reverence and justice in order for a polis to arise'[35] The question posed earlier of 'what is *politikē aretē* ' or as commentators ask: what does Plato mean by 'citycraft' demonstrates the discursive intention. The question of what is *aretē*, requires no firm answer for the point is to converse daily about *aretē* to acquire a greater self-realisation for as Plato states 'the unexamined life is not worth living'.[36]

PROTAGORAS' CLAIM

Protagoras continues to elide the move from *technē* to *aretē*. Protagoras claims to teach excellence through teaching citizens to hone the skills inherent within them; that is their 'god-given' sense of justice and common sense. In the citystate, everyone teaches *aretē*, just as everyone teaches the language of Greek, that is, the citizen learns to be a citizen as he learns to speak his own language. Plato uses *politikē technē* to denote the science of politics as something that one can practice.[37] *Politikē technē*, political skill or, more broadly conceived, 'the art of living in the polis', is instilled in members of the polis, through the very social bases of the state itself, as one learns a language, in contrast to technical skill, passed on through a specific, narrow course of instruction. Protagoras' claim that makes him special is that he is better at it than others.

Different translations open up the discussion. Translations also limit our interpretation. Translations differ, and sometimes say the same thing. For example, 'altogether weaker' and 'weaker in all things' mean relatively the same thing but city craft and art of running a city and art of politics or political skill do not. In another example, in the text, *dikē* and *aidos* are not always in the same order and in some translations they are always the same but others follow the source text. Translators suggest *aretē* is translated as virtue and excellence with equal measure. The use of *aretē* in this period demonstrates the fluidity of language and shift in focus of what is important. Greek conceptions of what made a person an excellent or admirable one differed widely at different periods. Traditionally *aretē* denoted excellences that would ensure success, prosperity and stability of the group to whom the citizen felt loyalty. In Homeric times this was through bravery, brute strength and cunning. In the time of Pericles and the Peloponnesian wars *aretē* extended to administrative and political skills. Excellences that once inferred an individual's success in competing in battle began to be used to refer to individuals supporting one another in cooperation.

In the centuries between Homer and Plato, the meaning of *aretē* changed as the need for different kinds of city administrators changed. The highest human excellence results from one's own making; a reflexive self-consciousness, a vision of human meaning quite distinct from Homeric values of bravery by which one vanquished one's enemy. In Protagoras time, excellences were those qualities deemed most likely to ensure the success, prosperity, and the stability of the group. This emphasises the need for community in order to survive. In the current era being a 'good person' is not the same as being a 'good leader' and pursuing what is best for oneself is often at odds with pursuing what is best for the city. These qualities do not necessarily concur with Homeric values. We look to leaders to be self-less and not self-serving or self-interested, quite different from the single-minded and physically courageous heroes of Homeric times.

It may be that there was confusion of thought of what an *aretē* was at the time, or Protagoras, as a distinguished Sophist may be doing this on purpose to slip in political skill as an excellence, one that he can teach. It is also how a *technē* becomes an *aretē*, one which each must share in equal measure. Plato states this clearly:

> *Is there, or is there not, some one thing which it is essential that all the citizens have a share of if there is to be a city? Here, if anywhere, is where the solution of your difficulty is to be found. If there is, and if this one thing is not carpentry or metalwork or pottery, but rather justice, prudence and what is holy – human goodness [aretē] to give it a single name.*[38]

A sense of justice and respect enable humans to acquire *aretē* that has connotations suggesting it is higher than *technē*. *Aretē* denotes excellence but also virtue. As Arendt describes: Excellence itself, *aretē* as the Greeks, *virtus* as the Romans would have called it, has always been assigned to the public realm where one could excel, could distinguish oneself from all others.[39] *Politikē aretē* which is simply the excellence of the good citizen [*agathos politeis*] and was a skill has now become an assemblage of moral excellences, that include collegiality or administrative skill, that is, being a good leader. As Plato suggests in another dialogue: To state that a democracy such as Athens is unable to govern is to belittle its *aretē*.[40] Civic *aretē* has been a goal from Homeric times and proof, if it is needed, that the term is awkward or ambiguous to translate is apparent not just in the multitude of translations, but in the example of classical scholars who not only leave it in the original but keep both *technē* and *aretē* in the Greek characters.

The dialogue commences with the two main protagonists holding one position and after both *muthos* and *logos* concludes with Protagoras and Socrates having exchanged philosophical stances. Both fable and rational discourse are examined from the stance of the architect and urbanist. For the ancient Greeks everything exists for the good of the polis and living in a polis means that everything is decided through words and persuasion and not through force and violence.[41] The polis requires an order that determines the structure, and, like following the rules of a game, justice consists in more than just the observance of the rules of the order, but also invites one to push the limits, held back from going too far by our sense of justice and good sense.[42]

No amount of rhetoric or intellectual skill can replace human goodness as essential constituent of the public realm. Arendt's territory of statecraft approaches Richard Sennett's least defined version of 'craft' in citycraft. Sennett's citycraft is reflective of the Enlightenment legacy that all things are improving and working towards a better future, in a manner that bridges the social and political realms. Arendt suggests however that statecraft is a self-standing domain of expertise.[43]

So *aretē* or excellence is teachable while political science is a gift of the gods – surely in contemporary times we might see this the other way. We interpret it differently according to our interests and understanding of what politics, cities, and excellence are. The first aim of government and administration is to secure the safety and prosperity of the polis. Such *aretē* requires courage, initiative, and the willingness to take risks to achieve a desired end.

CONCLUSION

Here we return to the myth and turn to Bernard Stiegler who, in as captivating manner as any Sophist, expounds on the role of *technē*. We had the knowledge and technical ability to build cities, but were unable to live in them until we received the divine gifts of *dikē* and *eidos*. As humans, we possessed the means to make war before we had the means to keep peace among ourselves. This ability to make war is what Stiegler refers to as the fault of Epimetheus, that we have *technē*, fire and knowledge of how to use it. Our ability to live with one another came later, as a corrective gift from the most powerful of gods.[44]

The fault of Epimetheus is that we, as humans do not have built in protection, we must think for ourselves and plan ahead. Our ability to develop the art of cities and living in them is the result of a forgetting, and of a theft; a double fault. Prometheus and Epimetheus need to work together – we can plan ahead, but only based on past experiences.[45] Epimetheus' name suggests heritage and the knowledge that accumulates from experience so that we may learn from our mistakes. Epimetheus has an important place for us in the understanding of cities and how we live in them, why we build them, and their relation to justice. Epimetheus also helps us to understand the relation of *eidos* to *dikē*, and how a *technē* became an *aretē*.

Where lies the 'truth' or *eletheia* in the discussion? Justice is always justice. No matter who translates it, or when it is translated. As Arendt points out, in the Athenian polis the main concern of citizens was 'talking with one another'.[46] Questions reveal more answers, and through interpretation and translation we can only hope to discover our own interpretation of the city of justice or justice in the city. Simonides suggests that 'the city teaches a man', and again, in the poem discussed in the *Protagoras* suggests:

> *A sound and healthy man, one who well knows*
> *Justice, the city's profit ...*[47]

The notion of the polis, political community, or citystate, draws attention to the theme of how we live together in cities. While Plato's *Protagoras* compares 'learning' justice to learning to play a flute, Aristotle's *Politics* suggests that the citizen is the flute-maker, and the city leader is the flautist 'laying out a masterful and compelling tune across the city'.[48] Humans, may have been forgotten by Epimetheus, but through sneakiness and ingenuity, have gained divine qualities that promote the success of the community as a whole. The point of the myth is that not only do we all have justice and a sense of moderation but that these are divine gifts of the highest order. Prometheus may have been afraid to go directly to Zeus for qualities to steal but humans get something anyway. They are evenly distributed, and all have them.

The dialogue presents us with the Socratic method of learning, and while each, Socrates and Protagoras begin at one side of the argument of whether or not *aretē* may be taught, they end on the other demonstrating just how this kind of method operates. In this sense Protagoras resembles Epimetheus: he enters the discussion like a Sophist, as a mere 'contest of words' but without foresight as to where it will lead him.[49] At the conclusion while Protagoras and Socrates have somewhat reversed their positions the actual issue has not been resolved. The *Protagoras* ends with the conclusion that until we know what *aretē* really is we may not know if it is teachable. And we end our discussion as Plato concluded his dialogue:

> *(...) 'with that we left.'*
>
> *'That ended the conversation and we left.'*
>
> *'Having said and heard these things, we went away.'*
>
> *And*
>
> *'Here our colloquy ended, and each went his way.'*[50]

NOTES

1 Plato, *Protagoras,* trans. C.C.W. Taylor (Oxford, 1889); Plato, *Laches, Protagoras, Meno, Euthydemus*, trans. W.R.M. Lamb (Cambridge, 1924); Plato, *Protagoras*, trans. M. Ostwald (New York, 1956); Plato, *Plato's Protagoras*, trans. B.A.F. Hubbard and E.S. Karnsofsky (Chicago, 1982); Plato, *Gorgias, Menexenus, Protagoras*, ed. M. Schofield, trans. T. Griffith (Cambridge, 2010).

2 Plato, *Protagoras*, trans. Taylor, 322d and 323b.

3 Edward Schiappa, *Protagoras and Logos; A Study in Greek Philosophy and Rhetoric* (Columbia, 2003).

4 Richard Kraut, *The Cambridge Companion to Plato* (Cambridge, 1992), p. xii.

5 Plato, *The Protagoras of Plato*, trans. E.G. Sihler, ed. H. Drisler (New York: Harper and Brothers, 1881) and A.W.H. Adkins, 'Αρετη, Τεχνη, Democracy and Sophists in Protagoras 316b–328d', in *Journal of Hellenic Studies*, vol. 93 (1973).

6 Plato, *Republic*, trans. A.D. Lindsay (London), 433a–b.

7 Adkins, 'Αρετη, Τεχνη'.

8 Plato, *Thaeatetus*, *Sophist*, trans. H.N.Fowler (Cambridge, 1921), 152a2–4.

9 Plato, *Protagoras*, 356–7a.

10 Hermann Sauppe and James A. Towle, *Commentary on Plato: Protagoras* (Boston and London, 1889).

11 Plato, *Protagoras*, 318e–319a.

12 Plato, *Protagoras*, 319a3.

13 Adkins, 'Αρετη, Τεχνην'.

14 Plato, *Protagoras*, Sauppe and Towle.

15 Leslie Kavanaugh, 'The architect as humanist', in *The Humanities in Architectural Design* (London, 2010), p. 37.

16 Plato, *Protagoras*, trans. Taylor; Hubbard and Karnofsky; Griffith, 319a.

17 Plato, *Protagoras*, trans. Taylor; Lamb; Ostwald; Hubbard and Karnofsky; Griffith.

18 Adkins, 'Αρετη, Τεχνη', p. 5.

19 Plato, *Protagoras*, 320c–328d.

20 Adkins, 'Αρετη, Τεχνη'.

21 Plato, *Protagoras*, trans. Hubbard and Karnofsky, p. 85.

22 Michael White, *Political Philosophy; An historical introduction* (Ann Arbor MI, 2003), p. 69.

23 G.R.F. Ferrari, 'Plato and Poetry', in G.A. Kennedy (ed.), *The Cambridge History of Literary Criticism*, vol. 1 (Cambridge, 1989).

24 Aeschylus, *The Persians and Other Plays; The Persians/Prometheus Bound/Seven Against Thebes/The Suppliants*, trans. Alan Sommerstein (London, 2009).

25 Hesiod, *Theogony and Works and Days*, trans. M.L. West (Oxford, 2008), pp. 511 and 522.

26 Plato, *Protagoras*, 320d–321b.

27 Hesiod, *Theogony* 566: 'and I discover the secret source of the fire filling the hollow of the reed' also translated 'within a hollowed fennel stalk'; also Hesiod, *Works and Days*, 50–53: '… Prometheus, … In the hollow of a fennel stalk he slipped it away, unnoticed by Zeus … ' Plato presents Olympus as a city of his own era, in which the rulers occupy the citadel and the people the lower city.

28 Plato, *Protagoras*, trans. Lamb, 322a.

29 Plato, *Protagoras*, trans. Ostwald, 322a.

30 Plato, *Protagoras*, 322b5–323b.

31 Plato, *Protagoras*, trans. Taylor; Lamb; Ostwald; Hubbard and Karnofsky; Griffith.

32 Plato, *Protagoras*, 322b3.

33 For the distinction between *politikē* and *polemike technē* see A.W.H. Adkins, *Merit and Responsibility* (Oxford, 1960). Also see *technē* as art of war in Aristotle, *Nichomachean Ethics*, 1094a.

34 Larry Goldberg, *A Commentary on Plato's Protagoras* (New York, 1983).

35 Plato, *Protagoras*, 322d.

36 Plato, 'Apology', in *Dialogues of Plato; Containing the Apology of Socrates, Crito, Phaedo, and Protagoras*, trans. Henry Cary (London, 1888), 38a.

37 Plato, *Gorgias*, 521d8.

38 Plato, *Protagoras*, trans. Griffith, 324d–325.

39 Hannah Arendt, *The Human Condition* (Chicago, 1958), p. 48.

40 Plato, 'Meno', in *Laches, Protagoras, Meno, Euthydemus*, trans. W.R.M. Lamb (London, 1924), 73c9.

41 Arendt, *The Human Condition*, p. 26.

42 Jean-François Lyotard, and Jean-Louis Thébaud, *Just Gaming*, trans. W. Godzich (Minneapolis, 1999), p. 100.

43 Richard Sennett, *The Craftsman* (London, 2008), p. 291.

44 Bernard Stiegler, *Technics and Time, 1: The Fall of Epimetheus* (London, 1998).

45 Stiegler, *Technics and Time*, 192.

46 Arendt, *The Human Condition*, p. 27.

47 Plato, *Protagoras*, 346c.

48 Adkins, 'Αρετη, Τεχνη'.

49 Sauppe and Towle, *Commentary on Plato: Protagoras*, p. 14.

50 Plato, *Protagoras*, trans. Taylor; Griffith; Hubbard and Karnofsky; Lamb, 362a3.

17

Ensemble Performances: Architects and Justice in Athenian Drama

Lisa Landrum

This chapter attests to the antiquity of architecture's practical and poetic involvement with justice by describing three ancient Greek plays in which 'architects' figure into the dramatization of just acts. The plays to be discussed include: Aeschylus' fragmentary *Dikē Play,* Aristophanes' comedy *Peace,* and Euripides' satyr play *Cyclops.*

FOUNDING INSTITUTIONS AND DISTRIBUTING HONOUR: *ARCHITECTING* IN AESCHYLUS' *DIKĒ PLAY*[1]

Among the fragments of Athenian drama one finds a few lines of tattered script belonging to a play by Aeschylus in which the activity of Dikē, the personified figure of Justice and daughter of Zeus, is arguably cast in terms of 'architecting'. Although the textual remains of this play are slight, one can nevertheless discern from them that a pivotal scene is unfolding: Dikē, having arrived as a stranger to an unnamed land, is in the midst of persuading a group (presumably the play's chorus) to receive her kindly. As Dikē explains, ever since Zeus 'justly' overcame Kronos, she has shared a place of honour on Zeus' throne. Now, at Zeus' bidding, she has descended from her divine seat with a beneficent intent. Prompted by questions from the chorus, Dikē pronounces her name: 'Justice, who has the greatest primacy in heaven.' She then elaborates on her special role, or office: for 'the just' she extends their 'life in justice'; for the brash, she chastens them. How does she do this, 'by the charms of persuasion, or by the method of force?' the chorus asks. 'By writing', Dikē responds, 'by writing their transgressions on the tablet of Zeus', then disclosing these inscriptions at the ordained time. In the last intelligible fragments of this play, Dikē testifies to her benefits by recalling how she once reformed the most violent of gods: presumably Ares, whom she brought to trial before a divine assembly, thereby founding Athens' first court.[2] Finally we learn how Dikē is likely to be received, for the chorus predicts that the 'people' will welcome this divine stranger who brings procedures for fair treatment and proof of her civilizing benefits.

Being the only surviving Greek drama in which Justice performs as a personified agent, this play of Aeschylus, partial as it is, nevertheless contributes to our understanding of the institution and representation of justice in the fifth century BCE.[3] Yet, more to the point, this rare dramatization of a personified Justice also adds to our understanding of architectural performance, since upon learning Dikē's name the chorus asks her a leading question:

> *What sort of honour do you architect?*[4]

Dikē responds, as mentioned above, by indicating that she rewards 'the just' by extending their life 'in justice', and chastens the brash by making their transgressions known. If a long life 'in justice' is the sort of 'honour' Dikē brings to mortals, then her manner of extending, withholding, distributing and adjusting such honour, as well as her mode of making dishonour apparent, must together qualify her role, or office. It is this complex office that the chorus suggestively introduces as *architecting*.

Given the fragmentary status of this script – including a gap of several letters in the critical verb – it is risky to say more about its architectural implications. However, in spite of this risk, the suggestion that the office of Justice is associated with *architecting* warrants further consideration, especially since Aeschylus made this association in the mid-fifth century BCE – at a time when architects (as we know them) were only just beginning to gain that title and so appear for the first time as figures of public significance.[5] Thus, before introducing later plays in which 'architects' are more definitively involved with justice, it is productive to ask: what may have prompted Aeschylus to qualify Dikē's distribution of honour as an architectural activity?

One may approach this question by considering the historical context – the contemporaneous ground of the play's performance. It is appropriate, however, to first seek out the poetic grounds for Aeschylus' trope. In this respect, Justice herself provides a clue to the mythic model Aeschylus had in mind when choosing his figure of speech. This clue points directly to Zeus and his triumph over Kronos. According to Hesiod's *Theogony,* after overcoming Kronos, Zeus commenced his first official business: re-distributing 'honour' to each and every god Kronos had oppressed. Hades, for instance, was allotted the honour of influencing the dead, while Poseidon earned dominion over the sea. Aphrodite gained sway over the alluring ways of women, and so on for each of the immortals. Like the 'honour' Dikē purportedly *architects* in Aeschylus' play, the 'honour' Zeus allocates in the *Theogony* is also called *timē*. For Hesiod, however, Zeus did not 'architect' this *timē*, instead, he 'declared', 'arranged', 'apportioned', 'divided' and even 'subdivided' it. Such manners of distributing honour suggest that Zeus not only entitled each god to influential powers and privileges but also arranged appropriate accommodations for them. Indeed, just as one (in the position to do so) might divvy-out spoils among comrades after a lucrative raid, or partition land among citizens when founding a city, Zeus allots to each god both an appropriate mode of influence and a correspondingly influential placement. Zeus himself, as the new sovereign, fittingly ascends to a new place of honour: high atop Mount Olympus. Other Olympians rise as well to dwell there with him. Hades and Poseidon come to be situated elsewhere: below the earth and within the sea, respectively. Yet, it is not only these new ruling gods who earn honours and placements from Zeus, since the poet also sings of the revised honours and reordered arrangements of other more contentious and marginal agents. The transgressive Titans, who had brashly attempted to overthrow Zeus' rule, are stripped of honour, banished and imprisoned deep below the earth in Tartaros. The gigantic Hundred-Handers, who had helped Zeus resist the Titans, are deployed to an appropriately supportive place: beneath the sea 'at Ocean's foundations'. The monstrous Gorgons, and other agents dangerous to mortals, are placed at another limit: beyond Oceanus – 'at earth's end'.

This survey of gods receiving 'honours' in the *Theogony* could be expanded, yet it is sufficient to show how Zeus' distributive activity is not only resonate with the office of Justice (as presented by Aeschylus) but also analogous to *architecting*. For, in having declared due honour for each god, Zeus concurrently elaborated a broadly differentiated topography of upper, lower and liminal regions. And within these differentiated regions diverse agents – both complementary and conflictual – were appropriately accommodated: in poetic correspondence to their unique mode of influence; in telling relation to one another; and in anticipation of mortals, who would come to dwell diversely and in conflict in the terrestrial region bounded in their midst. Although Zeus is not said *to architect* this topography in the *Theogony,* he does acquire a capability to which Hesiod gives a tectonic title. Upon rising to his new office, Zeus takes for himself (indeed swallows) his first wife named Mētis, who personifies 'cunning intelligence', and who Hesiod qualifies elsewhere as a *tektōn* of *dikaion*: an 'artisan of just judgements', or 'fabricator of what is just'.[6] It is only after assimilating this discerning feminine agent – who might 'advise him in matters good and bad' – that Zeus' governance begins to prosper.[7] And, so, together with Zeus, and the story of his original distribution of honour, Aeschylus may have also had Mētis in mind – as first '*tektōn* of what is just' – when he figured the discerning office of Dikē in terms of *architecting.*

Before moving to other examples, I must touch on the play's performative context. Although the dating and circumstances of this play involving Dikē are not certain, some scholars contend that the fragments belong to Aeschylus' most unique drama: neither a tragedy nor a satyr play (as he annually composed for the Dionysian festival in Athens), but rather an aetiological composition – a dramatization of origins – commissioned by Hieron, the new ruling tyrant of Sicily, to celebrate his founding of Aetna in 476 BCE. Ancient testimony tells us that Aeschylus put forth such a drama optimistically as 'an omen of good life for the settlers of the city'.[8] If the founding of Aetna was indeed the occasion for this play's performance then it would only have added to the aptness of Aeschylus' architectural trope, for the arrival of Dikē to this newly founded land would aim to initiate – most dramatically and auspiciously – both the beginning of justice for the settlers and a just beginning for the city they would build.

I must forego a discussion of this play's colonial implications in order to introduce two complete scripts in which 'architects' again become involved with justice, but in different contexts and with different motives, tactics and mythic models in mind. I will first treat Aristophanes' *Peace*, a comedy staged at the Dionysian festival in Athens in 421 BCE (fifty-five years after the optimistic founding of Aetna), during the tenth agonizing year of the Peloponnesian War.

RESTORING COMPREHENSIVE JUSTICE: DARING *TO ARCHITECT* IN ARISTOPHANES' *PEACE*[9]

Unlike Aeschylus' *Dikē Play*, which features a divine Justice descending to a receptive mortal plane, Aristophanes' *Peace* begins with a discontented mortal rising boldly to the heavens in search of a comprehensive justice, which the region has not yet found. In a parody of war-weary Athens, *Peace* depicts the city's institutions as dysfunctional and its citizens as self-interested sycophants, who reluctant to compromise are eager to condemn.[10] Caught in this problematic situation, Trygaeus, a farmer, decides to take his concern for society's well-being directly to the highest authority: Zeus. However, after flying a dung-beetle to the heavens, Trygaeus discovers that Zeus has abandoned his post. Only Hermes remains to explain that Zeus – having himself become fed-up with warmongering mortals – has allowed War to take over his place. When Trygaeus learns that War has imprisoned Peace in a pit and resolved to destroy the cities and citizens, he initiates a plan to rescue Peace (sister to Justice) and, thus, restore order to all.

Trygaeus begins his plan with a summons, to which a chorus of labourers responds. As this group bursts into the orchestra in exuberant dance, their own leader calls out to Trygaeus:

> *If it is necessary for us to do anything (in view of peace),*
> *direct us and architect.*[11]

Following this performative command, given as an imperative verb (*architektonei*), Trygaeus begins more officially and collaboratively what he had himself already begun: restoring Peace, a task that now involves directing others in a common purpose so that, together, they may hoist Peace up from the pit.

Subsequent events in the play reveal plenty about architectural activity, for when Peace finally appears she appears as an appealing statue, which Trygaeus ceremoniously 'installs'.[12] However much this installation may have reflected an aspect of architectural work at the time, our attention here must focus on how justice figures in the architect's overall scheme.

In addition to figuring in absentia into those situations of injustice that motivate Trygaeus to act in the first place, justice also performs overtly in the paradigmatic stories prefiguring Trygaeus' deeds. For, in flying a dung-beetle 'straight to Zeus',

Trygaeus mimes the extraordinary flights of certain justice-seeking heroes known from myth. These paradigms for just action include: Bellerophon, who took flight on Pegasus to slay beasts on behalf of society; and a tiny dung-beetle, who in a fable of Aesop flew directly to Zeus, boldly seeking justice against an eagle on behalf of a wronged rabbit. In *Peace*, Trygaeus evokes both the flight of 'Pegasus' and the story of 'Aesop', just as he commences his own justice-seeking ascent on behalf of others.[13] Where Trygaeus appears willing to engage more conventional procedures, it is to boldly indict Zeus. For, as he takes flight on the 'beetle', he warns that if Zeus refuses to reveal a plan for restoring worldly harmony he will 'write him up' – the same mode of prosecution that Justice herself claims as a definitive part of her office in Aeschylus' *Dikē Play*.[14] Trygaeus' comic appropriation of such divine and mythic agencies of justice is heightened by his use of the 'beetle', since this 'beetle' was the *deus ex machina* – the theatrical stage-machine, which typically enabled gods to bring resolution to earthly conflicts.

Aside from figuring in the situations and stories that motivate and guide Trygaeus, justice is found also in the peaceful conditions he leads others to recover. When Trygaeus and the chorus draw Peace out from the pit and into the light, comprehensive social justice is drawn out with her: people are released from military service to return to healthier pursuits; farmers are freed from fortified cities to resume agrarian livelihoods; and citizens of formerly conflicted city-states are 'reconciled'.[15] By drawing-out Peace, a vital prerequisite for open-minded governance is also recuperated, since Theōria, a lively personification of 'Beholding', emerges together with the statue of Peace and is restored directly to Council. Trygaeus himself accomplishes this reparation by leading Theōria to a prominent place among Councillors seated in the theatre's front row. This meta-theatrical episode is one of many in *Peace* wherein the intimate bonds between political and theatrical representation are made dramatically apparent.[16]

Along with these social and institutional reparations, recovering Peace also revitalizes a more elemental justice, since alongside Peace and Theōria comes 'Harvest', a voluptuous figure of agricultural abundance whom Trygaeus (whose own name implies 'Harvester') ultimately takes as his bride.[17] Trygaeus and his collaborators draw-out this fertile figure both physically, with their rope, and verbally, with catalogues of earthy benefits. These show forth palpably in song as plentiful produce, seasonal regularity, and proper mortal toil, such as ploughing fields, planting crops, harvesting produce, preparing feasts and marrying brides. This bountiful and vigorous imagery not only projects a prodigious future but also recalls a mythic past, since the imagery resonates with scenes of peace and prosperity in Homeric poetry. These exemplary scenes, which Trygaeus (and Aristophanes) must have had in mind when pursuing (and composing) *Peace*, include: the scene of ploughing, reaping and 'harvesting', as animated on the shield of Achilles; and the comparable scene of an ever-blooming orchard and vineyard, together with their rhythms of 'harvesting', as portrayed in the land of the Phaeacians.[18] And within each of these peaceful scenes, one finds as well the enactment of justice: situated within the ring of cultivated land on the shield of Achilles is a circle of elders, who are each deliberating judgment on a case;

and bounded by the generous orchard and vineyard of the Phaeacians is their hospitable palace hall, where a stranger (Odysseus) is kindly received, judged on the merits of his speech, and duly awarded honours.

If the peace and justice that Trygaeus (and Aristophanes) sought *to architect* were modelled after these Homeric scenes, then we ought also to regard how each scene entails architectural conditions. Upon the shield of Achilles, such conditions are found in the configuration of deliberating elders, who are seated in a 'sacred circle' upon a ring of 'polished stones', as well as in a configuration of circling youths, 'running round with cunning feet' upon a 'dance floor' modelled after the *choros* of Daedalus.[19] Similar conditions are actively initiated by Phaeacian officials as they prepare a 'dance floor' by levelling the ground and marking its limit. Architectural conditions are also woven into the hospitable Phaeacian halls – with their golden doors, silver doorposts, bronze threshold, and elaborate walls with fixed seats extending 'from the threshold to the innermost chamber' – wherein Odysseus' stories are shared and judged.[20] What must be emphasized here is that each of these architectural settings – the sacred circles, dance floors and ornamented halls – are not only elaborately crafted and appropriately arranged for dwellers and their activities, but are also active in sponsoring practices constitutive of peace and justice: deliberating judgments, hosting strangers, and exchanging stories. Taken together with the ever-blooming orchards and vineyards (and their related activities), these original situations of peace and justice may be regarded as the bases for Trygaeus' and Aristophanes' schemes – the exemplary 'beginnings' from which *Peace,* the play, and peace, the comprehensive condition, gain poetic orientation, mythic depth and enduring relevance.

To early Greek poets, such 'beginnings' were known as *archai,* which were more like poetic foundations than philosophical principles.[21] Given that Trygaeus was seeking *to architect* such founding conditions, it is not surprising that the Peace he recovers is repeatedly associated with *archai* in the play: Peace is said to re-inaugurate, or 'begin', many good things; to revive choral performances with 'original' themes; to reinvigorate 'ancient' customs; to recall 'archaic' ways of life; and to remix amiable affiliations – just as these were 'in the beginning'.[22] Conditions of *archē,* then, are also drawn-forth when this architect-protagonist draws-up Peace: not only Peace and her benefits but her *pre*-conditions. And Trygaeus makes these *archē*-conditions apparent for others not by pointing forlornly to some abstract peace lodged inaccessibly in the distant past, but by revealing Peace as a vital potentiality, the 'beginnings' of which are available to all those assembled right there in the present. For, in spite of the dramatic conceit that Peace lay hidden in a remote heavenly pit, Trygaeus and his collaborators draw her out from the very grounds of the theatre. They then give this act more enduring presence by refounding 'archaic' Peace anew: 'installing' her appealing statue as a dramatic figure in the orchestra. From this position on the 'dance floor', Peace not only becomes available for all to 'behold', but also re-activates the theatre as a primary arena for such peace-building activities as deliberating judgments, hosting strangers, and exchanging stories.

By his bold initiatives, then, this architect-protagonist reveals the 'beginnings' of peace and justice as being latent within the very situation that he, the chorus, the poets and diverse spectators share.

AGENTS OF POETIC JUSTICE: ARCHITECTS IN THE LAND OF THE CYCLOPS[23]

Within a few years of Aristophanes' *Peace*, Euripides presented *Cyclops* at the Dionysian festival in Athens (circa 424 BCE). Being a satyr play, *Cyclops* would have been staged after a trio of Euripides' own tragedies, thus culminating a day of tragic immersion with a kind of comic relief. As its title suggests, the plot of *Cyclops* follows the story Odysseus tells in book nine of the *Odyssey*. Euripides departs from his Homeric model, however, in a number of significant ways: by setting the action in Aetna (instead of a mythic terrain); by eliminating the obstructive stone at the mouth of Polyphemus' cave (replacing it with the traversable opening of the skēnē); by involving a requisite chorus of satyrs and their father Silenus (devotees of Dionysus); and by implicating 'architects', since Odysseus confers this plural title upon himself just as he reveals his scheme to punish Polyphemus. For Euripides, then, the situation involving architects and justice begins as follows.

Like Aristophanes' *Peace*, Euripides' *Cyclops* begins with circumstances of injustice: at the beginning of the play Silenus and the satyrs are already trapped against their will on the island of Polyphemus. Having become shipwrecked, while searching for Dionysus, these revel loving creatures now suffer in servitude to a reclusive giant. Yet, the situation soon becomes hopeful: as the satyrs sing their desire for Dionysus and Dionysian ways, Silenus spots Odysseus' ship. Odysseus and his crew subsequently appear, pronouncing their own basic desire for food. Hence, Odysseus and Silenus initiate a trade. To Silenus' delight, Odysseus has wine to offer, and for just one cup of this Dionysian substance, Silenus is prepared to give away all of Polyphemus' flocks, cheese and milk. But this exchange is interrupted when Polyphemus suddenly struts into the orchestra. Silenus, now terrified at being caught giving away the food, misrepresents Odysseus and his crew as hostile bandits. Neither Odysseus' verbal self-defence, nor the satyrs' protest that Polyphemus do no 'injustice' to the strangers, nor even Odysseus' elaborate attempt at dissuasion succeed in moving the giant, who, in response to these pleas, delivers a detailed counter-argument upholding his Cyclopean ways. He then demands that Silenus ready the fire and sharpen his knives, for he shall roast (not host) these strangers. As Polyphemus forces the hapless crew into his cave, Odysseus utters a prayer soliciting the vigilance of Zeus. Then, he, too, disappears behind the skēnē, leaving the chorus of satyrs to musically conjure the hidden horrors of the cannibal's meal.

But Odysseus eludes the beast. Sneaking out of the cave and into the orchestra, he delivers vivid testimony: two sailors have already been devoured, and those remaining (himself included) will soon be killed, cooked and eaten if he fails to act. And, so, Odysseus has risked crossing the cave's threshold to persuade the satyrs to collaborate in his scheme to subdue the giant (by wine), then blind and flee the beast. If successful, his scheme will release the endangered sailors, free the captive chorus, and allow Odysseus himself to resume a homeward course. But that is not all. Odysseus also emphasizes that his scheme will appropriately punish Polyphemus. Thus, having fully disclosed the improper conditions within the cave and the many details of his 'retribution', Odysseus urges his potential collaborators with these pivotal words:

> *Be silent now – for you know my scheme completely – and*
> *when I command, be persuaded (to follow) the architects.*[24]

Although, when the time comes, the satyrs will not follow Odysseus' command directly, Odysseus ultimately leads his scheme to completion. For, with the help of the satyr's song (and other influential agencies), Polyphemus is, in the end, blinded and left alone on his island, while the full ensemble of satyrs and mortals – liberated – together flee.

There is much in this play for architects to consider, but the ways in which justice performs in Odysseus' scheme must remain our focus. To begin, Odysseus acts justly because, like Trygaeus, he acts on behalf of disadvantaged others: ostensibly, the sailors and satyrs. Like Trygaeus, Odysseus also exposes injustices: notably, the cannibal's consumption of men within the cave. More important than the horrific details of this transgression, however, are the underlying injustices that the extreme physical mistreatment allegorizes.

Much in the same way that War's concealment of Peace makes mortal's obstruction of peace alarmingly apparent in Aristophanes' comedy, Polyphemus' enslavement of satyrs and murderous consumption of sailors in Euripides' satyr play provide extreme dramatizations of basic improprieties: namely, the abuse of 'customs' (*nomoi*) associated with Dionysian rites and hospitality. Polyphemus himself makes this abuse clear by arrogantly dismissing all 'customs' as trivial ornaments to life. Over the course of the play, we gradually learn the full scope of this dismissal. Polyphemus renounces not only hospitality and Dionysian rites (musical expression, dancing and wine-drinking), but also poetic language and honest discourse, for he censures Odysseus' 'well-shaped words' and dismisses the satyrs' moralizing speech, while embracing Silenus' flattery as 'most just'.[25] Polyphemus also rejects working in harmony with the seasons and the land, for he cultivates no grain and nurtures no vines. Correspondingly, he has no concern for the weather, no interest in portents (such as thunder), and no thought for the future. Having founded neither cities nor households he fosters no institutions or laws, and follows no rules beyond the unquestioned rule of the self. Finally, in maintaining no altars, he worships no gods besides his own belly, 'the greatest of divinities', which he singularly honours and ceremoniously sacrifices to.[26]

With such impious, asocial, anarchic and apathetic demonstrations, one recognizes that in the land of the Cyclops not only are there no social 'customs' but there are no conditions for architecture. It is no wonder, then, that an 'architect' would lead a scheme to flee such a land and attempt to restore those improperly confined there to more propitious dwelling conditions, for Odysseus specifically promises to return his mortal crew to their homeward bound ship, and to restore the devout satyrs to the 'halls of Dionysus'.[27]

Like the protagonist of *Peace*, the 'architect' in *Cyclops* restores displaced and disempowered individuals – both mortal and divine – to appropriate settings supportive of those individuals and their vital modes of being. Yet, Odysseus' full range of action may resemble more the manifold office of Dikē as portrayed by Aeschylus. For, like Dikē, Odysseus not only extends honour but also makes dishonour apparent by graphically blinding Polyphemus. As aggressive as this mode of 'retribution' seems, the Greek word for it (*timōria*) suggests a more broadly sanctioned act meant to safeguard 'honour'. This is because *timōria* is a compound term, joining together *timē*, 'honour' (such as Dikē and Zeus distribute), and *oromai*, the act of keeping watch or 'looking on' with vigilance.[28] Such vigilance is demonstrated at a critical moment in the satyr play: as the sailors are forcibly marshalled into the cannibal's cave, Odysseus implores Zeus to 'look' and see the injustice underway: 'Zeus, Protector of Strangers… *look* upon these things'.[29] In performance, Odysseus' command would have appealed not only to Zeus in the heavens but also to the spectators in the theatre. Thus, *all* eyes would turn to witness the dramatic events as violations of honour.

Bearing all this in mind, Odysseus' blinding of Polyphemus can be regarded somewhat more positively and reciprocally. For, by turning away Cyclopean vision while simultaneously turning collective attention toward the 'customs' that such vision threatens, Odysseus restores the primacy of those contested 'customs' and renews appreciation for the 'social order' (*eunomia*) that their continued practice aims to ensure.

Although Odysseus' restorative aims in Euripides' *Cyclops* liken him to Trygaeus and Dikē, his performance also diverges in telling ways. Where Odysseus diverges most from these kindred 'architects' is in his tactics. For, Odysseus neither 'writes up' transgressions on behalf of Zeus nor 'raises up' himself and absent gods with stage machines. Instead, this oddly plural 'architect' brings about his scheme of restoration, liberation and retribution with a subtler mix of agencies: persuasive speech, alluring props and potent wine. It is the wine in particular – itself representative of dramatic transformation and Dionysian influence – that is most closely linked to *dikē* in the script, and most palpably felt to bring about cultural renewal in the land of the Cyclops. This is because just before blinding Polyphemus, Odysseus first intoxicates him, by treating him – in a feigned symposium – to a strong taste of the very 'customs' (hospitality and Dionysian rites) he had previously denied. In this dramatic and ironic way Odysseus accomplishes poetic justice, chastening Polyphemus while symmetrically restoring manifold honours: to the mistreated sailors and satyrs; to the dishonoured gods, Zeus and Dionysus; to the disrespected 'customs' these gods exemplify; and to the spectators, who had themselves assembled for the Dionysian festival to participate in the very social and sacred practices Odysseus defends.

At the end of *Cyclops*, then, as at the end of *Peace*, comprehensive order and justice are dramatically reconstituted by an architect-protagonist, who leads others to collectively rediscover desirable conditions and practices latent in their midst.

PRE-PHILOSOPHICAL GROUNDS OF ARCHITECTURE AND JUSTICE

The plays introduced above do not present a philosophy of justice. In fact, it is their *pre*-philosophical (symbolic, allegorical and situational) manner of dramatizing certain dilemmas and deeds of justice that make them so strangely important for understanding the gradual emergence of justice as an abstract moral concept.[30] It is worth recalling that Plato, who would eventually ask 'what *is* justice' in his *Republic,* was himself but a child when *Peace* and *Cyclops* were performed. We are perhaps right to wonder, then, whether the injustice in Polyphemus' cave and the idealism of comic heroes like Trygaeus remained active in the philosopher's imagination as he later crafted the *logos* of his philosophical dialogues. In lieu of elaborating on the relevance of these plays to philosophy, I offer in conclusion a way to consider these three unique dramas (involving three different dramatists and three distinct genres) as a meaningfully coherent trio involving architecture and justice.

It is no doubt an accident of history that the surviving corpus of Athenian drama contains only three protagonists – Dikē, Trygaeus and Odysseus – who are each qualified as 'architect' while acting as an exemplary proponent of justice, peace and social order. This particular trio of conditions, however, was not a random cluster in Greek myth and thought. Neither was their association with architectural beginnings unprecedented. For these three vital conditions – Justice, Peace and Social Order – were together known as the Hōrai, daughters of Zeus and Themis.[31] As agencies constitutive of worldly harmony, these three sisters not only figured into the genealogy of gods but also the genesis of cities, since the lyric poet Pindar portrayed Justice, Peace and Social Order dwelling among mortals as the 'firm foundation for cities.'[32] This image of architectural and civic cohesion reminds us that Justice, Peace and Social Order are palpably vital yet vulnerable conditions that any architect-protagonist may endeavour to establish, defend, honour and restore.

NOTES

1 Unless otherwise noted, all translations follow Alan H. Sommerstein, *Aeschylus III: Fragments* (Cambridge MA and London, 2008), pp. 276–87.

2 According to myth, the site of this trial was thereafter named the Areopagus, or 'Hill of Ares'. Aeschylus' *Orestia* dramatizes an alternative version of this founding myth.

3 On the representation of Justice in epic and dramatic poetry, see Eric A. Havelock, *The Greek Concept of Justice* (Cambridge MA, 1978); and Hugh Lloyd-Jones, *The Justice of Zeus* (Berkeley CA, 1971).

4 *Dikē Play* 16, author's translation. This translation accepts the reconstruction of *architektoneis* by D.L. Page, 'P.Oxy. 2331 and Others', *Classical Review, New Series,* 7/3–4 (Dec. 1957): 189–92.

5 The earliest 'architect' term is otherwise found in Herodotus' *Histories,* circa 425 BCE. The earliest inscription bearing 'architect' (*IG* i³ 32) dates to 447/6 or 432/1 BCE, see Hendrik Svenson-Evers, *Die Griechischen Architekten Archaischer und Klassischer Zeit* (Frankfurt am Main, 1996), pp. 237–43.

6 Frag. 343/294.14, Glenn W. Most, *Hesiod II* (Cambridge MA and London, 2007), pp. 351–3.

7 *Theogony* 900. On the importance of Mētis for Zeus' governance, see Marcel Detienne and Jean-Pierre Vernant, *Cunning Intelligence in Greek Culture and Society* (Hassocks, 1978), pp. 57–105.

8 *Vita Aeschyli* 9, with C. J. Herington 'Aeschylus in Sicily', *Journal of Hellenic Studies,* 87 (1967): 74–85; Lloyd-Jones, *Justice of Zeus*, p. 100; and Sommerstein, *Aeschylus,* pp. 6–9.

9 Unless otherwise noted, all translations follow Jeffrey Henderson, *Aristophanes II* (Cambridge MA and London, 1998). My interpretation of *Peace* has been enriched by the detailed introduction and commentary of S. Douglas Olson, *Aristophanes' Peace* (Oxford, 1998).

10 On *Peace's* relation to contemporaneous circumstances in Athens, including the 'Peace of Nicias', see Olson, *Peace*, pp. xxv–xxxi.

11 *Peace* 305, author's translation.

12 *Peace* 923ff. This 'installation' is dramatized as a *hidrusis*—a veritable rite establishing a divinity's influence at a particular site. See Walter Burkert, *Greek Religion* (Boston MA, 1985), pp. 88–92.

13 *Peace* 76, 129–34. On other mythic schemas underlying *Peace's* plot, see A.M. Bowie, *Aristophanes: Myth, Ritual and Comedy* (Cambridge, 1993), pp. 142–50.

14 *Peace* 107; *Dikē Play* 21.

15 *Peace* 540, 526–55.

16 *Peace* 877–908. On metatheatricality in Aristophanes, see Niall W. Slater, *Spectator Politics* (Philadelphia PA, 2002). See also Lisa Landrum, 'Performing Theōria: Architectural Acts in Aristophanes' *Peace*', in Marcia Feuerstein and Gray Read (eds), *Architecture as a Performing Art* (Farnham and Burlington VT, 2013).

17 On Trygaeus' special name, see Olson, *Peace,* note to line 190; and Edith Hall, *The Theatrical Cast of Athens* (Oxford, 2006), pp. 321–52.

18 *Iliad* 18.541–572; *Odyssey* 7.112–132.

19 *Iliad* 18.503–504, 590–606.

20 *Odyssey* 8.258–264; 7.81–102.

21 See William Mullen, *Choreia: Pindar and Dance* (Princeton NJ, 1982), pp. 116–17.

22 Each quote denotes a word cognate with *archē* (singular of *archai*) in *Peace* 436, 780, 572, 694, 996, 1327.

23 Unless otherwise noted, all translations follow David Kovacs, *Euripides I* (Cambridge MA and London, 2001). I must also acknowledge my debt to Richard Seaford's detailed introduction and commentary, *Cyclops of Euripides* (London, 2003).

24 *Cyclops* 476–8, author's translation.

25 *Cyclops* 274.

26 *Cyclops* 335.

27 *Cyclops* 430.

28 Fiona McHardy, *Revenge in Athenian Culture* (London, 2008), p. 3.

29 *Cyclops,* 354.

30 See Havelock, *The Greek Concept of Justice*.

31 Hesiod, *Theogony* 901–3.

32 *Olympian Ode* 13.6–7.

18

The Architecture of Lincoln Cathedral and the Institution of Justice

John Hendrix

18.1 View of the nave elevation and vaulting of Lincoln Cathedral (photo by author)

The façade of Lincoln Cathedral reinforces the authority of the kings and Old and New Testament figures. The organization of the cathedral reinforces the hierarchical organization of a just society based on Christian morality, in facilitating the rituals of the worshippers and the clergy in the liturgical mass. The Dean's Eye and Bishop's Eye, the stained glass windows at the north and south ends of the great transept, reinforce the authority of the Dean and Bishop of the cathedral in the maintenance of the Christian ideal of the just, or the good. Most importantly, all of the details of the architecture of the cathedral reinforce the intellectual comprehension of the just or the good on the part of the worshipper. The details are designed to facilitate the ascension of the mind of the visitor from the physical particulars of sensual reality, the temptations of which are the source of unjust acts, to the intelligible universals of a metaphysical reality, which reinforce justice in the concept of the good, the universally just state.

In the *Republic* of Plato, a just, well-ordered state depends on the just, well-ordered soul of each individual. The cathedral institutes the well-ordered soul of each individual in order to facilitate a just state. The soul of each individual becomes well-ordered, through the experience of the architecture, as it ascends from the multiple particulars of experience to the universal laws which govern experience. This is enacted in the architecture through the transition from the compositions of the elevations and vaulting (Fig. 18.1), in geometrical and mathematical relations, to the purity of the light in the stained glass windows, the spiritual light, or *lux spiritualis*, which conveys the universal concept of the just

18.2 View of the Dean's Eye, Lincoln Cathedral (photo by author)

or the good. The mind of the viewer ascends from its material intellect, the *nous pathetikos* of Aristotle, which is passive and easily influenced, to an active intellect, the *nous poietikos* of Aristotle, which is a universal, divine intellect. As the active or divine intellect begins to participate in the mind of the viewer through the experience of the architecture, the viewer begins to understand the concept of justice in morality, in universal truth rather than individual need or desire.

The remains of the original Norman wall in the west front contain Norman sculpture from the time of Bishop Alexander. The figures represent incidents from Biblical history but are haphazardly arranged, suggesting that they were not original to Lincoln. The figures are three feet six inches tall, and are placed above eye level. From north to south, the figures depict the torments of the wicked, and Christ triumphant over Satan in the jaws of Hell. Jamb figures represent saints, Christ weighing souls, Lazarus taken up to Heaven, the expulsion of Adam and Eve, the call of Samuel, Samuel and Eli, and God's injunction to Noah. Other figures on the wall represent Man tilling the soil, Noah building the Ark, entering the Ark, and Daniel in the lion's den. More statues were added later in the mid-fourteenth century by Treasurer John Welbourne, of English kings from William I to Edward III.

The main source of light in the cathedral is the rose windows. At the north end of the great or west transept is the Dean's Eye (Fig. 18.2), and at the south end is the Bishop's Eye (Fig. 18.3). The windows are the best example of stained glass in the early thirteenth century in England, preceding the stained glass at Canterbury. Both windows in the transept are twenty-four feet in diameter. The Dean's Eye retains its original tracery, while the tracery of the Bishop's Eye is from the Decorated Period in the fourteenth century, inserted around 1320 in honor of John of Dalderby. Both windows are described in the *Metrical Life of Saint Hugh*, and they would have been completed during the bishopric of Robert Grosseteste. The Dean's Eye faces the deanery to the north, while the Bishop's Eye faces the bishop's palace to the south, next to the Galilee Porch, the ceremonial entrance to the cathedral for the bishop. As described in the *Metrical Life of Saint Hugh*, the Dean's Eye protects the cathedral from the spirit of the Devil to the north, while the Bishop's Eye invites the Holy Spirit to the south into the cathedral. The *Metrical Life* was the second biography of Bishop Hugh of Avalon, written by Henry of Avranches, a friend of Grosseteste, between 1220 and 1235, when Grosseteste became Bishop of Lincoln.

The subject of the images in the glass of the Dean's Eye is the Church on Earth, the Church Militant, paired with the Church in Heaven, the Church Triumphant, in sixteen circular openings surrounding a quatrefoil. Christ is seated in the center surrounded by the blessed in Heaven. Four compartments surrounding the central image, which are probably not in their original positions, forming the quatrefoil, show various subjects, including the relics of Saint Hugh. Subjects in the sixteen outer circles of the window include angels with the instruments of the Passions, Saint Peter conducting people to Heaven, the Resurrection, and bishops and archbishops. Below the window, five lancet windows can be seen through an arcade of seven lancet arches. Large lancet windows on either side of the Dean's doorway, dating from the fourteenth century, contain images of angels playing musical instruments and geometrical patterns. The musical instruments of the angels are a reference to the *musica cosmica* in contrast to the *musica mundana*, that there corresponds to all music created by human beings a celestial music from above, in the same way that the geometrical patterns represent a celestial intelligence in relation to human intelligence.

In the *Commentary on the Posterior Analytics* (I. 17)[1] of Robert Grosseteste, a *lux spiritualis* floods over intelligible objects, or *res intelligibiles*, like the light through the stained glass window in the cathedral, and over the mind's eye, or *oculus mentis*, and stands to the interior eye, or *oculus interior*, and to intelligible objects as the corporeal sun stands to the bodily eye and to visible corporeal objects,[2] following Aristotle, Themistius, Alfarabi, Avicenna, and Averroes. The *lumen spiritualis*, the light produced by the *lux spiritualis*, allows the mental sight, the *visus mentalis*, to apprehend the intelligibles in the *virtus intellectiva*, or *nous poietikos*, as the light of the sun, the *lumen solare*, makes vision possible. The *lumen spiritualis* is the 'first visible' in interior sight, *visus interior*, as the coloured body is the first thing receptive of the light of the sun (I. 19). The coloured glass in the stained glass window corresponds to the *lumen spiritualis* in the *oculus mentis*.

The more receptive the intelligible object, the *species apprehensibilis*, is to the *lux spiritualis*, the more visible it is to the *oculus mentis*. The object which is most similar to the light, the least material, is the most receptive of it. The power of the mind, the *acies mentis*, is a spiritual light, an *irradiatio spiritualis*, which operates in the *virtus intellectiva* to illuminate the *species apprehensibilis*, and the *virtus* is strongest when the object is the least material and conforms most easily to the immaterial *species*. The architecture of the cathedral presents a hierarchy of materiality in forms, like the hierarchy of the celestial spheres, following the 'principle of divisibility' of Scholasticism, in the multiplication and division of the architectural forms, culminating in the pure *lux spiritualis* which enters through the stained glass window.

Each of the stained glass windows at Lincoln is the *oculus mentis* of the body of the cathedral. The coloured glass is the *lumen spiritualis*, and the geometry of the tracery is the *species apprehensibilis*, the intelligibles of the architecture, and the structure of the cosmos, visible to the *oculus mentis*. The sight of the mind, the *visus interior*, is turned toward darkness and idleness when deflected from the *lumen spiritualis*, and is occupied with 'corruptible bodily things' (I. 14), as Grosseteste describes in the *Commentary*, but when it perceives a trace or *vestigium* of the *lux spiritualis*, it seeks it out, as the visitor to the cathedral seeks out the stained glass window, and then the *visus interior* is able to perceive the *lumen spiritualis* within.

The analogy of spiritual light to corporeal light was applied by Grosseteste to elements of the operations of the Church. In *De Libero Arbitrio*, or *On Free Will*, the analogy is applied to the Trinity, as the *lux spiritualis* is the mediation between the intelligible and material in the same way that the Holy Spirit is the mediation between the Celestial Father and the Body of Christ. In *De Libero Arbitrio*, the light shining through the stained glass window of the cathedral is seen as the operation of divine grace through free will. In his *Epistolae*, Grosseteste compared his relationship as Bishop to the clergy of the cathedral, and the relationship between the Pope and his prelates, including Grosseteste, to a mirror reflecting light into dark places. The Bishop illuminates the minds of the clergy by reflecting the *species apprehensibilis* by the *lux spiritualis* into the *oculus mentis* of the clergy, so that the *species apprehensibilis* can become the *species sensibilis*, sensible or perceived form, as a tangible rule of operation, in the correct operations of the Church, and the Bishop can assert his authority. The universal law is translated into material operations.

In the *Metrical Life of Saint Hugh*, the round stained glass windows are compared to heavenly bodies, whose 'circular display, facing the north and south, outshines all the rest [of the windows in the cathedral] with its twofold light'.[3] While the two windows in the transept can be seen as the sun and the moon, the rest of the windows 'may be likened to common stars'. The two windows are not only like the sun and the moon, but 'they excel: for the sun, reflected on the clouds, produces the rainbow; while these two flash without the sun …' The windows represent the Bishop and the Dean, as the Bishop, as described by Grosseteste in the *Epistolae*, illuminates the minds of the clergy by reflecting the *species apprehensibilis*, the intelligible form provided by the *lux spiritualis*, as through the stained glass window, into the *oculus mentis* of the clergy, in order to establish the rules of operation for the church. As Grosseteste explained in *De Libero Arbitrio*, the light shining through the stained glass windows is the 'operation of divine grace', as a light without a corporeal source. Inscriptions above the windows describe 'dwellers in the Heavenly City and the weapons with which they overcame the Stygian Tyrant', of the River Styx, so that the windows

18.3 View of the Bishop's Eye, Lincoln Cathedral (photo by author)

represent the heavenly cities, as in the *De Civitate Dei* of Saint Augustine. The windows allow the architecture to play the role of reinforcing standards of Christian justice in medieval society.

The Bishop's Eye is the greater of the two windows, because it faces south to receive the Holy Spirit, while the Dean's Eye faces north to protect the church against the Devil. The two windows illuminate the cathedral from the 'lantern of heaven', the great transept, which 'with these eyes surveys the gloom of Lethe', the oblivion of the river of forgetfulness in Hades. While the two great windows symbolize the Bishop and Dean, the clerestory windows below symbolize the canons, and in the aisles, the vicars, in a descending hierarchy from spiritual to more material affairs. The hierarchy of windows can be seen as a diagram of the order of the Church, an *imago generalis ecclesiae*, and as the reflection of light described by Grosseteste in his *Epistolae*, from the Bishop to the clergy of the cathedral.

In the *Metrical Life*, the colours of the body of the church represent the virtues of the heavenly cities. 'The hewn white stone stands for the chaste and wise: whiteness is decency [and purity] and its shaping, doctrine [or justice].' In the dark marble, 'smooth, shining, dark, is signified the Bride [or the virgin Mary], frank, virtuous, afflicted. Its smoothness truly exemplifies her utter candor, the polish her virtues, and the darkness her distress.' The colours are the product of the *lumen spiritualis*, the spiritual light reflected in the corporeal world, in the *species sensibilis*, by the *lux spiritualis*.

The 'consummation of the whole allegory' of the church is that 'the insentient stones conceal the mysteries of stones that live; the fabric made with hands

18.4 View of Saint Hugh's Choir, Lincoln Cathedral (photo by author)

displays that of the spirit; the outward appearance of the church shines doubly, enriched with twofold array.' The architecture of the church combines the material and the spiritual, the *virtus cogitativa* and *virtus intellectiva* in intellect. The architecture is the imprint on matter of the idea of the architect, participating in divine intelligence, discernible to someone whose intellectual ascension allows divine intellect to participate in their material intellect. As in the *Republic* of Plato, the mental faculty of the initiate described by Socrates 'will not rest content with each set of particulars which opinion takes for reality, but soars with undimmed and unwearied passion till he grasps the nature of each thing as it is' (490).[4]

In the architecture of Lincoln Cathedral, the Trinity is present especially in Saint Hugh's Choir (Fig. 18.4), in the grouping of three lancet windows per clerestory bay, and in the triradial vaults in the ceiling, where three tierceron ribs emanate from each boss along the ridge pole, causing the asymmetrical syncopation. In the choir the *lux spiritualis* shines through the triune lancet windows and mediates between the spiritual and physical, as in the Trinity, and shines the *species apprehensibilis*, represented by the forms of the glass windows, onto the *oculus mentis*, the mind's eye of the observer, in the form of the *species sensibilis*, represented by the triradial ribs in the vaulting, as they take the form of corporeal geometry, in mathematical relations.

The transition from the windows in the clerestory to the vaulting of the ceiling represents the transition from the *species apprehensibilis* to the *species sensibilis*; it represents the formation of matter through light, where matter becomes denser and more substantial as the lines of the rays of light become more multiple and the *virtus* becomes stronger, in the process of condensation and rarefaction; and it represents the formation of the material world from the point to line to surface in the two-dimensional pattern of the lancet windows, and the line to surface to solid in the vaulting pattern, concave surface, and volume of the vault. Conversely, the transition facilitates the ascension of the soul, or *anima rationalis*, of the viewer, from *nous pathetikos* or *virtus cogitativa*, reason connected to material things, to *nous poietikos* or *virtus intellectiva*, reason which is disconnected from material things and composed of intelligibles, in particular the concept of the good, or what is universally just. *Virtus intellectiva* involves the participation of *intelligentia*, divine intelligence, as described by Grosseteste in his *Commentary*.

The architecture is an *edificium* of the hierarchies of intellect described by Grosseteste, and it is a talisman for the intellection of the observer; the perception of the catechism of the architecture inspires the viewer to engage the *virtus intellectiva*, to understand the relation between reason and intellection, material world and spiritual world, body and soul, and to transcend the dictates of the body in the material to the dictates of universal laws in the spiritual. Saint Hugh's Choir consists of four bays. There are two arches in each bay of the triforium, each divided into two sub-arches, with trefoils and quatrefoils in the tympanum above, corresponding to the trivium and quadrivium of Scholasticism, heaven and earth. The Trinity, which is the manifestation of the One, divine *intelligentia*, transforms the *lux spiritualis* through the windows into the *lumen spiritualis* reflected in the choir, and the *lumen spiritualis* is further materialized through the Trinity, as it presides over the corporeal world, in the form of the triune groupings in the vaulting, which describe the structure of the corporeal world.

Peter Draper[5] compared the contrapuntal arcading in the aisles of Saint Hugh's Choir to an illustration in the *De statu ecclesiae* of Gilbert, Bishop of Limerick, the first papal legate in Ireland, which can be found in Cambridge University Library. In the illustration, tiers of arches are arranged in a complex pattern of arcading to illustrate the hierarchy of the Catholic Church. The arcades are offset so that the shaft of one arcade overlaps the arches of the arcade underneath, as in Saint Hugh's Choir. The arches represent the people of the Church, which is seen as a macrocosm or organism as represented by the system of arcading. The arcading represents a diagram of the order of the Church, in what the text calls an *imago generalis ecclesiae*. The arcades are organized in a series of pyramids; the smallest units are at the bottom, and work up to the largest units at the top. The basic units are the parish, run by the priest, and monastery, run by the abbot. The units are divided into ranks and categories, including *oratores*, or those who pray; *aratores*, or those who plough; and *bellatores*, or those who fight. The parishes and monasteries are governed by the diocese, which is governed by the archdiocese, the district of the archbishop, which is governed by the highest ranking bishop, *primatus*, of the Church. The Church is governed by the pope, who is governed by Christ. A secular hierarchy is established to correspond to the ecclesiastical hierarchy.

The arcading of the illustration is set on a continuous plinth, as in Saint Hugh's Choir, and the Gothic pointed arches are set on piers with bases and capitals. The continuous plinth represents the broad base of the Church and its open arms in embracing all people. The pointed arches in the upper level represent the more narrow and disciplined life, the *arcta via*, of religious and ordained people. The intersection of the arches as they overlap represents the close relationships between those religious or ordained. The arcading is set inside a major arch, representing the macrocosm of the Church, the *ecclesia generalis*. The arcading set inside the major arch represents the ability of the Church to subsume variation, particularities and individualities under an overarching whole. Romanesque towers appear at the top of the arcading. The Romanesque towers contrast with the delicate membrification of the arcading, which reflects the emphasis on light, transparency, structural clarity, and progressive divisibility, the principle of the *manifestatio*, associated with Gothic architecture. The illumination is an *edificium* in the same way as the cathedral; it is a catechism of a structure of knowledge, and the institution of justice, communicated in visual and structural terms.

The analogy between scripture and building as edifice is found in the *Moralia in Job* of Gregory, and the *Didascalicon* of Hugh of Saint-Victor. The edifice of scripture has both a structure, or history, and a superstructure, or allegorical content, in the same way that architecture has both a structure and an allegorical or metaphysical content, the ideas associated with its forms. In the *Metrical Life of Saint Hugh*, Lincoln Cathedral is compared to a honeycomb, yielding sweet inner meaning, the allegory of divine communion. Hugh of Saint-Victor compared history, as the foundation and principle of sacred learning, to a honeycomb, from which the allegory is extracted as honey. The structure of the cathedral corresponds to the history of the Church, its foundation of learning and institution of justice, and the metaphysical role of the architecture in communicating ideas corresponds to the allegorical content of spiritual development. The image of the honeycomb can be compared to the tiered arcading of the illumination of Gilbert, and to the syncopated arcading of Saint Hugh's Choir. In each case the reticulation, as an instrument of the progressive divisibility of the *manifestatio* in Scholasticism, contains the synthesis of reason and faith, in the comprehension of the good and the justice of the ecclesiastical hierarchy. The reticulation also occurs in the masonry of the crossing tower and the west front, in the Y-tracery of the stained glass, and in the vaulting of Saint Hugh's Choir, the nave, the Morning Chapel, the Consistory Chapel, and the chapter house at Lincoln.

In a letter written by Robert Grosseteste from Oxford, in around 1200 or 1225, to Master Adam Rufus, a former student, Grosseteste began, 'To make clear how God is the form of his creatures ... the meanings of this word "form" must be explained.' Here the Latin *forma* can be translated as design, form, mould, pattern, or shape.[6] 'It is said that the design is the model (or *exemplar*) to which the craftsman looks to make (or *formet*) his handiwork, in imitation of it and in its likeness.' Grosseteste continues, 'Thus the last [a block shaped like a foot], to which the cobbler looks to form the sole accordingly, is called the pattern of the sole.' The basis for the design of the architecture is the basis for the activity of any artisan, any urban professional of the era. 'Thus too the lives of good men, which we regard in order to form the manners of our life in their likeness, are called our pattern of living.' Grosseteste likens good design to ethical and moral behavior, on the model of the good; the basis for all artistic activity is also the basis for the ethics and morality of the era.

In the letter to Adam Rufus, Grosseteste asks the reader to 'imagine, even though it be impossible, that the will [or *solertia*] of the same architect wishing to build the house were so powerful that this will alone need be applied to shape the material into the house of the design in the architect's mind, so that by this application will be fashioned into the house'. The process of architectural design requires the penetrating ability and clarity of vision of the *oculus mentis* in relation to the divine *intelligentia*, as aided by the *irradiatio spiritualis*, in the intellectual ascension of the *virtus intellectiva*. If the process of architectural design is successful, then the architecture will accommodate the same intellectual ascension in the mind of the viewer, and the same vision of an ordered and just society.

NOTES

1 Robert Grosseteste, *Commentarius in Posteriorum Analyticorum Libros*, ed. Pietro Rossi (Florence, 1981).

2 Steven P. Marrone, *William of Auvergne and Robert Grosseteste: New Ideas of Truth in the Early Thirteenth Century* (Princeton NJ, 1983), p. 196.

3 *Metrical Life of St Hugh, Bishop of Lincoln*, ed. J.F. Dimock (Lincoln, 1860), ll. 833–965, quoted in John Harvey, *The Medieval Architect* (New York, 1972), pp. 237–9.

4 Plato, *The Republic*, trans. Desmond Lee (New York, 1955).

5 Peter Draper, *The Formation of English Gothic: Architecture and Identity, 1150–1250* (New Haven CT, 2007).

6 John Harvey, *The Medieval Architect* (New York, 1972), p. 23.

19

Politics and Architecture

Raymond Geuss

In 2001 some of the Faculties of the University of Frankfurt began to move physically from the often shoddy and distinctly run down looking post-war accommodation that had served them since the early 1950s into an architecturally spectacular set of buildings designed by Hans Poelzig in the late 1920s and set in a large park with an impressive view over downtown Frankfurt. Unfortunately, these buildings, known collectively as the 'Poelzig-Bau', had served as the Corporate Headquarters of I.G. Farben between 1931 and the occupation of the city by the US Army in March of 1945. What this means is that in the year 2009 a student could find that he or she was taking a seminar on Descartes, on Rimbaud, or on early Church history in the very rooms in which in the early 1940s gas chambers and crematoria for extermination camps were designed. In the period between 1945 and 1995 the complex served as the Headquarters of General Eisenhower and then of the Fifth US Army. When the US military moved out upon German re-unification, the question arose of what to do about the huge I.G. Farben complex, and it was only after a certain amount of political wrangling that the decision was taken to move the University into it. There was finally a sense that if the complex was not simply to be torn down, it would have to be symbolically detoxified, but how could that be done? The solution finally reached was that a permanent exhibition about its history would be installed in the building, which would be as uncompromisingly truthful about its past as possible, the main building itself would retain the historical name 'I.G.-Farben-Haus', and the large and impressive open space one encounters upon first entering the building, which is now the student café, but in the late 40s was the antechamber of Eisenhower's offices, would be named the 'Eisenhower Rotunda'. Finally, one of the squares on the new campus would be named after a former forced labourer in one of the I.G. Farben Works: 'Norbert Wollheim', a name that has special resonance for a philosopher because it is the surname of an important British philosopher, Richard Wollheim, who happened himself in the second World War to have participated in the liberation of Belsen. It is possible, in fact almost inevitable, that there will be no consensus on whether this series of decisions and actions was in fact appropriate and adequate – that is in the nature of a complex historical and political process like this one – but I would ask you now to accept for the sake of argument my view that this was a reasonable and laudable attempt to deal with a difficult situation. Let me, however, now engage in some counterfactual history. Suppose the Supreme Allied Commander in Europe had not been the traditionally conservative Eisenhower, but Field Marshal Douglas MacArthur, who was during the same period effectively Supreme Commander in the Pacific. MacArthur was a man of extreme right-wing political views, who came to be notorious for his persistent advocacy of the use of nuclear weapons against the North Koreans and Chinese during the Korean War. MacArthur saw this as a prelude to the extension of the war to be conducted with nuclear weapons into China proper, which he also advocated. When he failed to obtain authorisation for this policy, because the then US-President Harry Truman refused to countenance it, he tried in various ways to use his military position to undermine or circumvent the civilian political apparatus in the US, until Truman was finally forced to dismiss him from his post. I suggest that naming the entrance to Poelzig's complex the 'MacArthur Rotunda' would not have had the same effect of at least partially rehabilitating the building. On one final note, I should mention that parts of the Poelzig-Bau served as the Headquarters of the CIA in Germany, and that in the 1970s and 1980s it was the object of three terrorist attacks, probably by members of the RAF ('*Rote Armee Fraktion*'), a splinter group that had its origin in the German Student Movement of the late 1960s. In a bomb attack by the RAF on 11 May 1972, one US officer was killed and thirteen further people wounded.[1]

I would not now be discussing this case at all if I did not think that the Poelzig-Bau was a most impressive piece of architecture. However, the more I think about this, the more difficult it seems to me to separate the strictly architectural aspects of my reaction to this building from the historical and political, and, what is more, I do not think that this is so unusual.

The very term 'architecture' itself suggests a closer connection with politics than might be thought to be the case with any of the other arts or crafts. The Greek word 'ἀρχιτέκτων' signifies the person who is in charge of and has control over builders. 'ἄρχω'/ 'ἀρχή' in fact is one of the usual terms for a political relation of domination. On the very first page of his treatise on the good human life, *Nichomachean Ethics*,[2] Aristotle appeals to the example of the architect to discuss the notion, especially important for him, of the hierarchical relation of human activities one to another, and the differential forms of value which such hierarchically ordered activities have. The study of ethics, for Aristotle, is subordinated to that of politics just as the builders are subordinated to the architect. This metaphor of the 'architectonic' is one that recurs in many later views to refer to relations of subordination between different parts of a theory. Such relations may, of course, be ones of mere logical, epistemological or paedagogical dependence or of pragmatic subordination, rather than specifically political subjection. It is not, in any case, as easy as it might initially seem to say exactly what a 'political' relation, for instance a relation of political subordination in the relevant sense, is.

It has often been pointed out that there is a basic ambiguity in the concept of 'politics'. There is what I will call a 'wider', 'broader' or 'less specific' construal of the term, and a narrower or more specific construal. In the broader and less specific sense, 'politics' means simply any human activity of structuring or directing or coordinating the actions of a group. So we can speak of a 'politics' of the family or gender politics. The actions of different human beings can be 'co-ordinated' in any number of different ways. Thus, if one thinks of a pre-industrial society living in a small mountain valley, there may be a very high degree of 'co-ordination', in the sense of simple regularity, exhibited by the action of the members of that society. For instance, if there is only one pass over the mountains, it might well be the case that virtually anyone who ever tries to leave the valley in the winter does so through this pass. This is certainly a regularity we might observe to hold, but it is not *in itself* an archetypically political phenomenon because we think that using this pass to exit from the valley is a matter of simple necessity. That one goes through this exit, if one leaves at all, is not anything that is 'in our power' or 'up to us', and that means it is not itself a political matter but simply a natural fact. In addition, however, to such 'natural' co-ordination, there is also co-ordination that results from specific forms of human intervention such as persuasion, emulation, or coercion, and these are the characteristics of politics.

Thus, when certain philosophers have called freedom a precondition of politics or politics a 'realm of freedom', they are most sympathetically understood as making not some kind of ontological claim, but rather as describing a way of looking at the world. 'Politics', that is, especially in this first wide sense, is best understood as referring not to a special *domain*, like biology or astronomy, but to a way of seeing or considering the human world. The basic statement in politics is not: 'This is a political phenomenon' as parallel to 'This is an organic (or inorganic) compound' or 'this is a prime number'. Rather the paradigmatic claim is 'this is a political *question* or *issue*'. 'This is a political matter' means it is a matter considered in some sense to be potentially in our power and up for decision, and which we have some potential interest in dealing with in one way rather than another.

If this is right, three further things would seem to follow. First, although in a primitive society the weather might simply be a given, not *in itself* a matter for political discussion, the question of what we might *do* about the weather can well be a political issue: Do we distribute umbrellas to everyone or not? Do we put up a communal awning or tarpaulin on poles over the village green? Or do we let everyone fend for themselves?

Second, what *is* a political question or issue is itself historically variable in a way in which questions like 'What is an organic compound?' or 'What is the sum of seven and nine?' are not. What are political changes with changes in what we can and could do.

In pre-industrial times the weather is not in itself a political issue, subject to the caveats just mentioned above, but if we were able technologically to change and control the meteorological conditions, then it might very well become a political matter, in the weak sense, whether it rains on a certain day or not. That would mean that someone had decided to make it rain on that day *or had failed to decide anything*, leaving it up, as we might say, to 'nature'. Note that in the pre-industrial period people were not *failing* to decide on the weather, since they had no control over it, it was just there as a brute fact, a matter not of politics, but of natural necessity.

Third, suppose it really is the case that politics concerns things that are either in fact in our power or at any rate which we could imagine might come to be in our power, and suppose then further that any state of affairs that cannot be other than it is (such as whether a certain number is prime) stands outside the domain of political deliberation. If, then, I have a special interest in maintaining some feature of the present social or political regime, for instance, because it differentially benefits me, I may have a strong interest in trying to present this feature as a part of the order of 'natural necessity'. Think of Margaret Thatcher's constant refrains about the ineluctable necessity of tolerating unemployment as a means to controlling inflation, or of bowing to the imperatives of the market. This is the point at which it is sometimes tempting to appeal to claims about the objectivity of scientific results, and, of course, there often are well supported scientific results that are relevant to political decisions. However, it is also the case that sometimes political agents have a strong motivation for presenting as the only possible reading what is in fact only one specific reading of the existing evidence among others, namely that reading which seems to give support to their own projects and interests. The appeal to 'objectivity', whether justified or not, is so effective because it is responsive to deep-seated and perfectly comprehensible human needs. We seem to have good inductive reasons to cultivate our existing desire not to be grossly deceived about the world in which we live, if only because in most cases we have found that complete illusions turn out to have very painful consequences for us. This comprehensible desire for what we call 'objective truth' can often come into a sometimes slightly unholy connection with our human need to find, or invent, determinacy, stability, fixity, at almost any cost. The world is unstable and insecure, and our life in it is uncertain. It is painful for us to confront this fact. It also is exhausting having constantly to calculate again, to exercise context-dependent judgment or reopen questions apparently definitively settled. In the face of 'objectivity' we can relax and succumb to inertia, simplifying some aspects of the painful process of decision by leaving it, as it were, up to reality itself. Unless the shoe pinches us *very* badly so that we cannot overlook it, we would like to think the form of the shoe which happens to be customary in our society is the natural one or the 'objectively' given one. The idea that humans 'naturally' like 'freedom' or 'choice', if that means that they like continually to have to exercise their unbridled judgment or make decisions under the conditions of great uncertainty, is unfounded. This does not mean, of course, that they like to be in painful bondage, and much of human life is an attempt to find a path through the world which is responsive to the two forces of avoidance of novelty, and choice and avoidance of the painful consequences of failing to revise one's beliefs and attitudes when that is necessary.[3]

So much, then, for the first, the wider and weaker, which does not, of course mean 'less important' of the two concepts of politics. 'Politics' in this wider sense is a matter of any form of co-ordinating action regardless of the means used to achieve this coordination. Our more usual, or what I will call the 'narrower', concept of politics contains some further components in addition to those that constitute 'politics' in the wider sense. These are that the 'political' coordination of social action makes use of at least the threat of recourse to coercion, force or violence, and that there is some appeal to systematic forms of legitimation. So in the wider sense of 'politics' I can speak of the politics in a chess club as people jockey for influence, a certain kind of power, and a certain advancement through established offices. However this structure is not directly connected to the possible use of force. The Chairman of the chess club may make decisions about who plays which game against whom in which room and at what time, may adjudicate disagreements etc. and in these matters his word may be Law, but he cannot whip, or probably even threaten to whip, any of the members or lock them up against their will. On the other hand, a gangster can assault me, lock me up, and take away my possession by force, but does not make a claim that what he is doing is either morally good or politically legitimate. The full and narrower sense of politics comes into play only when the use of force or the threat of the use of force is a possibility, and when the potential recourse to coercion, force or violence is presented as being not merely a fact to be accepted, but as in some way 'legitimate'. The major agency in the modern world that makes this claim to legitimate use of coercive power is the state. 'Political' in the narrow sense means having to do with coordination of action through the use of state-power, or with the attempt to influence, infiltrate, or put oneself into a position to exercise that state-power.[4]

'Architecture', too, is a term which is used ambiguously, although the ambiguities are comparatively harmless. Thus it can either mean a certain skill, craft, or artistic ability or the exercise of that skill or craft in the activity of designing and constructing physical objects of a certain kind. Or finally it can refer to the objects thus designed and constructed themselves. Architecture seems to be different from many of the other arts in several ways. First architectural objects are palpably physical and inherently public: they are large objects, literally almost always bigger than any individual person, and they stand out, form physical obstacles to free movement, and shape the very space in which we live. Of necessity, then, they affect us a way that is different from the way in which most novels, pieces of music, or easel-paintings affect us. If I do not like the novel or poem I am reading, I can shut the book; if the picture displeases me, I can turn my head away. I cannot so easily exit from a large cathedral in which I find myself placed, or change the properties of the houses that face onto the streets down which I must pass to get to the city centre. This at least mildly and potentially more coercive feature of architectural objects makes them more political than the products of the other arts. It could, of course, be argued that every painting I see shapes my perception in a potentially permanent way and therefore makes me see everything in the world in a different way. Still, I do not usually have to look any particular painting. I do, however, have to live in whatever building or part of the city I happen to live in. I can, of course, choose to live in one kind of building rather than another, and can change the building I live in either by moving or by reconstructing it, but I cannot in the twenty-first century simply do without some built surroundings, as I can do without easel-paintings. It is, of course, true that this difference between architecture and other arts became even more pronounced during nineteenth and the twentieth century, when forms of literature, music, and aspects of the graphic arts became highly privatised, than it was in some previous periods. Thus, in the ancient world the basic form of consumption of what we now call 'literature' would not have been silent reading in an empty room, but the massive choral singing and dancing which was characteristic of the performance of a tragedy in Athens, or a public performance of epic by a rhapsode or the reading of a speech or dialogue by a slave to a group of gentlemen of leisure. Nevertheless, a constructed object like a house had in one obvious sense a firmer place as an opaque, solid, intransigent, three-dimensional part of the public fabric of a city than any ephemeral grouping of citizens did.

There is, therefore, an important further political issue here. Should buildings be unobtrusive, retreating into the background to allow agents to pursue their own self-chosen goals, as far as possible without *apparent* obstruction? If one has the view that *any* building in one way or another structures the space in which it stands, then this might seem slightly dishonest, a way of covering up what is in fact a choice about structuration and allowing it to pass unnoticed. The building may come to be taken as 'a fact of nature' in the urban landscape rather than the result of distinct intervention. Surely, however, one might think, the consequence of this should not be that buildings should be hyper-assertive, constantly calling attention to themselves and their effects. There is no optimal resolution to this tension. Perhaps for that reason reflecting on and theorising about architecture will always have a place in our intellectual life.

Furthermore, given the persistence of the material from which most buildings are made, the structuration of the environment which they produce also extends into the indefinite future, and thus concerns an indeterminate number of 'anonymous' other humans, who by the very nature of the case cannot be consulted. Architectural works completed now impose on future people a way of living by channelling the way human activities will be able to proceed. It is, then, coercing them at any rate in a minimal sense, making it *easier* for them to live in *this* way, and more difficult for them to live in *that* way, so any present construction is an act of political faith in a certain possible future.

Architecture has also often been held to be different from other arts in that it straddles the distinction between craft and fine art, between producing practical objects of use in a relatively predictable way, which is assumed to be the basic characteristic of a craft, and producing potentially unique aesthetic objects, which is associated with our modern idea of fine art. This dichotomy might also be associated with the distinction between being a 'mere' builder and being a proper architect. There is a functional dimension in architecture and also an expressive dimension, and much of the discussion at least during the past two centuries or so has revolved around the proper understanding of each of these dimensions, and, most importantly perhaps, the proper relation between the two of them.

It is also an important fact about our society that people do not simply engage in the activity of designing and building, but some of them also do this *as a profession*, and in our society 'profession' designates a very specific social role with associated legal rights, social and legal duties, and expectations.[5] As a professional architect in our society, one is embarking on a life of entering into contracts with people to build things which they, within certain limits, specify. This immediately raises straightforwardly political issues. Do you enter into contract with just anyone, on what conditions, for whose benefit? Last month I happened to meet and have a conversation with a German engineer whose family had built up the oldest and largest cement works in Central Europe (Dyckerhoff), and who were understandably very proud of the extremely high quality of their cement. During World War Two they had provided the cement for the building of the 'West Wall', the line of German fortifications on the coast of Western Europe designed to protect the Continent from Anglo-American invasion. When my new acquaintance's grandfather was called to account for this by the US occupation authorities after the war, the elderly patriarch produced the original set of specifications and contracts for the building of the large pediment on which the Statue of Liberty in New York Harbour rests. In these contracts it was specified that the pediment must be made of Dyckerhoff cement ('or cement of similar quality', as the contract apparently specified). In fact Dyckerhoff & Co. provided the 8,000 'bins' of cement from which the pediment was constructed. This line of response was apparently immediately accepted by the occupation forces without further question. Regardless of what one might think of the substantive rights and wrongs in this case, the issue is not whether the occupation forces ought to have accepted what might seem to us to be something too pathetically weak even to be called an 'argument'. It was merely an attempt, successful as it turned out, by the accused to evoke certain sufficiently strong positive sacral associations in the mind of the accusers as to blind them and deprive them of the use of whatever weak ratiocinative faculties they may have had in the first place. The real question, however, is what this tells us about the nature of our own conceptual space. These are in no sense irrelevant or unimportant questions, but they have more to do with the social role 'architect' than with the inherent nature of what the architect does. We might think that a doctor is, or should be, by virtue of his or her very role immune from politics. A military doctor should care for *all* the wounded on the battlefield, friend or foe, and civilised countries make it a point of pride to provide equal care for all combatants and for civilian victims including those who are now usually subsumed under the rubric 'collateral damage'. This does not mean that there is no politics in being a doctor, but only that we have decided that it would be a good idea, *not* an idea proposed to us by any notion of 'justice' but by such notions as humanity, decency, charity, benevolence, and also probably by various utilitarian calculations, artificially to *insulate* the practitioners of the medical profession from making certain everyday political discriminations.

There is yet a further way in which architecture was traditionally distinct from other arts, and this is in the more inherently social, and potentially political, nature of the activity itself – the activity of collective building. Aristotle's architect had the power to exercise a kind of social control, namely to give orders to the people who actually do the building. This power was not arbitrary, it did not come from nowhere, and it was not unlimited. It was a power based on the authority purportedly provided by knowledge (and perhaps also secondarily by experience, although many builders have more experience of construction than younger architects do). This immediately raises the question of what kind of knowledge there can be in this area. This question is especially pressing for architecture, more perhaps than for many other areas of human endeavour because precisely of the binary nature of the enterprise, that of designing and producing practically useful *and* aesthetically pleasing buildings. We do not have much difficulty in understanding the kind of knowledge that will contribute to making it likely that the building will be useful. It will have to stand up, and the technical discipline of statics gives us a relatively straightforward answer to that. But what notion of 'knowledge' underlies the claim of the architect to produce an object of great expressive value?

The problem for the architect, then, is that if his authority is based on knowledge, the builder and engineer *also* have *that*, but if what makes him distinct from the (mere) builder, and hence entitled to some special kind of authority, is the aesthetic or expressive dimension of the product, *that* seems more reasonably to be construed as having to do with faculties like that of 'taste' rather than with any form of knowledge. How does 'taste' give authority? It is completely unclear what kind of authority an architect can deploy and in particular whether the architect has any *coercive* authority at all.[6]

In the previous discussion of 'politics' in the narrow sense, I left one important aspect of the concept unexplored. I spoke in a vague way about politics as being a realm of coercion, force, or violence, as if these three things were the same, or at any rate did not need to be distinguished. It is not obvious, though, that coercion and violence are at all the same thing. I can be reasonably said to have been 'coerced' to do something in many kind of circumstances *even if* no one uses anything we would naturally call 'violence'. If you lure me into a room and lock the door, you have forced me or coerced me into staying in that room until you unlock it, but you do not seem to have used 'violence' on me in the same way you would have, had you bodily picked me up and thrust me into the room. Similarly, it does not seem odd to say that by lying to me you can 'force' me to do various things, in the sense that if I believe you, I might think I have no alternative to the course of action you wish me to take. Still, it seems a stretch of our current linguistic usage to call 'lying' a form of violence.

A further relevant distinction is that between active and passive or doing and permitting/ allowing to occur. This distinction is highly controversial among philosophers, or rather it is controversial whether it has any deeper significance. At an everyday level it is perfectly clear:

a) active: I push you into the water so that you drown.
b) passive: I fail to respond to your cries for help even though I easily could.

The reason this distinction is of relevance to this discussion is that political theory, especially of a liberal kind, has tried to focus on active, even deliberate human intervention. Politics then is construed as in the first instance about preventing other people from actively using violence on others. The result however is to skew the political realm. This is especially important for architecture because a building was historically an archetypically inert, but persistent, structure. I, or rather the builders, may have been active in putting it up, but once it was up, it was just there, and could be expected to stay there, if it was properly built, for a very long time. It can change its function over time, as when buildings originally constructed as fortresses become prisons, so whose deliberate intentions are significant, the person who built or those who now use? It is the very geometric structure of the building that forces people to act in one way rather than another, and also to fail to act in certain ways; if the structure works, it prevents the inmates from 'escaping'. This passive nature makes coercion 'softer' and harder to see as it were from the outside, although not to feel, if one actually must live in such a structure. It makes it also no less effective, and the question is whether it is not equally reprehensible.[7]

I have spoken of important ambiguities in the concept of 'politics' and of various different ways in which we speak of 'architecture' as a skill, an activity, a kind of object or a profession. It will then come as no surprise that I also think that the concept of 'justice' is multiply ambiguous. I would like to distinguish at least four rather distinct notions.

First of all, 'just' designates that which accords with existing, established, legal codes. Second, we call that 'just' which accords with what we – whoever 'we' in each case happen to be – think 'ought' to be the enforced legal code. Third, 'justice' is used simply, as Aristotle put it, to refer to 'all the human excellences together'.[8] That is, in this third sense 'just' refers in a rather indeterminate way to that which is socially excellent, desirable, etc. in whatever sense and for whatever reason. I note that it is extremely important not to confuse this third sense of the term with the second because there might well be things we think are *socially desirable* which we also think cannot for various reasons be formulated in a legal code. Thus I might think it highly desirable that people in a society be grateful to those from whom they have received benefits, but I might also think it completely wrong for this to be formulated as a requirement of any kind of *legal* code. First of all, a legal code must be enforceable by reference to external indicators, and I might think 'gratitude' is not the kind of thing that is sufficiently close to any external indicators to figure in a legal code. Second, I might think that precisely an important part of the value of gratitude is that it be exhibited *without* it being the case that it is legally required, and would be sanctioned. Its virtue is that it is extra-legal, not forced, etc.

The fourth conception of justice is one which focuses on questions of distribution. There has recently been significant disagreement among theorists about what it is that is supposed to be distributed, whether goods, welfare, opportunity, or the possibilities of agency, and there is a similar disagreement about whether the principles of distribution should be some version of equality or of proportionality, for instance that goods and benefits should be distributed equally to each or to each proportionally to their perceived merit or contribution, whatever 'merit' or 'contribution' mean.

Recently, meaning during the past forty years or so, there has been a strong tendency to understand politics in a highly artificial, restrictive, and impoverished way. Following John Rawls many theorists have essentially tried to construe politics as a form of human behaviour devoted primarily to the attempt to realise one particular social ideal, the ideal of justice.[9] They have then further eviscerated the concept of 'justice' so as to construe it merely as some general property of the distribution of goods and services in society.

I think that this multiple ambiguity in the concept of 'justice' has been a source of almost inestimable confusion. If 'justice' is used in the third sense, namely that is just which is in any sense socially desirable, then of course, it is no news that all politics is about justice. It is no news because it is just a tautology. However, it is easy to move, without noticing it, from that tautology to something that is by no means a tautology, namely to the claim that all politics is appropriately construed as concerned with the equitable or proportional distribution of pre-existing goods and benefits.

If one starts from the notion of politics which I sketched at the beginning, it is not difficult to see that not all politics is about justice, but also *at least* about the coordination of action, the exercise of influence and the control of the use of force (among other things). Arguably, 'justice' is not even one of the more important human values which can be instantiated in the political or social sphere. This is particularly clear in emergency situation, but, putting them aside, think, for instance, of welfare, efficiency, humanity, activity, security, dignity, and decency, not to mention creativity, a sense of self-affirmation and aesthetic grace. All of these are important social virtues, and none of them is self-evidently completely detached from the world of the political (at least in the wider sense).

In short, then, two associations of the concept of 'justice' seem to me unfortunate and unhelpful in the context of architecture. The first is the presumption that justice will have something to do with codes, rules, and conformity to such existing codes, or, for that matter, with conformity to a better set of ideal rules. The second that justice has to do with properties of distribution of goods that are considered to exist antecedently. When Marx in the nineteenth century attacked the focused attention which the political theory of his day turned on 'justice', it was because justice-centred theories took the goods in question at face value, as objects that had come into existence in ways that it was irrelevant to discuss.[10] Rather, Marx suggested that political theory should look carefully at the activities through which such goods were produced in the first place, and at the social relations that structured those productive processes. These, he thought, were the most important features of any society, and the rules of distribution, that is both justice in the sense of conformity to a legal code and justice in the sense of some scheme of distribution, were secondary.[11] What I would like to suggest is that architecture would do well to concentrate on the generation and fostering of varieties of free activity, and on the structure of the relations that will hold between the humans who need to interact, rather than on justice in the sense either of conformity to some code or the distribution of goods.

Unfortunately, then, I must disagree with one of the basic assumptions on which this conference is based. The prospectus for the conference states that 'Justice is fundamental to our notions of societal order, that is to the order sustained between ourselves without recourse to force.' When I say I disagree with this, I do not mean to say that I think that this assertion is incorrect in the sense in which it is, for instance, incorrect to think that the sun moves around the earth. Rather I disagree with it because it gives the strong impression of being a clear substantive claim, but on closer inspection it turns out to be no such thing. On some of the readings it expresses an unobjectionable or even tautological claim. If what it means is, 'We tend to use the word 'justice' to refer to whatever we discover is essential to the maintenance of our social order', then this may be true, but it is uninteresting. Even here, to be sure, one might wonder whether we wish to say that justice is whatever is fundamental to our existing social order or whether what we really have in mind is that justice refers to what would be essential to some ideally desirable order we can envisage. The trivial readings of this claim about 'justice' are, however, easily confused with other uses in which the statement expresses a highly contentful and controversial claim, for instance that equal (or proportional) distribution of goods is in fact fundamental to our social order, or to an ideally 'good' social order. In addition, I might add, what is so special about '*our*' notions of societal order? Are we to be satisfied merely with recognising that they are the conceptions we, for whatever reasons – good, bad, or indifferent – happen to have acquired?

Note, too, that this formulation seems to make the tacit assumption that societal order is good in itself, and 'our' conception of social order especially good, and that force plays no major constitutive part in our society. I take it that tacitly this includes the *threat* of the use of force. What if some use of force turns out actually to be required to maintain 'our' social order? This possibility does not seem even to be canvassed. So there is a highly specific set of liberal assumptions built into the very way in which this text is formulated which I, for one, would be inclined to reject.

I spoke earlier about our horror at the uncertainty of human life, about the vertigo we experience in the face of the indeterminate. and about our anxiety at having to exercise judgment and decide in each case afresh how to act toward our world. This is part of the strongest motivation for the focus of politics on the concept of 'justice', as it is part of the motivation to cling with limpet-like inertia to theories we have once committed ourselves to, even when they have revealed themselves to be seriously flawed. This is also part of the origin of our tendency to exaggerate the level of determinate objectivity we have been able to discern in our world. To start from 'justice' gives one the illusion that there is at least one distinct kind of determinate thing out there to which all the multiform indeterminacies and incommensurabilities of our forms of valuation can be reduced. If that were the case, we think, to some extent we would not need to exercise judgment. This, however, is exactly the problem with trying to reduce politics to discussion of 'justice'. This does not, in turn, in any way imply that political discussion is merely indeterminate or merely a matter of arbitrary choice. There are things which at any given time we have no real alternative but to accept, and valuing one thing is often really incompatible with valuing something else equally. No one can be a champion boxer in the morning and a subtle and accomplished violinist in the evening. Merely employing the term 'justice' to cover whatever we find of value will not in itself either solve any problems or cause there to be more unity and coherence among what we value than there otherwise would be.

To return once again to Aristotle, he thought that politics was in itself a constructive and 'architectonic' activity. It was really about creating the conditions for free, valuable action and the social genesis of the right kind of person, the proper citizen of the city-state. Aristotle also thought that the city-state was the only social form within which the highest and most complex kinds of human activities could be carried out. One can accept Aristotle's general claim that politics, and (by extension) architecture, are about enabling positively valued forms of collective human activity and about creating a certain kind or type of person without necessarily accepting his hierarchical views about human activities or the further claim that the most valuable life is possible only within the rigid format of an ancient city-state.[12]

Of course, the routine tasks of everyday building have to go forward, and of course architects have to honour their contracts, take care for whom and with whom they build, and what effects their building will have on the minimal provision of necessary goods, but architecture might also be seen, and has in the past been seen, to have an aspirational component, to be attempting to be 'constructive' in more than just the literal sense. In the nineteenth century some philosophers spoke of the basic task of the architect as being to build a dwelling suitable for God.[13] We twenty-first century atheists don't use this kind of religious language any more, but it is not difficult even for us to associate a clear and plausible meaning with that thought.[14] Architects should try to create structures which by channelling human energies in novel ways focus and intensify some of them while thwarting and dispersing others. We have a variety of complex reasons for judging that the intensification of some activities has made our lives richer and more worthwhile, or that, alternatively, it has been a huge mistake.

Thus, we judge that forms of human interaction, of relation to self and other, have become more or less efficient, more or less focused and intense, more or less socially aware and benevolent, more or less constructive in relation to other valued outcomes, and so forth. Some of these ways of evaluating it we call 'moral'. Also there is no particular reason to expect that the standards or criteria we now use for judging will never change. In some cases they will change as a result of interventions we make. If I were an architect, it would be the highpoint of my life to discover that people who antecedently knew, as it were, all there was to know about the building I designed for them and who thought they had good reason to detest it, came through living in it to change their minds and love it. I would have helped them to change their way of looking at the world, their standards for evaluating what is good, and their taste. Perhaps one could appeal to various systematic considerations to argue that some particular change had not been for the better – after all, sheer habituation has caused people to come to think they liked some extremely peculiar things – but the argument would need to be made in detail and evaluated on its merits.

Not all the evaluative standards we use in political philosophy, then, can reasonably be thought to be subordinated to a single notion of 'justice'. If the demand that architecture should take account of 'justice' is merely an exhortation to architects to look beyond their fees, and consider the different ways, for good or for ill, in which their buildings will be used, and the different ways in which those buildings will encourage or discourage certain uses, then this is unobjectionable, but also rather trivial. To put emphasis on its aspirational and humanly constructive component is to try to think about architecture in a way that very much goes beyond the framework of thoughts about 'justice'.[15]

NOTES

1 See *Von der Grüneburg zum Campus Westend*, brochure by University of Frankfurt (2007) to accompany the permanent exhibition in the I.G.-Farben-Haus. I am also grateful to Prof. Axel Honneth of the Philosophisches Institut of the University of Frankfurt for discussion of some of these issues.

2 *EN*, 1094a-1095a, 1141b; *Metaphysica*, 980a–981b.

3 Friedrich Nietzsche, *Sämtliche Werke: Kritische Studienausgabe*, ed. Colli and Montinari (Berlin: De Gruyter, 1967), vol. 1, pp. 875–90, vol. 5, pp. 15–39, vol. 6, pp. 88–97, *et passim*.

4 Max Weber, *Politik als Beruf* (Berlin: Dunker & Humblot, 1977).

5 This line of thought has been very fruitfully developed by Zeev Emmerich in a recent, as yet unpublished work, and in general I am very indebted to him for discussions of the topics in this paper.

6 For what is still one of the most interesting discussions of this topic, see Friedrich Schiller's, '*Über die ästhetische Erziehung des Menschen in einer Reihe von Briefen*', in *Sämtliche Werke*, ed. Fricke and Göpfert (München: Hanser, 1967), vol. 5.

7 Michel Foucault, *Surveiller et punir* (Gallimard, 1975).

8 *EN*, 1129b–30.

9 John Rawls, *A Theory of Justice* (Harvard, 1971).

10 See *Marx-Engels-Werke* (Berlin: Dietz, 1968), vol. 19, pp. 18–22; *Ergänzungsband*, 1, pp. 534–5.

11 Karl Marx, *Grundrisse* (Berlin: Dietz, 1974), pp. 5–19.

12 See Karl Marx, *Grundrisse* (Berlin: Dietz, 1974), pp. 387–8.

13 See G.W.F. Hegel, *Werke in zwanzig Bänden*, ed. Moldenhauer and Michel (Frankfurt: Suhrkamp, 1970), vol. 14, pp. 266–72.

14 See Friedrich Nietzsche, *Sämtliche Werke: Kritische Studienausgabe*, ed. Colli and Montinari (Berlin: De Gruyter, 1967), vol. 3, pp. 524–5.

15 Stuart Hampshire, *Thought and Action* (1970) and *Justice is Conflict* (London: Duckworth, 1999).

Index

MIX

Papier | Fördert gute Waldnutzung

FSC® C083411

Kolibri 360 GmbH
Ferdinand-Jühlke-Straße 7
99095 Erfurt, Deutschland
produktsicherheit@kolibri360.de